D1709635

THE SIRDAR

Sir Reginald Wingate and the
British Empire in the Middle East

Wingate in old age. At his death he was the senior general in the British army.

THE SIRDAR

*Sir Reginald Wingate
and the
British Empire in the Middle East*

by M.W. Daly

American Philosophical Society
Independence Square ◆ Philadephia
1997

Memoirs of the American Philosophical Society
Held at Philadelphia
for Promoting Useful Knowledge
Volume 222

ISBN: 0-87169-222-8   L.C.: 96-79457
US ISSN: 0065-9738

Contents

Part Three: Egypt and Beyond

Acknowledgments

This long book about a long life has had a long gestation. It stems from work undertaken fitfully during the past twenty years on the modern history of Egypt and the Sudan. In that work, as in the preparation of this volume, the help and example of Mr. Richard Hill and Prof. P.M. Holt have been continuous. In connection especially with the present work I must thank Mrs. Jane Hogan, archivist at Durham, for constant cheerful and professional help. I am very grateful to Mrs. Guy Street for access to and permission to use family documents, and for kind hospitatlity. Dr. H.P. Wilmott, the Hon. Alec Cumming-Bruce, Miss Caroline Mason, Dr. Muhammad Said al-Qaddal, Prof. Hasan Ahmad Ibrahim, and Prof. G.N. Sanderson all gave generously of their time in various ways. It is a pleasure to acknowledge the support of the American Philosophical Society, the unsung heroes of so much historical writing, in both the research and publication stages of the project. I would finally acknowledge those officers of the University of Tennessee, whose assurance of institutional uninterest in the project provided the challenge I needed to finish it.

Abbreviations used in the Notes

CAIRINT: a classification of the National Record Office, Khartoum
CB1: F.R. Wingate's commonplace book
CB2: Catherine Wingate's commonplace book
FO: Foreign Office
IRE: *Intelligence Report, Egypt*
JAH: *Journal of African History*
MECOX: Middle East Centre, Oxford
PRO: Public Record Office, London
SAD: Sudan Archive, Durham
SGA: Sudan Government Archives (National Records Office, Khartoum)
SIR: *Sudan Intelligence Report*

Part One: For Egypt, For Empire

Wingate with Khedive of Egypt, Abbas Hilmi II, at Port Sudan, 1909.

Aerial view of Suakin.

Wingate interrogating the Amir Mahmud Ahmad after the Battle of the Atbara, 1899.

Kitchener and Wingate on the S.S. *Dal,* Fashoda, 1898.

The bodies of the Khalifa Abdallahi and the Amir Ahmad Fadil on the
battlefield at Unam Diwaykaret, 24 November 1899.

Slatin Pasha, posing in "Dervish" costume after his escape to Egypt, 1895.

Wingate with his daughter, Victoria, at the Palace, Khartoum, c. 1907.

Wingate's official arrival at Port Sudan. Note the purpose-built car.

Wingate (second from right) with his staff at Nahud in March 1916,
about to launch the invasion of Darfur.

General Sir. R. Wingate with party of Sudanese at Regent's Park Zoo, 1937.

Governor-General's "office" on trek, Kordofan, 1916.

Wingate in old age.

Chapter One
Introduction

Sir Reginald Wingate intended Knockenhair, the house he built outside Dunbar, to be a family seat for generations. By Edwardian standards it is a country cottage rather than a stately home, made imposing by its hilltop setting. Wingate spent summers there with his family until the First World War, and it remained his home during a long retirement. After his death in 1953, his son, unable to find a buyer in a depressed market, gave the house to Dunbar council. It has since been divided into four apartments that overlook golf courses and housing estates, where once there were vistas to the sea.

At Dunbar Wingate is still remembered as "the Sirdar." Townsfolk recall noble and royal visitors, but more vividly Wingate's Sudanese servants. A local merchant hints darkly of "odd stories" he "wouldn't tell now"; old ladies attest to "black slaves buried in the back garden"! Stories abound of "the stuff they took out of" Knockenhair after Wingate died: the zebra-skin rugs, Remington rifles, Mahdist spears, Bija swords, war-drums, and animal heads—a mixture of English suburban villa and Ottoman provincial harem. Above all, there was paper.

For two days porters removed Wingate's private archives. Guard boxes, leather-covered tin-lined traveling cases, trunks, portmanteaux, wardrobes, steel cabinets, tied bundles, file cupboards and bookcases, albums and letter-books held the raw material of a lifetime. Whole rooms had been filled with files: the third-floor billiard room, the long-disused night nursery, Wingate's writing-room, even the chauffeur's quarters in the garage. From the time he was commissioned in 1880 Wingate had saved indiscriminately. An undated inventory of files at Knockenhair runs to thirty-three typed pages; after professional cataloguing at the University of Durham Library his papers occupy 1,671 files in 190 boxes. These deal with every aspect of Wingate's public and private life, and of the history of the Near and Middle East between 1880 and 1920.

Several circumstances make Wingate's papers especially important. His prodigious writing—of diaries, reports, minutes, and especially official and private letters—was characteristic of the Victorian colonial administrator. Their sheer volume and variety testify to the energy of their author. That Wingate had a higher opinion than others of his historical importance, a bureaucrat's recognition of the importance of records, and a conspirator's suspicion that these might one day be needed, led to conservation. As a junior officer under Kitchener and the khedive he learned lessons that served him well as sirdar and proconsul.

Despite these riches and his importance, no biography of Wingate has appeared, apart from *Wingate of the Sudan*, Ronald Wingate's work of filial piety published in 1955. There are several reasons for this. Wingate was (to borrow Acheson's phrase) "present at the creation" of the British Empire in the Near East. For almost forty years, as soldier, spy-master, propagandist, administrator, and statesman he played a central and astonishingly continuous role in the region's affairs. But although Wingate's life has much to teach of modern history and politics, his personality never captured the imagination of contemporaries or historians; as volumes on Gordon and Lawrence proliferate, other figures have been forgotten. And in judging the relative importance of people, historians have been like tourists rather than travelers: the inconvenience of Wingate's papers at Durham has, like that of its cathedral, made more estimable the merely more accessible.

That obscurity is doubly ironic, for while in later life Wingate resented his own eclipse, his very success had helped to bring it about. In charge of military Intelligence in Egypt from 1889 to 1898 he knew everything but could disclose little; he would later be remembered as the man who arranged the escape of an Austrian adventurer. As progenitor of three influential books of war-propaganda he has been dismissed by historians as an amateur, only to be made much of by amateurs themselves; few have recognized what he was up to. As governor-general of the Sudan from 1899 to 1916 he lived in state in a Palace in Khartoum, but the peace he maintained in that war-torn land ensured his anonymity in Britain. His role as commander-in-chief of Hijaz operations during the First World War—that is, as director of the famous Arab Revolt—was never even publicly announced, in deference to Muslim opinion; the names of subordinates became household words. At the crowning moment of his career, as high commissioner in Egypt, Wingate was overshadowed by British soldiers in the deserts of Arabia and Egyptian nationalists in the streets of Cairo. Finally, the method of his removal from Egypt in 1919 was designed by an ungrateful government to blame and then merely to discard one of the most distinguished of British administrators in the Near East.

In Wingate's day biographies were still parables. The lessons of his life are of the evanescence of honors, the duplicity of the ambitious, the falseness of fame, and the value but insufficiency for success of hard work in a hard world. Wingate was one of many British (indeed Scots) colonial administrators who learned with regret that a ruler of millions in the East was still a politician's pawn at home: the "Master" (as lieutenants called him) of oriental intrigue was no match for the mandarins of Whitehall. Thus it is only on the Nile, as at Dunbar, that Wingate's name still epitomizes an era, and for people who have little idea of why.

Chapter Two
Early Life

Francis Reginald Wingate was born on 25 June 1861 at Port Glasgow in Renfrewshire, the last of eleven children of Andrew and Bessie Turner Wingate. Andrew Wingate, son of a Glasgow textile merchant, had lived there since his birth in December 1813. After entering the family business he had married, on 5 June 1845, Bessie, the daughter of Richard Turner of Dublin. Between March 1846 and 1861 they had seven sons and four daughters. Francis (who seems to have been called Reginald even as a child) was born at Broadfield, his parents' house, and was baptized three weeks later by his future brother-in-law, the Reverend Thomas Walpole; the godparents were an uncle and aunt Mackenzie.[1]

Wingate's youth was difficult. In May 1862 his eight-year-old brother George died of scarlet fever. Six weeks later his father died at the age of forty-eight.[2] The family business had faltered, and his widow was forced to sell Broadfield and move with her children to Jersey in May 1864. There they occupied a series of small houses in St. Helier until October 1877, when Bessie Wingate herself died, aged fifty-five. Meanwhile her eldest son, Andrew, had died in April 1868; another son, Henry, a midshipman in the mercantile marine, had died at sea in August 1872 at the age of sixteen.[3] Most of Reginald Wingate's early life was spent in relative penury on Jersey. He attended St. James's Collegiate School there, under the direction of A. G. Thompson and the Rev. G. Thompson, from 1868 to 1878.[4]

With this background the most promising career was the army. In December 1878, at the age of seventeen, Wingate passed seventeenth in the entrance examination for the Royal Military Academy, Woolwich. He was appointed on 3 January 1879, and joined the

---

[1] CB1; Wingate's Bible.

[2] CB1; Cf. Wingate, *Wingate of the Sudan*, London 1955, 29.

[3] CB1; Wingate's Bible.

[4] Wingate's Bible; Wingate, *Wingate of the Sudan*, 30.

academy on the fourteenth, in a division of forty "gentlemen cadets."[5] Wingate was both fortunate and successful at Woolwich. Because of a shortage of officers in the Artillery, his division's course was accelerated, and he was passed out in July 1880. Furthermore, in 1880 the rank of second lieutenant in the artillery was abolished, so Wingate was a member of one of the first divisions to win commissions as lieutenants. In the order of merit he was tenth of thirty-nine. Only the top five cadets were usually offered commissions in the (much more remunerative) Royal Engineers; thus a month after his nineteenth birthday Wingate was gazetted a lieutenant in the Royal Artillery.[6] He was posted to a Heavy Battery at Kandahar in Afghanistan, and after a further five-month course at Shoeburyness and Woolwich, and a month's leave in Scotland, he sailed for India in March 1881.[7]

India left no noticeable impression on Wingate. He was there for only about a year, much of which was spent in language study. In later official and private correspondence he made little mention of the place or of his experiences there. Upon arrival in Bombay in late March 1881 he found that his battery had been transferred to Kolaba, so he was able immediately to take three weeks' leave, pending its arrival. He spent the leave with his brother Richard, a revenue official in the Bombay administration, at Kanara.[8] A diary entry during the steamship voyage from Bombay to Kumta notes that a fire on board was extinguished before reaching the cargo of baled cotton and explosives. Otherwise this first taste of the East was uneventful, and after ten days of hunting and riding he returned to Bombay on 21 April and drove to Kolaba to take up his post.[9]

The life of a young lieutenant of artillery in peacetime Kolaba was quiet. Routine duties occupied a few hours a day, and leave time was generous. Within days of arrival Wingate was hard at work on Hindustani with a fellow officer and a tutor. His diary records a desultory round of drills, inspections, and office work, and long

---

[5] CB1; H. P. Wilmott to the author, 3 April 1991. I am indebted to Dr. Wilmott for details of Wingate's Woolwich career.

[6] CB1; H.P. Wilmott to the author, 3 April 1991, citing *Records of the Royal Military Academy 1741–1892*. Cf. Wingate, *Wingate of the Sudan*, 30.

[7] CB1; Wingate's Bible.

[8] CB1; Wingate's Bible; Wingate, *Wingate of the Sudan*, 31.

[9] Diary entries for 7–22 April 1881, SAD 102/8.

hours of billiards, cards, and private correspondence.[10] In July 1881 Wingate had ten days' leave at Deolali, and in November visited his cousin, Andrew Wingate, Resident at Chittore in Rajputana, on the occasion of the viceroy's visit to the Maharana of Udaipur. He passed the lower standard examination in Hindustani in July 1881, and in December the higher standard, giving evidence both of the linguistic ability that became a hallmark of his career, and of his ambition to advance quickly.[11]

In April 1882 Wingate learned that his battery's service in India might be extended for two years, and he began actively to look for ways out. The Punjab Frontier Force and the Ordnance and Staff Corps were possibilities; Wingate asked the advice and help of senior officers in arranging a transfer. Meanwhile his battery was sent to Aden, then under the government of India's administration, and on 4 March 1882 Wingate found himself quartered at "the camp" there.[12] On his twenty-first birthday, 25 June 1882, Wingate re-read his journal entry of a year before: "I wonder where I shall be this time next year—not in Aden I hope"; it was, he wrote, probably the worst place in the world.[13] Ironically, it was also to prove the making of his career.

As a young lieutenant Wingate won the friendship of successive senior officers. In Aden he was taken into the family of General Blair, the commanding officer, who brought him to the attention of Sir Evelyn Wood, in July 1882 the newly-appointed chief of staff of the British Expeditionary Force to Egypt. Expectation was high that Wingate's battery would be sent to Egypt, and with that in mind he withdrew from consideration for positions in the Hyderabad Contingent and in China. Even before his transfer to Aden Wingate had begun to study Arabic, and once there had applied himself diligently to that task. On 6 November he passed the higher standard Arabic examination (despite officially protesting its unfairness), and was therefore disappointed to learn, in February 1883, of his immediate transfer, not to Egypt, but back to India, and a mountain battery at Khandala.[14]

---

[10] Diary entries for 14 April–14 June 1881, SAD 102/8.

[11] CB1.

[12] CB1; diary entries for 9 April, SAD 102/9.

[13] Diary entry for 25 June 1882, SAD 102/9.

[14] Diary entries for 12 April; 21 June; 8, 22 July; 1 September; 6, 7 November 1882; 4, 23 February 1883, SAD 102/6; CB1.

Wingate's second tour of duty in India was unsuccessful. Relief at leaving the "barren rocks" of Aden on 1 March soon gave way to a series of disagreeable incidents with his new commanding officer.[15] Indeed, in his commonplace book Wingate later listed as the "principal incidents" of that tenure his mauling by a panther, the murder of an Indian sergeant major and ensuing "mutinous feeling," the robbery of the Battery Chest, and the public execution of a murderer in the battery lines.[16] It was with unconcealed glee that on 17 April Wingate received a letter from Wood offering an appointment in the Egyptian army. General Blair had intervened; Wingate could "hardly believe the good news."[17] Wingate's diary entry for 18–19 May captures the mood:

> Smyth surprised me by telling me that my orders to go to Egypt had come . . . to proceed forthwith provided my transit did not cost the government of India anything. I at once decided on starting by the French Line sailing on the 20th and so had little time to lose. . . . got all my luggage packed with the assistance of some gunners—at 12 o'clock went down to the station with horse and syce, put them into a carriage and saw them safely off to Bombay—returned at 1.30 and wrote chits etc. till 3, had a couple of hours sleep, . . . got all my luggage on a couple of big gharries, bid adieu to servants etc., paid off all outstanding bills, . . . got last pay certificate . . . drew horse allowance . . . and started off from the mess at about quarter to 7. . . . arrived in Bombay at 12.30 . . . and then hurried off to pay office and thence to D.A.G.'s, then back again. . . . I only just arrived in time to get paid up to date . . . got my final leave certificate after some trouble. . . . Then went to Grindlays' and found that . . . the Capt. of the French boat had refused to take the horse. Went over to the French Compys. office with Wilson, met the Capt. who consented to take the horse provided I got a horse box—another difficulty—it was impossible to hire one—so I went straight to Major Seton's . . . and after some bother succeeded in getting him to sign an order for a horse box from Govmt. . . . Got box . . . and with all my heavy luggage proceeded to Princes Docks—got horse shipped and luggage stowed away—then returned to Bombay, sent Chokra to Watsons with light baggage, got £50 from Grindlays—went to telegraph office

[15] Diary entries for 23 February; 14, 21 March 1883, SAD 102/6.
[16] CB1.
[17] Diary entry for 17 April 1883, SAD 102/7.

and sent a line to Genl. Wood saying "orders received. Start twentieth in Canton."[18]

The day he left Khandala cholera broke out.[19] Wingate never returned to India.

---

[18] SAD 102/7.

[19] Diary entry for 20 May 1883, SAD 102/7.

Chapter Three
British Egypt

When Wingate arrived in June 1883 the British had occupied Egypt for less than a year. The nature and mechanics of the occupation, its duration, and its legal status were still unclear; indeed lack of clarity would characterize the regime. But what had brought the British to Egypt would keep them there until the 1950s: the need to secure the main route between England and the Indian Ocean, an object symbolized but not encompassed by the Suez Canal. The process of regularizing the British position involved Great-Power diplomacy, deep political divisions in Britain, and epochal repercussions in Africa, and it took many years. Egypt thus offered a stage to ambitious soldiers and administrators who, in other circumstances, might have had only supporting roles in the imperial drama: Cromer, Kitchener, Gordon, and their understudies—a whole generation that included Reginald Wingate.

In the British occupation of 1882 can be discerned echoes of Napoleon's invasion in 1798. The threat this seemed to imply to British interests in India had been short-lived: Nelson's victory at Abuqir, Bonaparte's ignominious scuttle, and his army's evacuation in the face of Anglo-Ottoman arms ended the French presence in 1801. The ensuing British withdrawal led to a struggle between the Ottomans and local Mamluks, whom defeat by the French had discredited. The weakness of both sides gave advantage to a third, an Albanian contingent of the Ottoman army, to whose leader, Muhammad Ali, the governorship of Egypt fell in 1805. During a long rule (1805–48) he ended the threat of Mamluk resurgence, and consolidated his and his family's positions through military and administrative reforms. The dynasty he established lasted until 1952, under nominal Ottoman suzerainty until the First World War and various degrees of British control from 1882.

Muhammad Ali and his successors, Abbas (1848–54), Muhammad Sa'id (1854–63), and Isma'il (1863–79), made Egypt the leading regional power.[1] Beginning in 1820–21 with the invasion of Sinnar and Kordofan, an empire extending from the Red Sea to Wadai and as far south as the Great Lakes was won, at great cost. In the 1830s Muhammad Ali conquered Syria and threatened the Ottoman sultanate itself, only to be stymied by Great-Power intervention. Maintenance of the Ottoman Empire served British interests; these in turn favored Egypt's continuing autonomy during the Ottoman revival of the 1850s. Subsequently it was not Ottoman but European, especially French, encroachment that most threatened. That new danger was symbolized during the reign of Sa'id by a concession to de Lesseps for building the Suez Canal. Ottoman and British opposition was overcome, and in 1869 the canal was inaugurated by Isma'il Pasha, amid much fanfare.

The canal was the most famous of many projects taken up by Isma'il, who in 1867 won from the sultan acknowledgment of the title khedive (Farsi: *khidiv:* king). His brilliant reign was marked by increasing effort to assert Egyptian independence, and ended with his deposition, a nationalist rising, and European occupation. Isma'il's designs were unmatched by his resources. Hampered by the Capitulations (Ottoman treaties, applicable in Egypt, that gave privileges to foreigners), and by the interference Egypt's debt to Europeans allowed their governments to exert, Isma'il eventually lost room to maneuver. In 1876 he set up the *Caisse de la Dette Publique,* with four European commissioners to restructure Egypt's debt; British and French controllers were appointed to oversee the government's revenue and expenditure. But when it became clear that Isma'il would not act as agent of the European bondholders, Britain and France induced the sultan to depose him in June 1879.

The open interference of the European Powers, and their attempts to manage Egyptian affairs through a weak new khedive, Muhammad Tawfiq, provoked a reaction. In 1881 army officers, whose grievances had been neglected, mutinied. In successive confrontations the khedive backed down, and the officers' standing grew. Alarmed, Britain and France agreed to support the khedive through a naval demonstration at Alexandria in May 1882. In a showdown, however, the khedive again gave way, and rioting at Alexandria on 11 June ended in the slaughter of Europeans. On 11 July the British fleet bombarded Alexandria. Attempts to organize international action,

---

[1] For a survey of the period see P.M. Holt, *Egypt and the Fertile Crescent 1516–1922,* London 1966, 176–217.

especially French participation, failed. With unusually broad domestic
support, the British government resolved to act. In August the Suez
Canal was secured, and on 13 September at the battle of al-Tall al-
Kabir, a British expeditionary force decisively defeated the Egyptians.

Intervention to restore the khedive's authority become permanent occupation. Although the British took immediate steps to evacuate their forces, it was clear that strategic interests could be secured
only by reform of Egypt's finances and administration. This would
take years, and was moreover beyond the power of the khedive, who
had been discredited by foreign intervention itself. Temporary measures were negotiated or imposed by the British in the face of intense
European, especially French, opposition. The resulting "anomalies"
(a recurrent word in Anglo-Egyptian history) were personified by Sir
Evelyn Baring, who came in September 1883[2] as British agent and
consul-general, but remained for a quarter of a century as virtual ruler
of Egypt.

One of many British difficulties was the defense of Egypt. The
Egyptian army had been disbanded after al-Tall al-Kabir. Most
schemes to replace it posed political or financial problems. A permanent British force would be expensive and belie promises of early
evacuation. Therefore it was decided to raise a new Egyptian army,
under British command. In December 1882 Sir Evelyn Wood was
appointed *sirdar* (commander-in-chief), and charged with the task.
He recruited twenty-six British officers, including in January 1883
Herbert Kitchener,[3] and in April, through the good offices of General
Blair, the young Lieutenant Reginald Wingate.

In June 1883, when he arrived, Egypt was thus in a state of flux.
The khedive (still legally a vassal of the Ottoman sultan) was a pup-
pet; his rebellious army had been humiliated and disbanded by foreigners. The Turco-Egyptian ruling class had shared the khedive's and
army's disgrace. The government was unable to pay its debts; the
events of 1880–82 had deepened the financial crisis. The mass of the
population, landless *fallahin* (peasants) or small-holders, was sullen
but expectant; its lot had been worsened in the 1870s by rapacious
landlords and incompetent government, by low Niles and poor har-
vests. Adamantly opposed to Christian European rule, defeated
nationalists nevertheless suspected British motives for retaining insti-

---

[2] Earl of Cromer, *Modern Egypt,* London 1908, I, 345.

[3] See E.W.C. Sandes, *The Royal Engineers in Egypt and the Sudan,* Chatham 1937,
52–54.

tutions of the old regime. Even with the best intentions British officials would face European interference, notably French participation
in the revived Dual Control of Egyptian finances. Thus the British
had responsibility in a complex and dangerous situation, but without
the complete authority needed for control.

Such issues did not concern the twenty-one-year-old lieutenant
who arrived at Suez, after a stormy passage from India, on 3 June
1883.[4] Wingate was unknown and unconnected. His personal
finances, always worrying, had been recently improved by an uncle's
legacy of £650, part of which he invested in government bonds; he
dreaded falling into the hands of money-lenders.[5] Nor did he have the
characteristics that propelled fellow officers such as Kitchener:
Wingate was short (about 5′6″), portly, and slightly owlish-looking;
what others won easily with flair, he would achieve through hard
work, or not at all. Senior officers in Egypt found him a dutiful subordinate and pleasant companion: never having known his father,
Wingate formed lifelong attachments to several early chiefs—most
notably, Sir Evelyn Wood. In any case the British establishment in the
new Egyptian army was so small as to give even the most junior scope
for advancement. Wingate's greatest advantage in Egypt was to have
won appointment.

Wingate arrived in Cairo on 4 June, checked into Shepheards
Hotel, reported immediately to Wood, the sirdar, and was posted to
the 4th Egyptian battalion under Major Wynne. He himself became
immediately third in command; no British officer could serve under
an Egyptian, so Wingate was now a major (*bimbashi*) at a salary of
£E440 (or £450) a year. On the sixth, after his second lunch in two
days with the sirdar, he had an audience with the khedive at Abdin
Palace. All this was exciting; practical problems of his new posting
soon intruded. Wood made clear why he had wanted an Arabist:
Wingate was to assist in translating the army drillbook.[6] He had found
himself unable to converse with the man in the street, and when his
Arabic tutor arrived from Aden at the end of June, Wingate housed

---

[4] Wingate's commonplace book is contradictory on the date of arrival, giving both
3 and 4 June (CB1).

[5] Wingate, diary entries for 28 July; 2 August, SAD 102/5; 28 September 1882,
SAD 102/6.

[6] CB1; Wingate diary, entries for 4, 5, 6, 7 June 1883, SAD 102/7; Contract of
service with Egyptian Army, 17 July 1883, SAD 233/6; "Pay of army," n.d., SAD
250/1/659.

him across the hall from his quarters at Abbasiyah. Comic-opera aspects of his position were fully revealed when Wingate, ignorant of the Turkish commands the Egyptian army used, and unable to resort to colloquial Arabic, had to drill NCOs in bayonet exercises he did not know. Yet Wingate easily passed the colloquial Arabic examination on 12 July. By then he had already been told—after four weeks in Egypt—that when Wynne went on leave he would command the battalion.[7] Nature intervened.

In July 1883 cholera broke out in Egypt, first in the Delta, then in Cairo, where it quickly spread to the army. On the fourteenth Wingate was made commandant of a special quarantine camp, which he had to set up himself. From the twenty-second, when the first case was admitted, Wingate and a few others worked night and day amid a mounting death toll. On 8 August he fell ill himself, not with cholera but typhoid. Fortunately there had arrived in Cairo a few days earlier a British doctor, T. D. Acland, who took special interest in the case. Wingate acknowledged that he owed him his life, and a lasting friendship began.[8] By 16 September Wingate was well enough to travel and was invalided home. At the Cairo station General Grenfell presented the first of Wingate's many decorations, the Osmaniah (4th class), for services during the epidemic; Grenfell's report noted especially his handling of Egyptian soldiers. On the ship to France Wingate met Sir Edward Malet, whom Baring had just succeeded as agent and consul-general; and Sir Colin Scott-Moncrieff, the irrigation expert newly appointed to the Egyptian Ministry of Public Works.[9] After reaching London on 1 October Wingate went to Scotland for six weeks, a period, he said, that "seemed to me almost the happiest time of my life."[10]

During this Scottish convalescence (which included much travel and visiting), Wingate fell in love with Norah McFarlane. When he went to Cannes in mid-November (on doctor's orders), it was in fact to visit her. He stayed there for three weeks, until recalled to Egypt in mid-December. There his hopes were dashed when Norah's mother

---

[7] Wingate, diary entries for 9, 27 June; 7, 12 July 1883, SAD 102/7.

[8] Wingate diary, entries for July and 8 August 1883, SAD 102/7; CB1.

[9] Wingate diary, entry for 8 August 1883 (recording events through 21 December), SAD 102/7; "Extract from report on cholera in the Egyptian Army," in Grenfell to Consul General Cairo, 8 August 1883, SAD 155/1/41; CB1.

[10] Diary entry for 8 August 1883, SAD 102/7. See note 9.

wrote and asked that he stop writing to her daughter. He recognized error in not having informed Norah's family of his intentions, but blamed his situation—that of a poor man, without prospects—for the inevitable disappointment.[11]

Events in Egypt left little time for brooding. On 5 November, at Shaykan in the desert of Kordofan, an Egyptian army under the British general William Hicks was destroyed by the Sudanese forces of the Mahdi. Hicks and his European officers were among the thousands killed. News of the debacle reached Cairo on the twenty-second, causing consternation. The army destroyed had been survivors of al-Tall al-Kabir, not Wood's new force, and Hicks had been acting in Egypt's name, not Britain's. But the occupying power could hardly evade all responsibility, either for the disaster or for what it portended on Egypt's southern border. When Wingate returned to Egypt on 20 December he was immediately brought into the War Office as ADC to General Wood,[12] and his duties soon involved the crisis in the Sudan.

---

[11] Diary entries for 8 August; 22, 23–26, 27, 28 December 1883, SAD 102/7.

[12] CB1; diary entries for 8 August; 22 December 1883, SAD102/7. Hicks was a retired Indian Army colonel hired by the Egyptian government and given the rank of *fariq*.

Chapter Four
The Sudan

———◁◦◦◦▷———

Although he served in the Egyptian army for thirty-two years—from 1883 to 1885, and 1886 to 1916—it is with the Sudan that Wingate's name is most closely associated. While the Egyptians and British had been occupied with events in Egypt itself, revolution had erupted in Egypt's empire to the south. The Mahdi's revolt, the death of Gordon and fall of Khartoum, the Khalifa Abdallahi's turbulent reign, and the Anglo-Egyptian conquest of the Sudan in 1896-98 comprise a long and much-thumbed chapter in imperial lore. The Mahdiyya has usually been seen as hopeless, backward-looking, and romantic; a stage-setting for the drama of British conquest; even as epitomizing the diabolic childishness with which Africa confronted Europe. Reginald Wingate did much to foster such views. As the Sudanese Mahdiyya was the making of Wingate, so the outside world's version of it was largely his creation.

Egypt and the lands south of the first cataract at Aswan are united by the Nile. Political, religious, and economic relations have been continuous and pervasive. By the early nineteenth century, when Egypt again sought to extend its rule there, the Sudan was a frontier zone between the Muslim world and Africa. In its Nilotic north, Islam and Arabic bore witness to and amplified the influence of Egypt. To the south, however, difficult communications and the resistance of Nilotic peoples and institutions barred the way to the Upper Nile and the lands drained by its tributaries. Of these Egypt knew little more than Europe.

Muhammad Ali's invasion of Sinnar and Kordofan in 1820–21 was intended mainly to win control of rumored riches. The long decline of central authority had left resistance to invasion weak; the Funj sultanate of Sinnar had largely been superseded by tribal confederacies and local chieftaincies. With a few famous exceptions the Egyptian campaign went smoothly. By 1822 the local forces along the main Nile and in Kordofan had been beaten. Kassala (or Taka) was subdued in 1840, the region of Fashoda in 1863. The far south

19

now lay open to Egypt, which by mid-century enjoyed the advantages of modern rifles and river steamers. Equatorial Province was established in 1871, the province of Bahr al-Ghazal two years later, and, in 1874, the lands of the old Fur sultanate were formally annexed.

Imperialism took on a logic of its own. The search for gold had been disappointing, that for ivory insufficiently remunerative; the need for slaves led to ever-deeper penetration of the Sudan. The Upper Nile fed the slave markets of the Near East and of the northern Sudan itself. Merchant-princes arose who, although Egyptian subjects, exercised sovereignty in remote stations; Zubayr Pasha Mansur, the most famous of the slavers, conquered Darfur in 1874. When, from the 1860s, Europe, especially Britain, exerted pressure on Egypt to halt this trade, a necessary condition was the further extension of Egyptian authority. Thus by the mid-1870s Egypt's empire reached the Great Lakes in the south, Wadai in the west, and the Eritrean coast of the Red Sea.

Egyptian rule in Africa, like that of its European colonial counterparts, was largely indirect. Denied easy wealth, Egypt was unwilling to invest heavily in government. Administrative policy was pragmatic, designed to finance the regime, maintain order, and encourage trade. This policy had mixed results. Relative security in the north led to urbanization. Khartoum, in 1821 a village near the confluence of the Blue and White Niles, by the 1870s resembled a well-built Mediterranean town. Wad Medani, El Obeid, and other centers were similarly developed. Communications were improved by regular steamer services and an extensive telegraph network. Trade, both foreign and internal, was enhanced, in ivory, gum, grain, ostrich feathers, animals, hides and skins, cloth, and other goods. Modern education and medicine were introduced, mainly for Egyptian personnel and their families.

On the other side of the ledger were problems and abuses which, in the 1880s, would lead to revolution. Determined to limit expenditure, the Egyptians raised taxes, especially on agriculture. This stimulated the slave trade, both because more land had to be cultivated, and because farmers were forced to turn to trade, notably but not exclusively in slaves. Traders in turn enlisted their own slave-soldiers, whose privileged status depended on commerce. From 1865, when the regime tried to control, then suppress, the slave trade, it therefore threatened the livelihoods of widespread and important elements of the population. Khedive Isma'il's use of Christian foreigners such as

Samuel Baker, Romolo Gessi, and Charles Gordon to carry out this policy added fuel to an issue already stoked with religious feeling. Taxation likewise alienated the populous Baqqara tribes of the west who, after Darfur was annexed in 1874, discerned little benefit in their altered status. But while these and other complaints were serious, it was a fortuitous combination of Egyptian collapse and unprecedented Sudanese unity that brought about the downfall of the regime.

In Islam messianic traditions center around an ultimate savior, the Mahdi (or divinely-guided one), who at the end of time will deliver Muslims from evil and restore justice to the world. Over the centuries, the circumstances of claimants to this role have engendered a body of traditions about the genealogy, appearance, and functions of the Mahdi. Popular reception of a claim to mahdi-ship has depended upon the contemporary social and political milieu: difficult times clarify the need for deliverance, and discount deviation from tradition while exaggerating points of compliance. In the Sudanese case there is evidence of interest in Mahdism in west and central Africa, and elsewhere in the Nile valley, including Egypt, earlier in the nineteenth century.[1] By the 1880s the idea had currency, and Sudanese had motives for revolt. The Mahdi's charismatic moment came with Egypt at its weakest and the Sudanese aggrieved, transforming provincial revolt into millennial movement.

Muhammad Ahmad ibn Abdallah was born in 1844 in Dongola, the son of a boatbuilder. After a traditional religious education he entered the Sammaniya sufi order, gained a reputation for piety and learning, and won a circle of followers. From Aba Island in the White Nile he issued, in March 1881, his declaration of mahdi-ship. This was followed by public manifestation and calls for adherence. Bungled attempts to arrest him enhanced his authority. Having crossed into Kordofan in August 1881, the Mahdi ambushed and destroyed an Egyptian force, capturing quantities of arms and the imagination of the tribes. A long campaign against Egyptian garrisons ensued. In January 1883 he took El Obeid, capital of Kordofan and main town of the western Sudan. The government of Egypt, buffeted by revolt and occupation, sent Hicks, the retired Indian army officer, to defeat the Mahdi; in this strategy the British acquiesced. Hicks's expedition into Kordofan was doomed from the start, and on 5 November 1883

[1] For a summary of Mahdism see Holt, *The Mahdist state,* 22–31.

his army was destroyed at Shaykan. With his powers seemingly confirmed and arms immensely reinforced, the Mahdi turned his attention to the east and Khartoum.

Although the British government had avoided official involvement in the Sudan, as the occupying power it had a responsibility to
defend Egyptian interests. London now decided that those would
best be served by abandoning the Sudan altogether, except for the
Red Sea ports.[2] When the British insisted, the Egyptian Ministry of
Sharif Pasha resigned in January 1884; his successor, Nubar Pasha,
agreed to British wishes. Few if any military men thought the Sudan
tenable without European troops, or worth their commitment. Nor
was there any evidence that Europeans could beat the Mahdi. There
remained, however, the task of salvaging the Egyptian civilian and
military population in the Sudan, and the Sudanese who wished to
leave. This was the assignment of General Gordon.

So much has been written about Gordon that any summary of his
last mission seems repetitive or simplistic. The main facts (but not the
details, which hagiographers continue to dispute) are clear. British
policy, which Gordon explicitly endorsed, was to evacuate the Sudan.
From the time of his recruitment in London in January 1884 until his
departure from Cairo less than a fortnight later, however, Gordon was
loaded down with documents (some of which, in Arabic, he was
unable to read), that obscured this central point, while his own imagination added daily to the scope of his mission. Ill-assorted hopes and
expectations of the British public, press, and politicians—and of
Gordon himself and his superiors in Cairo—were based on ignorance
of the Sudanese situation and exaggeration of his ability. Gordon was
the wrong man for the task at hand and was selected for the wrong
reasons; Baring, if not his superiors in London, was alive to the dangers Gordon posed. Those lay ahead when on 25 January Reginald
Wingate met "the celebrated Gordon Pasha" in Cairo; Wingate was
among the British officers who bade farewell when Gordon left for
the Sudan the next day.[3]

To an inexperienced young officer the prospect of war in the
Sudan was exhilarating. Having returned from sick leave on 20
December 1883, Wingate began work in the Egyptian War Office as

[2] Granville to Baring, 20 November 1883; quoted in Cromer, *Modern Egypt*, I,
373.

[3] Diary entries for 25, 26 January 1884, SAD 102/7.

"a sort of assistant or secretary" to Sir Evelyn Wood.[4] But hopes of active service were soon curtailed by news of Egyptian defeats in the Sudan. While the Mahdi himself had reduced the west, in the eastern Sudan the rebellion was directed from mid-1883 by Uthman Diqna (Osman Digna), later the most famous Mahdist *amir*. Exploiting sectarian rivalries within the Bija tribes, Uthman won a following, adopted the tactics of guerrilla warfare, and was soon strong enough to besiege Egyptian garrisons. Unchecked, Uthman might cut communications between Egypt and Khartoum. A force of Egyptian military police under British officers was therefore sent to Suakin, whence it set out on 4 February 1884 to relieve Tokar. Confronted by a Mahdist force, the Egyptians fled in disarray, losing more than two thousand men. British reinforcements arrived too late to relieve Tokar. Wood and his officers felt disgraced by this turn of events: the "death-knell of the Egyptian Army" was Wingate's reaction.[5] But the humiliation of British officers in Egypt had only just begun.

Now General Gordon made a fatal mistake. On 13 February at Berber, en route to Khartoum, he announced the khedive's decision to abandon the Sudan. Subsequent attempts to dilute the impact on public opinion were futile. Sudanese who had remained loyal or neutral now faced a choice: to come to terms with the Mahdi or leave the country. That Gordon believed he could reach a settlement with the Mahdi, buy him off, or at least arrange an orderly transition, was not only naive but now irrelevant to the urgent calculations of the Sudanese.[6] From Khartoum Gordon's messages to Cairo and the Mahdi were equally unavailing: neither Zubayr, the merchant he proposed to rule the Sudan, nor British troops would be sent; while the Mahdi, to whom he offered a sultanate and a suit of clothes, replied with the promise of Paradise and a patched *jibba*.[7]

By the autumn of 1884 the fall of Khartoum was inevitable. The British, and now the Egyptians, had written off the Sudan. Only the political impact of a debacle—the capture or death of Gordon, the massacre of Egyptian garrisons—concerned British officials in Cairo and London. In August the British government had felt forced to act,

---

[4] Wingate, diary entry for 22 December 1883, SAD 102/7.

[5] Diary entry for 15 February 1884, SAD 102/7. For the defeat near Suakin see Holt, *The Mahdist state*, 84n, 86.

[6] See Holt, *The Mahdist state*, 93–95.

[7] The patched, homespun *jibba* symbolized Mahdist asceticism. See Holt, *The Mahdist state*, 93, 95–98.

and had sanctioned an expedition in relief of Gordon. It was only on 5 October, however, that Lord Wolseley, appointed to command, reached Wadi Halfa. Meanwhile participation of the Egyptian army had been authorized, and from August, following the decision to relieve, Wood and his staff had been engaged in preparing an advance.

The main task of the Egyptian Army was to secure communications between Wadi Halfa and Khartoum. General Wood, with Wingate as acting A.D.C., arrived at Wadi Halfa on 29 August; Wingate remained there until 23 December. By then Wolseley was ready to proceed, and Wingate accompanied Wood to Kurti, Wolseley's forward headquarters.[8] Traveling mainly by camel and along the Nile, he closely observed the countryside and made frequent contact with villagers. On 4 January Wood's party reached Dongola, and was received with much fanfare by the governor. They reached al-Dabba on the ninth and Kurti, Wolseley's headquarters, on the eleventh.[9] There the relief expedition divided into two forces: one to cross the Bayuda Desert to al-Matamma, north of Khartoum; the other to follow the Nile. Wingate's diary gives details of the failed relief mission and of this first active service of the future sirdar.

Wingate's role as A.D.C. was mainly clerical, although in so small a headquarters his duties varied; often he found himself overseeing bivouac arrangements and interviewing local notables. Much time was spent ciphering and deciphering Wood's telegrams, occasionally all day and through the night. But neither routine duties nor the occasional excitement of the advance distracted him from personal disappointment. All his life Wingate would be sensitive to treatment by superiors; as the most junior British officer in the Egyptian army he had filed a complaint about an Arabic examination. Now, on campaign, he fretted about performing the duties of the sirdar's A.D.C. without the title or pay. He wondered why Wood withheld the appointment, but thought that if offered it he must refuse, lest in maintaining his station he fall heavily into debt. He had lent money to fellow-officers; they had not repaid him. On the day after news reached camp of the British victory at Abu Tulayh (Abu Klea), Wingate recorded an excess of expenditure over income of £161 (the equivalent of five months' pay); this would preclude "all possibility of . . . ever getting home [on leave] or ever getting

---

[8] CB1.

[9] Wingate, diary of the relief expedition, SAD 102/3.

out of debt."[10] The next day General Buller criticized the "slipshod way" in which Wingate ran Wood's office.[11] For another week he brooded, until Buller left to command the Desert Column, and Wood, appointed chief of staff, showed confidence by appointing Wingate A.D.C.[12]

There was little time to celebrate. Khartoum had fallen to the Mahdi. The approaching Desert Column had spurred a general assault on the city. On 4 February Wingate privately recorded receipt of the news in a dispatch from Buller: on 24 January Sir Charles Wilson and a forward force on two steamers had with difficulty reached the mouth of the Blue Nile when, in Wingate's words, "heavy fire was poured upon them from 5 points and from Khartoum itself which they could see plainly and which appeared to be wrecked—the Government house had no flag flying and all seemed to point to the town being in the hands of the enemy."[13] "Staggered by the news," Wingate and fellow officers were especially affected by the two-day gap between Gordon's death and Wilson's arrival off Khartoum,[14] a misapprehension that has become embedded in popular imagination. For the Mahdists had stormed Khartoum *because* the British were near: they would in any case have arrived "too late."

The expedition to relieve Khartoum became a mission to retake it. This reversal of policy was based on sentiment: British officers had been humiliated, and argued that Egypt would never be secure until the Mahdi was destroyed. Orders were given to defend Sudanese districts as yet "undisturbed," pending a decision about an advance to Khartoum. But the force available was insufficient for offensive operations, and the Mahdists continued to press. In mid-February Wood and his staff were ordered to Jakdul, half-way along the desert route to al-Matamma, where they were concerned mainly with evacuating casualties. By mid-March the entire Desert Column had retreated to Kurti. Operations could not resume before autumn. Meanwhile in Britain realism asserted itself, and by April the government had resumed its policy of abandoning the Sudan.

---

[10] Diary for 22 January 1885, SAD 102/3.

[11] Diary for 23 January 1885, SAD 102/3.

[12] Diary for 29 January 1885, SAD 102/3.

[13] Diary for 4 February 1885, SAD 102/3.

[14] Diary for 5 February 1885, SAD 102/3. For continuing debate over Gordon's death see Douglas H. Johnson, "The death of Gordon: a Victorian myth," *Journal of imperial and commonwealth history* X, 3, May 1982, 285–310.

While still engaged in the details of retreat Wingate faced decisions about his own future. In March Sir Evelyn Wood, unfairly sharing the blame for the failure of Anglo-Egyptian arms, resigned the
sirdarship. Wingate's contract would expire in June. Sir Francis
Grenfell, the new sirdar, offered to keep a place for him should he
leave the Egyptian army and later wish to return. With this in mind
Wingate, still at Kurti with Wood, studied for the higher standard
Arabic examination.[15] The announcement on 22 April that the British
had decided to withdraw from the Sudan clarified his personal position: the future seemed bleak for British officers in the Egyptian army.
Meanwhile Wood was ill and advanced his own date of departure. On
7 May he and his staff left al-Dabba. On the eleventh, at Dongola,
Wingate recorded the good cheer of British officers who had only
that morning received the order to "scuttle." Wood had offered to
make him A.D.C. at his new command in Colchester once he passed
the examination for promotion to captain, so Wingate too decided to
go.[16] On 20 May near Akasha, Wingate met Grenfell and, in "perhaps
the most unpleasant quarter of an hour" of his life, resigned without
mentioning Wood's offer.[17]

What Wingate believed were his last days in Egypt began on 1
June when he reached Cairo. On the second he took the Arabic examination which, after irregular proceedings, he passed with honors; this
carried a bonus of £100, and let him leave Egypt in about the same
financial condition in which he had arrived two years earlier.[18] Other
honors were withheld: at a farewell audience the khedive gave thanks
but no decoration (thus winning Wingate a £1 wager with Leslie
Rundle); disappointment made it easier to leave.[19] On the fourth he
resigned from the Egyptian service, and on the fifth officially returned
to the English army. Having thus resumed the rank of subaltern—"I
don't much feel my fall in rank" he confided in a diary—Wingate left

---

[15] Diary entries for 14 March 1885, SAD 102/3; 23, 25, 31 March; 1 April 1885,
SAD 102/10.

[16] Diary entries for 22 April; 4, 9, 11, 19 May, SAD 102/10.

[17] Diary entries for 20 May; 4 June 1885, SAD 102/10.

[18] Diary entries for 1, 2, 3 June 1885, SAD 102/10. The examiner wrote that
Wingate had passed "with honours" even though his score was one or two per-
centage points below that rank (diary entry for 3 June).

[19] Diary entry for 3 June 1885, SAD 102/10.

Cairo on 6 June.[20] At Ismailia he and Wood boarded the P.& O. liner *Sutlej*, whose passengers included the duke and duchess of Connaught. This first encounter with the royal family made an impression. The duke greeted them in pajamas, but the firing of salutes, "the honour of being invited to the Royal Table," and the luxury of first-class travel after the bivouacs of the Bayuda were as alluring to Wingate as they were tedious to Wood.[21] Wingate would soon have time enough to remember an important fact of life: in Egypt his social rank had been elevated by his race; at home he would be just another junior officer.

---

[20] Diary entry for 5 June 1885, SAD 102/10.
[21] Diary entries for 6, 7, 8, 9 June 1885, SAD 102/10.

Chapter Five
The Defense of Egypt

————⊰◯◯◯⊱————

W ingate's sojourn in Britain was a turning point in his career. Talented but impecunious, he found living expenses beyond his means and his Eastern experience of no account. Sir Evelyn Wood was his only friend in high places. By May 1886, when Wingate engaged to marry, it was clear that leaving the Egyptian army had been a mistake, and when an opportunity arose to return he took it without delay.

Wingate's luxurious voyage to England ended on 15 June 1885, and he began three and a half months' leave. In August the official dispatches of the Khartoum Relief Expedition were published; Wingate received his first "mention in Despatches." On 28 September he joined the Depot Battery, Southern Division, at Fort Rowner, Gosport, and immediately began preparing for his promotion examination. He passed in January 1886, and on 1 April, as arranged, was appointed A.D.C. to Wood, at the Eastern Command, Colchester. A week earlier the khedive had sent him the Medjidia order (4th class) for his services in Egypt.[1] How this affected his wager with Rundle is unrecorded.

A greater debt had in any case accrued. When Wingate arrived at Gosport in September 1885 he was joined by Rundle, newly returned from Egypt. Seven months later, on 1 May 1886, Wingate became engaged to Rundle's sister, Catherine, and resigned as Wood's A.D.C. Having accepted Grenfell's invitation to rejoin the Egyptian army, as assistant military secretary to the sirdar, Wingate sailed on 19 May, and took up his appointment in Egypt on the thirty-first.[2] He had been away a few days less than a year.

As assistant military secretary, then (from August 1886) also as assistant adjutant-general for recruiting, and finally, from 1888, as assistant adjutant-general for intelligence, Wingate was closely involved in the military administration of Egypt. Britain's ambiguous position, a partly consequent reliance on personal relations rather

---

[1] CB1; Wingate's Bible.
[2] CB1; CB2.

than official organization, and a small complement of British officers (and even fewer with useful languages and expertise) tested Wingate's undoubted capacity for work. Later in life, in high office, he would have to delegate; now, as an energetic bureaucrat, he was the object of superiors' reliance. Soon taken for granted, Wingate learned that ability alone would not guarantee preferment. This bred resentment, suspicion, jealousy, patience, and determination, for all of which Egypt offered ample scope.

It was the English cost of living and the prospect of marriage that had brought Wingate back to Egypt. Neither he nor Catherine Rundle had significant private income, so they had to delay the wedding until he established himself. Upon rejoining the Egyptian army, Wingate automatically became a local major, at £E540 per year. In May 1887 he was promoted senior major (*bimbashi*), at £E720. Despite promotion and increased responsibilities, he had no further increase in salary until May 1894. Lack of money was a theme of his early married life—as, indeed, it would be from time to time ever after.

On 18 June 1888 at St. Mary Abbot's, West Kensington, Wingate married Catherine Leslie Rundle, the only daughter of Captain Joseph Sparkhall Rundle, R.N., and Renira Catherine Leslie, both deceased.[3] It was by all accounts a happy marriage, and they had four children. Although propriety precluded a large official role, society expected more than homely virtues, and "Kitty" Wingate would play a continuous part in her husband's career. In Egypt British officials and officers, however junior, were a ruling class; as elsewhere in the empire, the manners and customs of home were not only upheld but exaggerated. Exchanging the banal security of the English middle class for the artifice and anxiety of a foreign elite, Catherine Rundle, like other British wives, took refuge in formality. She embodied Victorian qualities of propriety, dignity, and rigidity, kindness, sentimentality, and ambition. The Catherine Wingate of photographs and officials' memoirs is a stiff, severe, even forbidding public person; that of diaries, intense private correspondence, and family memories a vulnerable and sensitive wife and mother.

---

[3] CB1; Catherine Rundle was born on 26 October 1858, and was thus almost three years older than her husband; she never revealed her birthdate to her children and grandchildren, or, it seems, to her husband. See Genealogy of Rundles, n.d., SAD 234/7.

Abandonment of the Sudan had altered the role of the Egyptian army. British officers had two reputations to retrieve: that of the Egyptian soldier, diminished at al-Tall al-Kabir and destroyed in the Sudanese desert; and their own, tainted by the failure to rescue Gordon and by subsequent retreat. Moreover, the death of the Mahdi and the accession of the Khalifa Abdallahi in 1885 left unaltered the expansionist ideology of Mahdism: the message was universal, not national. Anglo-Egyptian authorities therefore prepared to defend Egypt itself, without an accurate appreciation of the threat they faced. During the spring of 1885 Grenfell established a Frontier Force, with headquarters at Aswan and a brigade at Wadi Halfa. In December, at the battle of Qinis, an Anglo-Egyptian force defeated the local Mahdists; amid mutual misreading of intentions, the Frontier Force then withdrew. Egyptian troops, having fought creditably at Qinis, were left to man the forward position at Halfa, which was fortified. The Mahdists, fully engaged elsewhere, likewise adopted a defensive strategy.[4] A similar stalemate prevailed in the eastern Sudan, where Suakin remained in Anglo-Egyptian hands.

As a staff officer based in Cairo, and still more as assistant military secretary and deputy adjutant-general for recruitment, Wingate was fully occupied in bureaucratic routine. The new Egyptian army had been recruited from 1883 in disregard of Egyptian law, and the recruitment system of the old army remained legally in effect. When it was realized in 1886 that a new draft would soon be needed, the recruiting law was amended. But village registers and census figures proved unreliable, as did local *shaykhs* empowered to conduct lotteries. In January 1887, therefore, recruiting commissions were established, and in May a khedivial general amnesty erased old offenses against the recruiting laws. Recruitment based on this reform was time-consuming, however, and Wingate proposed a system of annual (rather than five-yearly) recruiting.[5]

When Wingate returned to it in 1886 the Egyptian army consisted of some ten thousand men, organized into two brigades of five battalions each. Most of the men were native Egyptian conscripts, although, starting in 1884, Sudanese battalions had been raised,

---

[4] See Holt, *The Mahdist state,* 142–43, 175–77.

[5] Wingate, Report on recruiting operations, n.d., SAD 155/3.

mainly from among southerners who had remained loyal to Egypt or deserted the Mahdi. In 1886 two more Sudanese battalions were created, in 1887 a fourth, and in 1888 a fifth. By 1891 the army's strength was between twelve and thirteen thousand, and its budget about £E500,000. British officers numbered only sixty-four. Indeed, Wingate's time as assistant adjutant-general for recruiting coincided with important changes in the army: increases in its budget and establishment; greater professionalism; more reliance on Egyptian officers; growing confidence; and removal of the military threat thought to have been posed by Mahdism. Within a few years a compact force capable of defending Egypt's southern border had been created.

Like other bureaucracies, the Egyptian army rewarded good work by assigning more. Within months of re-appointment in 1886 Wingate was devoting time to military intelligence and to staff duties unrelated to recruiting. In February 1888 he was made responsible for civilian employees of the adjutant-general's office and for supervising civilian affairs at the frontier. By March Wingate had reaped the consequences of over-work, and an inspection of the frontier was in fact a "working holiday" to cure insomnia and other symptoms; after that he took care of his health, and tried to fit golf or tennis into every day.[6] But in October 1888, when a new army intelligence office was formed from existing personnel, Wingate was placed in charge; to circumvent the budget this arrangement went unannounced, and he retained the title, and duties, of assistant adjutant-general for recruiting.

Intelligence would make Wingate's name in Egypt. After home leave in 1888 he returned to Cairo with his new wife on 6 October. On 14 January 1889 he was promoted captain in the Royal Artillery, and the next day brevet major for services in 1884–85. A month later he was formally put in charge of intelligence, and promoted to the Egyptian rank of *kaimakam* (lieutenant colonel).[7] This rapid progress—Wingate turned twenty-eight in June 1889—was impressive, but the size of the British cadre, and consequent piling on of duties, qualified the ascent. In fact, again for budgetary reasons, Wingate's headship of the intelligence sub-office in the adjutant-general's department went unannounced, his transfer from recruiting

---

[6] CB1.

[7] Ibid.

duties was notified only verbally, and as late as 1893 he was still shown in some army orders as assistant adjutant-general, recruiting.[8]

Wingate chafed at this proliferation of ill-assorted duties. When in the autumn of 1888 Uthman Diqna laid siege to Suakin, the Red Sea port still held by Anglo-Egyptian forces, Grenfell and most of his staff went with reinforcements from Cairo, leaving Wingate almost alone and "overwhelmed with work" at the War Office.[9] His very competence made him indispensable in the office and thus unavailable for active service. "Most of my juniors," he wrote to Sir Evelyn Wood in January 1889, "are running up a mass of good reports . . . while I drift into insignificance"; he had become "a sort of handy Billy to any . . . Dick, Tom or Harry who enters the office." For this he blamed Grenfell, who never thanked him, paid no attention to career prospects, and (as Wingate told Grenfell's predecessor) had allowed standards to deteriorate.[10]

It was at this trying time that Wingate was promoted brevet major and put in charge of the new intelligence office, a development that captured his imagination and restored his equanimity. From early 1889 his time was spent mainly on this new duty, and to him belongs credit for organizing the Egyptian army's intelligence system. His long experience in this field would have important consequences for Egypt, the Sudan, and the outside world's understanding of them, as well as for his own conduct in future offices. At the outset, however, and until the possibility of an Anglo-Egyptian advance in the Sudan was mooted, Intelligence remained under-manned and under-funded, and was undertaken only because the British army of occupation itself refused to pay for frontier intelligence.[11] Wingate nevertheless turned the office into his own bailiwick. He regularized its affairs, expanded its duties and area of operation, brought its work to the attention of officials in London, and added to its purpose of collecting and disseminating information the advocacy of policy.

Wingate moved quickly to define the role of the Egyptian intelligence office. Discussions with the deputy assistant adjutant-general of the army of occupation delimited respective spheres. In February 1889 the office's functions were enumerated in a War Office memorandum. These included collecting information about

---

[8] Wingate, "Organization. Military Intelligence," n.d., SAD179/3.
[9] Wingate to Sparkes, 30 December 1888, SAD 155/3.
[10] Wingate to Wood, 13 January 1889, SAD 155/4.
[11] Wingate to Dalton, 23 December 1888, SAD 155/3.

the frontier and in the Sudan, and coordination of activities with the British army in Egypt. "Branch offices" were established at Suakin and Wadi Halfa,[12] but Wingate retained control. From the very inauguration of the office he corresponded directly with the War Office in London; a letter from March 1889 shows the direction his thoughts had already taken: "I feel sure that we have means . . . of assisting you [the War Office] considerably—not only as regards Egypt itself but many of the adjacent Mussulman countries. . . . there is lots of information to be had if one only knows how to set about getting it."

On the one hand over-reaching, Wingate in the same letter asks the War Office for "printed matter on Egypt": he was "sadly deficient of copies of . . . reports on. . . Egypt, the Sudan, the Arab tribes etc."[13] Two weeks later he asked London, again without irony, for "any reports etc. on the mode of working an Intelligence Deptmt."[14]

Examination of Wingate's early forays into intelligence-gathering and analysis illustrates an imbalance of enthusiasm and technique. In 1888 rebellion against the Khalifa Abdallahi broke out in the western Sudan. Its leader, called Abu Jummayza, rallied the tribes and defeated Mahdist armies sent against him. The movement lacked cohesion, however, and after initial victories Abu Jummayza died, his followers melted away, and the Mahdists reasserted control.[15] Wingate's rendering of these events was confused. After misidentifying Abu Jummayza as a deputy of Muhammad al-Mahdi al-Sanusi, shaykh of the Sanusiyya, and reporting wrongly that "the whole of Kordofan and Darfur" had risen up behind him, Wingate preposterously reported "every probability that the leader of the movement" would "oust the present Khalifa." Taking this for granted, he went on to suggest negotiations to recognize the Senussi's "spiritual supremacy over the Sudan," while establishing there a regime "compatible with the present policy of the Egyptian Government."[16] In a letter to the War Office in London a month later, however, Wingate called the Senussi news "exaggerated"; three days later he privately criticized his superiors for calling the Senussi a mere "local rebel"; and at the end of May wrote, with perhaps a new appreciation of his

---

[12] Wingate, "Organization. Military Intelligence," n.d., SAD179/3; Wingate to Dalton, 13 January 1889; 17 February 1889, SAD 155/4.

[13] Wingate to Callwell, 3 March? 1889, SAD 155/5.

[14] Wingate to Dalton, 16 March 1889, SAD 155/5.

[15] Holt, *The Mahdist state*, 157–59.

[16] Wingate, "Memorandum. The Senussi movement," 6 April 1889, SAD 155/5.

sources: "No news about Senussi except that he is reported to be dead or defeated and therefore I conclude he is more alive than ever."[17] But Wingate had made an important discovery, that "information" might be less valuable than even contradictory or erroneous "conclusions": in order to persuade London to keep British troops in Egypt, Baring and Grenfell were altering or even suppressing his reports.[18]

This episode illustrates several points of Wingate's method. He recognized early that his office would be bombarded with rumors, and that part of his work was to analyze, not merely report. But even in the rhetoric of everyday life the mere mention of a rumor lends it credence; while the terms in which reliable information is expressed can shed doubt on it, impugn its source, taint the motives of those who retail it and thus discredit the course of action it supports. Control of intelligence can silence critics, embarrass rivals, and reward friends, can indeed *create* "facts" and thus ensure outcomes that mere reporting would not support. Wingate learned that blame for erroneous assertions can be deflected by the way in which they are phrased; that British ignorance of Sudanese affairs was great enough to admit even gross distortions, without penalty to the reporter; and that his superiors were more likely to credit what they wished to hear. Information cannot be separated from its uses; in short, knowledge is power, and Wingate set out to harness it.

On the fate of distant revolts Wingate could afford to speculate, but accuracy about the frontier was essential to Egyptian security. For this Wingate had a requisite penchant for intrigue. In recruiting spies, sifting information, investigating tribal and personal motives, phrasing secret messages and interpreting replies, Wingate found a true vocation. In contrast to the quality of his reports on the Senussi, Wingate's intelligence on, for example, Mahdist troop movements was detailed and assured. By late May 1889 he had accurate information about the force advancing under the Amir Abd al-Rahman al-Nujumi down the Nile toward Egypt, and about its objectives. Most importantly, Wingate also had a clear appreciation of the difficulties al-Nujumi faced and the odds against his success.[19] While the unreliability of Sudanese informers continued to frustrate him and his colleagues at the frontier—diaries and correspondence relate the "dou-

---

[17] Wingate to Callwell, 14 May 1889; to Dunning, 17 May 1889; and to Prinsip, 30 May 1889, SAD 155/6.

[18] Wingate to Dunning, 17 May 1889, SAD 155/6.

[19] Wingate to Prinsip, 30 May 1889, SAD 155/6.

ble game" of the Ababda and Kababish[20]—Wingate correctly appreciated al-Nujumi's predicament long before his superiors did.[21]
Characteristically, he also considered in advance of battle the political
impact in England of the *manner* of victory: a massacre of Sudanese
camp-followers would bring an adverse reaction at home. Wingate
therefore drafted a letter from Grenfell to al-Nujumi, calling for surrender, and Grenfell reluctantly sent it. The letter alternated grue-
some warnings with the promise of leniency, and al-Nujumi sent the
expected reply: he and his men feared God alone.[22]

Confirmation of Wingate's Intelligence (and, more importantly,
of successful reform of the Egyptian army) came at the battle of
Tushki (Toski) in August 1889. In May al-Nujumi had set out from
Dongola for the long-delayed invasion of Egypt. Poorly provisioned
from the outset, his forces faced starvation by the time they reached
the Egyptian frontier, and were depleted by mass desertions. On 3
August at Tushki, downstream from Wadi Halfa, the Egyptian army
destroyed the Mahdist force; al-Nujumi himself was killed, and
any remaining Mahdist threat to Egypt ended. The battle has been
widely seen as having turned the Mahdist tide. In fact it revealed the
limits of Mahdism's expansionist ideology. For Wingate, who was present, it had personal significance: he witnessed vindication not only of
British military reform in Egypt, but also, and in detail, of his own
Intelligence efforts.

Wingate's success was marred by his mixing of private and public affairs. His wife, expecting their first child, had gone to England
earlier in the summer, and both worried about their finances. Wingate
had therefore agreed to act as a correspondent for Reuters while on
campaign. He was paid 20 Francs per short telegram, 40–60 Francs
for longer ones. Never at a loss for words, Wingate let loose a barrage
of long and colorful wires. One of these contained an estimate of al-
Nujumi's strength. At this, General Dormer, commanding the army
of occupation, ordered Wingate to end his correspondence. Reuters
intervened, and Dormer agreed to a system by which its Cairo agent

[20] Wingate to Callwell, 19 May 1889; Wingate to Dunning, 14 June 1889, SAD
155/6.

[21] See, e.g., Wingate to Prinsip, 30 May 1889, SAD 155/6; Wingate to Callwell,
22 July 1889, SAD 155/7.

[22] Wingate to his wife, 18 July 1889, SAD 233/7. Partial translations of the correspondence are in Holt, *The Mahdist state*, 180–81.

would omit from transmission to London anything he thought Dormer might like withheld. Wingate resumed the correspondence, and apologized to Dormer for the embarrassment. When he went on leave to London in August Wingate called at the Reuters office, solicited an additional "honorarium," and was paid sixty guineas more.[23] Easy money (and public recognition) opened Wingate's eyes to a second career.

Wingate's leave after Tushki was eventful. On 6 September he received his second "mention in Despatches" for intelligence work before the battle, and was awarded the Distinguished Service Order.[24] On the thirtieth his first child, Ronald Evelyn Leslie Wingate, was born in London. (The godfathers were two sirdars and future field-marshals, Wood and Grenfell.) Meanwhile Wingate had written a memorandum on the life and death of al-Nujumi, a copy of which he sent to Queen Victoria—Grenfell had already sent the amir's "armour"—thus modestly beginning a long association with the royal family.[25] He returned to Cairo on 31 October refreshed, delighted with his enlarged family, and expansive with plans and projects.

After the battle of Tushki, Egypt's southern frontier grew quiet, while in the eastern Sudan there was continuing stalemate. British officers in Egypt pressed for advances into Mahdist territory, but were rebuffed by London.[26] This was a period of frustration for the Anglo-Egyptian military establishment, of intramural disputes and personal conflicts, during which enhancement of reputation depended on developments subtler and less predictable than the tide of battle. For Wingate the period between November 1889 and October 1891 witnessed continued intelligence routine at a time when modest success had made him impatient for advance.

Soon after his return from leave Wingate became involved in another disconcerting episode with superior officers. Since undertak-

---

[23] Wingate to his wife, 20, 27 July 1889, SAD 233/7; Rees (Reuters agent for Egypt) to Wingate, 5 July (two telegrams), 18, 19, 30 July 1889; Wingate to Reuter, Cairo, e.g., 11, 13, 16 July, and (letter) 30 July 1889; Wingate to Dormer, July 1889, SAD 155/7; Griffith (Secretary, Reuter's Telegram Company) to Wingate, 4, 10, 12 September 1889, SAD 155/9. SAD 155/8 contains a series of Wingate's telegrams.

[24] CB1.

[25] CB1; CB2; Bigge to Wingate, 14 October 1889, SAD 155/9.

[26] See Holt, *The Mahdist state*, 190–92.

ing direction of intelligence he had communicated regularly with the intelligence department of the War Office in London and established close relations with officials there. This correspondence, undertaken with Grenfell's permission but "unofficially," had been unknown to both General Dormer and Sir Evelyn Baring, and when they learned of it in February 1890 Wingate was accused of underhandedness. The matter was quickly resolved, but an unpleasant aftertaste remained. The underlying problem was conflict between the ambitions of a young officer in a quiet, peacetime post and those of his military and political superiors.[27] These ambitions Wingate skillfully harmonized through his newly-discovered way with words.

---

[27] Wingate to "General," and Wingate to Callwell (draft), 11 February 1890, SAD 252/2.

Chapter Six
Author of Record

━━━◆◇◆◇◆━━━

Between the battle of Tushki in August 1889 and the Anglo-Egyptian capture of Tukar in February 1891 there was little activity on the frontier. In the eastern Sudan, stalemate had been broken in December 1888 with the Mahdist defeat at al-Jummayza, after which Uthman Diqna evacuated Handub and moved his headquarters to Tukar. Following Tushki the Khalifa Abdallahi, fearing a general advance from Egypt, tried to distract his enemies by exerting pressure on the isolated Red Sea posts still in Anglo-Egyptian hands. For their part British officers in Egypt, prevented from following up the victory at Tushki, now indeed turned their attention to the eastern Sudan, and pressed for a forward policy from the coast. Military intelligence proved an important factor on both fronts, in the war against Mahdism and in the battle to change British policy.

The chief obstacle to Anglo-Egyptian advance in the east was London's insistence on a defensive strategy. During 1888–89 the Sudan experienced famine, and an embargo on grain from Suakin rendered a Mahdist offensive all but impossible. During the winter and spring of 1890 British officers urged an offensive, citing not only the oppressed Sudanese but also the uncertain intentions of Italian forces in Eritrea. It was not until February 1891, however, that the generals, supported by Baring, won London's approval for an advance on Uthman Diqna's headquarters at Tukar.[1]

Although he was present during the final stage of the Tukar campaign, Wingate's contribution to its success was political. After an inspection of the frontier in February and March 1890, Wingate had returned to routine duties in Cairo. His intelligence reports on the frontier and Suakin gave useful support for an advance from the coast. Wingate's role in producing these reports was usually that of editor or transmitter, since information from officers (and through them, from agents and spies) was often published verbatim. Much of this material found its way into Wingate's first book, *Mahdiism and the Egyptian*

---

[1] Holt, *The Mahdist State*, 190–92.

Sudan, the drafting of which was under way. In January 1891 Wingate again inspected the frontier, this time in the party of the khedive. He returned to Cairo on 2 February, and on the eighth left to take part in the expedition against Uthman Diqna.[2]

The battle of Tukar was a turning point in the war in the eastern Sudan. An Anglo-Egyptian force of two thousand under Col. Charles Holled-Smith left Trinkitat on the coast on 16 February, and reached the vicinity of Uthman Diqna's camp at Afafit, near the ruins of Tukar, on the morning of the nineteenth. The Mahdists put up stiff resistance in the battle that followed, and several times nearly overwhelmed elements of the allied force. But at the end of the day the Mahdists had been routed, with heavy casualties, and the threat to Anglo-Egyptian supremacy on the coast removed. Uthman Diqna retired to Adarama on the lower Atbara, and the Tukar district was organized for civil administration. Grenfell returned to Cairo with his staff, including Wingate, on 14 March. Among the honors subsequently conferred was the 3rd class Medjidia, awarded to Wingate in June.[3]

Wingate's exposure to the limelight and lucre of news reporting during the Tushki campaign had suggested a solution to the dual problem of his career. At twenty-eight he had already enjoyed a pleasing degree of success. But with a wife and child his financial problems had worsened, while in the aftermath of Tushki no career-enhancing campaigns could be foreseen. Bureaucratic burial in the Cairo War Office, while contemporaries made their names on active service, was not a prospect to relish. Wingate would be neither the first nor last to turn, in such circumstances, to popular history in order to secure his future.

Even before Tushki, Wingate had contacted British publishers about a book on the Anglo-Egyptian campaigns of 1884–89. None was interested. Discovery on the Tushki battlefield of Mahdist documents, and the oral reports of Sudanese defectors who came in later, allowed him to try again. The so-called "letter-book of al-Nujumi" (a collection of correspondence and proclamations of the Mahdi and Khalifa Abdallahi) was given to M. Shakoor, a clerk in the intelligence office, to translate.[4] Meanwhile Wingate inflated the importance of

---

[2] CB1.

[3] CB1; Wingate, *Mahdiism and the Egyptian Sudan,* London 1891, 492–508; Holt, *The Mahdist state,* 191–92.

[4] Shakoor to Wingate, 30 September 1889, SAD 155/9. See Holt, *The Mahdist state,* 267.

these papers—by referring to them as "the Mahdi's diary"—in order to win superiors' permission to write a book.[5] Research and writing had, in fact, already begun, not by Wingate but by E. A. Floyer, inspector-general of telegraphs in Egypt,[6] and they formed a partnership. Grenfell, and with Grenfell's permission Wingate, supplied official information about the campaigns, while Floyer wrote an entire first draft, which Wingate only vetted.[7] Then the partners fell out.

To co-authors' ordinary disagreements had been added those of their superiors. Both Grenfell and, it seems, Wolseley were shown chapters as the work progressed. But when a complete draft was shown to Baring he objected to the tone and political content of the book and advised Wingate's withdrawal. Wingate protested that since the book was "essentially military Intelligence . . . Floyer's name alone [as author] would cause rather an anomaly."[8] And he told Grenfell:

> It was never my personal intention to enter into the political aspect of the question. Floyer as a non-military man naturally entered into this . . . and as he has done most of the writing I did not care to interfere with his deductions. Now, however, that Sir E. Baring's views have been obtained I am personally delighted that he has adversely queried these points which would undoubtedly have led to unpleasant criticism and an unnecessary stirring up of bygones. My view is . . . to avoid altogether political references or political deductions.

He could easily amend the offensive passages; could a final ruling await a revised draft?[9]

The different motives of the co-authors were clear. Floyer went to Baring, and concluded he could not produce a book such as Baring wanted. Historical accuracy demanded recognition of facts. "A number of Europeans most of whom are alive and most of whom behaved

---

[5] Wingate to Wolseley, 12 January 1890, SAD 252/1. In a letter to Grenfell (3 April 1890, SAD 252/1), Wingate states that Wolseley suggested the book.

[6] Wingate to Dalton, 8 December 1889, SAD 179/2. Wingate told Dalton that he "was going to help Floyer in his work connected with the history of the E.A. and the recent campaigns."

[7] Floyer to "General" (Grenfell), n.d., and Wingate to Grenfell, 3 April 1890, SAD 252/1. See also other correspondence in the same file.

[8] Wingate to Grenfell, 3 April 1890, SAD 252/1.

[9] Wingate to Grenfell, 6 April 1890, SAD 252/1.

badly" in the Sudan could not be omitted from the book, he told Grenfell, which indeed, he said, "must condemn Gordon not once but repeatedly": the facts were "unalterably" as he had stated them in the draft. Floyer therefore offered to finish the book as he had planned, hand it to Grenfell for his own and the army's use, but "draw back" from publication.[10]

Floyer had described the book as "most interesting work or rather pleasure";[11] to Wingate it was more, and he now hurried to salvage it. He altered the tone of Floyer's draft, cut offensive passages, deleted some difficult sections, and submitted the result bit by bit for superiors' approval. He told Grenfell that Floyer would "not probably like his name to be connected with so 'illiterary'" a result; it would not be "altogether a misfortune" if Floyer simply bowed out.[12] Floyer obliged, asking only, if the book were published, that "some tiny souvenir (a copy of it)" be sent him.[13] *Mahdiism and the Egyptian Sudan* was published by Macmillan in October 1891, under Wingate's name alone; in the "author's preface," Floyer is given "the writer's" thanks for unspecified "most valuable assistance and co-operation in the early part of this work."[14]

Mahdiism deals mainly with the military history of the period 1883–89. A first chapter on the social and religious background of the Mahdiyya is weak (as indeed Floyer had contended it must be), for lack of sources;[15] identification of Muhammad Ahmad al-Mahdi as the hidden twelfth *imam* of the Shi'a exemplifies Wingate's unconcern with the subject.[16] There is much detail about the campaigns, especially in the years 1885–89, based on intelligence reports. A supplement, including translations of captured correspondence of Uthman Diqna, was added at the last minute, after Wingate's return

---

[10] Floyer to Grenfell, n.d., SAD 252/1.

[11] To Grenfell, n.d., SAD 252/1.

[12] Wingate to Grenfell, 5 May 1890, SAD 252/1. See drafts and proofs of the book in SAD 216, for indications of Baring's vetting.

[13] Floyer to Wingate, n.d., SAD 252/1.

[14] *Mahdiism,* xxiii. Neither Ronald Wingate, who noted the first draft's "sweeping political criticism," nor Grenfell, who commented in his introduction on the absence of such, even mentioned Floyer (*Wingate,* 88; *Mahdiism,* xix). P.M. Holt, in writing an introduction to the second edition (London 1968), was therefore unaware of Floyer's role.

[15] Floyer to "General" (Grenfell), n.d., SAD 252/1.

[16] Holt comments on this in his introduction to the second edition (x–xi).

from Tukar. Appendixes provide documents and statistics. Wingate dealt with "political" subjects largely by quoting official reports, or not at all. Gordon's conduct and that of the British government in sending and relieving him, are described without comment or omitted altogether. Details of his death, which has assumed mythic proportions, are left to Bordayni Bey, whose account, published verbatim, includes not only the received version of events but the revealing note that he witnessed none of them.[17]

In publishing *Mahdiism* Wingate's motives were fame and fortune. Twenty-eight presentation copies went to the queen, the khedive, Grenfell, Wolseley, Wood, Baring, Buller, Sir Samuel Baker, Lord Dufferin, and a score of others. Reviews were favorable. The British press had no obligation to avoid "political" references or deductions. The *Saturday Review* called the book "a godsend, especially just before a general election." The *Athenaeum* claimed the book had been "written with the manifest object of bespeaking favour for an Egyptian reconquest of the Soudan," and warned against "further English meddling." Baker, writing in the *Anti-Jacobin*, used the book to justify meddling: the Sudan "alone could supply the looms of Lancashire with the required amount of cotton, and could fill the granaries of England with supplies of wheat."[18] Indeed, it was only politics that gave the book interest: several reviewers criticized its style, and generally the book was judged dull. The public agreed: by the end of November only three hundred copies had been sold, and the publisher was far from breaking even; when Wingate suggested a "popular" (cheap) edition, Macmillan declined.[19]

Wingate learned from this experience. *Mahdiism,* a dense (and expensive) book of more than six hundred pages, could never have achieved mass readership. Censorship had cleansed it of controversy, for which Wingate had not provided a popular substitute. Many books about the Sudan campaigns had already been published, retailing adventure, personality, and gore, in stirring prose; *Mahdiism* was

---

[17] Ibid., 163–72. See Douglas H. Johnson, "The death of Gordon: a Victorian myth," *Journal of imperial and commonwealth history* X, 3, May 1982, 285–310. For Uthman Diqna's correspondence see Wingate to Marriott, 30 March 1891, SAD 252/1.

[18] *Saturday Review; Athenaeum;* and *Anti-Jacobin,* 31 October 1891. Clippings in SAD 252/1.

[19] Reviews, SAD 252/1. George Macmillan to Wingate, 27 November 1891, SAD 252/1.

dry and full of detail. The partnership with Floyer, although supply-ing Wingate with a draft, had been awkward, embarrassing, and almost fatal to the project. Without business experience, Wingate had reached unsatisfactory terms with Macmillan. Much work had pro-duced little reward. Articles he submitted to magazines did no better: an account of the siege of Khartoum in the *United Service Magazine* appears to have yielded £12, most of which went to a translator, clerk, and typist. And when Wingate submitted a synopsis on the Egyptian army to *Harper's Magazine* it was rejected.[20] His next assault on the reading public would be different in several respects.

While *Mahdiism* later seemed the first stage in a propaganda cam-paign, at the time it appeared more likely to mark the end of Wingate's Egyptian career. Late in 1891 Grenfell made known his intention to resign. The new sirdar was to be Col. Kitchener, the adju-tant-general, with whose fortunes Wingate's would be mingled for the next quarter-century. Kitchener was widely disliked by fellow officers and subordinates, including Wingate; his biographer claims that Kitchener's appointment as sirdar "was received with surprise and dis-gust by the entire Egyptian Army."[21] Moreover the new adjutant-gen-eral was to be Wingate's brother-in-law, Rundle, a prospect Wingate likewise viewed with dismay. Just as he had complained to Wood about Grenfell, now Wingate wrote to Grenfell about the new regime:

> I am not a persona grata either to Sirdar or A.G. [adjutant-gen-eral (Rundle)] nor are they to me. I have many points of difference with the latter and I foresee possible rows. . . . My seniority . . . precludes me from the hope of higher billets[,] and service under chiefs in whom I have neither much confidence nor very much respect is likely to become difficult. . . . With such sentiments as these[,] service in the E. A. . . . has become distasteful and . . . the time is coming when I must cast about for more congenial work. . . . [L]eave I feel I must and I am not a little perplexed at what is the best line to take up. . . . [22]

---

[20] Editor, *United Service Magazine,* to Wingate, 15 May; 2 July 1892, SAD 252/1; Osgood, McIlvaine and Co. to Horsley, 13 October 1892, SAD 230/5.

[21] Philip Magnus, *Kitchener. Portrait of an imperialist,* New York, 2nd ed., 1968, 80. Cf. Wingate, *Wingate of the Sudan,* 93. See also Grenfell to Wingate and Wingate to A.G. [Kitchener], 12 June 1891; and Wingate to Grenfell, n.d. (draft), SAD 252/2.

[22] Wingate to Grenfell (draft), n.d., SAD 252/2.

One possibility had arisen from Wingate's relations with the intelligence department of the War Office in London. In December 1891 Wingate was asked whether he would be interested in the military attaché-ship in the embassy at Constantinople, if Col. Herbert Chermside decided to retire. Wingate replied immediately that the idea was "most pleasing," but that he would have to look into the financial implications. He consulted Grenfell and Wolseley, as much to win support as to solicit advice, but Chermside, a friend from the early days of the new Egyptian army, wrote privately that he would not be resigning soon. The prospect of Constantinople remained open for years. Meanwhile, in October 1891, while on leave in London, Wingate passed the interpreter's examination in Turkish, which earned him a gratuity of £200. While this would strengthen his case for Constantinople, he had in fact taken up Turkish, the language of Egypt's ruling class (and had even registered for the examination), long before that prospect had arisen.[23]

On 6 December 1891 word reached Cairo that Father Josef Ohrwalder, an Austrian priest taken prisoner by the Mahdists in 1882, had escaped from Omdurman and arrived in Egypt. Wingate, who was still on leave in England, had been largely responsible for organizing the escape. Upon returning to Cairo in mid-December Wingate interviewed the priest, whose knowledge of affairs at Omdurman was more detailed than any information Anglo-Egyptian officials had previously obtained. Deeply disappointed by sales of *Mahdiism,* and by the publisher's refusal to issue a cheap edition; distressed by changes at the top of the Egyptian army and his own dashed hopes of transfer elsewhere; and determined to make his mark, Wingate immediately recognized the political and personal potential of Ohrwalder's story. Working quickly, he issued the *General military report on the Egyptian Sudan 1891. Compiled from statements made by Father Ohrwalder* on 27 December. While officials digested it, and Wingate recovered from pneumonia, Ohrwalder, undoubtedly at Wingate's instigation, was already "preparing an account of his life in the Sudan."[24] It is charac-

---

[23] Callwell to Wingate, 1 December 1891; Wingate to Callwell, 12 December 1891; Wingate to Grenfell, draft, n.d., SAD 252/2. Wingate to Callwell, 25 January 1892; Callwell to Wingate, 2 February 1892, SAD 253/5. For the Turkish examination see Wingate to A.G. London, 17 July 1891, SAD 252/2, and CB1, 20 October. Cf. *Wingate,* 92.

[24] Wingate to Callwell, 25 January 1892, SAD 253/4. Other correspondence in the same file gives the illness as influenza.

teristic of Wingate that, in a letter noting Chermside's decision to remain at Constantinople he also asked the War Office about his own collaboration with Ohrwalder; there were few occasions in his life when Wingate dwelt upon disappointment.

The censorship that had rendered *Mahdiism* dull and unremunerative made Wingate cautious. At first he asked the War Office only for an opinion of his assisting Ohrwalder to "put his notes together." Charles Callwell replied that Wingate's "editing" of such a book would be "capital," so long as the sirdar approved.[25] Wingate had already offered Ohrwalder's account to George Macmillan, who, however, requested a sample of the manuscript and warned that the current prominence of the story did not guarantee the success of a later book. In May, having read the manuscript, he declined to publish. The "whole subject of the Sudan," Macmillan said, was "not now very attractive to the average English reader"; Ohrwalder's account did not dispel an impression that the Mahdiyya was "an old story . . . that might well be forgotten."[26]

Wingate, in Cairo, offered the book to at least one other publisher before receiving Macmillan's rejection. As in the case of *Mahdiism,* he feared that he might be "cut out" altogether from publication. This arose from the unusual circumstances of the manuscript's production. Ohrwalder, using *Mahdiism* for structural and other support, had quickly drafted his account in German. This had then been "roughly translated into English" by a Syrian clerk, Yusuf Effendi Cudsi. Wingate, in turn, edited and re-wrote that translation "in narrative form." Both Yusuf Effendi's and Wingate's versions survive, however, and show Wingate largely as copy-editor, correcting the English of a non-native-speaker: even highly rhetorical passages in Wingate's draft (and in the book as published) derive from Cudsi's version and therefore, presumably, from the German original. Now, while Wingate searched for a publisher, the Austrian Mission in Egypt contemplated publication of the German original. Such would not only diminish interest in any subsequent edition, but might even result in a publisher's commissioning an English

---

[25] Wingate to Callwell, 25 January 1892, SAD 253/4; Callwell to Wingate, 2 February 1892, SAD 253/5.

[26] George A. Macmillan to Wingate, 28 January 1892, SAD 252/1; and 26 May 1892, SAD 230.

translation of its own, without reference to Wingate. Thus Wingate was anxious to find a London publisher as soon as possible, and when Sampson, Marston & Low offered a contract he accepted immediately.[27]

Ten years' captivity in the Mahdi's camp was published in October 1892. Its complicated provenance is reflected even in its title page and preface. Wingate is shown as author, and in the preface writes that the book is not "a literal translation of the original manuscript, but rather an English version." The historian's verdict that the book is a "biographical gloss on Wingate's *Mahdiism*" seems therefore to fall on Ohrwalder rather than Wingate, since Wingate's role was mainly that of editing a translation of the priest's original—an original that indeed relied on *Mahdiism* for structure, tone, and much detail.[28]

Unlike *Mahdiism*, the book is personal, colorful, even lurid—designed to appeal to the general public rather than to specialists. It is, moreover, much less reticent in the area of "political deductions," a fact that may be ascribed to its equivocal authorship. Yusuf Effendi's translation of Ohrwalder, with which the book ends, asks: "How long shall Europe, and first that nation which has the next position on Egypt and the Soudan, and which has not unjustly the call to be well deserving of colonising and civilising savage peoples, look at the outrages of the Mahdia, and the cruel destruction of the Soudan people??" [29] Wingate left this rhetorical flourish (as edited) at the end of a long book, and reviewers duly repeated it in the press.

Ten years' captivity was an instant success. Within two months more than two thousand copies were sold. In 1893 a cheap edition of three thousand more was published, after which, however, sales abruptly fell; remaining copies were sold off in a still-cheaper binding. But by December 1894 Wingate had earned some £323 in royalties.[30] He was unsatisfied, however, complaining on the one hand about the marketing of the book, and arguing unsuccessfully on the other for an

---

[27] Wingate to Marston, 29 May 1892, and Wingate to Macmillan, 25 May 1892, SAD 230. SAD 228/15 contains Yusuf Effendi's translation; SAD 228/1-14 Wingate's manuscript, in 14 notebooks.

[28] P.M. Holt, "The source-materials of the Sudanese Mahdia," *St. Antony's papers, Number 4: Middle Eastern affairs, Number One*, London 1958, 110.

[29] SAD 228/15.

[30] Reid to Wingate, 28 December 1892; Wingate, note, 1 January 1893, SAD 230. Marston to Wingate, 15 December 1894, SAD 260/1.

"honorarium," because of the book's success.[31] Nevertheless, for a
kaimakam earning £E720 a year, the royalties were not insignificant.

For Wingate *Ten years' captivity* served several purposes.
Although on balance personal motives seem to have been decisive, he
was certainly aware of the political use to which the book could be
put. The roles of Floyer, Ohrwalder, and Yusuf Effendi in *Mahdiism*
and *Ten years' captivity* make it difficult to assess precisely his own
views. Rules for the transmission and collation of intelligence from
Suakin and the frontier before 1892 create a similar problem of iden-
tifying the authors of original sources. Several articles he published in
1892, however, clarify Wingate's views on the ultimate goal of
British policy in the Sudan. One, later reprinted as *The Sudan past
and present,* assumes an eventual forward policy and promises rich
rewards. Wingate repeats canards about the Mahdi, the khalifa, and
the late Turco-Egyptian regime, and assesses elements of the
Sudanese population. Thus dwellers in the northern towns were
"idle, dissolute, drunken, demoralised": "probably the most worth-
less" people in the world. But in the south were warlike peoples who
could "hardly be over-estimated," and "the European nation which
sooner or later extends its sphere of influence over these distant
lands" would "secure a recruiting ground for troops to whom for
reckless bravery and endurance it would be hard to find an equal";
they had "been truthfully described as creatures who 'eat, drink, and
fight, but never pray.'"[32]

Whatever Wingate's reasons for publishing before 1892, he
clearly favored Anglo-Egyptian advance into the Sudan. Changes at
the top of the Egyptian army; his own likely continuance in Egypt,
and promotion; reorganization of the intelligence service and greater
prominence for its director; and international developments during
the last phase of the European Scramble for Africa, all helped now to
concentrate Wingate's attention on a single goal: the overthrow of
the Mahdist state.

---

[31] Wingate to Marston, 5 December 1894 and 27 January 1895; Marston to
Wingate, 5 December 1894, SAD 260/1.

[32] Reprinted from *Proceedings* of the Royal Artillery Institution XIX, 14, Woolwich
1892.

Chapter Seven
Director of Military Intelligence

⟶∘◇∘⟵

Although discouraged by his failure to win appointment outside Egypt, and by the prospect of service under Kitchener and Rundle, Wingate saw possibilities in the new regime. His fondness for Grenfell had never depended on the old general's abilities; while Kitchener was notoriously difficult, he would reform the ramshackle arrangements that had grown up since Wood's day. Wingate had long complained about the difficulties under which he operated and the quality of intelligence that resulted. With Kitchener there would be no shortage of difficulties, but a rationally organized and centrally directed intelligence department, sufficient to prepare for the conquest of the Sudan, might be established.

In February 1892, while he toured the frontier and awaited the changing of the guard in Cairo, Wingate listed his complaints about the current intelligence operation.

> Anyone who has followed Sudan events [he wrote, could] see at a glance that the writers [of intelligence reports] know practically nothing of the situation in the Sudan and moreover almost every rule drawn up as regards spelling etc. is neglected. . . . I would strongly recommend that none of the reports recently received should be sent on; many of the statements are inaccurate and reflect discredit on the Intelligence Dep. . . . I really feel ashamed that . . . they should be solemnly printed as records of the Intell. Dep.[1]

There were other problems: expenditure exceeded the paltry budgetary provision, staff were too few (and during leave season there were none at all at some posts), collation and analysis of intelligence were haphazard or non-existent. Kitchener, adjutant-general since 1888, knew the system's weaknesses. His appointment as sirdar was gazetted on 18 April; on the nineteenth the intelligence was reorga-

---

[1] Wingate to General, draft, 24 February 1892, SAD 253/5. See also CB1. The complaint about spelling was not pedantic: inaccuracy could result in confusion.

49

nized as a separate department, Wingate was appointed director of military intelligence, and the office of assistant adjutant-general for intelligence was suppressed.[2]

After eight years in the Egyptian army Wingate knew that titles and appointments meant less than procedures and personalities. Now "the change of office," he told Callwell in London, was "merely a distinction without a difference."[3] Wingate was left in the dark about lines of communication with the sirdar and adjutant-general, with the Egyptian war minister, and even with intelligence officers in the field. Confidential correspondence and intelligence diaries continued to be sent to the adjutant-general before Wingate saw them.[4] Bitterness crept in. A personal argument, which stemmed from an Egyptian officer's asking Wingate's advice on a transfer before consulting Rundle, involved offensive language; Rundle's repeated apologies failed to satisfy, and Wingate nursed the grievance.[5] He complained to Kitchener of, among other things, Rundle's excluding him from ceremonies; the sirdar took the blame, hoping, he said, that Wingate and Rundle would "pull together."[6] Wingate discovered that an officer junior to him had been invited to succeed Rundle in commanding the artillery, a post he might have liked himself. He had had no increase in pay for five years, and even his new rank (*miralai* or colonel), was designated "local and temporary."[7] As often in his career, Wingate discerned personal slights, which, unredressed, seemed to multiply. Nor was Kitchener at the root of the trouble: even Grenfell, in confidential reports that later came into Wingate's possession, had judged him very highly in all areas but "tact" and the "power of commanding respect."[8]

---

[2] Holled-Smith to Wingate, 21 February 1892, SAD 253/5; *War Office Gazette,* No. 16, 18 April 1892; Egyptian Army, War Office, *Army Orders,* 19 April 1892. There is confusion about Wingate's successive promotions and titles. Cf. Wingate, *Wingate of the Sudan,* 82; Holt, *Mahdiism,* vi–vii.

[3] Wingate to Callwell, 17 April 1892, SAD 233/2.

[4] Wingate, "Registration of intelligence correspondence," 25 April 1892; Wingate, "Reorganization [*sic*] Intelligence Department" [April 1892]; Wingate to Colonel [Rundle], 25 April 1892, SAD 253/6.

[5] Wingate to Rundle, 23, 28, 29, 30 March 1892; Rundle to Benson, n.d.; Rundle to Wingate, 29, 30 March; 2 April 1892, SAD 233/2.

[6] Wingate to Colonel [Rundle], 28 April 1892; Kitchener to Wingate, n.d., SAD 253/6.

[7] Wingate to Colonel [Rundle?], n.d., SAD 253/6.

[8] Report for 1891–92, SAD 233/2. The report is copied in Wingate's hand.

For several months after Kitchener's appointment Wingate considered leaving Egypt. With Constantinople closed, he investigated eastern consular appointments, for which Arabic and Turkish (and Persian, which he now began to study) would stand him in good stead; these, he discovered, were few, and often involved expenses that exceeded their salaries.[9] He could return to the British army, but there again money would be a problem, he would have gained nothing in rank while away, and his special expertise would carry no advantage. Letters to Grenfell, and especially to Wood, won advice but not intervention. Wood wondered what Wingate had expected from the change in sirdar; he should not be "discouraged at finding that self-interest" was "now predominant amongst" his associates; rather "this must always be the case in such a Service" as the Egyptian army.[10]

By June Wingate had faced facts. "If I return to the Regiment and stay for a year in England," he told Wood,

> it would necessitate drawing on our small capital which I would not like to do. . . . Should anything turn up in England which would justify my throwing up my present £E720 a year here, I should be inclined to consider the English service as only temporary for . . . the career which is most suited to my acquirements [*sic*] and to my pocket, lies somewhere in the East, either India or Turkey. . . . The question therefore seems to resolve itself into waiting . . . and the question of where the waiting time had best be spent—England or Egypt—is a purely financial one.

His wife, expecting their second child in September, would stay in England during the winter of 1892–93; they had given up their rented house in Cairo; his bags were packed to "leave Egypt at a moment's notice." If a good opportunity arose while he was on leave in England, he would resign immediately and not even return to Egypt.[11]

---

[9] Chermside to Wingate, 26 April 1892, SAD 233/2. On Persian see Wingate to Duanitch, London, and Wingate to Delavage, 31 March 1892, SAD 233/2. Wingate apparently dropped Persian on discovering that the War Office awarded bonuses only for Arabic, Turkish, and Russian; he then briefly considered Russian (Delavage to Wingate, 2 May 1892, and Wood to Wingate, 15 February 1892, SAD 233/2).

[10] Wood to Wingate, 13 April 1892, SAD 233/2.

[11] Wingate to Wood, 27 June 1892, SAD 233/2.

Meanwhile, Wingate dealt as usual with disappointment by throwing himself into work. He pressed Rundle and Kitchener over intelligence organization, and was able gradually to erect a workable apparatus. By the end of March he had drafted a new standard of transliteration for Arabic and an index of Egyptian and Sudanese words.[12] By mid-May he had devised a plan to reorganize intelligence from the frontier. Under the old system his staff there consisted of an Egyptian officer, an interpreter, and twenty-one agents at Halfa, Korosko, Aswan, and Sarras; a British officer had part-time duties. The total budget for agents was £E89 a year. Nor were they of much use: the agents were "well known as such," probably "the last to know the intentions of the enemy," and were used mainly for patrol work that could be better done by local Shaiqi tribesmen. Wingate's plan proposed a new headquarters at Aswan, and a branch at Halfa under an Egyptian officer who would advise on the employment of secret agents for special missions. At Korosko and Aswan a similar "director of secret service" would supply spies, for which a small budget was required. Patrolling should be left to salaried Sudanese shaykhs.[13] Wingate's case was strengthened two days after he submitted his plan, when a Mahdist raiding party, undetected, ravaged the village of Samna, upstream from Sarras. Tribal patrollers—whom he saw as double-dealers—had failed again; reliance should be placed on agents who would infiltrate enemy territory and be paid "for intelligence in proportion to its value."[14]

Wingate had employed secret agents for some time. Ohrwalder's escape from Omdurman had proven the value of agents paid for special assignments. Even in Cairo Wingate relied on one or two Sudanese to inform him privately of arrivals from the Sudan. Only three people, including Wingate, knew how many agents he employed in Cairo or how he got his information. He strove to prevent any agent's knowing the identity of any other.[15] Essential for success was latitude with budgets. There is no evidence that Wingate recognized the flaws in this highly personal system: where secrecy was achieved, the spymaster could exercise control.

---

[12] Wingate to Dalton, 29 March 1892, SAD 233/2.

[13] Wingate to Sirdar, "Reorganization [sic]. Frontier Intelligence," 14 May 1892, SAD 253/7.

[14] Wingate to Callwell, 16 May 1892, SAD 253/7.

[15] Wingate to Kempston, 27 May 1892, SAD 253/7.

The problems and prospects of service under Kitchener and Rundle were put aside when Wingate went on leave to England at the end of July 1892. His wife had preceded him in May to rented rooms at Manstone Green, Isle of Thanet, Kent. On 27 August their second child, Graham Andrew Leslie, was born there. He lived for only two weeks, succumbing to an unspecified illness on 11 September.[16]

This bereavement occurred amidst activity frenetic even by Wingate's standards. He visited London frequently to confer at the War Office, to call on publishers, to attend meetings of learned societies. He spent weekends with General Wood and others. And he engaged in propaganda. The Liberals won the general election in July, and were expected to relax Britain's hold over Egypt and shun a forward policy in the Upper Nile. In August Wingate drafted a long memorandum on "The effect on Egypt of the withdrawal from Uganda,"[17] arguing that if France replaced the British there, Equatoria and thus the Sudan would fall under French influence and the "whole Egyptian question" might be revived. It is likely that the War Office had solicited this memorandum; it now requested a further paper on "the advantages to be derived from the occupation of the Soudan by us," especially as a "recruiting ground."[18] The Uganda memorandum was sent to the Foreign Office and to Lord Roberts in India. Meanwhile the author of *Mahdiism* was in demand. Wingate lectured to the Oriental Congress in London and at the Royal Artillery Institution (for a £5 "bonus"), in September, and was interviewed by Lord Rosebery, the new foreign secretary, in October. On 20 October *Ten years' captivity in the Mahdi's camp* was published, widening Wingate's recognition in Whitehall. By the time he and his wife returned to Cairo on 27 October Wingate better understood the potential of his position. He now set out to define his role as director of military intelligence in Egypt, and to use his unique knowledge to influence developments at home.[19]

Events in Egypt gave ample scope for a wider role. The Khedive Muhammad Taufiq had died in January 1892 and been succeeded by his eighteen-year-old son, Abbas Hilmi. Almost any prince would

---

[16] Wingate to Wood, 27 June 1892, SAD 233/2; CB1; SAD 233/3 contains messages of condolence from Grenfell, Rundle, Baker, and many others.

[17] 21 August 1892, SAD 253/10.

[18] Chapman to Wingate, 23 August 1892, SAD 253/10.

[19] CB1.

have seemed troublesome after Taufiq, and a reputation for anti-British views soon attached itself to the new ruler. By the end of 1892 his relations with Baring—who in March had been raised to the peerage as Lord Cromer—approached a showdown. The advent of a Liberal government in Britain added to the khedive's readiness to test his limits. Battle was joined in January 1893, ostensibly over ministerial appointments. In London Rosebery, under threat of resignation, carried the government in supporting Cromer, who insisted on putting the khedive in his place. Reinforcement of the British garrison in Egypt asserted continuity despite the change of government.

Throughout this crisis and before a more conclusive showdown in January 1894, Wingate was a principal source of intelligence for the War Office in London. In Cairo the British inspector-general of police lacked confidence in his (Dutch) head of secret police; Wingate was asked to supply political intelligence.[20] Couching his reports in diffidence over professional trespassing, Wingate nonetheless impressed London with command of the subject. In April he went so far as to provide the War Office with "the Khedivial genealogical tree"—for future reference.[21] In London the director of military intelligence welcomed independent and informal political information supporting his own and Cromer's views about how to deal with oriental potentates; Wingate armed the War Office for debate with the Foreign Office. In his official *Intelligence Report* for December 1892, for instance, Wingate cited a newly-arrived Sudanese merchant to support the view that only British occupation of Egypt prevented another Mahdist invasion. At the same time he told the War Office there was no "likelihood of a Dervish advance down the Nile," but that the opportunity was "being taken advantage of to ask for an increase of the Egyptian Army which is always a step in the right direction."[22] To the extent that (as often happened) the views he expressed to London did not coincide with Kitchener's, Wingate described them as "perfectly private."[23]

Although this method of "private" communication would cause problems throughout his career, it was not unusual. At this point it

---

[20] Wingate to Everett, 17 February 1893, SAD 255/2.

[21] Wingate to Everett, 12 April 1893, SAD 255/1.

[22] *Intelligence Report, Egypt, No. 9,* December 1892, 8; Wingate to Everett, 5 December 1892, SAD 253/14.

[23] See, e.g., Wingate to Everett, 29 January 1893, SAD 255/1.

was a way for Wingate to enhance his reputation and extend his influence. Kitchener was a master at claiming credit for subordinates' work; Wingate's private channels to London were rivulets compared to his own. Stymied, for instance, in official attempts to get more money for his department, Wingate repeatedly warned the War Office that intelligence from the frontier and Suakin would be unreliable until more was budgeted for it. In May 1893 he told London he had "no specially detailed officers for Intelligence" at either front: officers merely did intelligence work "in addition to their other duties," which took precedence. Wingate's correspondent at the War Office, noting the "private" designation of his letters, nonetheless knew that these were "written with a purpose" and passed them "to some one [*sic*] who" would "know what to do" with them.[24] When Mahdist raids met with any success, similar warnings were almost invariably advanced.[25]

While uncertainty reigned in Cairo—over Cromer's unfinished business with the khedive, new tensions in Britain's relations with other interested powers, and policy toward the Sudan—Wingate was more fully occupied than ever. When his wife returned to England in June he took a brief holiday in the Fayum with Dr. Acland (who had treated his typhoid in 1883), then studied for an examination for promotion.[26] This had two parts: drill, which he passed in Cairo in July, and tactics, topography, fortifications, and military law, which he would complete in London in November.[27] From the ultimate limit of dull routine to the most fanciful and extraordinary intrigue—such was the spectrum of Wingate's life in these years: after completing the Cairo portion of his examination he returned to plotting a British takeover of north-central Africa.

Rabih Fadlallah (also called Rabih Zubayr) was a merchant-warrior in the mold of Zubayr Rahma Mansur, whom Gordon had alternately seen as scourge and savior of the Sudan. In 1879 Rabih and some followers, checked by the Egyptian anti-slavery campaign, had set out on a career of conquest that culminated in his taking Burnu in 1893 and would end with his death in battle with the French in 1900.

---

[24] Wingate to Everett, 21 May 1893; Everett to Wingate, 25 August 1893, SAD 255/1.

[25] See, e.g., Wingate to Fairholme, 2 August 1893, SAD 255/1.

[26] CB2.

[27] CB1; Wingate to Milner, 23 July 1893, SAD 255.

News of his exploits was long in reaching the outside world, but was
of much interest to scrambling European imperialists, including the
British in Egypt. Rabih's attitude toward the Mahdist state was
uncertain: perhaps he could be used against the khalifa, perhaps
against the Belgians and French. In 1891 a plan to contact him was
rejected by the Foreign Office. But in February 1893 a messenger
from Rabih (with a letter written in 1891) reached Cairo.[28] Messages
were returned by the British and, at their behest, by Zubayr Pasha,
still living in Cairo. This diplomacy was conducted mainly from
Egypt, with Wingate as the principal conduit for the War Office.[29]

In August 1893 a plan was approved to send a delegation of
three—ostensibly pilgrims returning from Mecca—from Zubayr to
Rabih via England and West Africa. They left Alexandria on the
twenty-fourth for Liverpool, and after British second thoughts went
on to the Oil Rivers Protectorate.[30] (On 13 September a news agency
reported from Cairo that Rabih was in Bagirmi. Kitchener took the
opportunity to propose demarcation of a British sphere of influence
that would encompass the Sudan and almost all of what is today
Chad, and thus connect British lands in West Africa to British East
Africa.)[31] The messengers duly reached Calabar, whence, after long
delays while letters were re-drafted, they finally set out and, after
many adventures, found Rabih in late 1895.[32]

Wingate would return to the charge once more before events in
the Sudan outpaced trans-African communications. In April 1894,
upon hearing a rumor that Rabih had died, Wingate suggested sending Zubayr Pasha himself to Burnu to succeed his erstwhile vassal.
Once there, Zubayr could lead "an expedition, equipped and armed
by the British government and perhaps assisted by a few British officers," to "checkmate French pretensions" and "seriously menace the
authority of the Khalifa" in the Sudan.[33] Kitchener briefly took up the

---

[28] W.K.R. Hallam, *The life and times of Rabih Fadl Allah*, Ilfracombe, Devon 1977, 211.

[29] See SAD 255/1.

[30] Wingate to Cartwright, 23 August 1893; Wingate to Everett, and Wingate to Kitchener, 31 August 1893, SAD 255/1.

[31] Kitchener, Memorandum, 15 September 1893, SAD 255/1.

[32] Hallam, *The life*, 220.

[33] "Memorandum on the situation in the Western Sudan," 15 April 1894, SAD 257/1.

idea,[34] and Wingate privately told a friend that he hoped to be one of the "British officers" sent to "accompany" Zubayr.[35] Nothing came of the suggestion, which may be dismissed as a flight of fancy.

While Wingate was engaged in high politics in Cairo, his wife, who had returned to England in June, gave birth on 28 August 1893 to their third child, Malcolm Roy Wingate, at Newton Abbott, South Devon. Wingate joined them in September. On 6 November he passed the second part of his promotion examination, in London. By the twenty-second the family had returned to Egypt.[36] Any hopes that Kitty Wingate had for a quiet winter were soon dashed by the Anglo-Egyptian confrontation that had been looming for a year.

After the crisis of January 1893 British relations with the khedive had briefly improved, only to deteriorate again later in the year. The inevitable clash centered this time on control of the army. On 13 January 1894 the khedive embarked on an inspection of the frontier, accompanied by the war minister, the sirdar, and, among others, Wingate as director of military intelligence. The khedive repeatedly found fault in the appearance and performance of the troops, British officers, and Kitchener himself. Criticism culminated at Wadi Halfa on the nineteenth, when Abbas Hilmi told the sirdar that Egypt was disgraced by the army Kitchener had paraded before him. Kitchener offered his resignation on the spot. The khedive pulled back, assured the sirdar of his confidence, and belittled the whole episode. But just as the khedive's insults appear to have been planned, so Kitchener—and, sensing in Cairo the significance of events on the frontier, Cromer—now took full political advantage. In later conversations with the khedive and in reports to Cromer, Kitchener exaggerated what had happened. Although he had long been accused of a "want of tact with Orientals," Kitchener knew that in this case Cromer would welcome a pretext for action, and thus secured (rather than, as his British critics would have hoped, endangered) his position as sirdar. Even if Cromer agreed with the critics, he could hardly appear to accept the khedive's version of events over Kitchener's. Rosebery issued what amounted to an ultimatum, requiring the khedive to attest publicly to full confidence in

---

[34] Wingate to Milner, 21 April 1894, SAD 257/1.

[35] Talbot to Wingate, 25 April 1894, SAD 257/1.

[36] CB1.

his officers, British and other, and to replace his war minister with a British nominee. Kitchener was knighted.[37]

It had been left to Wingate to supply the version upon which his superiors based their successful demands for action against the khedive. Indeed, this would be the first of several important occasions when Wingate acted as Kitchener's draftsman and Cromer's source. On 23 January Kitchener sent him to Cairo, where he delivered Kitchener's report—which Wingate had written—and his own detailed diary of the khedivial tour.[38] Both documents were dispatched to London, where Rosebery used them to persuade a reluctant cabinet to act.[39] The resulting "check" to the khedive, pleasing to the whole British establishment in Egypt, marked for ardent imperialists the beginning, rather than the end, of a campaign to increase British control. Grenfell, for instance, interviewing members of the British cabinet, used the dispatches from Egypt to press for declaration of a protectorate.[40] Wingate himself told the War Office of his "absolute conviction that in dealing with orientals, half measures are fatal";[41] there "must sooner or later" be "another explosion," after which the khedive must go.[42]

The weight attached to his reports of the Frontier Incident transported Wingate again to the fringes of high politics where, despite protests, he longed to be. In a mass of letters he detailed the likely consequences of events he had reported and others now predicted. To the War Office, members of parliament, ex-sirdars, and others he proposed with apparent insouciance abolition of the khedivate and reimposition of an Ottoman governor under British protection. While assuring correspondents he had no "competence to discuss" such matters,[43] he outlined a plan and reached conclusions about its impact on the Eastern Question, British naval policy in the eastern

---

[37] Wingate, "Diary of H.H.'s visit to frontier," n.d., SAD 179/4; John Marlowe, *Cromer in Egypt*, London 1970, 172–75; Philip Magnus, *Kitchener. Portrait of an imperialist*, London 1959, 83–89.

[38] For Wingate's draft of Kitchener's report see SAD 257/1.

[39] Wingate to Fairholme, 5 February 1894, SAD 257/1. See also "Diary of H.H.'s visit to frontier."

[40] Grenfell to Wingate, 30 January 1894, SAD 257/1.

[41] 5 February 1894, SAD 257/1.

[42] Wingate to Milner, 12 February 1894, SAD 257/1.

[43] E.g., Grenfell, 15 February 1894, SAD 257/1.

Mediterranean, security of imperial communications, and so forth, all, as was by now usual for him, expressed "absolutely privately."[44] An example of this method, and of the conclusions Wingate now retailed, can be drawn from a letter to a newspaper correspondent:

> The Frontier incident having entered into the sacred realms of politics with which we soldiers are supposed to have nothing to do, precludes me from giving you any details which have not yet become public property[,] should it be your intention to make use in the press of information I might supply. But if . . . you merely ask me for information for yourself *privately,* then I have no hesitation in telling you that . . . I have never seen a more deliberate determined and badly-planned attempt to upset English influence in this country than that which the youthful Khedive and Maher [the war minister] have just perpetrated. . . . As regards the attitude of the Turk in this matter, I am inclined to think that he views with considerable alarm the escapades of the youthful Khedive. . . .[45]

The Frontier Incident ended in complete success for the British protagonists. Rosebery had carried a reluctant Liberal cabinet in reasserting British pre-eminence. Cromer and Kitchener, while ensuring the unending hostility of the khedive, had enjoyed and benefited from that reassertion; each now recognized his partial dependence on the other in the shifting sands of Anglo-Egyptian politics. Wingate, from this moment onwards almost uncannily in the right place at the right time, had solidified his reputation, strengthened contacts at home, and become emboldened by a new sense of mission. The international repercussions of the incident whetted an appetite for involvement in affairs, which would now be fed by the quickening pace of events in and about the Sudan. For years Wingate had tried to leave Egypt. Now, after the Frontier Incident, Grenfell congratulated him for his "really wise choice" in staying, adding laconically that he hoped one day to see him sirdar.[46]

---

[44] Wingate to Everett, W.O., 10 February 1894, SAD 257/1.

[45] Wingate to Dr. Russell, 21 February 1894, SAD 257/1. Emphasis added.

[46] 30 January 1894, SAD 257/1.

Chapter Eight
Suakin

The Frontier Incident was one of several developments that brought Egypt once again to the notice of the British government and public. Successful Mahdist raids on Egyptian positions in July and November 1893 seemed to portend another all-out attack (and were used by Wingate to support pleas for more money).[1] More provocative, from the British point of view, was increasing Great-Power involvement in the region. It was this, in the end, that would justify the winning of the Sudan. In the meantime, in 1894–95, Wingate, as director of military intelligence, continued both to involve himself in high politics and to find himself relegated to the dreariest duties of backwater administration.

In 1894 Italy, from its colony of Eritrea, moved to secure its position and reduce expenditure on defense by taking Kassala, the Sudanese border town on the Qash. Under terms of an Anglo-Italian agreement in 1891 this was allowed as a temporary defensive measure. Much of the diplomatic prelude to the move was played out in Cairo, where Wingate was drawn into discussions ostensibly about cooperation in intelligence. The Italians in fact proposed—as they had unsuccessfully before—a joint expedition against Kassala.[2] London had no intention of sanctioning an Anglo-Egyptian offensive, jointly with the Italians or alone, toward what would, in the event of success, be an expensive and isolated outpost. Intelligence cooperation between Cairo and Massawa was established,[3] but when the Italians advanced in July it was with British acquiescence, not participation.

That the interest of Wingate and fellow officers in this matter reflected a fear of losing the Sudan to European rivals is borne out by their reaction to developments on other fronts. By early 1894 French

---

[1] Wingate to Fairholme, W.O., 2 August 1893, SAD 255/1.

[2] Wingate, memorandum, 24 February 1894, SAD 257/1.

[3] Fairholme, W.O., to Wingate, 15 March 1894; Wingate to Fairholme, 19 March 1894, SAD 257/1.

attention to the Upper Nile had become obvious. A flurry of agreements between interested powers ensued. British attempts to block French advance from the west were defeated in February 1894 when Germany recognized a French sphere extending to the Nile. This in turn led to an Anglo-Congolese convention in May, by which new barriers, indefensible in international law, were erected. Meanwhile in Cairo the British response to Franco-German cooperation was furious but hopeful. "I should not be surprised," Wingate told the War Office, "if the rapidity with which events will march in these regions, will not force us into making some movement on the Egyptian Sudan from the North and East in order to prevent other powers from settling in the Nile Valley." By now, however, Wingate had recognized that arguments he and others had long proposed to justify such "movement" rendered them "alarmists" in London's eyes.[4] The French menace also explains Wingate's interest at the time in Anglo-Ottoman relations and his (otherwise bizarre) enthusiasm for the embassy to Rabih Zubayr. He was fast becoming the unofficial foreign-affairs advocate for the British military establishment in Egypt.

From involvement, however peripheral, in matters of state Wingate was now, in May 1894, sent to Suakin, the Egyptian Red Sea outpost, while the governor went on leave. The title of acting governor-general of the Red Sea Littoral and officer commanding Suakin carried less irony since the occupation of Tukar, but a summer away from the centers of affairs held no appeal.[5] It would not be a wasted season, however. With his usual industry (and despite intense heat and humidity) Wingate made several tours outside the town, gaining knowledge of the region and its peoples; was able, through the telegraph, to keep in touch with Cairo and London; had his first important experience in civil administration; and, as always, the ink was hardly allowed to dry on one report or memorandum before another was taken in hand.

After seeing off his wife, who would spend the summer in "some cheap and quiet spot in Switzerland,"[6] Wingate left Cairo on 22 May for the two-day sea journey to Suakin. Despite the charm of its coral buildings, Suakin was torpid with dengue fever. Archibald Hunter,

---

[4] Wingate to Fairholme, 23 March 1894, SAD 257/1.

[5] Wingate to Lloyd, 27 April 1894; Wingate to Grenfell, 14 May 1894, SAD 257/1.

[6] Wingate to Milner, 12 April 1894, SAD 256/1.

one of Wingate's predecessors, had described the town as a "d[amned] dirty and shamefully neglected dung pit."[7] Like him, Wingate found the administration, its officials, and soldiers in poor condition. But whereas Hunter had kept an Abyssinian mistress (whom he later brought to Cairo), and terrorized disgruntled under-lings,[8] Wingate seems to have kept his balance; little was expected of an "acting" governor in any case. On 1 June he inspected Handub and Tambuk. On the sixth he left for Tukar and Akik, returning to Suakin on the tenth. Between 28 June and 2 July (after a week of fever) he inspected Halaib, Ruwaya, Muhammad Ghul, and Darur, and on the nineteenth set out for Erkowit, Sinkat, and Tamanib, returning (in haste, at the rumored approach of a Mahdist force) on the twenty-third. Early in September he inspected Tukar again and Bahadur island, before returning to Cairo on the twentieth.[9] Visiting places he had dealt with for years as an intelligence officer but never seen was full of interest for Wingate, who would later, as governor-general of the Sudan, make his warm-weather home at Erkowit in the Red Sea Hills.

As governor and commanding officer, Wingate was responsible for all aspects of Suakin's administration, and he approached them with zest. But the work involved everything from defense to refuse dis-posal and was too much for one man. Upon his return to Cairo a sub-governor was appointed, to whom, Wingate recommended, many of the routine administrative duties should in future be assigned.[10] Commanding a garrison for the first time, Wingate gained experience of military administration. When Amarar tribesmen kidnaped a woman of the IXth Sudanese battalion, Wingate commuted the death sen-tence to life imprisonment and one hundred lashes; the public whip-ping reportedly gave great satisfaction, while commutation precluded a blood feud.[11] When trouble brewed at Tukar he found the British commander dependent on translators and unable to cope; language skills would in future contribute to Wingate's assessment of fitness to

[7] Hunter to Jim (Duncan Hunter), 22 July 1891, quoted in Duncan H. Doolittle, ed., *A soldier's hero. General Sir Archibald Hunter,* Narragansett, Rhode Island, 1991, 33.

[8] Ibid., 35, 39–40.

[9] Wingate, engagement calendar, Suakin, 1894, SAD 256/1; CB1; Wingate to Maxwell, 29 June 1894, SAD 257/1.

[10] Wingate to Lloyd, 24 October 1894, SAD 258/1.

[11] Wingate to Kitchener, 16 July 1894, SAD 257/1.

command.[12] In these and other practical ways Wingate's brief tenure at Suakin provided experience that a decade of staff work had not.

Wingate's administration at Suakin, and his relations with Kitchener while he was there, foreshadowed the contrast between the two as successive governors-general of the Sudan. Kitchener tended to see subordinates, whatever their ranks or titles in civil administration, as his local representatives; Josceline Wodehouse, for example, governor of the frontier province from 1888 to 1894, was driven to distraction by the sirdar's constant interference.[13] Wingate now experienced this in a new way, as he did also Kitchener's penny-pinching and cavalier treatment of subordinates, whether military or civilian, European or native.

On 12 June fire destroyed the "*harimat* lines"—housing for relatives and camp-followers—of the XIIIth Sudanese battalion at Tukar. Wingate immediately wired Egypt for financial assistance; sent tents for shelter and transport to bring the women to Suakin; expressed personal concern for the mother of a child who had been burned; and promised to back up the commander, H. W. Jackson, in any steps necessary to relieve distress.[14] Kitchener's response was characteristic. After complaining that Wingate was "extravagant with the telegraph," he denied government responsibility for *harimat* lines and told him to "stamp out any idea that the Govt. is going to house these ladies or pay for" houses they burned down. It was not "a good thing to pamper the blacks": this was "Jackson's failing."[15] Wingate replied respectfully but pointedly: the blacks should not be pampered, but was Kitchener aware of the condition of the XIIIth Sudanese? Jackson had single-handedly brought them back from near-mutiny before the fire, largely at his personal expense. And while Wingate might "lack experience in such matters," he could not ignore "facts which were so very patent."[16] Behind Kitchener's back and against his direct order Rundle thereupon found £15 to send Wingate for rebuilding. When a private subscription was suggested Kitchener would not allow it.[17]

---

[12] Wingate to Rundle, 16 July 1894, SAD 257/1.
[13] Wodehouse to Wingate, 29 May 1893, SAD 255/1.
[14] Wingate to Jackson, 13 June 1894, SAD 257/1.
[15] Kitchener to Wingate, 19 June 1894, SAD 257/1.
[16] Wingate to Kitchener, 1 July 1894, SAD 257/1.
[17] Rundle to Wingate, 5 July 1894, SAD 257/1.

While from Cairo Kitchener intervened in the affairs of the Red
Sea Littoral, so ironically did Wingate try to manage the Cairo intelligence from Suakin. In his absence Major J. G. Maxwell (a cousin of
Grenfell, the ex-sirdar) was in charge, and difficulties had arisen from
the start. It was "next to impossible," Maxwell told Wingate, to get
anything done, what with "a howling Zubair, a scented Kash. el Moss
[*sic*] or a mass of unimportant Consuls General asking you unimportant questions."[18] But Maxwell's unsuitability did not justify
Wingate's "private" communication with his subordinates. Maxwell
soon discovered this, and complained to Wingate, who described the
correspondence as trivial, himself as "hurt" by Maxwell's insinuations,
and his correspondent—a "weak-backed Syrian"—as to blame for the
trouble.[19]

In any case Wingate was fully engaged in intelligence work at
Suakin, which had always been a main conduit of information on the
Mahdist state. Plans—already under way—to extricate European
prisoners from the Sudan were advanced and monitored. Wingate
kept abreast of Mahdist affairs through interviews with merchants
and tribesmen. When the Italians took Kassala in July, it was Wingate
who notified Cairo.[20] His proximity to enemy territory gave rise to
rumors in the Egyptian press that he was supplying arms and ammunition to the enemy![21] After what Kitchener called a "gross attack" in
al-Ahram, a complaint was lodged with the minister of war, Wingate
privately offered to resign, and *al-Ahram* was forced to publish a
retraction.[22]

Remoteness stimulated his pen. The War Office still valued his
advice on general African affairs—"matters equatorial," as one official
put it—as well as his local intelligence reports.[23] There was no shortage of local rumors and international maneuvers on which to specu-

---

[18] Maxwell to Wingate, 31 May 1894, SAD 257/1.

[19] Maxwell to Wingate, 20 June 1894; Wingate to Maxwell, 29 June 1894, SAD
257/1.

[20] Wingate to Talbot, 2 July 1894; Wingate to Everett, W.O., 17 July; 1 August
1894, SAD 257/1.

[21] Wingate to Fairholme, 9 September 1894, SAD 258/1.

[22] *Al-Ahram,* 14, 16, 27 August 1894; Kitchener to Minister of War, 14 August
1894, encl. in Rundle to Wingate, 16 August 1894; Wingate to Sirdar, 23
August 1894, SAD 256/1.

[23] Everett, W.O., to Wingate, 22 June 1894, SAD 257/1.

late (though Kitchener complained of Wingate's costly telegraphy, and Wingate was vexed at being "dreadfully out of the world").[24]

Long nights at Suakin produced lengthy reports. One, "The Egyptian Army," a manuscript of 105 pages ending with the Frontier Incident, was written at Cromer's request and formed the basis for a chapter in his *Modern Egypt*.[25] Another, "Notes on the Egyptian fellah as a soldier and the Egyptian armies past and present," dealing with periods up to 1885,[26] may have been similarly commissioned. Wingate also wrote detailed personnel notes for Kitchener on British officers.[27] Heavy correspondence with Cairo and London continued, and Wingate used an exotic postmark to support his view, expressed with ever-increasing force, that the time was right for an advance against the khalifa.[28]

In this he was at one with Kitchener and other British officers in the Egyptian army. To them it was clear that the British government, notwithstanding assertions of preeminent rights in the whole valley of the Nile, might in the end give way to the French. Such a conclusion would be unbearable: they had not defended Egypt from the Mahdists only to lose control of Egypt's lifeline to the French. The only acceptable end to a confrontation already over a decade old was destruction of the Mahdist state. But Wingate, perhaps better than anyone else, knew that the weakness ascribed to the Mahdists was exaggerated, that it was "not the Khalifa's possible disintegration which will draw us into an expedition, it is the pressure of France and other European nations towards the Nile Valley which will force England to go to Khartoum."[29] In this view, then, French "pretensions" (as they were often called) actually helped the Anglo-Egyptian war party, whose difficulty lay in winning over a reluctant British government before those pretensions were realized.

When, during the summer of 1894, British officers pressed their point in England, they failed to convince either Lord Cromer or the Liberal government. Kitchener pressed for an advance up the Nile from Wadi Halfa to Dongola, and military circles in London and

---

[24] Wingate to Everett, W.O., 1 August 1894, SAD 257/1.

[25] SAD 179/4; see also SAD 218/4, rough draft and correspondence with Cromer.

[26] 19/9/94, SAD 258/1.

[27] Wingate to Kitchener, draft, n.d., SAD 258/1.

[28] SAD 257/1.

[29] Wingate to Maxwell, 29 June 1894, SAD 257/1.1

Cairo thought immediate action likely.[30] From distant Suakin Wingate
did his part, especially after the fall of Kassala to the Italians, to urge
a forward policy, arguing, as he would for the next four years, that in
the face of a powerful advance the khalifa would likely fall back on
Omdurman.[31] His superiors knew the ease with which a confrontation
with the Mahdists could be precipitated in the Red Sea Littoral, and
Rundle warned Wingate not to try—"it does no good," he wrote: the
British government had confirmed "a policy of do nothing."[32] Indeed
Wingate's arguments may have weakened the military's case.

On 20 September, after several postponements, Wingate left
Suakin for Cairo. (Kitchener had planned to recall him for a special
mission to London in June, but this fell through.)[33] His wife and children were in England, and for financial reasons Wingate was unable
to join them on leave. "Maintenance of three establishments" had
reduced him to "complete impecuniosity," he told his brother-in-law,
and he was in no need of leave. After four months in what Rundle
called "the most damnable place in the world," Wingate professed
himself "wonderfully fit."[34]

---

[30] Fairholme to Wingate, 25 July 1894; Maxwell to Wingate, 31 July 1894, SAD
257/1.
[31] See, e.g., Wingate to Everett, W.O., 1 August 1894, and other correspondence
in SAD 257/1.
[32] Rundle to Wingate, 30 August 1894, SAD 258/1.
[33] CB1; Kitchener to Wingate, 23 May 1894, SAD 233/4, and other correspondence in the same file.
[34] CB 1; Wingate's Bible; Rundle to Wingate, 30 August 1894; Wingate to Rundle,
31 August 1894, SAD 258/1.

Chapter Nine
Slatin Pasha

———◄◦◦◦►———

Although they had failed to persuade the government, British officers in Egypt took it for granted that an advance into the Sudan was necessary. By late 1894 their intramural argument concerned whether the advance would come in time to forestall the French. Speculation about French intentions fed the rumor-mill in Cairo. Wingate's old chief, Sir Evelyn Wood, disconcertingly honest as usual, told Wingate that an advance was at present unlikely, and of doubts at home that "Khartoum" was "worth the money."[1] It was left in some measure to Wingate to make the prize worthy of the race, through good fortune and a facile pen.

On 20 November 1894 Father Paolo Rossignoli, a missionary captured at El Obeid in 1883 and detained in Omdurman since 1885, arrived at Aswan with two nuns who had shared his captivity. Their escape had been the direct result of Wingate's endeavors. In March he had hired an Ababda tribesman to go to Omdurman and bring out either Karl Neufeld, a German merchant also held captive, or Rossignoli.[2] After twelve years in captivity, Rossignoli had much to tell; within days of his arrival in Cairo Wingate began plans for a memoir, and produced an outline for publishers. But one, Edward Arnold, seemed to speak for all in warning that British interest in the Sudan waxed and waned according to whether Egypt was in the news; any new book must be of "first-rate interest."[3]

Wingate had learned something about haggling. Already in correspondence with Sampson, Marston, Low about insufficient royalties from Father Ohrwalder's book, he extracted excellent terms from Arnold: an advance, and royalties of 20 percent on the first two thousand copies sold, rising to 25 percent on copies above that. The con-

---

[1] Wood to Wingate, 28 September 1894, SAD 258/1.

[2] The contract is printed in appendix A to *IRE*, November 1894.

[3] Arnold to Wingate, 17 January 1895, SAD 260/1. The outline and other correspondence are in the same file.

tract was between the publisher and Wingate alone, not Rossignoli.[4] Composition of the book, tentatively entitled "Rescued from Khartoum," followed the method used with Father Ohrwalder: Rossignoli's Arabic and Italian remarks were recorded and roughly translated into English for Wingate to re-work. Unfortunately for Rossignoli, another arrival from Omdurman completely eclipsed his own, and the collaboration was abandoned.

Of the Europeans in the Sudan none was more important than Rudolf Slatin, an Austrian soldier who had joined the Turco-Egyptian administration in the Sudan in 1879 and surrendered, as governor of Darfur, to the Mahdists in 1884. Several of Wingate's rescue efforts had focused on Slatin, and in 1892 the Austrian government, without Wingate's knowledge, had financed an abortive scheme.[5] Occasional communication between Slatin and the outside world whetted Wingate's appetite (and fed conspiracy theories in the Egyptian press). Slatin's ambiguous position in Omdurman—as a detainee but a *mulazim,* in attendance on the Khalifa Abdallahi—made escape more difficult. As in Rossignoli's case, contracts were drawn up between the intelligence department and would-be rescuers. One such arrangement finally succeeded. On the night of 20 February 1895 Slatin stole away from Omdurman on a donkey, rendezvoused with his deliverers, and sped north. After an eventful journey he reached Aswan on 16 March.[6]

Slatin's arrival had important results. His knowledge of the Mahdist state, its politics, personalities, military resources, and other subjects was of practical use to the intelligence department. His dramatic story contributed to the pressure for a forward policy in the Sudan. But it was Wingate's propaganda that ensured the enormous public reaction that ensued. With Wingate's (and the newspapers') help Slatin became the toast of Europe, and a living reminder of Britain's unfinished business in the Sudan. And with the help of the personality thus invented, Wingate too passed to a higher level of

---

[4] For correspondence, drafts, and other material related to the book see SAD 260/1.

[5] Wingate to Wodehouse, 17 March 1893, SAD 255/1.

[6] "Memorandum on the escape of Slatin Pasha," Appendix A to IRE, March 1895; Richard Hill, *Slatin Pasha,* London 1965, 29–34. For greater detail see Gordon Brook-Shepherd, *Between two flags. The life of Baron Sir Rudolf von Slatin Pasha,* London 1978, 106–21.

public and political notice. Indeed for Wingate the escape was an unmixed blessing, from which he reaped fame, honors, promotion, money, and support for the main prize: avenging Gordon and beating the French by conquering the Sudan.

Meanwhile there were other scores to settle. Within days of Slatin's appearance in Egypt, publishers' offers began to arrive, both for Slatin himself and for Wingate as potential editor or intermediary. Wingate engaged a London literary agent, A. P. Watt. Rossignoli's book, still in progress, posed a problem: "it would fall very flat if Slatin's experiences were published at the same time," Wingate noted.[7] He rejected Arnold's suggestion of incorporating "some of Slatin's adventures" with Rossignoli's.[8] Watt negotiated with Arnold. The Rossignoli contract was canceled, and a new one drawn up for a book on Slatin. This treated him and Wingate as co-authors, dividing royalties evenly, and provided for an advance of £300 payable upon publication.[9]

The authorship of *Fire and sword in the Sudan* was as unusual as that of *Mahdiism* and *Ten years' captivity*. It was initially agreed that a German edition would be published in Vienna at the same time as an English edition ("or version"), published "almost under identical arrangements as those made in the case of" Ohrwalder's book. The only difference would be to list Slatin as author and Wingate as editor, in order, it was said, to improve sales.[10] Early drafts were translated from the German by a local clerk.[11] By May Wingate claimed to have made so many "rearrangements and modifications" that the English edition must be considered the original and the German and any others as translations from the English.[12] Now difficulties arose over a French edition, which its publishers naturally wished to present as a translation from the German original (and not as a translation of

---

[7] Wingate to A.P. Watt, 28 March 1895, SAD 260/1.

[8] Arnold to Wingate, 20 March 1895, SAD 260/1.

[9] Contract, SAD 260/1. Rossignoli published a memoir, *I miei dodici anni di prigionia in mezzo ai Dervisci del Sudan,* in 1898.

[10] Wingate to Watt, 28 March 1895, SAD 260/1.

[11] Brook-Shepherd cites a letter Wingate wrote to Sir Arthur Bigge attesting to a Syrian translator. The same author credits Wingate with having translated Ohrwalder's German manuscript, but elsewhere confirms that Wingate did not know German. See *Between two flags,* 130–31, 138.

[12] Wingate to Watt, 8 May 1895, SAD 260/1.

a translation).[13] This problem was solved (for the publishers if not the student of Wingate's literary affairs) by suppressing Slatin's German original altogether. Manuscript was sent, in increments, to a translator in London (a Miss Joachim), whose English rendering was then edited by Wingate to create the English version as published. That version was in turn sent to the same translator to be rendered into German.[14] Thus despite showing Wingate's name on the title page as translator, *Fire and sword in the Sudan* (finally published in February 1896) is his edition of Joachim's English translation of Slatin's original; *Feuer und Schwert im Sudan,* published in Leipzig, is Joachim's translation of her own (edited) English translation of the original German.

Meanwhile, by other, more immediate means, Slatin's fame spread across Europe. Even before he had reached Cairo on 19 March wild rumors had told of his coming, and these Wingate fed by releasing only a brief, sensational account of the escape; another, more prosaic narrative followed later. While the sober European press took note of Slatin's importance for military intelligence, the lower end of the market was regaled with adventure and romance. Whatever their merit, most accounts made a hero too of the ingenious spy-master who, from a thousand miles away, had orchestrated the coup. The burst of publicity that accompanied Slatin came as a tonic to Wingate's flagging career.

Wingate had been suffering from continuing uncertainty about the future. For years he had been tantalized by the military attaché-ship at Constantinople. For various reasons—international crises, ambassadorial succession, the whims of Col. Chermside (who had held the post since 1889)—a definite offer had never been made. During the summer of 1894 another crescendo had been reached. Letters of recommendation (from Wolseley, among others) were dispatched to the War Office, and Wingate, immured at Suakin, went so far as to arrange a code for messages with Chermside. "Wingate Souakin. No." was duly sent in August when Chermside,

---

[13] Watt to Wingate, 20 July 1895, SAD 260/1.

[14] Watt to Wingate, 27 July 1895, SAD 260/1. Typescripts, with manuscript emendations by Wingate, are in SAD 443/1–2. Even Wingate's private explanations caused confusion: "Many thanks for telling me how Slatin's book was written," Sir Arthur Bigge wrote Wingate; "I conclude that *he* wrote it first in Arabic?" (22 April 1896, SAD 262/1).

citing no prospects for employment himself, applied for a further extension.[15]

Amidst this uncertainty came a bureaucratic controversy that painfully revealed Wingate's dependence on the goodwill of superiors in London and Cairo. We have seen that Wingate communicated routinely with the military authorities at home, both officially and "privately." The blurred boundary between the two categories, which allowed officials to convey information without taking responsibility for consequences, had caused trouble before. In October 1894 Hubert Foster at the War Office had written "personally" to Wingate on behalf of investors interested in a railway from Suakin to Berber. Wingate went to Cromer, who advised temporizing.[16] Then, on 29 October, Wingate told General Chapman, his prototype at the War Office, that Cromer was "extremely averse to any discussion of the project at present for political reasons," and that in any case the plan was unfeasible. Chapman was embarrassed by the implication that he or the War Office had had an interest in a commercial matter (and behind Cromer's back), and he supported his subordinates' complaint that Wingate should not have gone to Cromer with a "personal" letter.[17]

There the matter might have rested, had not Captain Fairholme, Wingate's regular correspondent at the War Office, raised the stakes. He too had written about the railway project, but only for "official" information. The incident, he told Wingate, had "left an impression . . . which must materially affect" their future correspondence unless Wingate could assure him that his letters would not be shown to anyone else. Wingate was forced to choose between Cromer and the War Office, at a time when his future depended upon the goodwill of both. He again consulted Cromer, who advised him to tell General Chapman that any letter, "private or other," on "official subjects" was "liable to be shown to the Sirdar or himself"; Cromer would write to the War Office to explain.[18] More correspondence ensued. Wingate

---

[15] Wingate, note, 17 June 1894; Wolseley to Wingate, 7 July 1894; Chermside to Wingate, August 1894, SAD 256/1.

[16] Foster to Wingate, 2 October 1894; Cromer to Wingate and Wingate to Foster, 18 October 1894, SAD 258/1.

[17] Wingate to Chapman, 29 October 1894; Chapman to Wingate, 7 November 1894, SAD 258/1.

[18] Fairholme to Wingate, 7 November 1894; Wingate to Chapman, draft, n.d., SAD 258/1.

passed it all to Cromer.[19] The matter was closed, but with what lasting effects Wingate could only guess.

While the Anglo-Egyptian world revolved around Slatin during
the winter and spring of 1895, Wingate had thus become concerned
about his own future. He had had no substantive promotion since
1889; Kitchener, pretending interest, took little, and was brusquely
critical of the intelligence department.[20] Wood, as always Wingate's
advisor, warned him too about trusting Cromer (to whom, even as
Wood's letter was en route, Wingate had just committed himself in
the controversy with the War Office): "what was sauce to me the
goose, may be sauce to you, the gander, or perhaps in our respective
positions we might call you the duckling," said Wood; Wingate's recognized competence, even Cromer's occasional praise, was no substitute for promotion.[21] The Constantinople attaché-ship was due to fall
vacant on 30 June 1895, and—in what he called "rather a momentous" step—Wingate told Cromer that without prospect of promotion he must take the post if it were offered.[22] Cromer took up the
matter, but as there was at least one officer ahead of Wingate for promotion the War Office appeared willing to consider only a higher
local rank.[23] Just at this point Slatin escaped from Omdurman. Wood,
having discussed Wingate's case at the War Office, now advised him
"after all . . . to stop in Egypt," a view shared by Grenfell and others
who took an interest. Meanwhile Chermside, at the behest of the
ambassador at Istanbul, yet again extended, until the summer of
1896, his stay there. Fairholme at the War Office told Wingate that
Chermside was "quite indispensable to the Embassy just now," confirming Wingate's lack of options.[24]

Following Slatin's escape Wingate remained in Egypt until July,
when he went to England on leave. The intervening months were

---

[19] Wingate to Cromer, 15 November 1894, SAD 258/1.

[20] Wingate to Wood, 9 January 1895, SAD 233/4. For insults see Rundle to
Wingate, April 1895; and Wingate to Rundle, 10 April 1895, SAD 233/4.

[21] Wood to Wingate, 18 November 1894, SAD 233/4. See also Wood to Wingate,
21 January 1895, SAD 233/4.

[22] Wingate to Milner, 11 February 1895, SAD 233/4.

[23] Cromer to Wingate, 13 February 1895; Wingate to Wood, 15 February 1895;
Wood to Wingate, 28 February 1895, SAD 233/4.

[24] Wood to Wingate, 1 April 1895; Grenfell to Wingate, 27? 1895; Chermside to
Wingate, 4 April 1895, SAD 233/4; Fairholme to Wingate, 26 April 1895, SAD
258/1.

filled with office work, informed by the special knowledge and credibility Slatin provided; by reports occasioned by the escape; by work on the book; and by the nagging problem of Wingate's own future prospects. *Fire and sword* would soon be used to sway public opinion in Britain toward intervention in the Sudan; Slatin himself was immediately put to the task in official circles, first in Egypt, then Britain. Wingate's *General report on the Egyptian Soudan, March 1895, compiled from statements made by Slatin Pasha,* was quickly produced. This masterful document intersperses military and political detail with argument and distortion. That Wingate had abandoned disinterested intelligence—at least in documents prepared for circulation outside the Egyptian army—is apparent. About the Bahr al-Ghazal, for instance, the southwestern region through which French or Belgian penetration to the Nile was likeliest, the *Report* states:

> Slatin Pasha points out that the geographical and strategical position of that province with reference to the rest of the Egyptian Soudan, renders its possession absolutely essential. The presence of foreigners unconcerned in the preservation of Egyptian interests, having at their command the vast resources of this great province, which are estimated at a much higher value in both men and material than those of any portion of the Nile Valley, would place them in such a predominating position as to render in a large measure valueless the occupation by Egypt of the remainder of the Egyptian Soudan.

The statement is both deeply erroneous and carefully exculpatory of its author. Possession of the Bahr al-Ghazal was not essential for control of the Nile, least of all because of its "vast resources." Elsewhere in the *Report* the region's population is given (on the authority of Slatin, who had no way of estimating it) as "between five and six millions" of "by far the most warlike" people in the Sudan: rent by mutual animosities, however, they might be both easily conquered and molded into "an efficient local army." Such contradictions passed unremarked. The Bahr al-Ghazal was far away, few Europeans had visited it, Slatin was one of them, and the Scramble was entering its final phase.[25]

---

[25] See also Wingate to Fairholme, W.O., 8 April 1895, SAD 256/1 for Wingate's use of Slatin's expertise in this matter. The foreign secretary, Kimberley, called the report "very important. We have never before had any real knowledge of the state of affairs" in the Bahr al-Ghazal (Kimberley to Cromer, 22 March 1895, FO 633/7/162).

Indeed, Slatin's escape concentrated Wingate's mind on great things. Secret, detailed plans for an advance as far as Berber had been drawn up in February. Fitful interest in Rabih Zubayr flared anew. In April Wingate drafted a letter to Cromer suggesting omission altogether of public reference to British claims in the Upper Nile, substituting instead support for Ottoman or Egyptian claims, against which France, champion of an indivisible Nile, could raise no objection.[26] (At Fashoda, in September 1898, he would have occasion to reiterate.) On 5 April the Austrian minister presented Wingate the 2nd class of the Iron Crown of Austria, conferred by the Emperor Franz Josef for his role in Slatin's escape. Cromer wrote an official dispatch to the Foreign Office in praise of Wingate's work; Lord Kimberley, the foreign secretary, brought Wingate's services to the attention of the Egyptian government;[27] and on 24 May he was made a Companion of the Bath in the Queen's birthday honors list. (This was particularly gratifying because, the year before, Kitchener had dangled before him the possibility of a C.M.G. that, in the event, had failed to materialize.)[28] Now Rosebery, the prime minister, gave private assurance that Slatin's escape had been "only the last of a long series of services" for which Wingate deserved a reward.[29] By the time he left Cairo on 2 July, for a season full of promise in England, Wingate's star had brightened again.

It was reflected glory. In congratulating him on the Austrian order an officer joked of "Baron Wingate von Ohrwalder von Slatinstein."[30] The khedive made Slatin a *pasha* of Egypt; Wingate

---

[26] For the Berber plans see SAD 258/1/597-728. For Rabih see Wingate, "Resumé of a conversation which took place on 1st April between Lord Cromer and Zubayr Pasha, at the British Agency," 1 April 1895, SAD 258/1. For Wingate's letter (undated, April 1895) about the Upper Nile: SAD 261/1.

[27] Kimberley to Cromer, 25 April 1895 (MS copy in Wingate's hand), SAD 262/1; CB1; Cromer to Sanderson, 10 April 1895, FO 633/5/609; Kimberley to Cromer, 26 April 1895, FO 633/7/164; see Cromer to Wodehouse, 29 March 1895, FO 633/5/607.

[28] Wingate to Milner, 12 April 1894; Milner to Wingate, 20 May 1894; Kitchener to Wingate, n.d. (August 1894), SAD 256/1; Wingate to Wood, 9 January 1895, SAD 233/4. Kitchener "implore[d]" Cromer to get the C.M.G. for both Rundle and Wingate or for neither: Rundle was senior to Wingate, there was rivalry between them, and when he was not decorated, neither was Wingate (Cromer to Wodehouse, 29 March 1895, FO 633/5/607).

[29] Rosebery to Wingate, 14 June 1895 (MS copy in Wingate's hand), SAD 262/1.

[30] Rogers to Wingate, 6 May 1895, SAD 115/9.

remained a *bey*. A pattern emerged by which the ambitious bureaucrat acted as agent for the colorful adventurer. Fresh from a round of receptions, audiences, and honors in Vienna, Slatin reached England at the end of July. Wingate had already laid the groundwork by, among other things, sending a souvenir of Slatin to Queen Victoria and announcing his planned arrival. Through Grenfell came an invitation to dine with the duke of Connaught (for "Slatin and yourself").[31] The Prince of Wales asked Slatin to Marlborough House; "perhaps you would kindly come with him" was the wording of Wingate's invitation.[32] Wingate corresponded with Sir Arthur Bigge, the queen's private secretary, over several weeks, to extract an invitation to Osborne House; when it finally came it was for Slatin, Bigge adding that the queen wished to see Wingate "at the same time."[33] There on 19 August Slatin and Wingate—in knee breeches (Bigge had lent a pair of tights)—dined with the queen. After dinner she invested Wingate with the C.B. and had a full account of Slatin's experiences. Although in her diary the Queen described Wingate as "a very clever distinguished officer," it was—as he himself must have known—as Slatin's "great friend" that he would be remembered.[34]

Queen Victoria had taken an immediate liking to Slatin. What appealed to her is uncertain: his escape had been exciting, but no more than others'; they spoke about it in German, but so could have Father Ohrwalder, without the same rapport. In any event, on 20 August Bigge wrote to Wingate that the queen had been "much interested with [*sic*] your and Slatin's visit" and wished "to see the latter again"; Bigge added that the queen and Princesses Louise and Beatrice wished to have photographs of Slatin. In mid-September the queen arranged through Wingate for Slatin's portrait to be painted ("in his Dervish dress") for her while he was visiting Vienna.[35] Wingate began to write to Bigge (and others, including Wolseley), about a British decoration for Slatin, and managed, in the course of correspondence, to get an invitation to Balmoral a week before Slatin

---

[31] Grenfell to Wingate, 24 July 1895, SAD 256/1.

[32] Knollys to Wingate, 26 July 1895, SAD 256/1.

[33] Bigge to Wingate, 26 July 1895, 1 August 1895, SAD 256/1.

[34] Brook-Shepherd, *Between two flags*, 134–38, quoting Queen Victoria's diary; Court Circular, *Times*, 21 August 1895; see also Bigge to Wingate, 8 August 1895, SAD 256/1.

[35] F.J. Edwards to Wingate, 11 September 1895, SAD 256/1; see also Edwards to Wingate, 12 September 1895, SAD 256/1.

was due there.[36] Meanwhile Wingate ushered the celebrity from office to drawing room to learned society. "Slatin and I . . . are coming to London to-morrow," he wrote the prime minister in August, "and in case you should like to talk to him" they would call on him at home.[37] This hob-nobbing did not go unnoticed in Egypt: judging by the press accounts, Maxwell wrote, Wingate had become "nearly as ubiquitous as the Prince of Wales"; Kitchener, himself a master of the pacific arts, complained that he could think of no way of writing to the peripatetic Slatin "except c/o the Queen."[38]

The highlight and culmination of an eventful leave was the visit to Balmoral on 10–13 October, the first of many Wingate and Slatin would pay. Wingate had planted a seed in fertile ground: the queen invested Slatin with the military C.B.—a rare honor for a foreigner— as well as the Egyptian War Medal. Wingate was given a "portrait" (by which he must have meant a photograph) of the queen and copies of her books.[39] After another round of social engagements and hectic attention to the manuscript of *Fire and sword,* both Wingate and Slatin left England for Egypt via Vienna, reaching Cairo on 2 November.[40]

As exciting as these events surely were for a major in the Egyptian army, they exposed his personal predicament. Fame had not brought fortune, but had drained Wingate's meager resources. In May 1894 his army pay had been increased to £E840, but, after his expensive summer in Suakin, he had been unable to afford leave with his family. In March 1895 he was reduced to asking his Aunt Agatha for a loan of £50, to be repaid from proceeds of the Rossignoli book (which he hoped to edit in her billiard room). While Wingate edged into society with Slatin, his family settled into lodgings at Tunbridge Wells.[41] A crisis loomed, and the advance for *Fire and sword* seems to have been spent before it arrived.

---

[36] Bigge to Wingate, 20 August 1895, SAD 261/1; Wingate to Bigge, draft, 22 August 1895; Wingate to Wolseley, 22 September 1895; Wolseley to Wingate, 27 September 1895; Bigge to Wolseley, 30 September 1895; Bigge to Wingate, 2 October 1895, SAD 262/1.

[37] Wingate to Rosebery, draft, 23 August 1895, SAD 262/1.

[38] Maxwell to Wingate, 25 August 1895; Kitchener to Wingate, 4 October 1895, SAD 261/1.

[39] CB1; Bigge to Wingate, 2, 6 October 1895, SAD 262/1.

[40] CB1.

[41] Wingate to his Aunt Agatha, 3 March 1895, SAD 256/1.

Upon returning to Cairo, therefore, Wingate once again took up the question of his future prospects. In a memorandum dated October 1895 (perhaps drafted during the journey) he noted that his contract with the Egyptian army would expire in May 1896, and he had heard nothing of an extension. If the authorities wished him to stay, something must be done about salary and promotion; if no "guarantee" could be given for the long term (such as of future employment by the Foreign Office or Colonial Office, or at least of counting his Egyptian service toward pension), he must seek a "definite career" elsewhere. For all his recent success Wingate held a weak hand: no offers awaited his attention, and his limited means made return to England unfeasible.[42] He might threaten to leave; superiors knew he had nowhere to go. Patience enforced is no virtue, and Wingate was embittered by the procrastination, punctuated by assurances of regard, which by the end of 1895 had become routine. To higher authorities his was the common problem of the junior officer without private means in a peacetime army: when the army finally advanced, so would his career.

---

[42] Wingate, draft memorandum, n.d. (October 1895), SAD 262/1.

Chapter Ten
The Invasion

For all its seeming inevitability, the Anglo-Egyptian invasion of the Sudan in March 1896 stemmed from sudden decisions of a reluctant British government. During their last months in office the Liberals' abhorrence of a forward policy alarmed even Lord Cromer, who, since advocating withdrawal in 1884–85, had recognized an eventual need to occupy at least the Nile valley, if for no other reason than to keep out the French. When in March 1895 he told Kimberley that recent extension of the Egyptian telegraph from Korosko to the Murrat wells, and planned continuation of the Egyptian railway to Aswan, would both help in "the ultimate reconquest of the Soudan," the foreign secretary became alarmed.[1] Although publicly the government took exception to rumored French intentions in the Bahr al-Ghazal, Rosebery himself told Cromer that Britain would take "no initiative" in the Sudan: for various reasons, European and Egyptian, the "initiative should come from Egypt." What was more, in the current international situation even an "urgent request" for British collaboration would be denied.[2]

In the event, an urgent request came from Italy, not Egypt, and reluctance was overcome by fear of France, not the Sudanese. In June 1895 the Conservatives returned to power in Britain; in the general election in July they won a large majority. Meanwhile in March Italy, from its base in Eritrea, had invaded Abyssinia, where French influence had been rapidly increasing. Uncertainty demanded reconsideration of Britain's defensive strategy. In October Cromer expressed reluctance to embark on construction of the Aswan dam, lest Egypt want funds for a Sudan campaign.[3] Serious preparation began, however, only after the Abyssinians defeated the Italians at Amba Alagi on

---

[1] Cromer to Kimberley, 8 March 1895, FO 633/6/235; Kimberley to Cromer, 22 March 1895, FO 633/7/162.

[2] Rosebery to Cromer, 22 April 1895, FO 633/7/137.

[3] Cromer to Salisbury, 30 October 1895, FO 633/6/243.

7 December. This opened the way for the Mahdists to reoccupy Kassala or cut its communications with the coast. In London the Italian ambassador, as early as 10 December, asked for British help. The War Office mooted a diversionary "show of activity" on the Egyptian frontier or, from Suakin, occupation of Kassala by the British themselves, as a first step toward conquering the Sudan.[4] This was just what reluctant imperialists wished to avoid. Cromer thought the occupation of Kassala, for which Kitchener pressed, easy to achieve; he feared where it (and Kitchener) would lead, and even more what might result if the soldiers were let loose up the Nile.[5] As he told the Foreign Office in February, Kitchener was "a Jamesonian type," and needed to be "kept in hand."[6] Salisbury decided to await developments.

The possibility of an early advance in the Sudan affected Wingate personally. By mid-February 1896 he had still had no word about his Egyptian army contract, which was due to expire at the end of May. But reliable intelligence was now more important than ever. Calling Wingate "a perfect encyclopaedia . . . on all matters connected with the Soudan," Cromer asked the War Office to prolong his stay indefinitely.[7] In that case Wingate would stay or go as Egypt's and his own needs dictated; he had heard that Chermside would retire from Constantinople in October. Cromer's mistrust of Kitchener may have figured in this intervention. Wingate had shown loyalty to Cromer and could be expected to keep him informed, as the secretive Kitchener could not. When Kitchener claimed credit, in a thirty-second interview, for Wingate's contract extension, Wingate, knowing better, replied simply, "Many thanks. I am much obliged to you."[8] In fact, the extension, for two years, was granted only in mid-March, after the Anglo-Egyptian invasion had been decided.[9]

On 1 March 1896 the Italian army was routed by the Abyssinians at Adowa. The development awaited by Salisbury— "the long expected shake of the Kaleidescope," as Wingate called it—had occurred. On 12 March the British cabinet authorized an advance to

---

[4] Fairholme, W.O., to Wingate, 15 December 1895, SAD 261/1.
[5] Cromer to Salisbury, 18 December 1895, FO 633/6/247.
[6] Cromer to Sanderson, 9 February 1896, FO 633/8/22.
[7] Cromer to Wolseley, 13 February 1896, FO 633/8/25.
[8] Wingate to Milner, 21 February 1896, SAD 262/1.
[9] W.O. to Sirdar, 16 March 1896, SAD 233/6.

Akasha, midway between Wadi Halfa and Dongola up the Nile. This had two objects: to divert the Mahdists' attention from the Italians in the east, and "to plant the foot of Egypt rather further up the Nile."[10] For various reasons—European relations, Egyptian finances, military uncertainty—Salisbury and Cromer were reluctant to authorize an advance even to Dongola. Cromer feared irresistible pressure to continue the advance, pressure not only from the soldiers but now also from a British public suddenly aroused by *Fire and sword in the Sudan*.

The "shake of the Kaleidescope" had increased public interest in Slatin's memoir, which was fortuitously published in February 1896. Indeed, Edward Arnold, the publisher, joked that Wingate had "fomented" trouble in the Sudan "just at the right time by means of his secret Agents!"[11] Presentation copies were liberally distributed: to the queen, Salisbury, Wolseley, Grenfell, Cromer, Rosebery, Milner, the duke of Connaught, the Prince of Wales, Sir Thomas Sanderson, and others, as well as thirty-six British newspapers and magazines.[12] By the second week in April more than five thousand copies had been sold, and royalties of about £1,200 accrued.[13] Arnold argued for a cheap, abridged edition, which was finally published in 1897. By 1898 the book had "found its way into every Library" in Britain, and was often given as a prize in school competitions, much as Gordon's *Journals* had been.[14] *Fire and sword* was well received by the press. As in the cases of *Mahdiism* and *Ten years' captivity*, much of the reaction was uncritical, politically skewed, and dwelt on blood, slavery, sadism and, sexual excess. Reviews called attention to "unspeakable tyranny," "savagery," "lawless and corrupt oppression." The *Pall Mall Gazette* on 18 March reminded readers that Britain had "at least some responsibility" for the wreck of the Sudan, and joined Slatin in calling for its recovery. The *Belfast News Letter* of 7 April saw "no use looking for mysterious motives in the Nile expedition. The state of the Soudan" was "itself a sufficient explanation and justification." Criticisms of *Fire and sword* were few. H. G. Prout, an American former officer of the Egyptian army writing in the *New York Times*,

---

[10] Wingate to Milner, 7 March 1896, SAD 262/1; Salisbury to Cromer, 13 March 1896, FO 633/7/171.

[11] Arnold to Mrs. Wingate, 31 January 1896, SAD 260/1.

[12] "List A," 1 February 1896, SAD 260/1. See also another list in the same file.

[13] Watt to Wingate, 10 April 1896, SAD 260/1.

[14] Arnold to Slatin, 23 November 1898, SAD 432/80.

questioned the author's motives and veracity in his treatment of the Mahdi.[15] Most penetrating was a contributor to the *Saturday Review:* "The author has a thirst for revenge, which he apparently attempts neither to control nor conceal. When, therefore, he depicts the power of the Khalifa as broken, and predicts that on advance we should be welcomed as redeemers by the down-trodden tribes of the Soudan, we cannot but feel that the wish is father to the thought."[16]

Still, much more typical was the *Echo's* eloquent plea: the Mahdi had "launched into bestial excesses, of which he died. His successor is a still more horrible villain. A brisk kick from outside would knock over the Mahdist edifice. Who is going to kick?"[17]

Thus politicians, press, and public were ready, in March 1896, to invade the Sudan. The British government gambled that it would be able to stop at Dongola and, as Cromer feared, had no intention of paying for the campaign. If Italy could be helped, France warned off, the Mahdists frightened, Gordon "avenged," the Liberals embarrassed, the British public placated, and the Egyptians made to pay, then Dongola was a prize well worth having. To these many motives Wingate, remembering the humiliations of 1884–85, added another: "the success of the Black man against the White is at all times undesirable," he wrote. The Italian defeat held "evil consequences" for all European powers in Africa.[18] Taking the Sudan would restore order, not only in the Sudan, but to the affairs of Africa generally.

The first phase of the Dongola campaign proceeded quickly. On 18 March two columns set out from the Egyptian forward post at Sarras for Akasha, which was taken on the twentieth. Construction began immediately on a military railway between the two posts. On the twenty-first Kitchener and his staff, including Wingate, left Cairo for the frontier; Wingate reached Wadi Halfa, the base of operations, on the twenty-ninth. By 12 April the Egyptian forces between Sarras and Akasha numbered more than eight thousand. The Khalifa Abdallahi rushed reinforcements to the north. A skirmish occurred on 1 May, when the Mahdists were driven off into the desert four miles east of Akasha. By early June Egyptian railhead was within striking distance of the Mahdists, making it necessary to

---

[15] Cited in Hill, *Slatin Pasha,* 41, 155.
[16] 4 April 1896.
[17] 5 February 1896.
[18] Wingate to Gleichen, 7 March 1896, SAD 261/1.

dislodge them from Farka (Firket). In this, the first important
engagement of the campaign, Kitchener commanded some ten
thousand men. The Mahdists were defeated on 7 June, with heavy
casualties, and were forced to evacuate both Farka and Sawarda.
With the northern half of the old Dongola Province now in
Egyptian hands, the advance paused to await steamers that would
come with the rise of the Nile, and because of a serious outbreak of
cholera in the Egyptian army.[19]

Throughout this phase of the Dongola campaign Wingate
served as director of military intelligence and Press Censor. His work
was characteristically thorough and competent, and was widely
praised in military circles. Especially before the battle of Farka, the
timing of which he either brilliantly predicted or indiscreetly
announced in letters home, Wingate seemed totally in command of
the local situation.[20] But it was also characteristic that Wingate, as
censor, created problems by again combining incompatible public
and private roles.

Wingate's appointment as director of military intelligence to the
expedition was a formality, and combining it with the duties of press
censor was not unusual. But even before the appointments were
announced on 29 March there were hints of problems ahead. On the
twenty-first in Cairo, Arthur Conan Doyle, reporting for the
Westminster Gazette, asked Wingate for "a shove up"; there were
other such requests for special treatment. Worse, Wingate himself
now undertook, for about ten days, to act as correspondent for
Reuter. This raised questions about conflict of interest and unfair
competition. The editor of the *Times* even hinted at duplicity, since
Wingate had urged him to send a correspondent but had never said
he was available himself.[21] In mid-April, after Cromer relayed
reporters' complaints of favoritism, Wingate asked to be relieved of
the censorship. Kitchener accepted the resignation, which in turn provoked an effusive address by the reporters, denying all knowledge of

[19] CB1; *IRE,* 44 (February and March 1896); 45 (29 March–12 April 1896); 47
(26 April–22 May 1896); 48 (22 May–21 June 1896).

[20] See, e.g., Milner to Wingate, 1 July 1896, SAD 262/1; Fairholme, W.O., to
Wingate, 24 July 1896, SAD 261/1. See also Wingate, *Wingate of the Sudan,*
106–07.

[21] Conan Doyle to Wingate, 21 March 1896; Moberly Bell to Wingate, 10 April
1896, SAD 261/1.

complaints and recording "perfect confidence" in Wingate's "absolute impartiality."[22] Cromer added his own endorsement and, a regular Reuter correspondent having arrived, Wingate resumed the censorship. How had he expected to combine the roles of correspondent and censor? To Cromer he explained that the Reuter assignment had been temporary, during a period of little activity.[23] But whether he had seen in it only a little extra income or a way of directing British press accounts of the campaign, the episode raised doubts about his judgment.

In July cholera broke out at Aswan. Careless enforcement of quarantine resulted in its spreading southward to every Egyptian army post. By the second week in August, 260 Egyptian and 19 British soldiers had died, as had 183 civilians of the *harimat,* and some 457 other civilians.[24] Wingate was at Kusha, the Egyptians' forward post, when the epidemic reached there on 14 August.[25] By then the epidemic was apparently on the wane, and, with the rise of the Nile, resumption of the campaign was at hand.

The Egyptian advance from Kusha to Dongola began on 12 September. The main Mahdist force, under Muhammad Bishara, lay in a heavily fortified position at al-Hafir, north of Dongola. From the abandoned heights of Karma, on the right bank of the Nile opposite al-Hafir, the invaders bombed the Mahdist stronghold, then bypassed it with gunboats, threatening to surround it. The Mahdists therefore evacuated al-Hafir, leaving the way open to Dongola, which was occupied on the twenty-third. The Mahdists were now in full retreat: al-Dabba was occupied on the twenty-fourth and Marawi on the twenty-sixth, by small forces on gunboats. After a brief tour of the riverain towns Kitchener and his staff, including Wingate, returned to Cairo in early October.[26] The first phase of the conquest had been completed, cheaply and easily.

Egyptian *Intelligence Reports* indicate the scope of Wingate's work throughout the Dongola campaign. That the Egyptians encountered few surprises during the advance was widely ascribed to

---

[22] Wingate, memorandum, 16 April 1896; Various correspondents (unaddressed), 17 April 1896, SAD 262/1.

[23] Wingate to Cromer, 18 April 1896, SAD 262/1.

[24] *IRE* 49, 22 June–18 August 1896.

[25] CB1.

[26] *IRE* 50, 28 August 1896–31 December 1896; CB1.

the effectiveness of his intelligence arrangements. As the episode of the censorship indicates, however, direction of intelligence did not satisfy either Wingate's ambitions or his financial need. Extension of his contract to 1898, at an increased salary, had been improvised at Cromer's request. Throughout the summer of 1896, as the Dongola campaign progressed, Wingate was once more involved in correspondence over the military attaché-ship in Constantinople. In June he suggested to Fairholme at the War Office that Cromer be consulted again: if Wingate had to leave Egypt by May 1898 in any case, it would be "folly" to refuse an offer at the end of the present campaign.[27] Cromer himself, though still irritatingly non-committal, told Wingate that "in the public interest" as well as his own he "had much better stay in Egypt."[28] In the end, in circumstances now obscure, Wingate was passed over for Constantinople on the grounds that the Dongola campaign made him "not available," even though it ended before the post needed to be filled.[29]

Adding to Wingate's frustration were difficulties in his newly-revived literary career. The advance to Dongola created demand in Britain for a campaign history, while the success of *Fire and sword* and Wingate's unique access to information made him an obvious potential author. Several projects arose: a new book by Wingate and Slatin on the Dongola campaign; an updated edition of *Mahdiism;* and an abridgement of *Fire and sword*. In the end, only the last was published, and Wingate was left with little to show for it.

As early as mid-summer Wingate corresponded with Watt, his agent in London, about the current campaign. "I have no doubt," he wrote, that "newspaper correspondents and others . . . ignorant of the official circumstances," would produce books, but those could be little more than "personal narratives"; "with Slatin Pasha and myself the case is somewhat different."[30] Wingate wished to forestall competition and attract offers, but had not decided to attempt another book. In November Edward Arnold, publisher of *Fire and sword,* repeated a request for a campaign history, but suggested Wingate might wish to

---

[27] Wingate to Fairholme, draft, 28 June 1896, SAD 262/1. See also Wingate to Cromer, 28 June 1896, SAD 262/1. Wingate apparently wrote with Cromer's permission.

[28] Cromer to Wingate, 13 July 1896, SAD 262/1.

[29] Wingate to Milner, draft ("not sent"), November 1896, SAD 262/1.

[30] Wingate to Watt, 8 July 1896, SAD 260/1.

await the final showdown with the Khalifa Abdallahi.[31] By December Wingate had given up the idea,[32] perhaps because of difficulties that arose over a new edition of *Mahdiism*.

In 1896 *Mahdiism* went out of print, and Macmillan wished to produce an updated abridgement. Owing to the press of work, R. A. Marriott, who had helped to edit the first edition and was now commanding the Camel Corps, was given the task, at Wingate's suggestion and with his assistance.[33] No contract was signed. In July, at the frontier, Wingate received the first installment of Marriott's work and was "staggered" not only by "many points of divergence" but also by much that would be politically controversial. He therefore insisted that either Marriott refrain "absolutely from political discussion" and "from attacks on superiors," or that the project be abandoned.[34] Marriott made changes, then sent 120 pages, as revised for the press, to Wingate; if this draft proved unsatisfactory, Marriott suggested publication in his own name alone.[35] Wingate rejected that proposal in a way that annoyed Marriott, who now revealed that his "political" comments (about the need to push on immediately to Berber after the fall of Dongola) had been inserted at the suggestion of the War Office, where he had been told to "rub it in." "Riled," Marriott now "chucked the whole thing."[36] When Macmillan asked Wingate to revive the project, he refused.[37]

By the end of 1896, therefore, the only project still pending was an abridgement of *Fire and sword*. The Dongola campaign had rekindled interest in Slatin, whose fame Wingate continued to share and promote. (After the battle of Farka, for instance, Wingate had sent trophies to Queen Victoria in their names; further souvenirs were dispatched at intervals. In thanking Wingate, her private secretary, with the tact Wingate by now must have expected, noted "how keenly H.M. follows all that Slatin does.")[38] In October, after the Dongola

---

[31] Arnold to Wingate, 10 November 1896, SAD 260/1.
[32] Wingate to Watt, 12 December 1896, SAD 260/1.
[33] See Wingate, draft Introductory Note, 4 July 1896, SAD 260/1.
[34] Wingate to Marriott, 11 August 1896, SAD 260/1.
[35] Marriott to Wingate, 7 August 1896, SAD 260/1.
[36] Wingate to Marriott, 11 August 1896; Marriott to Wingate, 1 October 1896, SAD 260/1.
[37] Marriott to Wingate, 1 October 1896; Wingate to Marriott, draft, 25 October 1896; Wingate to Macmillan, 15 October 1896, SAD 260/1.
[38] Bigge to Wingate, 3 July 1896, SAD 262/1.

campaign had ended, Arnold suggested a cheap edition, omitting "all the historical matter" (the long introductory chapters for which Wingate himself was most responsible).[39] Wingate and Slatin collaborated in Cairo during the winter, and the book was published in mid-1897. Sales were brisk. In 1897 Wingate earned about £160 from the book.[40]

In the aftermath of the Dongola campaign Wingate's reward seemed slight. He won battle honors for his presence at Farka and al-Hafir, and in November was finally promoted brevet lieutenant colonel and awarded the Dongola campaign medal.[41] That was all. Wingate was disappointed: he had been treated no better than junior officers; the intelligence department's achievement was put on a par with that of British officers who had arrived in Egypt a few days before the campaign, and of whose preferment Wingate was clearly envious. In a letter left unsent to Milner, he complained of being tired, discouraged, and "burning from a sense of indignation."[42] It was left to Evelyn Wood to apply the cool hand of reason: senior staff officers in London were getting older, he wrote; they knew that many who were "next to them, or near to them in the way of seniority" did not "shine as men of exceptional merit"; they had therefore decided "to take advantage of the recent expedition up the Nile, to bring forward men, not for what they had done, but for what we hope they may do." Contradicting Wingate's assertion, from now made privately with increasing insistence, that no British officers should be brought into the Egyptian army above him, Wood held that the sirdar must do what was best for the army, "without any consideration of your's or anyone's seniority."[43]

The Dongola honors left Wingate with a grievance against Kitchener that would smolder for years, one based partly on the simple fact that his chief had never once shown gratitude for his services. Expressions of approval were important to Wingate, and often compensated for the slights he perceived in others' conduct. Wood's

---

[39] Arnold to Wingate, 19 October 1896, SAD 260/1.

[40] Wingate to Watt, 12 December 1896, SAD 260/1; Arnold to Wingate, 18 February 1898, SAD 227/1.

[41] CB1.

[42] Wingate to Milner, draft, "not sent," November 1896, SAD 262/1.

[43] Wood to Wingate, 18 January 1897, SAD 179/6. Cf. Hunter to George Hunter, 21 February 1897, printed in Doolittle, *A soldier's hero,* 107.

detached analysis made sense, but if superiors were satisfied with a job well done, he should have public recognition; if the War Office was bringing forward men for what it hoped "they may do," what were their hopes for Wingate? In 1896 Wingate was reminded again that, through diligence and hard work, he had achieved the status consistently reserved for the successful bureaucrat. He was naive to expect otherwise: as Archibald Hunter admitted, there had been so little fighting during the campaign that British honors—not the "soup plates" struck by the khedive—might begin and end with the sirdar.[44]

Preparations for the second stage in the conquest of the Sudan began soon after Dongola. Although Cromer, Salisbury, and indeed the British Treasury were, to varying degrees, determined to stop at Dongola for several years, the march of events was beyond their control. The easy Egyptian occupation of Dongola had relieved anxiety about the military and financial costs a further advance would incur. In an exercise in personal diplomacy Kitchener, during the summer of 1896, persuaded the British Exchequer to make a low-interest loan to Egypt to pursue the war. Persistent rumors of French moves into the Bahr al-Ghazal, from west and east, argued for a faster advance. In October 1896 even Cromer saw no "serious obstacles" to an advance in 1897.[45] Meanwhile the complicated diplomacy that would eventually lead to Omdurman—and to Fashoda—took Wingate away from Egypt, to the court of Menelik II, king of Abyssinia.

---

[44] Hunter to Duncan Hunter, 28 October 1896, printed in Doolittle, *A soldier's hero*, 94.

[45] Cromer to Salisbury, 30 October 1896, FO 633/6/264.

Chapter Eleven
Mission to Abyssinia

Menelik II's defeat of the Italians at Adowa in March 1896 was, as we have seen, the impetus for a British advance to Dongola. In the aftermath of Adowa, French (and Russian) activities in and regarding Abyssinia increased, and did not abate after the Egyptian occupation of Dongola in September. Indeed, Kitchener's invasion quickened the pace of Great-Power competition for influence over Menelik. It also revived Menelik's fear of hydra-headed European aggression: no sooner had he disposed of the Italians than the British, in the shape of Kitchener's Egyptian army, had appeared on the horizon. Distrusting all who sought his friendship, Menelik saw the Mahdist state as a potential bulwark against the Europeans. The British, in turn, aware of both Menelik's contacts with the Mahdists and the French presence at Addis Ababa, saw a need to forestall Franco-Abyssinian action in the Upper Nile—but not an urgent need: London hoped that diplomacy would allow postponement of an advance up the Nile to Omdurman.[1]

Thus in December 1896 Cromer suggested a mission to Menelik to convince him of Britain's good intentions. A letter was sent to the *Negus,* and in mid-February 1897 his reply, welcoming an embassy, was received. Rennell Rodd, chief secretary in the Cairo Residency and an old hand at Upper-Nile diplomacy, would head the mission, with Wingate as understudy. Captain Count Gleichen and Lord Edward Cecil, whose careers would from now on involve Wingate, were sent out by the War Office to accompany them. None of the principals spoke Amhara; a Shoan resident in Cairo was engaged to translate. The ostensible purpose of the mission was to establish relations with Menelik and settle questions involving the borders between the Somali Coast protectorate and the Abyssinian province of Harrar;

[1] For the diplomatic history see G.N. Sanderson, *England, Europe and the Upper Nile 1882–1899,* Edinburgh, 1965, 247–60, 292–99, et passim; "Contributions from African sources to the history of European competition in the Upper Valley of the Nile," *JAH* III, 1, 1962, 69–90; and "The foreign policy of the Negus Menelik, 1896–1898," *JAH* V, 1, 1964, 87–97.

the subject of a definite border between Abyssinia and the old
Egyptian provinces would be omitted unless raised by Menelik. By
the second week of March preparations for the journey had been
completed.² Wingate was evidently glad to get away on 10 March;
having had four months with his family in their new rented house,
Maison Rolo, he was, however, again suffering from insomnia, a lifelong problem he always attributed to overwork.³

Traveling from Ismailia via Aden, the Rodd Mission reached
Zayla on the Somali coast on 19 March. A caravan of almost two
hundred men transported them to the borders of Harrar, which was
reached in ten days; along the way bands of Italian prisoners from
Adowa were met and interviewed. From Harrar, where they were
received by Ras Makonnen, the governor, a difficult journey brought
them finally to Addis Ababa in mid-April.⁴ There, with little local
knowledge and encumbered with uncertainties about a rapidly-
changing international situation, Rodd and Wingate were no match
for Menelik.

Wingate and Gleichen, the mission's intelligence officer, learned
little about the Abyssinians' true attitude toward the Mahdist state. They
had to rely on translators, and Wingate was ill for much of their stay.⁵ A
Sudanese delegation, they were told, had recently been sent home
empty-handed; otherwise, Wingate admitted on 7 May, "no exact information" about it could be gleaned.⁶ In fact Menelik had approached the
Khalifa Abdallahi in July 1896 about an alliance against the Europeans,
and subsequent actions on both sides clearly indicate entente. Yet by the
treaty signed by Rodd and Menelik on 14 May the *Negus* agreed to prevent arms and ammunition from reaching the Mahdists through his territory, and declared them the "enemies of his Empire."⁷

---

² For the mission's instructions see Salisbury to Rodd, 24 February 1897, *Papers
respecting Mr. Rodd's special mission to King Menelek* [*sic*], F.O. Confidential Print,
September 1897. For accounts see Wingate, *Précis of information obtained by the
British Mission to Abyssinia, March to June 1897,* W.O. Confidential Print 1897;
and James Rennell Rodd, *Social and diplomatic memories* (second series)
1894–1901. Egypt and Abyssinia, London 1923, 109–86.

³ CB1.

⁴ Rodd, *Social,* 124–49; CB1.

⁵ Wingate, diary entry for 12 March 1898, SAD 102/1.

⁶ Wingate, draft memorandum, 7 May 1897, SAD 122/1.

⁷ "French translation of treaty, signed at Addis Abbaba [*sic*], May 14, 1897," encl.
in Rodd to Salisbury, 14 May 1897, *Papers respecting Mr. Rodd's special mission.*

In discussing Abyssinia's western boundaries the British mission was equally out of touch. When the subject was raised, Menelik referred to a circular he had addressed in 1891 to the European powers, notifying Abyssinia's ancient borders. Since these extended in the west to the White Nile, Rodd considered it inopportune to discuss them at all. Rodd and Wingate were told, however, or in any event they reported, that governors of Abyssinian border provinces were rapidly expanding their territory.[8] But on this subject too Wingate, in his own enquiries, met "considerable difficulty . . . as the Abyssinian officials observe[d] great reticence when asked questions on these matters." He nonetheless concluded that if the Mahdists faced an Anglo-Egyptian advance from the north, Menelik would opportunistically occupy territory up to the White Nile.[9]

What Wingate purported to fear was that Menelik, at French instigation, might attempt such an occupation *before* the British pushed south from Dongola. A draft of his 7 May memorandum on Abyssinian borders includes paragraphs (deleted from the version officially circulated) about Franco-Abyssinian intentions. There was no doubt, Wingate wrote, that Menelik was "to a very large extent guided by French counsel in all his undertakings." If the British were to make any territorial concessions to him "in the direction of Khartoum," they would be "augmenting French influence in these districts from which it would appear specially desirable to exclude it." On this erroneous premise Wingate based the conclusion that, far from cooperating with Menelik, Britain must take "some definite decision . . . in regard to the reconquest of the lost Provinces of the Sudan" before Menelik, as proxy for the French, took them himself.[10]

If, as has been demonstrated, Menelik's true policy was defensive, designed to play one European power against another, and to cooperate to that end with the Mahdist state, it must be concluded that Wingate was duped. If so he was a willing dupe. For if the mission had recognized (and reported) such a defensive policy, the French threat would have diminished in British eyes. And if Menelik's entente with the khalifa had been correctly portrayed as essentially anti-European (rather than anti-British), then the likelihood of his

---

[8] Sanderson, *England,* 153, 258–59; Rodd, *Social,* 168, 171.

[9] Wingate, Memorandum, 7 May 1897, *Papers respecting Mr. Rodd's special mission.*

[10] Wingate, draft memorandum, 7 May 1897, SAD 122/1.

advance to the Nile receded too. In both cases the threat of French occupation, either directly or under Abyssinian cover, would be reduced, and a strong new case for Egyptian advance from Dongola exploded. Like Slatin's reports on the Bahr al-Ghazal, Wingate's on Abyssinia relied for credence on a *lack* of information, and perhaps reflected what by then may fairly be called his and his fellow-officers' obsession with the conquest—or possible loss—of the Sudan.

The Rodd mission left Addis Ababa on 14 May. At a farewell audience with Menelik Wingate was presented with the Star of Ethiopia (second class). The party sailed from Zayla on 14 June for Aden and reached Port Said on the twenty-third. After reporting to Cairo Rodd and Wingate left for England on the twenty-sixth, and arrived in London on 2 July.[11]

In the months since the mission to Menelik had been suggested, the British government had discounted the danger he posed. Rodd and Wingate advised that Col. Macdonald, in Uganda, move down the Nile to Fashoda or, barring that, that British troops be sent to Egypt for an early advance from Dongola. Macdonald's ill-conceived mission had in fact already been authorized, but a mutiny of Sudanese troops in Uganda in September 1897, his own incompetence, and the magnitude of the task he had been given resulted in a fiasco.[12] In pressing for an Egyptian advance up the Nile the envoys were similarly unsuccessful. The push to Abu Hamad was in fact already under way, and its expected success would probably lead to the early occupation of Berber: that would be quite enough for the time being, as far as Salisbury and Cromer were concerned.

In these deliberations Wingate had a delicate task to perform. His very presence in London with Rodd was occasioned by Kitchener's desire to press privately, and against Cromer's wishes, for early dispatch of British troops with which to push on to Omdurman during the winter. Wingate's difficulty was increased by Kitchener's unwillingness to express this view himself in unambiguous terms. Ironically, Wingate claimed that Kitchener had even barred him from discussing military intelligence with General Grenfell (now commanding British troops in Egypt, and suspected by Kitchener as the War Office's choice to supersede him) and other senior British officers. This prohibition Wingate secretly defied. Indeed, in communi-

---

[11] CB1.

[12] Rodd, *Social*, 187–88. For Macdonald's mission see Sanderson, *England*, 255–58.

cating privately to Grenfell his own disagreement with both
Kitchener's and (even more circumspectly) Cromer's views, Wingate
tried to protect himself in the drawn-out, highly personal struggle
between Kitchener and the army establishment. The fact of this private communication was therefore more significant than its content.[13]
While Kitchener, not for the first time, exposed Wingate to the cross-
fire of powerful chiefs, Wingate too played a double, even triple,
game by informing Cromer of his own views before expressing them
in London, and by secretly siding with Grenfell against Kitchener.
Decisions reached in London were important not only for the future
of the Upper Nile but also for the careers of those British officials and
officers whose fate was so closely connected to it.

Wingate left London on 26 July empty-handed. That the Rodd
Mission had failed he later admitted, although he blamed this on
Rodd's and the government's refusal to act upon information
received.[14] He spent the first two weeks of August in Cairo before
going to Marawi, which he reached on the twenty-eighth.[15] During his
absence from Egypt—almost five months, except for three days in
transit between Abyssinia and London—the military situation on
Egypt's southern frontier had changed little. Indeed, the apparent
inability or unwillingness of the Khalifa Abdallahi to commit his forces
to defense of the new northern border (let alone to the reconquest of
Dongola) had raised hopes, not least in the mind of Cromer, that the
"Soudan nut" would be "less difficult to crack" than they had
thought.[16] By the end of July an Egyptian advance to Abu Hamad, at
the northernmost point on the great bend of the Nile, could no
longer be postponed. Kitchener's military railway across the Nubian
desert, by which the Egyptians' most serious problem, communications and supply, might be solved, was nearing that town. To protect
the advancing railhead, the Mahdists must be displaced. On 7 August
1897 Abu Hamad was therefore taken after a brief battle. Mahdist
delay in reinforcing the strategic center of Berber led to its evacuation
without a fight, and on 6 September an Egyptian force occupied it.[17]

---

[13] Wingate to Grenfell, draft, 25 September 1897, SAD 262/2. See Magnus,
Kitchener, 106–08.

[14] Wingate, diary entry for 6 February 1898, SAD 102/1.

[15] CB1.

[16] Cromer to Salisbury, 5, 6 June 1897, quoted in Sanderson, *England,* 260.

[17] *IRE* 54, 1 June–17 July 1897; *IRE* 55, 18 July–30 September 1897; Holt, *The
Mahdist state,* 233–35.

At this point the history of the Sudan campaign becomes insepa-rable from British politics, disputes within the British officer corps in England and Egypt, struggle between Cromer and the generals for control of the campaign, and, not least, the reaction of all of these with the situation in the Sudan as reported by Wingate. Occupation of Berber allowed reopening of the route between Suakin and the Nile, while extension of the desert railway to Abu Hamed in late October facilitated re-supply. The Mahdists made no attempt to dislodge the Egyptian forward forces, and occasional raids in the vicinity of Berber were ineffectual. Kitchener's immediate problem was not military but political. Gunboat reconnaissance up-river revealed that at al-Matamma the Amir Mahmud Ahmad had a force of some twenty thousand men, while Wingate's intelligence revealed that the *main* Mahdist army, much larger, remained at Omdurman. Kitchener had calculated that his rapid advance would force Cromer and Salisbury to send British troops sufficient to meet such forces and complete the conquest. But if reinforcements were denied, Kitchener feared a Mahdist counter-offensive would cut his long line of communication, with potentially disastrous results.[18]

Having thus set a trap for his civilian overlords, Kitchener now saw it closing on himself. Cromer argued that no British interest jus-tified a British expedition, and that since Egypt alone could not afford the conquest, the present line of advance should be held indefinitely.[19] Indeed, did the British want, for themselves or Egypt, "large tracts of useless territory"?[20] Kitchener, exhausted with worry, now threatened to resign. Described by Cromer as a "changed man. . . . a sick man" said to be "liable to fits of extreme depression,"[21] Kitchener, in Berber, in fact cabled his resignation to Cromer in mid-October, only to with-draw it a few days later. While this added to an impression of nervous indecision, it also ironically elicited the support Cromer always gave upon a prodigal son's return. While Salisbury continued to see no rea-son for immediate advance,[22] Cromer softened his own opposition.

---

[18] *IRE* 56, 6 October–12 November 1897; Magnus, *Kitchener,* 106–08.

[19] Cromer to Salisbury, 22 October 1897, FO 78/4959.

[20] Cromer, memorandum encl. in Cromer to Salisbury, 5 November 1897, FO 78/4959.

[21] Cromer to Salisbury, 23 October 1897, FO 633/6/285.

[22] Salisbury to Cromer, 29 October 1897, FO 633/7/183; Magnus, *Kitchener,* 109–11.

While these battles were fought at higher levels, Wingate did his part behind the scenes. On 5 October he set out on horseback from Marawi to Abu Hamad, arriving only on the eleventh, and rode on to Berber on the thirteenth, reaching there two days later. At the end of October he went to Dakhila (soon to be Fort Atbara, and later simply Atbara), at the junction of the Atbara and the Nile, the forward base for steamer operations. On 12 November he left Berber for Cairo, making the journey in seven days via Abu Hamad and Dongola.[23] This activity resulted in detailed intelligence summaries used to justify renewed advance. Cromer remained unimpressed. "Wingate is back from the Soudan," he wrote Salisbury wearily on 19 November. "He takes up the same line as the other soldiers . . . that a further advance ought to take place next winter."[24] By now Cromer discounted advice and even intelligence he received from British officers: not only Kitchener, who was "inclined to keep back facts," but "almost all the soldiers" had "some personal interest lurking behind" the views they expressed.[25]

The political impasse was broken in mid-December after Wingate, in receipt of fresh but by no means momentous intelligence, wired Kitchener at Wadi Halfa that a Mahdist attack on Berber was imminent. In a covering minute to an *Intelligence Report* issued in mid-January Kitchener wrote that there had been "no doubt that the Khalifa . . . had every intention of assuming an offensive policy, and of sending a large force from Omdurman to invade the Berber district." But the same minute noted the chronic shortage of food afflicting Mahmud Ahmad's diminishing army at al-Matamma, and did not reveal how a further Mahdist host would feed itself on the march or upon arrival.[26] Moreover the same *Report* encloses a note by Grenfell, briefly reporting that no such attack ever took place but stressing that Mahdist strength remained undiluted. In fact a Mahdist advance, when it finally came in March 1898, resulted from desperation rather than strength.

Wingate's warning was quickly and enthusiastically relayed. Cromer—not Kitchener—now advised Salisbury of the need for British troops, and on 23 December the Cabinet approved in princi-

---

[23] CB1.

[24] FO 633/6/287.

[25] Cromer to Salisbury, 24 December 1897, FO 633/6/292.

[26] *IRE* 57, 13 November–31 December 1897.

ple. Kitchener himself, who had long feared that with those troops might come War Office control and his own supersession, was now finally appointed to overall command. This fear, of having the prize of Khartoum snatched from him by Grenfell or another senior officer, had been Cromer's main hold over Kitchener for the past year. Even now, with Kitchener in command, Cromer would retain overall control, an arrangement in which Salisbury, intent on maintaining the Foreign Office's dominant role, concurred.[27]

Within the space of a week the military situation had in fact been transformed. Wingate left Cairo on 24 December to join Kitchener at Wadi Halfa, confident at last of a showdown with the khalifa. Sorry to miss Christmas with his wife and sons, Wingate yet recorded unfeigned joy at "the beginning of the end." He reached Wadi Halfa early on the thirty-first, just as rumors arrived that the khalifa's main army was on the march. While Wingate admitted privately that this news might be false—as he knew it must be—he nonetheless "thought it quite good enough to urge the Sirdar to call now for British troops." After characteristic indecision Kitchener agreed, and "at long last the momentous and important step was taken" of making the request. "It was astonishing," Wingate continued, "to see the difference" in Kitchener, once he had made up his mind.[28]

[27] Cromer to Salisbury, 24 December 1897, FO 633/6/292; 25 December 1897, FO 633/6/293; 8 January 1897, FO 633/6/294.

[28] Wingate diary, "Up Nile," entries for 24, 31 December 1897, SAD 102/1; CB1; Cf. Philip Ziegler, *Omdurman,* London 1973, 29-30.

Chapter Twelve
With Kitchener to Khartoum

With a British brigade on the way, the Sudan campaign entered its final phase. The rumored approach from Omdurman of the main Mahdist army, which had occasioned Kitchener's request for British troops, was soon discovered not to have taken place. But the issue had been forced not in December but in September 1897, when an advance to Berber had been authorized. Once Egyptian forces were there, the vulnerability of their supply lines would require further advance, and that would require British troops. Although Cromer and Salisbury had wished to call a halt, the specter of another Shaykhan or Khartoum weighed heavily. Wingate knew this, and indeed later worried that his own role in winning over civilian superiors would be held against him.[1] Where Gordon had failed, Kitchener, with Wingate's help, had succeeded in pulling British troops up the Nile before it was too late.

Although the mood of British officers was buoyant and expectant, problems remained, and in the end "Kitchener's luck" would be needed. Either because Wingate's view of the inevitability of Egyptian advance from Berber had not been widely shared, or (more likely) in order to convince Cromer than none was intended, steps necessary to supply a campaign had not been taken. Camel transport was scarce, and Berber suffered shortages of all kinds. Wingate put the number of camels needed at seven thousand; he asked Cairo to order three thousand from Somaliland, to be sent via Suakin. But Kitchener decided to await the rise of the Nile to facilitate re-supply by steamer. Meanwhile the 1st Lincolnshire regiment was due at Aswan on 12 January, the Warwickshire regiment on the fifteenth, and the Cameron Highlanders on the nineteenth.[2]

As a showdown loomed, tensions rose among the Egyptian army's British officers. A diary Wingate kept of the period details

---

[1] Wingate to Bigge, 3 January 1898; Wingate to Wood, 31 January 1898, SAD 267/1.

[2] Wingate, diary entries for 6, 7 January 1898, SAD 102/1.

disputes with Kitchener, secret telegrams, personal slights, disagreements about strategy and tactics. In all of this Wingate maintained the balancing act to which he had become accustomed. On Kitchener he had a moderating influence in political matters, often winning after hours of argument Kitchener's grudging agreement to cancel an untruthful telegram or alter a harsh order. In strictly military matters, over strategy, Wingate argued from the opposite pole. For Kitchener was a ditherer—and never more so than now, before the battle of the Atbara—who always needed "stiffening," and his secretiveness hampered Wingate's performance. Relations with officers remained poor, often because of deliberately offensive treatment: Slatin was routinely insulted; Rundle and much of the Egyptian army headquarters staff were kept in the rear with little to do; Wingate himself was as usual taken for granted, snubbed, forced to write deceptive dispatches for Kitchener's signature, and generally frustrated. Kitchener, he confided to his diary, was a "time-server," indeed "the quintessence of a coward."[3]

A crisis of sorts was reached in mid-February. When Wingate learned that Kitchener was about to go to Berber without him, Wingate wired his wife to meet him at Aswan. "Am looking forward to my darling's arrival with greatest delight," he recorded in his diary, as he did her fear that Kitchener might be angry.[4] Kitchener, a bachelor, had no patience with married officers' attempts to maintain family life. At the last minute, Kitchener told Wingate to stay at Wadi Halfa. No reason was given; Wingate was "furious" but had to delay his departure.[5] During a similar episode in May, Wingate told his wife that even mentioning her to Kitchener "always brings about a sneer in which he airs his views on the mistake of officers marrying, and I am not going to subject you or myself to his boorish insults."[6]

All was forgotten during the brief time he had with his wife and Sir Francis and Lady Grenfell, who were also at Aswan. Indeed in Grenfell, commanding the British army of occupation in Egypt, Wingate saw that his position was far from unique. Owing to the political arrangements Cromer had made, Grenfell was virtually at his beck and call; his own planned trip to Berber, already scheduled and

---

[3] 23 January 1898, SAD 102/1.
[4] Entry for 10 February 1898, SAD 102/1.
[5] Wingate, diary entry for 14 February 1898, SAD 102/1.
[6] Wingate to his wife, 15 May 1898, SAD 233/5.

postponed several times, was again put off, and he was now recalled
to Cairo, only to be allowed, at the last minute, to travel with Wingate
after all, but only as far as Wadi Halfa. It was "no easy matter,"
Wingate wrote on the way, "to steer a clear course amongst so much
double-dealing."[7]

Experience saved Wingate from new problems with the press.
When need arose in early January for a Reuter correspondent,
Wingate refused; Cromer arranged for a special correspondent to be
sent up from Cairo. Later in the month the *Standard* asked him to
report from the front; again he refused, this time annoying Kitchener
who disliked the alternatives. By the end of January many British correspondents had arrived, and while Wingate saw advantage in dealing
with some, he had difficulty avoiding others. The press, which a
younger Wingate had seen as a source of easy money, was now but a
necessary evil. For the rest of his career Wingate would use the press
but never trust it, and by 1898 the work of special correspondent,
while temptingly remunerative, in any case seemed beneath his dignity.[8] Now, as censor, he could also be reasonably sure of sympathetic
treatment *by* the press. As Archibald Hunter, then at Berber, wrote
privately: Kitchener, Wingate "& Co & Correspondents are to reap
all the kudos & other poor devils who keep watch & guard . . . we
could count for nothing."[9]

Having learned the hard way that the overtures of Fleet Street
could not be orchestrated from the Nile, Wingate negotiated instead
with publishing houses. We have seen how several projects mooted in
1896 failed. The main objection to a campaign history had been the
likelihood that further battles would render it out of date before publication. In February 1898 Edward Arnold, anticipating war correspondents' instant histories at the end of the campaign, asked
Wingate to begin "*the*" book at once, in order to publish as soon as
possible after the final battle. As incentive Arnold noted the continuing good sales of *Fire and sword,* an abridged edition of which had
been published in October, and that Wingate's royalties from it had
amounted to £160 in 1897.[10] A sixth printing of *Ten years' captivity*

---

[7] Diary entry for 26 February 1898, SAD 102/1. See also CB1.

[8] Wingate, diary entries for 2 January; 2, 3, 4, 5 February, SAD 102/1.

[9] Quoted in Doolittle, *A soldier's hero,* 150.

[10] Arnold to Wingate, 18 February 1898, SAD 227/1.

would appear in early September, at the very height of British interest in the Sudan. Having rejected in 1896 Macmillan's terms for a new edition of *Mahdiism,* Wingate had the satisfaction in March 1898 of their agreement to an abridged version, which, in the event, did not appear.[11] Indeed, despite negotiations and even agreements, Wingate never published another book. After the Sudan campaign, political risk outweighed financial gain; when in March 1899 Winston Churchill asked for his comments on a draft chapter of *The river war,* and disclaimed his rumored intention of "crabbing the Sirdar," Wingate nonetheless replied simply that he would "prefer to see nothing of a controversial nature."[12] There was no reason to take the risk, however small, of association with something beyond his control, a view Wingate shared with many experts acknowledged in the prefaces of embarrassing books. But as late as 1936—forty years after the fact—Wingate told the military historian E.W.C. Sandes that the "true story" behind the Egyptian advance from Dongola to Berber could not yet be put in writing: he would tell him about it when they met. It was "unfortunate . . . that political reasons frequently interfere with true history,"[13] but it could not be helped.

Upon returning to Wadi Halfa from Aswan Wingate went immediately to Berber, where he joined Kitchener on 3 March.[14] Amid final preparations for an advance against Mahmud Ahmad, Wingate's personal position was suddenly, and at last, secured. For his services he was promoted, on 11 March, full colonel and honorary aide de camp to Queen Victoria, and awarded another campaign clasp.[15] There is irony in the timing of this promotion. In September Wingate had written to Wood, complaining of the ingratitude and lack of recognition that continued to weigh upon him. As usual Wood had offered avuncular advice, in the end reminding Wingate that "with an Adjutant General [Wood] who knows you well, and a Commander-

---

[11] CB1; Wingate, diary entry for 12 March 1898, SAD 102/1.

[12] Churchill to Wingate, 30 March 1899; Wingate to Churchill, 31 March 1899, SAD 269/3. In a preface Churchill merely acknowledged the "Director of Military Intelligence" for help with maps.

[13] Wingate to Sandes, 3 February 1936, SAD 227/7. Wingate probably referred also to suppression of the details of his own supersession in Egypt in 1919.

[14] CB1.

[15] *London Gazette,* 11 March 1898. See also CB1. The promotion was retroactive to 12 December 1897.

in-Chief [Wolseley] who has a good opinion of you, . . . you need not be despondent as to your future."[16] Wingate had nonetheless continued to put himself forward in letters to Wood, Rodd, and others (and via these, even to the prime minister).[17] When he was finally promoted, among the congratulatory messages was one from Wood, who remarked characteristically: "I hope that you may live to profit by the 10/6 a day" the promotion carried with it.[18]

There was little time to celebrate, for the penultimate battle of the campaign was imminent. As Anglo-Egyptian forces gathered, the Mahdist commanders decided finally to advance to meet them. Uthman Diqna's Bija forces on the Atbara had reached Shandi on 8 January,[19] to be joined by Mahmud Ahmad's army from al-Matamma. From Shandi the combined force had marched north on the right bank of the Nile, then northeast, finally reaching the Atbara on 19 March. In response to Mahdist movements Kitchener had established a new forward base at Kannur, six miles downstream from Fort Atbara. He and the staff, including Wingate, arrived on 16 March. Uncertain of the Mahdists' plans, Kitchener ordered a further advance on the nineteenth, to the Ras al-Hudi, a bend in the Atbara where Mahmud Ahmad could be cut off if he tried to cross the desert to Berber. Reconnaissance located Mahmud's forces near Umm Dabi. There, short of food and suffering mass desertions, the *amir* fortified his position and awaited re-supply.[20]

Now, with a Mahdist army under famous *amir*s entrenched behind a thorn fence awaiting attack, Kitchener lost his nerve. Patrols failed to lure the Mahdists into open ground. Rather than storm their camp, however, Kitchener delayed, wiring even Cromer, in Cairo, for advice. While Cairo and London wondered, Kitchener's officers finally persuaded him to attack. On 8 April, Good Friday, the Anglo-Egyptian forces advanced on the Mahdist *zariba,* preceded by artillery bombardment and helped immeasurably by Maxim guns. The fighting was over in less than an hour. Mahdist losses were estimated at three thousand killed, Anglo-Egyptian at under one hundred. The

---

[16] Wood to Wingate, 29 September 1897, SAD 262/2.

[17] Wingate, diary entries for 14, 22 January 1898, SAD 102/1.

[18] Wood to Wingate, 17 March 1898, SAD 267/1.

[19] Wingate, diary entry, 9 January 1898, SAD 102/1; cf. Holt, *The Mahdist state,* 238.

[20] *IRE* 59, 13 February–23 May 1898; Holt, *The Mahdist state,* 237–38.

Amir Mahmud Ahmad was taken prisoner. Uthman Diqna escaped. Gunboats set off up the Nile as far as al-Sabaluqa gorge to raid, while patrols were sent up the Atbara after fugitives. The road to Omdurman lay open.

From the controversies over the conduct of Kitchener and his soldiers during and after the battle of the Atbara Wingate's name has been largely omitted. The taking of prisoners, treatment of the wounded, and looting of the Mahdist camp had nothing to do with him. He was present at the battle, and won two clasps to the Sudan Medal, but as director of military intelligence his work was done before, and after, the fighting. Following the battle Wingate accompanied Kitchener to Fort Atbara, where a service of thanksgiving took place on Easter, and to Berber, where a triumphal review was staged. Yoked and chained, whipped and abused, Mahmud Ahmad was made to walk through the streets behind Kitchener and his officers, treatment a biographer describes as "condescending to the primitive psychology of the natives"; Wingate recorded in his commonplace book only a "great function."[21] His interest in Mahmud was typically practical, as the subsequent *Intelligence Report* indicates. And a series of photographs taken when Mahmud was brought before him show Wingate, on foot, overweight and smoking a cigar—hardly the picture of a conqueror—conversing with the *amir,* still dressed in the patched *jibba* of Mahdism.

After the battle of the Atbara, Anglo-Egyptian forces went into summer camp while the ground was prepared for an assault on Omdurman. Following a reconnaissance with Kitchener up the Nile to al-Matamma and al-Sabaluqa at the end of May, Wingate returned via the military railway to Wadi Halfa and Egypt, arriving in Cairo on 10 June. After a week of office work he proceeded to England on leave. His elder son, Ronald, who with his brother had gone ahead of their parents, contracted pneumonia at sea, so Kitty Wingate had hurried to England (arriving before her sons) while her husband was still in the Sudan. Wingate's pleasure after the Atbara must also have been cut short by the death in Ireland, on the day after the battle, of his brother Richard at the age of forty-nine, from recurrent malaria contracted in India.[22]

---

[21] CB1; Magnus, *Kitchener,* 121–22. See also G.W. Steevens, *With Kitchener to Khartum,* Edinburgh and London 1898, 165–67.

[22] CB1; CB2.

Wingate's leave was brief. With the final push to Omdurman only three months away, it is a sign of Anglo-Egyptian confidence that he took leave at all. The highlight of an otherwise uneventful leave was a visit to the queen at Windsor, where the Wingates dined and stayed overnight, for once without Slatin. He, indeed, had been deliberately excluded because, in light of Kitchener's animosity, court officials feared the effect an invitation would have on his career.[23] But Slatin was more than ever in the old queen's thoughts: after the Atbara she had wired Aswan to enquire about him ("and also Colonel Wingate"),[24] and in June, although resisting an impulse to invite him to Windsor, she "could not bear to think" that "she might never see him again."[25]

Wingate returned to Cairo on 31 July and left immediately for the Sudan, traveling straight through to Fort Atbara, which he reached only on 12 August because of steamer breakdowns and other delays.[26] By then the advance to Omdurman was well in hand. Railhead had reached the Atbara, and the Nile had risen, allowing ten Egyptian gunboats easy access south. Egyptian and British reinforcements had swollen the combined force to almost 26,000 men, with eighty artillery pieces and forty-four Maxim guns. In early August the general movement up-river to Wad Habashi and Wad Hamid had begun, crucially re-supplied by the military railway and steamers. Mahdist positions along al-Sabaluqa gorge were abandoned, and by 23 August the invaders' advanced post had been established at Jabal Ruwiyan, about fifty miles downstream from Omdurman. Wingate had long predicted—and the khalifa's difficulty in provisioning large forces away from the capital had made likely—the decisive battle at Omdurman. Sandes has described the final advance:

> The Anglo-Egyptian force broke camp . . . on the 28th, . . . marching on a broad front up the left bank of the Nile. . . . The formation on the march was now a double line of brigades. . . . The left flank was protected by the gunboats. . . . ; the right flank was guarded by the Camel Corps. Each brigade, except Collinson's, was followed by a battery of field artillery; the cavalry and horse artillery covered the front; baggage and supply columns toiled in

---

[23] CB1; Bigge to Wingate, 24 June 1898, SAD 267/1. Cf. Hill, *Slatin Pasha*, 57–58.

[24] 18 April 1898, SAD 267/1.

[25] Bigge to Wingate, 24 June 1898, SAD 267/1.

[26] CB1; Wingate, diary entries, 1–12 August 1898, SAD 102/1.

the rear. At the head of the British infantry rode the Sirdar, leading the most powerful army the Sudan has ever seen.[27]

By the thirty-first they had reached Sururab, six miles north of Karari,
on the outskirts of Omdurman.

    Meanwhile the Khalifa Abdallahi and his *amir*s had resolved to
go out and meet the enemy (a decision Wingate later attributed to the
influence of his own agents).[28] A Sudanese historian writes:

> At dawn on Wednesday, 31 August the rhythm of the drums and
> the sound of the *ummbaya* [war trumpet] announced the advance
> of the armies of the Mahdiya to the battlefield. The various divi-
> sions gathered in the great mosque and in the space to the east of
> the *qubba* [the Mahdi's domed tomb]. At 0600 the soldiers began
> to march, four abreast, in their *rub's* [divisions] to the parade
> ground. Before each *rub'* rode an *amir* with his sword unsheathed.
> As they marched they cried, "There is no God but God . . . Fight
> the infidels for the cause of God."[29]

When the Anglo-Egyptian vanguard reached the Karari hills they saw,
below them on the plain, in formation, some fifty thousand Sudanese.

    The battle of Omdurman took place on 2 September on the
plains of Karari north of the city. The khalifa launched an all-out
assault on the Anglo-Egyptian forces drawn up in front of Iqayqa, a
village on the Nile. Reckless bravery was no match for modern
weapons, and the Sudanese were repulsed with heavy losses. Unaware
of the disposition of the Khalifa Abdallahi's Black Flag division,
Kitchener ordered an advance toward Omdurman. In this and in several lesser lapses lay the Mahdists' opportunity, but they were unable
to grasp it. Campaign historians were provided with a colorful cavalry
charge, some adroit maneuvering, and an hour's worth of tension,
but lack of coordination and inferiority of arms soon led to a rout.
The khalifa himself hurried back to the city, and thence into Kordofan
with some survivors, while Kitchener and his officers rode into
Omdurman, through a field of ten thousand dead.

---

[27] Sandes, *The Royal Engineers,* 254–55.

[28] *SIR* 60, 25 May–31 December 1898.

[29] 'Ismat Hasan Zulfo, *Karari,* trans. by Peter Clark, London 1980, 135.

The week following the battle was one of intense activity, interest, and emotion for Wingate. He had been at Kitchener's side during most of the battle which, albeit to his wife, he described as having "all the elements of excitement to make it really interesting."[30] Once the city had fallen, release of foreign prisoners was immediately taken up. Wingate later claimed to be the first European to reach the prison; at any rate he now met for the first time those whose information and escape had for so long concerned him, one of whom, Charles Neufeld, the only European actually a prisoner, was soon to give him trouble. On 3 September, with characteristic energy, Wingate personally toured the main repositories of Mahdist government documents and officials' papers, ordering that they be collected and guarded; the Mahdist archives are today a treasure of the National Record Office in Khartoum. (Among the papers Wingate immediately found the khalifa's Abyssinian correspondence, which proved that Menelik had outsmarted the Rodd Mission in 1897; Wingate sent the papers to Rodd in Cairo.)[31] On the fourth Wingate witnessed the dramatic memorial service held in the ruins of Gordon's palace at Khartoum, where the flags of the victors were raised and the anthems of Egypt and Britain played; his personal accounts of the day were soon dispatched to Britain.[32]

Even these events only punctuated a week of constant activity. "Everything," he later wrote to his wife, "seemed to be thrown into" his hands. As the sirdar's unacknowledged draftsman, Wingate was now more than ever occupied with communications. He began to compile long intelligence reports of the campaign, with many appendices on all aspects of the advance since June. Kitchener's official dispatch after the battle was—except for one paragraph, in praise of the intelligence department, which he wrote himself—written entirely by

---

[30] 6 September 1898, SAD 233/5.

[31] Wingate to his wife, 13 September 1898, SAD 233/5; Holt, *The Mahdist state,* 266–67, quoting Na'um Shuqayr. On prisoners' release cf. Henry S.L. Alford and W. Dennistoun Sword, *The Egyptian Soudan. Its loss and recovery,* London 1898, 275. On Abyssinian correspondence see also G.N. Sanderson, "Contributions from African sources to the history of European competition in the Upper Valley of the Nile," *JAH* III, 1, 1962, 69–90.

[32] See, e.g., Wingate to his wife, 13 September 1898, SAD 233/5. For full accounts see Sandes, *The Royal Engineers,* 275, and Bennet Burleigh (an eyewitness), *Khartoum campaign 1898, or the re-conquest of the Soudan,* 3rd ed. London 1899, 279–87.

Wingate; thus the words of lavish praise for the British commanders—
Kitchener had told him to "lay it on thick"—were his, the sirdar
grumbling in disagreement even as he signed the dispatch.[33] Wingate
interrogated Mahdist prisoners, *amir*s and important officials, many
of whom, with the flight of the khalifa, now transferred their loyalty
and services to the new rulers. Moreover, the routine work of his
department continued, as intelligence about the khalifa's and other
remaining Mahdist forces, scattered throughout the country, had to
be collected and analyzed. In much of this work Wingate was supported by Slatin, whose experience of the Mahdist capital was as long
and personal as Wingate's was official and brief.

Wingate's ubiquitousness after the battle, and his role as censor,
which demanded he read every news telegram before it was sent,
brought him into constant contact with the press and into countless
newspaper accounts and campaign histories. In these he made a useful foil for Kitchener. In appearance, personality, and manner, as in
other ways, the two differed greatly. While Kitchener, tall and dash-
ing, enigmatic and aloof, now was lionized almost to the point of
idolatry as a warrior-chief, Wingate, unremarkable, gregarious and
personable, was praised as the institutional memory of the campaign.
One sold newspapers, the other censored them. It is as difficult to picture Kitchener tied to a desk as it is to imagine Wingate dragging a
defeated enemy through the streets of Berber. Kitchener, despite his
flaws (and his contempt for reporters, which they privately reciprocated) became a national hero; Wingate, despite his successes (and his
cultivation of the press) lacked the traits that, with popular imagination, define the heroic.[34]

---

[33] Wingate to his wife, 13 September 1898, SAD 233/5. Cf. Steevens, *With
Kitchener*, 307–08.

[34] For correspondents' treatment of Kitchener and Wingate see, e.g.,Ernest N.
Bennett, *The downfall of the dervishes*, London 1899, 69–70, 94, 108–11, 128,
148; Steevens, *With Kitchener*, 292–93; Churchill, *The river war*, 2nd ed.
London 1902, 98, 138, 267; and especially Bennet Burleigh, *Khartoum campaign 1898*, London 1899, 64–66, 107–09. See also Magnus, *Kitchener*, 133–34.

Chapter Thirteen
Fashoda

Throughout the Nile campaign, and for years before it, prospective French occupation of the Upper Nile had been put forward as a reason for Egyptian or Anglo-Egyptian advance. By the time that advance reached Omdurman in September 1898 the French were already ensconced upstream at Fashoda. But the British government had recognized that this race would go to the strong, not to the swift. Mere occupation of a point on the Upper Nile did not grant title to it, let alone to the land beyond the rivers; Salisbury and Cromer knew how tenuous must be European control exercised from any direction but the north. A crisis precipitated by competing claims would turn not on which flag flew first but on the ability of each side to enforce its will. But whether the test of strength would end in war or peace in Europe might depend on the way claims were asserted or resigned in the Upper Nile.[1]

In the diplomacy of the Fashoda Incident, Kitchener, Wingate, and other soldiers played parts largely scripted by diplomats in London, Paris, and Cairo. There was, however, room to improvise, and personality was important in determining the success or failure of the actors (and the quality of the reviews that followed). In no other case is the nature of Kitchener's relations with Wingate so clear as at Fashoda; the sirdar was ineffective at center-stage, while Wingate, hardly noticed, prompted him from the wings.

On 5 September the Mahdist steamer *Tawfiqiya*, returning from the south, reached Omdurman unaware of the recent battle. Wingate, who "happened to be on the river bank," sent out a rowboat that returned with several Mahdist officers. One described a skirmish with Europeans at Fashoda. Wingate "asked him if he could see any flag flying at Fashoda, and, taking my walking stick, he drew on the mud

---

[1] Sanderson, *England,* 260–68.

bank a picture of the French Tricolor!"[2] No time had been lost in putting together a powerful force of five steamers, the 11th and 13th Sudanese battalions, a company of Cameron Highlanders, Maxim guns and artillery, which set out from Omdurman on the morning of the tenth. Wingate, "dog-tired" after the constant activity of the past ten days, traveled in the *Dal* with Kitchener. When not dealing with reports and correspondence, he spent much of the journey interviewing villagers and others about the movements of Mahdist fugitives from Omdurman. Near Renk on the fifteenth the gunboats exchanged fire with Mahdists camped on shore; one boat was badly damaged but the position was taken and the Mahdists captured or driven off. After this battle Wingate inspected the steamer *Safia*, the exploits of which during the Gordon Relief Expedition he had described in *Mahdiism*. Now he removed the boiler plate mended in 1885 and had it sent to Lord Charles Beresford, who had been in command.[3]

The Anglo-Egyptian flotilla was now well into Shilluk country, amid the low, monotonous scenery of the *sudd*.[4] On the sixteenth the two Shilluks on board were sent to summon their *reth*, or king. He, it transpired, had gone to see the French at Fashoda, so the flotilla continued upstream. The Anglo-Egyptian force thus approached Fashoda without current intelligence from local people or any contact with the French.[5]

The story of the Marchand Mission is well-known, justly so not only because of the international incident that would swirl around Fashoda, but also because of the epic journey that had brought it there. The mission had been authorized, after much intramural maneuvering in France, in November 1895. Great delay was encountered before the expedition left France, and more still before Marchand himself finally set off from Brazzaville in March 1897. Traveling mainly by river, portaging where necessary, the expedition

---

[2] Wingate to Prof. Harold Temperley, 31 December 1938, SAD 244/6. Wingate was writing forty years after the event. G.N. Sanderson points out that contemporary sources agree that the Mahdist informants gave no intelligible description of the flag flying at Fashoda (Letter to the author, 12 June 1995).

[3] Wingate, *Mahdiism,* 183–88; CB1.

[4] Ar. *sadd* (barrier): masses of floating vegetation that made navigation difficult or impossible.

[5] Wingate, diary entries for 13–19 September 1898, SAD 102/1.

reached Wau in the Bahr al-Ghazal in November. The steamer *Faidherbe*, which they had carried in pieces, was reconstructed and launched on the Sueh. After much travail in the *sudd*, Marchand reached Fashoda on 10 July 1898. Two days later, with a flag-raising ceremony, he took possession of the ruined fort there in the name of France.[6]

The nature of the mission was less complicated than its journey. Marchand's orders had changed during the three years he spent between Paris and Fashoda, but the real object had not: establishment of a French presence on the Upper Nile. On 25 August a Mahdist force, in steamers sent from Omdurman to collect grain from the Shilluk, attacked the French but were driven off with heavy casualties. A few days later Marchand signed a treaty of protection with the *reth* of the Shilluk. Although communications with his base were tenuous, Marchand was thus by early September rather comfortably in possession of Fashoda, well-supplied and well-fed, acting in the name of France.

The Anglo-Egyptian force that now approached from Omdurman had not been suddenly improvised. When in May 1898 the khedive had tried to assert himself over Sudan policy, Salisbury had reminded him that Britain alone would decide what role, if any, Egypt would have in the Sudan's future affairs. In fact the British had not determined how the Sudan should be administered once the conquest was complete, nor, indeed, which territories should be administered at all. In June Cromer had raised the question of sovereignty in the Sudan: after the defeat of the khalifa, when Anglo-Egyptian forces reconnoitered upper riverain regions, in whose name should these be claimed, Britain's or Egypt's or both?[7] Cromer drafted a memorandum embodying his own views, which in turn formed the basis for the policy adopted. At Khartoum both British and Egyptian flags should fly. Two flotillas should thereafter proceed up the Niles, with Kitchener himself commanding the White Nile expedition. No recognition was to be given any French or Abyssinian presence that might be encountered. Regarding the further policy to be adopted toward the French his instructions continued:

---

[6] Sanderson, *England*, 285–87; Darrell Bates, *The Fashoda incident of 1898*, Oxford 1984, 50–100.

[7] Cromer to F.O., 14 May 1898; Salisbury to Cromer, 15 May 1898; F.O. to Currie, 25 May 1898, FO 78/5185. See also Cromer, memorandum, 15 June 1898, FO 78/4956.

the course of action to be pursued must depend so much on local circumstances that it is neither necessary nor desirable to furnish Sir Herbert Kitchener with detailed instructions. Her Majesty's Government entertain full confidence in Sir Herbert Kitchener's judgment and discretion. They feel sure that he will endeavour to convince the Commander of any French force . . . that the presence of the latter in the Nile Valley is an infringement of the rights both of Great Britain and of the Khedive.[8]

The news that had reached Omdurman on 5 September had therefore perhaps hastened but had not caused Kitchener's departure for Fashoda.

On 18 September Kitchener's flotilla reached Fabiu, fifteen miles downstream from Fashoda. From there he sent a message, addressed to the "Chief of the European Expedition at Fashoda," which Wingate and he had drafted on the fifteenth and of which Wingate had made a fair copy the next morning. This announced the defeat of the Mahdists and the impending arrival of Kitchener's force. While at Fabiu awaiting the *reth* of the Shilluk (who did not appear), Wingate made his most important contribution to the Fashoda Incident. He argued that, at Fashoda, the Anglo-Egyptian force should raise only the Egyptian flag, and that, in effect, the sirdar should act in the name of Egypt. Kitchener allowed himself to be persuaded. As the flotilla approached Fashoda on the morning of the nineteenth, a small boat drew up with a message from Marchand acknowledging receipt of Kitchener's letter and welcoming him to Fashoda "in the name of France."[9]

Now again Wingate's influence was brought to bear. He and Kitchener had rehearsed what the sirdar would say to Marchand, but so bold a reference to French rights "rather staggered" Kitchener. Wingate "begged him to be firm" and to keep to the course they had set, and Kitchener recovered his composure.[10] At his invitation Marchand boarded the *Dal,* and Kitchener formally protested his violation of Egyptian and British rights. When Marchand stated that he was under orders to remain at Fashoda, Kitchener (dressed in the uni-

---

[8] Salisbury to Cromer, draft, 2 August 1898, FO 78/4955.

[9] Wingate to his wife, 18 September 1898, SAD 233/5; Sanderson, *England,* 333–34.

[10] Wingate to his wife, 23 September 1898, SAD 233/5.

form of the Egyptian sirdar) asked him whether he would resist re-establishment of Egyptian authority there. A tacit compromise was reached, whereby Marchand and his men would remain but would not resist the raising of an Egyptian flag nearby, at Kodok. Wingate himself, accompanied by Marchand's second-in-command, Germain, selected the site for the flag-raising. A ceremony was held, and the healths of Queen Victoria and the French Republic were drunk—in Champagne provided by Marchand in his hut.[11] An Anglo-Egyptian garrison was installed nearby. Just before reboarding the *Dal* Wingate delivered a formal note to Marchand, protesting French infringement of British and Egyptian rights. Kitchener and Wingate then proceeded to the mouth of the Sobat before reversing course and returning down the Nile—past Fashoda, without stopping—to Omdurman.

Although the sirdar and his staff had thus confronted and escaped the French at Fashoda without resort to force, the issue was far from resolved. Months of tense diplomacy would ensue. Nonetheless the confrontation itself, and its reporting, were crucial in determining the eventual outcome. While Kitchener's orders seemed to anticipate the possibility of a showdown,[12] references survive, in Wingate's diary and letters, to "private" instructions to avoid violence. On 17 September Wingate referred in his diary to "private letters which pointed to there being no fighting": if Marchand proved obdurate Kitchener would erect "a cordon round him and prevent him from communicating with anyone whatever and so force the govt. to demand of the French govt. the withdrawing of the French force." On the eighteenth Wingate wrote to his wife that Kitchener had "express instructions not to 'have corpses,'" and that while he, Wingate, would have immediately landed troops to occupy the old Egyptian fort at Fashoda, Kitchener's "private instructions" would "not allow of him taking so strong a line."[13] Adoption of the "one-flag solution" was thus crucial in allowing Kitchener to fulfill the terms of his mission.

Almost as important as British conduct at Fashoda was British control of information about it. Kitchener's northward bypass of Fashoda was in part intended to allow the British to avoid relaying

---

[11] CB1.

[12] Sanderson, *England*, 332.

[13] Diary entry for 17 September 1898, SAD 102/1; to his wife, 18 September 1898, SAD 233/5.

news from Marchand to the French government.[14] The incident at
Fashoda—indeed the very presence and condition of Marchand and
his men there—would thus be reported to France and the outside
world in general through the words of Anglo-Egyptian officialdom's
chief propagandist, Wingate. In describing the encounter privately to
his wife Wingate foreshadowed that official view: the "poor Froggies"
were "virtually our prisoners," indeed had been "rescued" by the
British from certain "annihilation" at the hands of the Mahdists.
Their position was "absurd," and while admiring their "pluck" in
crossing Africa, Wingate knew they realized the "futility of all their
efforts": "I suppose the 'conclusion' cannot be long in coming; for
the French govt., in the face of our rescue of their expedition, which
is now at our mercy, cannot fail to send them orders to return via
Cairo and in that case I shall hope to introduce to you my friend
Marchand!"[15]

On 22 September, en route to Omdurman, Wingate wrote the
official dispatch of the White Nile expedition. Two typed copies
were produced immediately, which Lord Edward Cecil, Lord
Salisbury's son and Kitchener's aide-de-camp, would deliver personally to the Residency in Cairo and his father in London.[16] This
stressed the hopelessness of the French position at Fashoda; it was
indeed a largely fictitious account, written in the euphoria of a
homeward journey, for an audience wholly unable to verify it.
Marchand's position at Fashoda was not only tenable but indeed
more secure and comfortable than that of the Anglo-Egyptian garrison that Kitchener had left there. But to the outside world the
French were depicted as brave and desperate men stranded by the
schemes of an irresponsible government.[17]

The dispatch concluded:

> M. Marchand is in want of ammunition and supplies, and any that
> may be sent to him must take months to arrive at their destination.
> He is cut off from the interior, and is quite inadequately provided
> with water transport. Moreover, he has no following in the coun-
> try, and nothing could have saved his expedition from being anni-

---

[14] Wingate, diary entry for 21 September 1898, SAD 102/1.

[15] Wingate to his wife, 23 September 1898, SAD 233/5.

[16] Wingate, diary entry for 22 September 1898, SAD 102/1.

[17] Sanderson, *England*, 337–39.

hilated by the dervishes if we had been a fortnight later in crush-
ing the Khalifa.[18]

This line—the hopelessness of Marchand's position; his "rescue"
by Kitchener—and the emphasis on Egypt's (rather than Britain's)
rights in the Upper Nile became the insistent refrain of British diplomatic activity in the tense weeks ahead. Nor was it one with which the
French government could easily argue. No report from Marchand
himself reached Paris until 22 October; before then French appreciation of events (and indeed that of the British press and public) was
dependent on Wingate's version: Queen Victoria noted in her diary
on 30 September that Marchand would have no choice but to leave
Fashoda, "for lack of provisions and water"![19]

On 24 September the *Dal* reached Omdurman, where Kitchener
and Wingate remained until 3 October. As early as the twenty-fifth,
Wingate described the sirdar as "very restless and anxious to get
away," and himself as "sincerely hope[ful] he will take me with him."[20]
Indeed, amid pacification and organization there was much concern
about the personal prospects of the Anglo-Egyptian victors. Kitchener
had learned on the Upper Nile of his peerage, and by Omdurman was
privately speculating that he might succeed Cromer in Cairo.[21] On the
thirtieth he finally told Wingate "the joyful news" that he could
accompany the sirdar to Cairo, a message he relayed in code to his
wife.[22] They set out on the *Dal* at 7:00 A.M. on 3 October, and sped
north, reaching Shallal in forty-eight hours. At Cairo on the sixth
their train was met by Cromer, Egyptian ministers, and a great
throng, and they proceeded in a parade through crowd-lined streets.
Wingate was made a pasha of Egypt and named adjutant-general of
the Egyptian army. On 11 November he was made a K.C.M.G. for
the Sudan campaign.[23]

The Fashoda Incident, like many episodes in the Scramble for
Africa, was decided in Europe. In the end it was the relative strength

---

[18] Cf. Sanderson, *England*, 338–39. Wingate's similar letter to Queen Victoria was
published: *The letters of Queen Victoria,* third series, vol. III, London 1932, 285–87.

[19] *The letters of Queen Victoria,* 289.

[20] CB1.

[21] Ibid.

[22] Ibid.

[23] Wingate diary, 3,4,5,6,7 October 1898, SAD 102/1; CB1.

of high-seas fleets, not of Nile flotillas and collapsible steamers, that won the day for the British. But the conduct of affairs at Fashoda had "avoided corpses," and thus had given diplomacy, however unsubtle, time to work. If Kitchener had insisted on raising the British flag at Fashoda, a shooting war might have been unavoidable. And if an accurate picture of Marchand's far-from-hopeless position there had gained currency in Europe, the French government might have lacked even the face-saving concern for intrepid explorers that publicly covered its humiliation. In advising Kitchener to raise an Egyptian flag of convenience, and by depicting him and Marchand to Europe as latter-day Stanley and Livingstone, Wingate both helped to set the stage and to write the script for Britain's peaceful victory on the Upper Nile.

Chapter Fourteen
Patience Rewarded

Fifteen months elapsed between Wingate's return to Cairo and his appointment as sirdar and governor-general of the Sudan in December 1899. Although he did not share in the adulation of Kitchener, there was wide public and private recognition of the central role Wingate had played in all aspects of the Sudan campaign. He received hundreds of telegrams and letters, from the queen and members of the royal family, government ministers, officers and colleagues, friends and unknown admirers. The press sang his praises. Yet the future was as obscure as ever, and still depended upon the maneuvers of politicians and superior officers.

Long before the twin victories of Omdurman and Fashoda, Wingate had calculated his future prospects in Egypt. During the late stages of the campaign he had watched with alarm the arrival of ranking British officers. When in January 1897 he had complained privately to Sir Evelyn Wood, his old patron had disagreed with the contention "that nobody should be brought into the Egyptian Army" over his head: Kitchener had to do what he considered best, "without any consideration of your's or anyone's seniority."[1] By June 1898 Wingate had become senior colonel in the Egyptian army and directly below his brother-in-law, Rundle, on the seniority list; ordinarily this should mean promotion to pasha, but in doubting Kitchener would recommend this dignity Wingate proved right.[2] Even on the way to Omdurman in August, Wingate worried about the aftermath of the impending battle. As he wrote his wife:

> If all goes well at Khartoum—you know my views about the future and I hope that you may perhaps in Cairo be able to put them forward. Of course I may be obliged to spend a few months in the Sudan, but what I really want is to be head of an office in Cairo which will connect the Cairo and Sudan Government[s]. It seems

---

[1] Wood to Wingate, 18 January 1897, SAD 179/6.
[2] Wingate to his wife, 8 June 1898, SAD 233/5.

to me that such a billet is what I am most fitted for and I should
like it, but I expect others think differently and no doubt there will
be other competition in the field. . . . We must carefully watch
events and in case of necessity—I shall probably wire to you what
line I want you to take.

Rundle and Hunter were the main competitors: if Kitchener left
Egypt, Hunter might become sirdar; if Kitchener stayed on, both
Hunter and Rundle, unwilling to continue under him, would go,
leaving the field clear for Wingate.[3]

After Omdurman and Fashoda, uncertainty was more keenly felt
because the possibilities seemed so great. During their sojourn at
Omdurman en route from Fashoda in September, Wingate described
the sirdar as "in a greater state of restless excitement" than he had ever
seen him, "owing principally to the peerage which seems to have generally upset his equilibrium." Kitchener wondered aloud about his
own future, as usual giving no hint about Wingate's, whose great fear
was that he would be left at Omdurman while Kitchener and Rundle
reaped the spoils in Cairo and London.[4] In the event, Kitchener
brought Wingate to Cairo, left him there to run the army, and
returned to the accolades of the government and people of Britain.

Ironically, Wingate's eventual success depended upon Kitchener's
lack of immediate prospects elsewhere and others' refusal to serve
under him any longer in Egypt. Despite the death of his wife, Cromer
decided to remain as agent and consul-general in Cairo, blocking that
avenue to Kitchener's advance. No first-class command in India was
available, so Kitchener decided to stay too, in the dual role of sirdar
and governor-general of the Sudan. When this became clear, both
Rundle and Hunter determined to go, Hunter to India, Rundle to
Britain (and both soon thereafter to re-join Kitchener in South
Africa).[5] Thus immediately upon arrival from Omdurman, Wingate
was finally made a pasha of Egypt and promoted adjutant-general of
the Egyptian army. He continued to dread a return to Omdurman,

---

[3] Wingate to his wife, 20 August 1898, SAD 233/5; See also Wingate to his wife,
28 September 1898, SAD 233/5. Hunter had expressed interest: see, e.g.,Hunter
to Duncan and Abby Hunter, 13 July 1896, *A soldier's hero*, 80; and 20 February
1899, ibid., 186, wherein he claims to have been offered the post of sirdar.

[4] Wingate to his wife, 28 September 1898, SAD 233/5.

[5] Hunter to Duncan and Abby Hunter, 20 February 1899 and 19 March 1899, in
Doolittle, ed., *A soldier's hero*, 185–88.

but in the end the sirdar needed Wingate's energy in Cairo more than his special knowledge of the Sudan in Omdurman. In addition to the duties of adjutant-general Wingate found himself charged with drawing up the Sudan's first civil budget and even writing Kitchener's speeches—"I am the Sirdar's creative slave," he told his wife.[6]

During the last months of the Omdurman campaign Wingate had maintained his extensive private correspondence. This included notably telegrams and letters to Queen Victoria, her private secretary, Sir Arthur Bigge, other members of the royal family, and government officials. Whether he was star-struck or calculating, honored or duty-bound, these missives served to keep him in mind, at a time when rewards must be debated. In this matter Wingate could not rely on Kitchener; he had been disappointed too often: "You know for how much I have to thank him in my career!!" he reminded his wife.[7] The sovereign was more appreciative than the sirdar: "I cannot tell you with what, I may say, rapture your letter . . . has been received by The Queen," Bigge told him in reply to a vivid account of the Fashoda Incident; "we know what a share you have had in these successful labours." (Bigge added that Slatin was to visit England "at The Queen's request.")[8] When at last, on 16 November the Sudan Honours were published, Kitchener and Grenfell were awarded the G.C.B., Gatacre, Hunter, and Rundle the K.C.B., and both Wingate and Slatin the K.C.M.G.[9] That he deserved the knighthood is undoubted; that he should be rewarded in the same degree as Slatin may have reminded Wingate that honors are not so much earned as bestowed.

While press and public were preoccupied during October and November with the Fashoda crisis, decisions were taken about the future of the Sudan. These were complicated by the multiplicity of British interests in the Nile Valley and their repercussions beyond. At Khartoum the flags of Britain and Egypt had been raised; at Fashoda Egyptian rights had been asserted; Egypt, although under British occupation, was itself still part of the Ottoman Empire. What was the status of the Sudan? As early as the Dongola campaign of 1896 this

---

[6] Wingate to his wife, 11 October 1898, SAD 233/5. SAD 226/3–6 contain hundreds of congratulatory messages regarding the events of 1898–99.

[7] Wingate to his wife, 11 October 1898, SAD 233/5.

[8] Bigge to Wingate, 27 October 1898, SAD 267/1.

[9] "Sudan Honours," 16 November 1898, SAD 226/2.

question had arisen, as lands won from the Mahdists had to be administered, at least formally. Now, after Omdurman and Fashoda, it became acute. Objections to British annexation were overwhelming: Egyptian and European opposition would be insurmountable, the expense of administering the country unacceptable. Re-incorporation with Egypt was likewise vexed: Wingate's propaganda had ensured that the British public would reject that option, which would in any case have hobbled the Sudan with the capitulatory and other international arrangements that complicated British rule in Egypt.

By November 1898 the question could no longer easily be deferred. European business interests were clamoring for concessions. What legal regime must apply to foreigners, and to their property? Cromer argued that a "compromise between the two extremes" of British annexation and incorporation with Egypt must be found, albeit "a status hitherto unknown in the law of Europe."[10] The compromise, moreover, should be embodied in an Anglo-Egyptian (not Anglo-Ottoman) convention, a draft of which Cromer drew from Sir Malcolm McIlwraith, judicial adviser to the Egyptian government. This, as amended in discussions involving Cromer, Kitchener, and Salisbury, formed the basis for two Anglo-Egyptian Conventions of 1899, together known ever since as the Condominium Agreement.

In its preamble, the first convention referred to "certain provinces in the Soudan which were in rebellion against the authority" of the khedive, and had been re-conquered by joint Anglo-Egyptian action, a share in the administration of which Britain had by "right of conquest." The laws of Egypt, and the capitulatory regime enforced there, were declared inapplicable in the Sudan. The convention vested "supreme military and civil command of the Soudan" in a governor-general to be nominated by Britain and appointed by the khedive. That officer would have full legislative powers, having only to make his acts known to the Egyptian government and the British agent in Cairo. (For this statutory latitude Wingate and his successors as governor-general had Kitchener to thank, for he had disputed Cromer's draft calling for *prior* notification of legislation.) Likewise over financial control Kitchener won Salisbury's support for a degree of independence from Cairo. In an oft-quoted line Salisbury told Cromer that "the Governor General of the Soudan is to govern, and

---

[10] Cromer, memorandum for Salisbury, 10 November 1898, FO 78/4957. For details of these deliberations see Daly, *Empire*, 11–18.

is to spend the money he has"; while he must of course defer to the Cairo agent, he should not be hamstrung by overly-detailed controls.[11] The Condominium Agreement was signed on 19 January 1899, and Kitchener was appointed governor-general of the Sudan. The bare constitutional bones of the convention would be fleshed out over years of Anglo-Egyptian and especially intramural British argument, mainly during Wingate's long governor-generalship.

Brief and unsuccessful, Kitchener's tenure as governor-general of the Sudan had important consequences for Wingate. Kitchener returned to Cairo from his triumph in Britain only in mid-December 1898, and almost immediately proceeded to Omdurman. He remained in the Sudan until May, and after a visit to Cairo went to Britain; he spent most of the autumn in the Sudan before his appointment in mid-December as chief of staff to Lord Roberts in South Africa. During the chaotic early months of his governor-generalship, Wingate bore the burden of affairs in Cairo. Under a dutiful and considerate chief these would have been onerous and complex, involving not only routine administration of the Egyptian army but also the embryonic civil government of vast new territories. But it was in a "mood of prickly impatience and overweening self-confidence"[12] that Kitchener returned to the Sudan in December 1898, and he soon proved impossible to work with. He busied himself with big projects—reconstruction of Khartoum, the hunt for the fugitive khalifa—and ignored and even hampered the country's recovery. His secretiveness and disdain for civil administration resulted in official disarray and unnecessary human suffering. His unconcern, even contempt, for officers and men led to mutiny.

The direst results of Kitchener's failings would confront Wingate only after he succeeded to the governor-generalship at the end of 1899. Until then he was fully occupied with the day-to-day conduct of affairs. Wingate's correspondence with officers in the Sudan is replete with their complaints about Kitchener's administration—indeed lack of administration—and a general lack of direction. A letter dated 2 November 1898 from his friend Milo Talbot, in Omdurman, is typical, and illustrates how quickly the rot had set in: Col. Maxwell was

---

[11] Salisbury to Cromer, 9 December 1898, Salisbury Papers, Hatfield House, 3M/A113/85. For details of the Agreement see Daly, *Empire*, 14–18.

[12] Magnus, *Kitchener*, 147.

worrying away at Khartoum preparing the site and laying out all
sorts of lovely squares, crescents etc. on the plan I prepared. . . . I
have been doing Chief of Staff to Maxwell as well as D.M.I.
[Director of Military Intelligence]. As the latter I have little to do.
We are still encamped in the old place and the natives come little
to me. Indeed I don't feel inclined to encourage them very much
to come to me as I've no intention of stopping here in my present
position. All this hunting slave girls and tracing stolen cows and
camels does not interest me and unless I get the position I want, I
trot off to India as soon as my year is up. . . . I'm sick of this atmosphere of lies and corruption and trying to make bricks without
straw. The Sirdar said he would write to me. . . . There's a great
deal of want here, if not actual famine. . . . I can't stand his way of
doing things. This is rather a growl, but I thought it was best to
let you know my intentions.[13]

None of this would have surprised Wingate, nor gone uncon-
firmed by many other sources. Although from January 1899 the
Condominium Agreement provided the bare bones of constitutional
government for the Sudan, Wingate knew from experience that the
conduct of affairs would depend on the views and relations of the
principals. Maneuvering and petty intrigue therefore continued, with
Cromer trying to maintain control of the Sudan from Cairo, and
Kitchener, newly armed by celebrity, chafing at any criticism of his
haphazard and irresponsible regime.

Not for the first time, Wingate found himself in the middle,
sometimes the referee, more often the bystander as superiors circled
each other in the ring. His great fear remained relegation to the
Sudan as Kitchener's place-man. He did everything he could to stress
the need for a Sudan government office in Cairo, and his own unique
ability to run it. This campaign involved not only the usual tireless-
ness in office routine, but also much private lobbying. In mid-
February 1899, for instance, Wingate wrote to Count Gleichen, his
intelligence colleague (and Queen Victoria's cousin):

I fear that you and my other friends in the Intell. Divn. [of the War
Office] will think that now that I am *nominally* no longer connected with the Intell. Divn. officially, I am [unmindful] of all you
have done for us and mean to "sever the connection". I, therefore,
hasten to tell you that this is not the case. I take just the same inter-

---

[13] SAD 266/11.

est as ever in the work. . . . I am just as much D.M.I. in Cairo as I ever was and more so because the Sudan civil work is now passing through the Intell. office. . . . I have reorganized [*sic*] it into two sections—*A*. to deal with Civil work . . . and *B*. Intell. and political. . . . However the Sirdar may determine to centralise in Khartoum, he cannot do without an office of this sort in Cairo which must for many years be his source of supply. . . . There is no one to work this office in Cairo but myself and therefore I have to do all the work passing through it— not as adjutant general, but as Wingate. . . . gradually the work of this Sudan office is growing considerably more . . . than that of the A.G. office. I have appealed in vain for more assistance in English officers but the Sirdar cannot spare them . . . Indeed I should not be at all surprised if, one fine day, I did not receive an order to report at Khartoum and what will happen to the work then I cannot say. . . .[14]

Having thus alerted the War Office, Wingate turned also to Cromer. In March Cromer himself wired Kitchener that Wingate was greatly in need of help in Cairo, and that the combined duties of adjutant-general and Sudan affairs were too much for one man. "You probably have little idea of what the work here is," he added with customary tact.[15] Wingate duly drew up an elaborate plan to separate the two areas. This called for a Sudan Office (with an "under Secretary of State for the Sudan" drawing £E1,500 a year), to deal with its financial, administrative, and political affairs.[16] No such position was created, for while Kitchener was sirdar he would never permit the centralization in Cairo such an office would entail, and Wingate, once he succeeded Kitchener, likewise had no use for it.

The Nilotic summer intervened. Kitchener went on leave to England in May. Wingate had fallen ill with influenza or pneumonia (or both) in April, and had barely recovered by 20 May, when he too left for four months' leave.[17] When he returned it was indeed to Khartoum that he proceeded, not to the sirdarial clerkship he had feared but to his one real taste of military glory.

Since his defeat at Karari on 2 September 1898 the Khalifa Abdallahi had been a fugitive in Kordofan. But he was not alone.

---

[14] 19 February 1899, SAD 269/3.

[15] N/d, SAD 269/3.

[16] Wingate, "Notes on the creation of a Sudan Office," 10 March 1899, SAD 269/3.

[17] CB1.

Although he never regained the power to challenge the new regime in a pitched battle, his freedom bred insecurity in the land, served as a focus for die-hard elements, and embarrassed Kitchener and his officers. Anglo-Egyptian patrols, including one under Kitchener's brother, failed to corner him or retreated in the face of his superior force. Hemmed in in southern Kordofan, however, his fighting strength gradually declined. By the autumn of 1899, both sirdar and khalifa had had enough of the chase: Abdallahi led his force northward, in the direction of Omdurman, while Kitchener determined finally to crush him.

During his summer leave the sirdar planned a major expedition against the khalifa. In September he and Wingate returned to the Sudan, where renewed operations failed to bring the khalifa to battle. In late October, from his base aboard a steamer in the White Nile, Kitchener sent an infantry column under Wingate fifty miles toward Jabal Qadir, but the khalifa got away. Kitchener thereupon went to Cairo for meetings with Cromer, leaving Wingate in command. The noose was closing on Abdallahi; it was Wingate's good fortune to preside. In Kitchener's absence he led a column of some 3,700 men to a place called Umm Diwaykarat, where on 24 November the decisive engagement took place. His own diary account for Kitchener not only tells the story, but also illustrates Wingate's way with words: "It was now obvious [on 23 November] that our occupation of GEDID had placed the Khalifa in an unfavourable position strategically, his route to the North was barred, his retreat to the South lay through waterless and densely wooded districts, and as our seizure of grain supplies . . . would render his advance or retirement a matter of considerable difficulty, it seemed probable that he would stand. I therefore decided to attack him at dawn on the 24th." The diary continues:

> At 3 a.m. the enemy's position was reported about 3 miles distant and the force was deployed into fighting formation. . . . in the distance the beating of "NOGGARAS" and the blowing of "OMBEYAS" was suddenly heard. . . . At 5.10 a.m. . . . the indistinct form of the advancing Dervishes became visible. The line was immediately prepared for action and at 5.15 a.m. the guns and Maxims opened fire, followed by Infantry volleys. . . . As the light improved large bodies of shouting Dervishes were seen advancing, but our steady volleys and gun and maxim [sic] fire kept theirs

under and it gradually slackened. The whole line was now advanced down the gentle slope towards the Dervish Position, and moving forward at a more rapid pace, soon drove the retiring enemy towards their camp which lay concealed in the midst of trees. . . . Cease fire sounded at 6.25 a.m. and as the troops advanced towards the camp numbers of the enemy surrendered. . . .

What of the Khalifa Abdallahi, and the other lieutenants of the Mahdi, whose downfall had so fully occupied Wingate for fifteen years?

Immediately in front of the line of advance of the 9th Sudanese, and only a few hundred yards from our original position . . . , a large number of the enemy were seen lying dead, huddled together in a comparatively small space: on examination these proved to be the bodies of the Khalifa Abdulla et Taaisha, The Khalifa Ali Wad Helu, [the amir] Ahmed el Fedil, the Khalifa's two brothers Sennousi Ahmed and Hamed Mohammed, the Mahdi's son Es Sadik and a number of other well known leaders. . . . At a short distance behind them lay their dead horses. . . . [W]e learnt that the Khalifa, having failed in his attempt to reach the rising ground . . . had then endeavoured to make a turning movement which had been crushed by our fire: seeing his followers retiring, he made an ineffectual attempt to rally them, but recognising that the day was lost, he called on his Emirs to dismount from their horses, and seating himself on his "furwa" or sheepskin . . . as is the custom of Arab Chiefs who disdain surrender . . . he had placed Khalifa Ali Wad Helu on his right, and Ahmed Fedil on his left, whilst the remaining Emirs seated themselves around him, with their body-guards in line some 20 paces to their front and in this position they had unflinchingly met their death.

The Mahdist losses were reported as 1,000 killed or wounded; 9,400 prisoners, including camp followers, were taken. The Anglo-Egyptian force lost but 4 killed and 29 wounded.[18]

Considering both the drama likely to surround the final battle of the Mahdiyya, and the personalities involved on the British side, it remains surprising that Kitchener let Wingate command. The superiority of Anglo-Egyptian arms had meant that, barring a miracle or ineptness, victory was likely if the khalifa could be brought to battle. A biographer states that Kitchener, knowing he would soon leave the

---

[18] Wingate to Kitchener, 25 November 1899, SGA, CAIRINT 1/66/340. For an account of the expedition see Sandes, *The Royal Engineers*, 297–301.

Sudan and eager to have Wingate succeed him, deliberately deferred in order to forestall other candidates.[19] Nothing in their previous relations supports that theory.

Following Umm Diwaykarat Wingate returned immediately to Khartoum. (By one account he left the battlefield the same day, and went sleepless for four nights.)[20] As always, however, there was time to send and receive messages. Soberly he cabled Cromer: "Mahdism received its coup de grace on 24th and I hope a new era will now open for the unfortunate Sudanese people." To his wife Wingate telegraphed an economical "Hurrah Mahdism finished"! And to Slatin he wired ironically, "MABRUK YA ABDELKADER."[21] By return cable came news of the birth of a daughter, Victoria Alexandrina Catherine Wingate, in Cairo on 25 November. Lady Wingate had received word of the khalifa's defeat in a note from Cromer five hours earlier: "'Rex' has smashed up the Khalifa and killed him and all his principal Emirs. I am so glad on every count." From Queen Victoria came cabled congratulations over both events, the victory and the birth. Slatin's message said much in a few mangled words: "Hurrah well done. . . . Now I may say 'you did nt [*sic*] only your best to save me—but also you revenged me'! . . . I received the first news from Windsor through Her Majesty. . . . I was really toucht—God save the Queen. Isn't old K. a little jealous?"[22]

Speeding northward, Wingate reached Aswan on the thirtieth (where he met Sir John Aird, who immediately commissioned a painting by Gow of the "Battle of Gedid"), and Cairo on 2 December.[23] On the fifteenth he wrote at length to Queen Victoria, through her private secretary, to thank her for agreeing to be godmother to her namesake:

> It is impossible for me to express to you with what feeling of heart-felt gratitude and devotion my wife and I read that most gracious message in which her Majesty has so highly honoured us and our little daughter. . . . I do not imagine any Sovereign in the world is

[19] Sir George Arthur, *Life of Lord Kitchener,* London 1920, I, 262.

[20] Sandes, *The Royal Engineers,* 301n. Sandes's source was likely Wingate.

[21] To Lady Wingate, 24 November 1899, to Cromer and Slatin, 25 November 1899, SAD 269/11. "Congratulations, Abd al-Qadir." Abd al-Qadir was the name Slatin took when he converted to Islam at the court of the Mahdi.

[22] Slatin to Wingate, 27 November 1899, SAD 226/5.

[23] CB1; CB2.

so dearly loved as our Queen. . . . I long to pour out my heart in feelings of the deepest gratitude for this most highly prized favour. The good news has done more than anything else to hasten my wife's recovery, and it is such an inexpressible joy to us both to feel that we are so honoured . . . that we can scarcely realise our good fortune. . . .[24]

Meanwhile more mundane events a continent away were determining Wingate's future. In South Africa, October and November had witnessed a series of Boer victories. On 10 December the British were defeated at Stromberg, on the eleventh at Magersfontein, and on the fifteenth at Colenso in Natal. Lord Roberts was appointed on the eighteenth as commander-in-chief, with Kitchener as his chief of staff and second-in-command. Traveling by special trains and steamer Kitchener left Khartoum the same day, broke all speed records, and boarded a Royal Navy cruiser at Alexandria on the twenty-first. His train from Cairo had slowed sufficiently to pick up Wingate, who, on 22 December, was named to succeed him.[25] On the twenty-fourth came official announcement that "His Highness The Khedive has been graciously pleased by Khedivial decree to promote El Lewa Sir Reginald Wingate Pasha, K.C.M.G., C.B., D.S.O., A.D.C., to the rank of Ferik [Major-General], and appoint him Sirdar of the Egyptian Army."[26]

---

[24] *The letters of Queen Victoria,* 437–38.

[25] CB1; Magnus, *Kitchener,* 157–59.

[26] Special Army Order, War Office, Cairo, 24 December 1899, SAD 233/6.

PART TWO: GOVERNOR-GENERAL OF THE SUDAN

Chapter Fifteen
Wingate's Sudan

————◆◦◦◦◆————

At the time of his appointment Wingate had been associated with the Sudan for a decade and a half. He had served as governor at Suakin. For long years in military intelligence he had sent out spies, interviewed informants, and read and written hundreds of reports on conditions in the Sudan. He had helped to plan the Anglo-Egyptian campaign, had been present at the major engagements, including Omdurman, and commanded at Umm Diwaykarat the force that killed the khalifa. He had been to Fashoda. He had produced three books on which much of British public opinion about the Sudan was based. Since the fall of the Mahdist state, Wingate had coordinated from Cairo the affairs of Kitchener's makeshift regime at Khartoum. Now, on 22 December 1899 he was named sirdar of the Egyptian army and (on the twenty-third) governor-general of the Sudan. What was the nature of the dual appointment Kitchener broke speed records to relinquish? What reality lay behind the title with which Gordon before him had gone to Khartoum?

To appreciate Wingate's record as governor-general it is necessary to survey the prospect he faced at the end of 1899. Kitchener had negotiated with Cromer and Salisbury the Anglo-Egyptian conventions that comprised the Condominium Agreement, the only "constitution" this "hybrid form of government" would ever have. Other achievements of his year as governor-general are few. He had launched the fund-raising drive that created the Gordon Memorial College, and had involved himself in rebuilding Khartoum. Administration bored him. That Khartoum's reconstruction monopolized transport and contributed to famine elsewhere did not concern him. Mistrust of superiors and subordinates alike made him secretive and unresponsive; records were unkept, comings and goings unannounced. Large sums were spent on buildings, while in other areas parsimony ruled. By the end of a brief tenure Kitchener had failed to create a civil administration, and had exemplified how not to do it. When he left for South Africa, disgruntled British officers had preceded him in droves, his Egyptian men were on the brink of mutiny, and the Sudan was still unpacified after a generation of war.

131

While it is possible to reach general conclusions about the condition of the Sudan at the end of 1899, it is important not to rely on Wingate's own propaganda. The evil of the Mahdi and barbarism of the khalifa are naturally thematic in *Mahdiism, Ten years' captivity,* and *Fire and sword.* Contradictory evidence that could have harmed the war effort went largely unexpressed and unpublished. The private opinion of Archibald Hunter, written at Firket in June 1896, is worth comparing to the official view:

> It is all very well to indulge in tirades of the abuse of the dervish rule in the Sudan. It is certainly better than the American rule over the Red Indians, than the Turkish rule anywhere in Asia, Africa or Europe; than the Italian rule in Sicily or Erythrea. . . . The land has been allowed from Firket to the third Cataract to go out of cultivation, because the people most of them came to us, but the date trees are unharmed, the inhabitants cultivate the foreshore, & are fat & sleek & well. . . . Slatin, Wingate & others write the rounded periods of inconceivable horrors, torture & injustices . . . [but] from documents their taxation seems to be fair enough . . . & there is a total absence so far as I can see of any undue interference in the family life of the local inhabitant. . . . Men have been put in irons for harbouring our secret agents—and quite right too from their point of view. . . . if the choice were given me I sh'd elect to live in dervish Sudan instead of German East Africa . . . or in the Congo Free State . . .[1]

As governor-general during the formative years of the Condominium Wingate—not Hunter or other free-thinkers—determined the outside world's view, and not only of the Mahdist state, but also, by contrast, of the Anglo-Egyptian regime over which he presided. Thus official reports of the early Condominium are sometimes as gloomy as the propaganda of the 1890s. Whereas those anti-Mahdist books, tracts, and intelligence reports had been used to justify military action, their later repetition justified and extolled, by comparison, the successor state. While it can be stated with assurance that the condition of the Sudanese peoples improved under Wingate's rule, contemporary accounts were often designed to make that conclusion inescapable, and must be read critically.

One example illustrates the problem. To this day popular accounts conclude that the warfare and famine of the Mahdiyya car-

[1] Hunter to Sir Frederick Stephenson, 19 June 1896, *A Soldier's Hero,* 75–76.

ried off seven to ten million Sudanese. No evidence supports such figures or any other late nineteenth- and early twentieth-century figures on which current accounts are based. Moreover those sources vary incompatibly, while huge regions of the southern and western Sudan were unvisited by British officers at the time the figures were produced.[2] Nor can general conditions be accurately described from contemporary accounts. Regions most severely damaged during the Mahdiyya were those (along the main Nile north of Khartoum and in the more accessible parts of the Gezira south of it) where Anglo-Egyptian officers were likeliest, and in most numbers, to visit immediately after the fall of the khalifa. Less traveled paths took them (as less publicized reports show) to places like Wad Madani, al-Duaym, and Kawa, where W. E. Garstin found in 1899 flourishing markets, rich fields, and much evidence of long-distance trade.[3] Similar variations can be shown, or assumed, to have existed throughout the country.[4] The degree of recovery after the Mahdiyya must therefore, to some extent, reflect widely different degrees of disturbance during it.

None of this diminishes Wingate's achievement, or that of his subordinates. That he (and others) used inflated figures reflects the propagandist's appreciation for the single, striking "fact" that could, for an uninterested European audience, command the momentary notice needed to encapsulate success. For more attentive Egyptians—and Sudanese—policies, not just propaganda, had to be devised, and people had to be found to rule. It was in these substantive areas that Wingate succeeded, as during his long tenure the bones of the Condominium Agreement acquired flesh, an administration was set up, and policies evolved that would have a lasting impact on the Sudan and in the empire.

Wingate owed his appointment to Lord Cromer. We have seen how transfers and promotions had made Wingate, by June 1898, senior colonel in the Egyptian army and, by March 1899, second only to the sirdar. Private assertions of precedence, however, gave him

---

[2] For details see Daly, *Empire,* 18–23.

[3] Ibid., 21–22.

[4] See, for example, "Report to accompany sketch by Bimbashi Morant Inspector Kassala District," 15 April 1899, SGA, CAIRINT, 3/4/69; Boulnois, "Report on visit to ABU DELEIK made by Bimbashis Boulnois and Battley Jan. 1900," 13 February 1900, SGA, CAIRINT 3/4/70.

only a moral claim for consideration; he remained uncertain until his appointment. The way was prepared, ironically, by Kitchener, who, by his conduct in office, convinced Cromer that an entirely different character was needed in Khartoum. Apparently the appointment was Cromer's to make. As early as May 1899 Cromer had told Salisbury that Kitchener had "had about enough of the Soudan" and would likely leave soon; "I think Wingate, with Maxwell under him, would be able to get on. I do not, under any circumstances, want a new War Office man without local experience."[5] On 18 December 1899, the day on which Kitchener's appointment to South Africa was confirmed, Cromer wired privately to Salisbury; "I propose to submit Sir F. Wingate's name to the Khedive, as successor to Lord Kitchener. Is this approved?" It was, the next day, and the dual appointment was made.[6] There is no evidence of other candidates, or that thought was given to separating the two posts.[7]

Wingate's appointment was well received; Kitchener was in some respects an easy man to follow. Only because his conduct had alerted Cairo to the potential for trouble-making up the Nile did Kitchener's memory hamper his successor. A *Times* correspondent described as a "general expectation as of something springlike and mild" the British reaction to Wingate's succession.[8] His early conduct in office would show an ability to win the support of Egyptian subordinates. The Sudanese were not yet in a position to judge.

Wingate's first test in office came at the moment of appointment. For years Kitchener's policies and methods as sirdar had earned him the dislike of British subordinates and the disaffection of Egyptian officers and men. It was said that every British officer left the service with some grievance against Kitchener.[9] In March 1899 Cromer reported "a good deal of grumbling amongst the British officers"; the sirdar was "a somewhat exacting Chief who does not treat his subordinate agents with much consideration." An infor-

---

[5] Cromer to Salisbury, 9 May 1899, FO 633/6/313.

[6] Cromer to Salisbury, 18 December 1899, Hatfield House MSS 3M/A112/57; Salisbury to Cromer, 19 December 1899, 3M/A113/102.

[7] After announcement of Kitchener's appointment, Wingate's succession was apparently taken for granted in London. See, e.g., Prince of Wales to Bigge, 19 December 1899, *The Letters of Queen Victoria*, 442.

[8] Quoted in Gabriel Warburg, *The Sudan under Wingate*, London 1971, 8.

[9] See Daly, *Empire*, 33.

mant, returning from the Sudan, told him that British officers looked "like so many hunted animals."[10] They eluded the predator by leaving the Egyptian army. The result was secondment from Britain of younger, greener officers with neither the experience nor the Arabic needed to command.

The mistreatment that induced British officers to leave drove Egyptian officers to mutiny. To them service in the Sudan seemed indefinite exile, made worse by Kitchener's economies and by neglect of the ill-will these engendered. Even he admitted, in March 1899, "discontent" over pay: without reference to political authority he had canceled special field allowances for soldiers stationed in the Sudan, and used the money for other purposes. He seemed deliberately to provoke the Egyptians, and to despise them the more for tolerating his abuse. As often in such cases, it was left to others, undeserving of the chore, to deal with the crisis.

In December 1899 events combined to produce mutiny. British defeats in South Africa, a consequent exodus of British officers, and wild rumors that Egyptian troops would soon be forced to follow, increased tension. This was mishandled by the commander at Omdurman, Col. Maxwell, who saw an opportunity to reduce the size of Sudanese battalions by retiring "bad characters" and "weedy old men who cost money and do nothing":[11] "economy should be observed," he claimed, imitating Kitchener at a moment that called for imagination.[12] Ostensibly because deteriorating ammunition had caused accidents, Maxwell ordered its withdrawal from troops and return to the armory. This, to unhappy and suspicious men, was ominous of action planned against them. On the night of 22 January they rushed the armories and made off with ammunition. Scuffles broke out, and Maxwell had to compromise to restore order: a quota of ammunition was returned to each battalion. There the matter could not of course be allowed to rest. Settlement awaited the new sirdar, Wingate, who was still in Cairo.[13]

Rumors of imminent trouble had circulated in Cairo for weeks. Cromer had reported them to London; Wingate later claimed to have

---

[10] Cromer to Salisbury, 26 March 1899, Hatfield House MSS 3M/A112/27.

[11] Maxwell to Wingate, 26 December 1899, SAD 269/12.

[12] Maxwell to Wingate, 19 January 1900, SAD 270/1/1.

[13] For details of the mutiny, see M. W. Daly, "The Egyptian Army mutiny at Omdurman, January–February 1900," *Bulletin of the British Society for Middle Eastern Studies* 8, 1, 1981, 3–12.

been told by Princess Nazli that disaffected officers had approached the khedive for support. Before leaving for the Sudan, Wingate therefore had an audience with the khedive, during which Abbas Hilmi strenuously denied any knowledge of or association with the mutiny. Wingate entrained at 8:00 P.M. on 29 January, for his first trip to the Sudan as sirdar and governor-general. In a note he wrote decades later Wingate claimed to have asked the khedive

> to hand me a letter giving me *full powers* to deal drastically with the outbreak. . . . I had previous knowledge of his sympathetic attitude to the Native officers when they, clandestinely, complained to him of my predecessor's financial reforms. . . . The letter was duly drafted in strong terms in Arabic, the Khedive deprecating bitterly the tarnished honour of his Army, and urging me to lose no time in restoring order and punishing the guilty. . . . The letter was never used by me, nor did I divulge its existence but the fact that it was in my possession precluded the possibility of collusion between the mutineers and the Palace.[14]

Wingate reached Omdurman on 4 February, reviewed the situation (unresolved and in some respects deteriorating), and called a "levee" for the next day. The Egyptian officers were allowed to choose seven representatives. Their spokesman in turn put their grievance: Kitchener's financial reforms. If these were withdrawn, he said, "all this trouble would at once cease." According to Wingate, his own reply was "instantaneous": the officers were holding a pistol to his head, and he would not even discuss their grievances until all missing ammunition was accounted for and all men had returned to army discipline. If order were not restored immediately, "a large force of British Troops" would be dispatched to the Sudan.[15]

While Wingate later recalled an abrupt end to the mutiny, in fact insubordination continued for several weeks. He appointed a commission to investigate, but while it deliberated, defiance of orders continued. Cromer began to question Wingate's strategy: on 20 February he told Wingate that if the commission did not report soon, it might be necessary to dissolve it, "cashier" the ringleaders, and,

----

[14] "Memoirs. Note by R. W. On the mutiny in Omdurman Dec. 1899–Jan. 1900," n.d., SAD 270/1/1.

[15] Ibid.

with British troops and loyal Egyptians, "shoot down without mercy anyone who shows the least hesitation or reluctance to obey."[16] On the twenty-second, however, Wingate was able to report the commission's recommendations. Several officers would be dismissed (not by court-martial, because no witnesses would come forward); they were publicly drummed out of the army two days later. Meanwhile, under terms of a compromise, armory windows were left open one night, during which most of the ammunition was returned.[17]

No outcome of this crisis would have been fully satisfactory. Whether settled by compromise or suppression, open defiance of orders must depress morale, unsettle relations among the ranks, and provide a precedent for future grievances of the Egyptians and fears of the British. Indeed, although the mutiny ended without bloodshed, there was little to celebrate. The causes remained debatable, and, from one point of view, irrelevant; complicity of politicians (and the khedive himself) in Cairo remained widely suspected and wholly unproven; Wingate's settlement solved the immediate problem but held mixed lessons for the future. Indeed, this first matter with which Wingate had to deal as sirdar and governor-general would affect, in one way or another, the whole range of policy during his long tenure, and would have consequences until the end of the Condominium.[18] Security remained the watchword, "bluff" the strategy of the regime. Always there were memories of Gordon. Wingate's long-sought prize of office was depressingly tarnished from the start.

To what extent Wingate's handling of the Omdurman mutiny affected his reputation at this crucial turn in his career is unclear. There was no question of his sharing responsibility with Kitchener (and Maxwell) for the grievances that had led to mutiny. But was the "mildness" expected to characterize his regime, in contrast to Kitchener's, seen in February 1900 as weakness? Praise of Wingate's role in ending the crisis was faint. Evelyn Wood's cable was typical in content (and characteristically blunt in tone): "I can quite understand that he who sowed has left you to reap the unpleasant crop."[19] Cromer, never profligate with praise, nonethe-

---

[16] Cromer to Wingate, 20 February 1900, F.O. 78/5087.

[17] Wingate to Cromer, 22 February 1900, W.O. 32/6383, and 24 February 1900, F.O. 78/5087.

[18] See Daly, "The Egyptian Army mutiny," 10.

[19] 9 March 1900, SAD 270/3.

less told Salisbury, when the crisis had passed, that the British had "been perilously near a serious upset"; Wingate's "conduct of the whole business has been marked by great judgment."[20] In a later, private, note he was more pointed: "When Kitchener left," Cromer wrote in April, "he said something to me about coming back here. . . . his return is out of the question. He would not be able to hold the Soudan without a large British force."[21]

Karari, Fashoda, Umm Diwaykarat, Kitchener's departure, his own succession, the Omdurman mutiny, and the task that confronted him in the Sudan all contributed to a shift in the emphasis of Wingate's and other British officers' sense of mission in the Nile Valley. For two decades Sudanese "fanatics" had been the enemy, whose rebellion, to be sure, had been sparked by the oppression of Egypt. Now, with the Mahdiyya ended, the main threat to British interests was posed not by Sudanese religion but by Cairene politics. British reports on the Omdurman mutiny and its aftermath are remarkable for detecting the baleful influence that Egypt and Egyptians, military and civilian, were having and were bound to have in the Sudan. For their part, destruction of the Mahdist State allowed Egyptians to renew attention to the central fact that Britain occupied Egypt. The Sudanese—largely rural, tribal, conservative, unsophisticated—were soon seen to respond favorably to the British brand of good government. To Wingate, his subordinates, and their successors, the Egyptians were thus at best a necessary evil, supplying trained manpower and revenue, but always a danger. As the Egyptian army guarded the regime from Sudanese fanatics, British troops guarded it from the Egyptian army. Thus did the victors over Mahdism fall out, within a few months of the khalifa's death, and a struggle begin, for the hearts and minds of the Sudanese, which would end only with the Sudan's independence in 1956.

---

[20] 25 February 1900, Hatfield House MSS, 3M, A112/95.
[21] Cromer to Salisbury, 27 April 1900, FO 633/6/324.

Chapter Sixteen
Governing The Sudan,
1899–1907

———◆◇◇◇◆———

Although a soldier all his adult life, Wingate made his name as an
administrator, and it is partly for this reason that his role in the
history of the modern Middle East has been obscured. In the Sudan,
Wingate's legacy has been greater, longer-lasting, and influential on
more lives than that of any other Briton. But in a consciously analyt-
ical age a "Hero of Bureaucracy" is unlikely to stir much interest.
Cromer, the epitome of proconsular *gravitas,* recognized this; in a
career lacking episodic thrill and popular adulation he wielded
immense power for a quarter of a century. Wingate, an unwilling
understudy, affected but never matched "the Lord's" cool detachment; he took pride in the creative role he was called to play on the
imperial stage, and thereby set a pattern, adopted by hundreds of
British officials who followed him, of proprietary, paternal involvement in what his son later called "the making of the Sudan."

Only the administrative scaffolding erected by the Condominium
Agreement was in place before Wingate took office. Survival of old or
traditional authority both eased and complicated Wingate's task: the
Sudan was not the clean slate popular writers have frequently discerned. Wingate and his officials revived government at the central
and provincial levels, quickly pacified most of the country and
enforced a high degree of personal security, and won the trust or
acquiescence of most of the people. In this they were helped by the
exhaustion of the country, the particularism of its peoples, ironically
by an acute shortage of revenue and manpower, and crucially by a
spirit of pragmatism and compromise. The Sudan Government under
Wingate was personal, undogmatic, and utilitarian; by rejecting system, it became a unique colonial administration.

Even after his appointment as governor-general of the Sudan,
Wingate evidently hoped to spend most of his time in Egypt. He had
immediately arranged Maxwell's appointment as commandant at
Omdurman and deputy governor-general, a new position, and given

him use of the Palace at Khartoum: after his own arrival he would
need only a few rooms—his wife would not be joining him.[1] It may
have been the Omdurman mutiny that changed his mind, or realization that independent action would be impossible in Cairo. In any
case, although until 1914 Wingate spent six weeks or more in Cairo
every year, there was never again a question of where his principal residence would be. But even in the wake of the mutiny Wingate, suffering from influenza and the insomnia that always followed over-
work, was able to leave the Sudan for seven months.[2] The work of
establishing administration continued, as it had begun, by correspondence with men on the spot.

What seems unconcern or negligence in fact reflected both the
Sudan Government's origins in departments of the Egyptian army
and a military view of the Sudan as Egyptian hinterland.
Throughout the Mahdiyya Suakin and Wadi Halfa had remained in
Egyptian hands, and the Anglo-Egyptian advance up the Nile that
began in March 1896 brought Dongola, then Abu Hamad and
Berber, the northern Butana and other areas under the conquerors'
control; administrative decisions could not await the last battle.
After the fall of Dongola, a Sudan Bureau had been set up in the
Egyptian army's intelligence department; it and a similar section in
the army's finance department were meant as expandable nuclei for
civil administration. Vestiges of that plan survived: the head of the
finance department's Sudan section, for example, became the first
financial secretary of the Sudan Government; the office of civil secretary, eventually second in importance only to the governor-generalship, emerged soon after Omdurman in the person of an army officer "to do intelligence and secretary for civil govt. to the G.O.C."
In the provinces Egyptian offices were revived. In Dongola the
British commander became *mudir* (governor), combining military
and civil functions the governor-general and sirdar would embody at
the center. The "province" of Dongola was divided into districts,
each under an Egyptian *ma'mur*. This system was maintained under
the Condominium Agreement. One or two British officers
appointed as assistants to the *mudir* were later called inspectors

---

[1] Draft telegram, Wingate to Maxwell, n.d., December 1899; Wingate to Maxwell,
    24 December 1899, SAD 269/12; "Extracts from the Muayad. 1st January
    1900," SAD 265/3.
[2] CB1.

(*mufattashin*), forerunners of the civilian district commissioners at the core of the Sudan Political Service. The early administration thus combined aspects of Turco-Egyptian government with elements of Egyptian army bureaucracy.

In this and other respects the Sudan Government differed from British colonial regimes elsewhere. Condominium, in Wingate's day, meant that sovereignty was shared by Britain and Egypt, no matter how unequally they exercised it. The Sudan's affairs were overseen in London not at the Colonial Office but by the Foreign Office, where Cromer's Condominium was merely a diplomatic device and the Sudan a barbarian land needing occupation to ensure Egypt's security. From the start, therefore, prospects for progress, for anything more than the minimum needed to maintain order, were poor. Two factors account for the success that was achieved: Egyptian money and the efforts of Wingate and his officials.

For them, civil administration was a novelty. Military careers flourished in active service, not office work. Many senior veterans of the 1896-98 campaigns had left the Sudan immediately for South Africa, India, or other fields of glory. Of those who stayed to try their hands at government, some proved inadequate or unsuitable and soon left; others built careers. Replacements were always hard to find, and secondment from the British army meant that officers' services could be required elsewhere at short notice. This uncertainty led to employment of civilians and eventually changed the character of the administration. Under Wingate, however, officers predominated in a system ideally suited to his temperament and methods.

Wingate acted early to remove rivals. His appointment had come only after retirement or transfer of better-connected or more illustrious officers; Cromer would have no qualms about replacing him if problems arose. Wingate had little administrative experience, a minor military record, and, apart from Wood and a few others, no personal support in Britain. After the rush of officers to South Africa, however, only two competitors remained in the Egyptian army, Maxwell and Herbert Jackson; there had been rumors that Maxwell would succeed Kitchener. When Wingate was preferred, Maxwell, at Omdurman, asked to be made commandant there and "wakil" (deputy) governor-general, at the same time admitting that "the Cape is the place for a soldier": were he offered a place there he "would go off like a shot."[3]

---

[3] Maxwell to Wingate, 26 December 1899, SAD 269/12.

The Omdurman mutiny provided the powder. Wingate, who had voiced concern about "denuding" the Egyptian army of British officers, wrote privately to Wood (at Cromer's instance, he said) that "one exception should be made, viz. Colonel J. G. Maxwell." Cromer had foreseen friction, and cabled Salisbury that Maxwell, "though an excellent officer in every way," seemed to be cast in the Kitchener mold: "I should be very glad of the Transvaal excuse to get him away." Wood, as usual, not only saw the light, but found simple words to describe it: "Understanding that you particularly wished Maxwell to be given employment," he wrote Wingate, "and believing that you might have special reasons for urging his claims," he had arranged Maxwell's transfer to South Africa.[4]

Jackson's case was more vexing, and its result less clear. Of British officers only Jackson had more experience in Egypt and the Sudan than Wingate. He had fought in major battles against the khalifa, and had been left in command at Fashoda after Kitchener's meeting with Marchand. He had brought the Omdurman mutiny to a peaceful end; his personal relations with the army rank-and-file were unequaled. Soon after his own appointment Wingate named Jackson civil secretary, a nebulous post but clearly meant to use his knowledge of and sympathy with the Sudanese. In that office Jackson reportedly disappointed, but his fall had a personal element now obscure. Several unconvincing versions are extant, involving alleged insults to Slatin Pasha or Lady Wingate, the flaunting of Sudanese mistresses, and "disloyalty" to Wingate by direct communication with Cairo.[5] Jackson was demoted to Berber as *mudir*, and, a few months later, to Dongola. Cromer saw in the incident symptoms of a deeper problem. There was no doubt, he told Lord Lansdowne, "that the sympathies of all the army, British and Egyptian, will be with Jackson; that service under Wingate is unpopular with the British officers; that it is in many respects a more objectionable form of unpopularity than that which Kitchener excited, for they were all afraid of Kitchener and respected him."[6] For the rest of his career Wingate would be charged with

---

[4] Wingate to "General" (Wood), 9 January 1900, SAD 270/1/1; Cromer to Salisbury, 28 January 1900, Hatfield House MSS, 3M/A112/72; Wood to Wingate, 25 January 1900, SAD 270/1/2. For Cromer's pre-mutiny reservations see Cromer to Lansdowne, 10 January 1900, FO 633/8/247.

[5] See Wingate, diary entry, 23 March 1902, SAD 272/8.

[6] 19 January 1902, FO 633/6/336.

removing rivals in favor of young and pliable subordinates. The charge withstands scrutiny; Wingate had been taught by masters.

The most important relations of Wingate's early years in the Sudan were with Lord Cromer, who had been in Egypt as long as he had, and had reached a pinnacle of personal power and prestige. During a long official acquaintance there was never doubt as to which had the upper hand. No less as governor-general than as junior officer Wingate was subordinate to "the Lord," and he acted accordingly. Notwithstanding Wingate's experience of Anglo-Egyptian intrigue, no evidence has arisen of his having challenged Cromer's authority. Dealing with Kitchener had taught Cromer what he wanted in Khartoum, and in most ways Wingate suited him. "The two Sirdars differ in every respect,"[7] he wrote in early 1900, which meant that in almost every respect Wingate was an improvement.

During discussions that had led to the Condominium Agreement, as in early implementation of it, Cromer had lost several battles to Kitchener. In December 1898 Salisbury, in an oft-quoted letter, told Cromer that on "two main points" of dispute Kitchener was "probably right. They are that the Governor General of the Soudan is to govern, and is to spend the money he has. In both cases he is of course to obey orders received from you, and his proceedings may be revised and altered by you: but . . . he shall not by a formal document be forbidden to pass an ordinance, or to spend £100 without a preliminary approval."[8]

The Condominium Agreement therefore gave wide powers to the governor-general, who had only to inform the co-domini of his acts. This statutory latitude was never matched in fact, even under Kitchener. Moreover Cairo had other ways of asserting control. Separate Financial Regulations gave ample scope for Cromer and his successors to interfere, for at least as long as Khartoum depended upon Egyptian subventions.

The exact nature of the relations between the British representative in Cairo and the governor-general in Khartoum was therefore largely left to the two to decide. Although their relative strength ebbed and flowed with each change in office, the trend throughout the Condominium was toward Khartoum's greater independence. Whereas in 1899 Cromer claimed that all he wanted was control of

---

[7] Cromer to Barrington, 28 February 1900, Hatfield House MSS, 3M, A112/97.
[8] Salisbury to Cromer, 9 December 1898, Hatfield House MSS, 3M, A113/85.

"big questions,"[9] those with foreign or major Egyptian repercussions, in fact he clashed with Kitchener repeatedly over what was "big." With Wingate Cairo's interference was constant and detailed, at times extremely so, as befitting relations of minor bureaucrats rather than proconsuls.

What they confronted (and Cromer recognized) was the age-old problem of reconciling central control with local autonomy. Thus in 1904 Cromer could write—he never joked—that his control over the Sudan Government was light. Yet he "constantly" noticed "a tendency to consider the Soudan as a separate independent Government, more or less unconnected with Egypt. It is nothing of the kind." Indeed, he added, "the only reason why . . . the Soudan has a Governor-General and special Laws is to avoid the capitulations and the rest of the international paraphernalia" afflicting Egypt.[10] He often returned to the theme. "I doubt," he told Wingate expansively in May 1904, "whether anywhere in the world the principles of decentralisation are carried so far as in Egypt, and still more in the Soudan." For Khartoum to be "left without some effective control" was "a most pernicious dream" that would end in detailed control from London.[11]

Cromer preferred control from Cairo. This is illustrated by procedures adopted for Sudan legislation. Although by the Condominium Agreement Wingate had only to notify his laws to Cairo, in practice Cromer notified him. In 1905 Cromer described the method precisely:

> The Ordinance is drafted by the Legal Secretary of the Soudan Government. . . . then sent by the Governor-General to me. I always send it to the Department of Justice, where it is fully examined by . . . the [British] Judicial Adviser. . . . If, as generally happens, some remarks have to be made, the draft Ordinance is then returned to Khartoum for reconsideration. It then comes back to me. If . . . I am satisfied with the changes which have been made, I cause the Ordinance to be submitted, by the Financial Adviser, to the Egyptian Council of Ministers. He then notifies to me their assent, or their observations if they have any to make. I then inform the Governor-General that the Ordinance may be issued. It

---

[9] Cromer to Kitchener, 19 January 1988, PRO 30/57/14.

[10] Cromer to Wingate, 25 January 1904, FO 633/8/390.

[11] Cromer to Wingate, 3 May 1904, FO 633/8/396.

is issued in the *"Soudan [sic] Gazette"*, and I send a copy to London.[12]

What Cromer claimed as Khartoum's defense against London's control Wingate and his subordinates saw as Cromer's personal interference. Cromer's hand was heavy; his lack of tact was defensible as businesslike and impersonal, but cannot always have been so received. In 1900 he drafted and dispatched the Sudan Government's *Annual Report* to London without even showing it to Wingate. In subsequent years Wingate drafted a report, which Cromer and his advisers amended, sometimes drastically, before submitting it, a procedure with which Wingate pretended to agree. Indeed in 1901 he invited Cromer to take a "red pencil" to the "many imperfections" of his "long-winded" draft, and he later thanked him for deleting comments about Kitchener: "I felt it incumbent on me to say something about my predecessor," he wrote, and was "much pleased" that Cromer had erased it.[13] Many such remarks adorn their correspondence. But Wingate put another view to Lord Edward Cecil in 1905: "I really believe he . . . would rather I wrote nothing but there are a few points I must bring out, even if he pigeon-holes them which is probable."[14]

Cromer involved himself in details of insignificant departments. He asked why scissors for cutting ostrich feathers could not be supplied the governor of Kordofan; he complained about, and recommended, textbooks used in the schools.[15] Among subjects recorded in Wingate's log of incoming correspondence with Cromer in 1904–05 are "Guard of Honour Dukes Visit"; "Land reclamation works"; "Annual Report"; "Dhurra ration"; "Table allowances"; "Evelyn name for paddle steamer"; "Locusts"; and sundry other points: sixty-six letters are entered under one official class alone.[16] One of many aides-memoires Wingate prepared for meetings with Cromer lists a score of topics, not all concerned with

---

[12] Cromer, "Soudan Legislation," 20 April 1905, FO 78/5430.

[13] Wingate to Cromer, 30 January 1901, SAD 270/1; 18 February 1901, SAD 271/2. See also Daly, *Empire*, 43–44.

[14] Wingate to Cecil, 10 January 1905, SAD 276/1.

[15] Cromer to Wingate, 9 February 1904, REPORTS 3/1/2; 3 February 1904, SAD 275/2.

[16] "From Lord Cromer. Contents," SAD 234/4.

"big questions."[17] Yet it was without irony that Cromer urged Wingate in 1906 to "abridge your telegrams somewhat; otherwise you will run up an enormous telegram bill."[18]

In other ways Cromer's interference was continuous and intense. He corresponded with Wingate's subordinates, and met them when they passed through Cairo. Wingate's own presence in Egypt, required annually for meetings about the budget and other matters, gave occasions for close consultation. Cairo's control of the Sudan budget allowed—or as Cromer put it, required—scrutiny of all aspects of policy. When Cromer complained about spending, Wingate apologized, referring to himself as Cromer's student, servant, agent, or "wakil." The following, from 1905, is one example of many:

> Your instructions will of course be carried out in their entirety. I do not for a moment question the absolute soundness of all you say. You naturally come down on what you consider dangerous to proper financial equilibrium and therein to my mind lies the value of the Cairo financial control. . . . You very kindly give me an amount of latitude and independence here which greatly facilitates my task but I hope that I never forget that my position here is rather that of a Lt. Gov. under you as Viceroy.[19]

A few weeks later Wingate honored Cromer with the name of a new Sudan Government steamer.[20] In this context Wingate's spelling of "Sudan" without the "o" that Cromer always used reveals assertiveness and small-mindedness as much as changing conventions.

There is no evidence that Wingate's manner raised his credit with Cromer, and some reason to suppose it reduced it. Willingness to adopt as his own any "principle" Cromer advanced left an impression of weakness and vacuity. Kitchener—devious, ambitious, and untrustworthy—had threatened Cromer's power in Egypt; Wingate's very pliancy devalued the expertise that had made his appointment a good one. But unlike Kitchener, Wingate had nowhere to turn in London for support; he had neither the means to afford dismissal nor the prospect of high employment elsewhere. Before retiring in 1907

---

[17] "Notes. Lord C.," 20 October 1905, SAD 234/4.

[18] Cromer to Wingate, 4 July 1906, SAD 279/1.

[19] Wingate to Cromer, 27 April 1905, SAD 276/4.

[20] The *Evelyn*. Wingate to Cromer, 10 May 1905, SAD 276/5; Cromer to Wingate, 16 May 1905, SAD 234/3.

Cromer told Grey, the foreign secretary: "Wingate has done very well in the Soudan. He is popular with his officers, and possesses considerable authority. . . . But I cannot conceal from myself the fact that he is very local, and has not got any firm grip of the main principles on which the Government of the Soudan, or indeed of any other country, has to be conducted. Also, he is ignorant as a child of everything connected with financial affairs."[21] Once again, and from afar, it was Sir Evelyn Wood who most accurately summarized Wingate's situation: "Twenty years ago," he wrote in 1902, "I never looked to your writing to me from a Palace! Perhaps some day you will sit on the Khedivial Throne. [But] I fancy his Lordship of the Norfolk watering place, has most of the power."[22]

Wingate's relations with subordinates resembled his own with Cromer. To be sure, an ingredient in his success was an essentially personal method. Although often unimaginatively correct, he disregarded channels to advise, befriend, and correspond informally with junior officials. Although at times pompously insistent on precedence, he had a hearty common touch. The inconsistency is less striking in one who rises from obscurity to high office; for soldiers unequal relations are normal. With Cromer Wingate did what he was told; to Evelyn Wood, his subordination was natural and filial, and no rivalry or tension could arise. With junior officers and officials he assumed a paternal role; he could afford informality because none doubted who was in command: in 1907 one young official remarked that "to criticise the Government there . . . is like giving your opinion on the Kaiser in Berlin."[23] Difficulty arose when precedence was unclear, as when military seniority left him inferior in some other way. Thus Maxwell, a fighting soldier, not a staff man, had to go; Jackson, beloved of the troops, was a threat. Slatin, however, an Austrian with useful connections but ineligible for highest office, became boon companion, and many younger officers, green but enthusiastic—as Wingate had been when Wood had taken him on—were carried along despite their failings.

Almost all high officials of the early Sudan Government were British officers seconded to the Egyptian army. All provincial governors and inspectors were officers, and mass resignations and transfers after the battle of Omdurman resulted in almost complete turnover in

---

[21] Cromer to Grey, 19 April 1907, FO 633/13/2. Cf. Cromer to Lansdowne, 19 January 1902, FO 633/6/336.

[22] 12 May 1902, SAD 272/2.

[23] F.C.C. Balfour to his mother, 14 January 1907, SAD 303/6.

the cadre. Wingate was able therefore to fill vacancies with men of his own choice, either from the depleted Anglo-Egyptian officer corps or directly from Britain. Some were personal friends, like Count Gleichen, whom he made Sudan Agent in Cairo, and Milo Talbot, director of surveys. Most were officers first, administrators second, and few remained when the period of secondment expired. The government thus had a military character in its official relations and methods of control, which were stronger than in a civilian regime. Bureaucratic continuity, however, was cut by the double-edged sword of secondment: while the government could dispense with an officer at the end of his contract, he always had the option to leave on a few months' notice. Even before the Omdurman mutiny, Cromer had joined in asking London to help keep experienced officers in the Sudan;[24] sudden replacement of seasoned Arabic-speakers by junior officers fresh from England was later generally agreed to have been a cause of that revolt.[25] Informed by visitors passing through Cairo, Cromer moreover concluded that even good officers were inevitably hampered by reliance on Egyptian and Sudanese intermediaries; mastering Arabic took time. The "only remedy," he decided, would be a civilian cadre "prepared to stay in the country and acquire a thorough knowledge of the language."[26] The result was recruitment, beginning in 1901, of British university graduates for posts in the civil service; later termed the Political Service, they worked mainly in administrative capacities in the provinces—as inspectors, later as *mudir*s, and eventually in high offices of the central government.

Far from creating the Political Service (which later gained fame as an elite corps), Wingate disliked the need for it, promoted members slowly, and tried to postpone demilitarization of the Sudan Government. In 1900 Maxwell had suggested that the civil secretary should be a civilian—all five of Wingate's successive appointments to the post were soldiers. He delayed appointment of the first civilian *mudir* until 1909. Even after civilian recruitment had been well-established, he continued to bring in officers at higher civil ranks, thus hampering civilians' advance and dampening morale. He justified this, and

---

[24] Cromer to Salisbury, 20 March 1899, Hatfield House MSS, 3M, A112/23.

[25] See, e.g., Jackson to Wingate, 4 March 1900, Hatfield House MSS, 3M, A112/113.

[26] Cromer to Salisbury, 8 June 1900, FO 633/6/325. Cf. Ronald Wingate, *Wingate*, 134.

a preference for officers generally, by arguing that the dual nature of his own and *mudirs'* posts made civilian appointments inefficient. Yet it was he, strongly backed by Slatin, who insisted on retaining the dual system, even when officers had been so far removed from military affairs as to be civilians in all but name. In 1902 he wrote that merely to discuss separation of civil and military functions "would result in confusion and chaos."[27] Wingate's rationalizations do not ring true; he feared separation of his own dual role as sirdar and governor-general. Only the First World War and its demand for soldiers made the Sudan Government irrevocably civilian in its upper echelons.[28]

The central government under Wingate had three secretaries; civil, financial, and legal. The financial secretary was important because the Financial Regulations and Cairo's supervision gave him a degree of independence from the governor-general. Soon after taking office Wingate, in consultation with Cromer, appointed E. E. Bernard, who was a thorn in his side ever after. Under Cromer, Bernard interfered in all areas of government; under Cromer's successors he was brought under greater control. The nature of the post condemned him to difficult relations with Wingate. Moreover Bernard was Maltese and a Catholic, enough in the world of British officialdom to provide pretexts for disagreement. Notably open-minded in this respect, Wingate could not resist holding Bernard's background against him in political disputes; he tried to forge with others a bond of shared dislike. Wingate's correspondence is replete with references to Bernard's failure to "see things like an ordinary Englishman": if Bernard "had only been anything else but what he is," then all would have been well; "Et hoc genus omne," was the tag he used to deride Bernard to Cecil, whose own "attitude towards Bernard's 'Israelitistic'" qualities he in turn criticized to others.[29] A 1905 letter to Cromer is so laden with motives as to defy classification: "for a number of years," Wingate wrote, "I have been almost the only supporter he [Bernard] has had. I long ago recognised his sterling financial qualities but of course his methods and his natal origin have been against him and you know far better than I do how diffi-

---

[27] Wingate to Cromer, 23 May 1902, SAD 272/2.

[28] See Daly, *Empire,* 82–91. For Slatin's views see, e.g., Slatin to Wingate, 15 March 1908, SAD 282/3/1.

[29] Wingate to Cecil, 20 August 1905, SAD 277/2; Wingate to Phipps, 14 August 1904, SAD 275/6.

cult it is to get the average English gentleman to submit to somewhat Levantine methods."[30]

Yet Wingate was no virulent racist: he enjoyed the very "Levantine" company he seemed to disdain; his friend Slatin was an Austrian Jew. Rather, Wingate played on the prejudices of others when it served his personal or political purpose. Occasionally this caused difficulty, as when an anti-Semitic remark to a Muslim audience was publicized in 1914. To what extent correspondents recoiled at his vulgarity rather than warming to his overtures cannot be gauged.

Wingate's relations with the other two secretaries were less complicated. He was served by a succession of civil secretaries whose records support the view that he saw strong subordinates as rivals. Two nonetheless stand out, P. R. Phipps (1905–14) and L.O.F. Stack (1914–16). The duties of the post evolved to encompass aspects of civil administration that were not assigned elsewhere. Phipps became a personal friend, Stack a trusted confidant. The third secretaryship, the legal, was the only one occupied by a civilian under Wingate. This was Edgar Bonham Carter, whom Wingate inherited from Kitchener. While he was instrumental in establishing the Sudan Government's legal system, his impact beyond the department appears to have been slight, and his relations with Wingate were warm.

The most interesting of Wingate's appointments was Slatin's. Like the position of Sudan Agent in Cairo (to which he appointed several well-connected friends), that of Inspector-General of the Sudan was invented by Wingate himself; he created it for Slatin, who had left the army after Karari because of Kitchener's dislike. Duties were spelled out, and in the early years Slatin made long treks in the provinces. In no other post did the Sudan Government so closely approach the "Oriental" methods it was meant to eschew, for Slatin had scores to settle, debts to repay, and prejudices to act upon in matters of policy. Contemporary evidence of unease about Slatin's conduct is far from general, though later accounts make it clear. Wingate insisted that he needed Slatin's advice, the product of unequaled experience during the Mahdiyya. In fact, their relations were mutually beneficial, Wingate providing a well-paid position to Slatin's liking, while Slatin played the adjunct whose legendary exploits admitted Wingate to European circles otherwise closed. By 1914 the social side

---

[30] Wingate to Cromer, 27 April 1905, SAD 276/4.

of Slatin's life had eclipsed the official, and murmurs were heard of redundancy. That he was trapped in Europe when war was declared was in retrospect fortunate for all concerned.[31]

The policies of the Sudan Government under Wingate evolved as resources, necessity, and officials dictated. That Cromer controlled "big questions" is certain, but does not mean that Wingate disagreed. Over religious policy they differed little, over taxation not at all. In military matters Cromer's interest was lightly felt. Wingate wisely deferred to Cairo in the minefield of international affairs—relations with neighboring territories, control of Nile waters, the status of Europeans in the Sudan. But Cromer's putting Egypt first inevitably led to disagreement over economic policy. His insistence on continuity and expertise—not Wingate's genius for administration—led to creation of the civilian Political Service. It is important finally to note that Cromer's interest is not itself proof that his wishes were carried out.

The tacit bargain of condominium was that the British ruled while the Egyptians paid. Until 1913 the Sudan's annual budget was balanced only through Egyptian subventions totaling over £E5m. During the same period development loans, for railway and telegraph construction, the building of Port Sudan, and many other projects, amounted to another £E5.4m. Since the subvention was negotiable annually, and reflected not only what the Sudan needed but what Egypt could afford, Cromer and his financial officials had good reason for supervision. The Sudan Government had no alternative: Britain refused to contribute, and the Sudan was poor. Cromer, for economic reasons, and Wingate, concerned with political consequences, agreed on a policy of low taxation. Not until 1909 did the government's annual revenue exceed £E1m, and although changes were made in the system, the principle remained sacrosanct. Enforcement of the Financial Regulations thus involved scrutiny from Cairo and conflict between Wingate and Bernard, the financial secretary. Willing economy was as uncharacteristic of Wingate in government as it was in private life, and when these overlapped, trouble resulted.

---

[31] Slatin's appointment may have been suggested by Cromer: See Cromer to Salisbury, 8 June 1900, FO 633/6/325.

In light of Cairo's control credit must be given Wingate for the size of Egypt's contribution. In winning this his main weapon was the "recrudescence" of Mahdism—the threat that "fanatical" Sudanese would rise again unless some policy or project, unfortunately costly, were undertaken. Egypt was in the Sudan, the argument ran, to protect its own southern borders; better to buy peace through Sudanese contentment than through constant resort to arms. Many civilian projects were thus defended as essential for security. A railway extension to open up Kordofan was justified by a need to bring turbulent western tribes under closer control. Mosque-construction, tax-forgiveness, subsidies for the pilgrimage to Mecca, land grants and special privileges for notables, even costly public works in the Three Towns of Khartoum, Khartoum North, and Omdurman were similarly linked to security rather than admitted as domestic spending. Cairo, and more so London, in political self-defense if a rising ever *did* take place, heeded Wingate's warnings, backed as these were by his (and Slatin's) vaunted expertise. Nor was Wingate above wheedling, misrepresentation, and inspired bookkeeping.

In any case the results of the period are impressive. Most of the Sudan's railway system was built during Wingate's governor-generalship. The telegraph system was a creation of his early years. Wingate was the main proponent of a new deep-sea harbor on the Red Sea to replace outdated Suakin; the result was named Port Sudan—Cromer having suggested Port Wingate, Wingate having preferred Port Cromer—and officially opened by the khedive in 1909. At considerable cost and with great human labor the *sudd*, vegetation blocking the Upper Nile and other southern rivers, was cleared and regular steamer traffic inaugurated. These expensive projects were made possible by Egyptian loans and subventions, won by Wingate in weeks of negotiation every year.

A similar case of Cairo's useful involvement in a "big question" and Wingate's implementation concerns the Sudan's legal system. Foundations—a penal code and code of criminal procedure—were laid in Cairo by W. E. Brunyate, legal adviser to the Egyptian government; Bonham Carter drafted the Civil Justice Ordinance. The difficult, time-consuming, and sensitive work of land settlement was a major accomplishment of the Wingate years. The basis for a regime of Islamic law was laid by ordinance in 1902. That these and other major reforms were enacted without serious disruption, and that they remained basic to the Sudan's legal system even after independence, testifies to the achievement of their authors.

Another issue with economic as well as religious aspects, and involving Cairo as well as Khartoum (and London) was labor, or more precisely slavery and the slave trade. Wingate was aware—perhaps to the point of uncritical reliance on old certainties—that Egyptian attempts to end the slave trade had won support for the Mahdi's revolt in the 1880s. It was, however, one of the new regime's stated purposes to eradicate the trade and free unwilling slaves; European eyes, including the Anti-Slavery Society's in Britain, watched. But Wingate and most British officials believed that the Sudan's recovery depended on agriculture, which required that labor remain on the land. This view was buttressed by the stigma attached to slaves and ex-slaves. Slatin called them "god-forsaken swine," blacks lazy by nature, who if freed would become thieves and prostitutes, a drag on the economy rather than an engine.[32] In no area did the Sudan's remoteness better serve its government's purpose. Europe was assured of determination to end slavery, while Wingate fought to control (in order to weaken) the Egyptian government's department for the suppression of the slave trade: this, after a decade of controversy, he succeeded in doing in 1911. For Wingate slavery was a problem of public relations, not morality, an indigenous institution sanctioned by Muslim law, the abolition of which courted risk of violent Sudanese reaction in exchange for no benefit to government, masters, or even slaves themselves. Cromer fully supported him.[33] Reports to London were vague, laced with misleading statistics, or simply false. His comment to Cromer in 1907, when forwarding a new circular on slavery, sums up the prevailing attitude: it had been so worded that "if it ever became necessary to publish our arrangements, we could, without much fear of difficulty, publish this document as it stands."[34] Nor did that attitude change subsequently, a conclusion reflected in a scandal that beset the Sudan Government a generation later.

Overarching Wingate's views on slavery, taxation, internal security, education, and many other questions, was the importance he attached to religion. Every area of administration had a religious aspect. In this more than in any other way, the policy that evolved from Wingate's experience survived his tenure as governor-general and helped to shape the modern history of the Sudan. Fifteen years of Wingate's life had been absorbed in defeating the Mahdist state;

---

[32] Slatin to Bigge, 6 September 1897, SAD 238/653. See also Slatin to Wingate, 27 January 1900, SAD 270/1/1.

[33] See Cromer to Salisbury, 10 February 1899, FO 633/6/309.

[34] Wingate to Cromer, 30 January 1907, SAD 280/1.

notwithstanding triumphal telegrams after Umm Diwaykarat, Mahdism was not dead. His policy toward the cult was suppression: its texts were proscribed; its surviving notables remained in prison or under restriction; the Mahdi's tomb, desecrated by Kitchener in 1898, was left in ruins. Mahdist eschatology predicted the Second Coming of Jesus; claimants to the mantle were hunted down, executed, or locked up, as were revivalists. Although popular support of these was limited or non-existent, they reminded the British of Sudanese susceptibility, and were used to remind Cairo and London of the need to support Khartoum's budget requests. In creating an image Wingate thus drew a fine line between a popular administration in confident control and a lonely band of foreigners governing by "bluff" a host of die-hard fanatics

To check the appeal of Mahdism, and of the Islamic mysticism whence it seemed to have arisen, Wingate upheld orthodoxy and cultivated responsible notables. In 1901 he created a board of *Ulama* in order to give a Muslim stamp of approval to the government's acts.[35] A grand *qadi* presided over Shari'a courts; a *mufti* of the Sudan duly approved government innovations. Friday, not Sunday, was made a day of rest. The pilgrimage to Mecca was facilitated at government expense. Mosques were subsidized but left free from interference. Significantly, *sufi shaykhs* willing to cooperate were treated with respect, and a few with great honor: Sayyid Ali al-Mirghani, whose family's Khatmiyya *tariqa* had opposed the Mahdi, reemerged as the leading religious notable.

Quieting Sudanese Islam meant offending the Church Militant. In this Wingate was at one with Cromer. Both saw in the Mahdiyya a reaction against the European Christians who had implemented unpopular policies of the old regime. Even before the battle of Omdurman, British missionary societies and others were eager to memorialize Gordon through rapid proselytization in the Sudan. Wingate supplied local arguments, backed by undoubted expertise, that Cromer used diplomatically to deflect pressure. They delayed appointment of European clergymen, creation of an Anglican bishopric, even the opening of mission schools in the Muslim north.[36]

---

[35] Wingate to Cromer, 13 June 1901, SAD 271/6.

[36] See, e.g., Cromer to Salisbury, 2 February 1899, FO 633/6 /308; to Bishop Blyth, 8 February 1900, FO 633/8/254 and 23 February 1900, FO 633/8/256; and to Gwynn, 13 March 1903, FO 633/8/351.

With unimagined results they prevented missionary activity altogether among Muslims, instead allowing it among the non-Muslims of the South. Mindful of European rivalries rather than Sudanese welfare, Wingate designated a "sphere" for each denomination or missionary society. Pressure for access to Northern Muslims was met by reminders of insufficient effort among the pagans of the South.

There was one object for which Cairo's support, essential in the areas of slavery, missionary activity, and much else, could not be invoked, for it contradicted Cromer's own policy: despite Wingate's deference, in many ways he worked to separate the Sudan from Egypt. When Cromer angrily called attention to this "tendency," Wingate invoked ignorance, error, excessive enthusiasm, faulty communication. But just as the ties between Egypt and the Sudan were strong, so were the ways in which existing differences could be enhanced and new ones created. The Condominium Agreement itself was a two-sided coin, for it exempted the Sudan from Egyptian laws and international treaties as applied in Egypt. Some degree of independence was therefore necessary in, for instance, postal regimes, application of international conventions, and foreign credit; the number and variety of these increased over time. Partly for financial reasons Wingate established an officers' training course at Khartoum, and new battalions of Sudanese (and, for the first time, Arab, that is, northern Muslim), soldiers, the nucleus of the separate army created in 1925. Port Sudan and the Atbara-Red Sea railway eclipsed the Nile route through Egypt. In the name of security, the Egyptian press was heavily censored in the Sudan. The hatred Sudanese supposedly bore Egyptians was used to justify everything from the training of local replacements for government posts to restrictions on Egyptian visitors. The British side of condominium was emphasized, as much as was possible in the light of Egypt's financial support. Even economic development, specifically later cotton-growing schemes, had as one object the independence of the Sudan from Egypt. It is difficult therefore to separate out the results of Wingate's and his officials' efforts from those that past and future social and economic developments would anyway have produced. But there is ample reason to suppose that a formal policy, actively pursued, to strengthen rather than weaken Egypt's historic ties would not have culminated in the creation of an independent Sudan.

Chapter Seventeen
Master

During the early years as sirdar and governor-general Wingate developed a pattern of work and style of life that would affect not only the rest of his career but also the history of the Nile Valley countries. Despite Cairo's control—the practical effects of which ebbed even in Cromer's time, and rapidly thereafter—Wingate enjoyed in many ways almost a free hand in Khartoum. Military matters, especially those limited to the Sudan (where most of the Egyptian army was stationed), gave him great latitude. In provincial affairs Cairo's interest was usually piqued only by controversy, and was then as ephemeral as the dust that collected on its expressions. Wingate and Slatin had made careers of secrecy, and the outside world, even Cairo, was far away. Most importantly, the advent of a new regime assigned fortuitously to Wingate the role of setting precedents, and thus of creating, often routinely, models by which history would judge his successors.

Wingate undertook with relish the public side of his duties. Twenty years as adjutant, assistant, and deputy, as adviser, planner, indeed prompter to powerful chiefs had readied him for the perquisites of office. Obeisance to Cromer in Cairo rarely checked viceregal pretensions in Khartoum. The energy and enthusiasm that characterized Wingate's whole life were moreover now given new scope. His first years in the Sudan appeared to involve constant motion between Khartoum and the provinces, the Sudan and Egypt, the Nile Valley and Europe. For this period Wingate's and his wife's commonplace books provide a detailed record, and illustrate his energy, interests, and the sudden change in circumstances that his appointment involved.

After the Omdurman mutiny in 1900 Wingate, ill with pneumonia, went on leave to England. While there he was summoned to Balmoral, and later accompanied the khedive to Windsor and to court functions in London. His holiday in Scotland, spent mainly at Dunbar, was marked by the award of the freedom of the borough.

He returned to the Sudan in November, his wife accompanying him to Khartoum for the first time. A month later Cromer arrived for Christmas at the Palace, his first visit during Wingate's tenancy. A week after Cromer left, the guest quarters were occupied by Princess Henry of Battenberg and Princess Beatrice of Saxe-Coburg, first in the long line of royal visitors distinguishing Wingate's regime. Another hallmark, frequent provincial tours, began in January 1901, when Wingate left, by camel, for El Obeid, a journey that took ten days. He returned to Khartoum via al-Duaym on 18 February, and only a week later was off again, for the eastern Sudan. He visited Abu Haraz on 28 February, Gadaref on 6 March, Gallabat on the eleventh, and Kassala, via Gadaref, Seti, and Tomat, on the twenty-first. On 3 April Wingate reached Suakin, where he embarked for Egypt. He spent three weeks there with his wife (who had traveled by the Nile route), and saw her off for England before leaving for Khartoum on 1 May. The dates of his own leave that year are uncertain; he traveled via Egypt and Marseilles, and after an audience with the king in London joined his family at Dunbar.[1]

By 1902 a pattern was emerging. In February Wingate inspected the army's artillery camp at Wad Ban Naqa, then welcomed the Egyptian war minister before leaving for the Upper Nile on the twenty-second, a tour that took him to Gondokoro and back by 12 March. After a week in Khartoum he went to Cairo, returning to the Sudan on 13 April. By late May Wingate was in Egypt again, en route to the coronation of King Edward VII, but the king's sudden illness forced postponement, and an outbreak of cholera in Cairo recalled Wingate to Egypt. In October, back in Khartoum, Wingate received Lord Kitchener, who formally opened the Gordon Memorial College on 27 October and remained until 19 November. Wingate then went to Egypt with his wife for inauguration of the Aswan Dam on 10 December; they returned to Khartoum on the fourteenth. After Christmas Wingate took a large party, including Lord and Lady Cromer, to the Upper Nile as far as Gondokoro; they returned to Khartoum on 27 January. With the Cromers Wingate then attended army exercises for four days.[2]

In March 1903 Wingate took his wife and daughter to Cairo, saw them off for England, then returned to Khartoum via the Dongola

---

[1] Wingate's Bible; CB1; CB2.
[2] CB1.

Reach. He visited Dongola and Marawi, Berber for the annual agricultural show, then Shendi and al-Damir, before reaching Khartoum
on 14 April. Two weeks later he left for a tour of the Gezira, inspecting Masid, Kamlin, and Rufaa on 28–30 April, and al-Masallamiyya
on 1 May. He spent 2–4 May at Wad Medani, Birtingayil, and
Manaqil, reached al-Duaym on the sixth, and returned to Khartoum
on the seventh. A week later he left for Cairo where, having finally
given up his house, he stayed with Lord Cromer at the British Agency.
Wingate went on leave on 6 June, reached England on the twelfth
and Dunbar, by now his summer home, on the eighteenth. From
there he attended the king's dinner for the khedive on 29 June, a
royal ball for President Loubet on 6 July, the Prince of Wales's ball on
the thirteenth, and other social events before returning to Dunbar.
There Wingate, an avid golfer (with a handicap of eighteen), won the
Roxburghe gold cross and other prizes, and was made captain of the
Dunbar Golf Club. In late September he and his wife went to
Traunkirchen in Austria to stay with Slatin, departing for Egypt via
Trieste on the twenty-ninth. They had two weeks at Alexandria,
where the Egyptian court spent the summer, then left for Cairo and
Khartoum.[3]

The 1903–04 round of inspections began, remarkably, only a
week later, when with his wife Wingate left Khartoum by steamer on
28 November up the Blue Nile. They visited Wad Medani, Sinnar,
Singa, Abu Nama, Rusayris, and Dinder before returning to Khartoum
on 9 December. Early in January they welcomed to the Palace (again)
Princesses Henry of Battenberg and Beatrice of Saxe-Coburg, Lord
William Cecil and his wife, and Mustafa Pasha Fahmi, the Egyptian
minister. On 1 March the Wingates left for Cairo. Lady Wingate
departed for England on the nineteenth, and Wingate started back to
Khartoum the next day. On 15 April he attended the agricultural show
and camel races at Berber, and the next day visited the railhead of the
Atbara-Red Sea line. After inspecting, by steamer, Umtiur, al-Damir,
Aliab, and Shandi, Wingate traveled by camel to Massawarat, Naga,
Dura, and Soba on 16–23 April. He returned to Khartoum to welcome General Slade, G.O.C. Egypt, and Sir William Garstin on the
twenty-seventh. On 15 May Wingate began a long tour of the White
Nile and Sobat, visiting Kodok (the re-named Fashoda) on the twentieth and Tawfiqiyya on the twenty-first, whence he steamed up the

---

[3] Ibid.

Sobat. He toured the American mission at Doleib Hill and Nassir post on 23 May, traveled up the Pibor past Khor Jokau to Itang on the Baro River, which he reached on the twenty-fifth, and visited Ideni, an Anuak village, before returning to the Nile. He inspected the Austrian mission at Lul on the twenty-eighth, Melut on the twenty-ninth, and Renk on the thirtieth, returning to Khartoum on 1 June. Less than a fortnight later Wingate went to Cairo on leave; he arrived in London on 1 July. After a few days he went to Dunbar. Leave was punctuated by several visits to London and elsewhere: on 14 July the Wingates dined with the Prince of Wales and the khedive, and on the sixteenth Wingate had an audience with the king. He and his wife left for Egypt (via Vienna and a brief visit to Slatin) on 27 September. Wingate returned to the Sudan at the end of October.[4]

The 1904–05 season began remarkably when Wingate set out for the remote Bahr al-Ghazal four days after returning from leave. The journey from Khartoum to Wau took eleven days. There a "durbar" was held with local notables. After a dinner with British officers about to leave on an expedition against the Azande prince Yambio, Wingate left Wau on 19 November and reached Khartoum on the twenty-seventh. In early December the G.O.C. Egypt and his party stayed at the Palace and with Wingate observed maneuvers outside Khartoum. From 28 December to 17 January Prince Leopold of Battenberg visited, then the duke and duchess of Connaught and their daughters arrived for a week. Two days after they left, Wingate was off via Atbara to Kassala and then, via railhead and Suakin, by sea to Egypt. He saw off his wife, who had traveled by the Nile route, on 24 February, then returned to Khartoum. A long bout of insomnia, Wingate's lifelong affliction, ensued, and may explain a lapse in activity. He left for annual leave on 28 May, visiting the Atbara railhead (then ninety-seven miles from the Nile) en route, and after only three days in Egypt sailed for Trieste and the first of what would be annual "cures," this time at Marienbad, where Lady Wingate joined him. They went to London on 25–26 June and then to Oxford, where Wingate received a D.C.L. degree, lunched at All Souls, and dined at Christ Church, where he gave a speech. Wingate won the Merchants' Cup at Dunbar that summer, a relatively quiet one, and with his wife and daughter returned to Cairo at the beginning of October.[5]

---

[4] CB1; CB2.

[5] CB1.

A tour immediately upon return from leave had by now become customary, and soon after arriving in Khartoum on 6 November Wingate was up the Blue Nile. On 15–19 November he visited Wad Madani, Sinnar, Singa, and Rusayris, and returned to Khartoum on the twenty-second. In mid-December Prince Leopold again came to stay, a visit so unremarkable that neither Wingate nor his wife recorded a departure. On 23 January they left for Port Sudan where, on the twenty-seventh, the Nile-Red Sea railway was inaugurated. They returned to Khartoum on the twenty-ninth with Lord Cromer. A series of private visitors occupied February. On 6 March Wingate left for Karima, where he opened the rail line to Abu Hamad before proceeding to Cairo. There he greeted the Prince and Princess of Wales on 29 March, and dined with them at Abdin Palace on the thirty-first. His wife left for Europe on 7 April, and Wingate returned to the Sudan, attending the Damir agricultural show en route. After three weeks in Khartoum, Wingate went on long leave; he met his wife at Marienbad on 28 June. This "cure" lasted a month, and they returned to England on 24 July. Wingate had his usual audience with the king on the twenty-sixth, attended a meeting of the Imperial Defence Committee, then went to Dunbar for two months. After visiting Balmoral in late September, Wingate returned via Vienna to Cairo and, after an unusually brief stop, reached Khartoum on 9 November.[6]

The autumn tour, this year to Kordofan, began on 20 November, and took Wingate to Bara, El Obeid, the Mahdist battlefield of Shaykhan, al-Rahad, Habila, Umm Ruaba, Umm Diwaykarat, where he had defeated the khalifa in 1899, and, via Kosti and Kawa, back to Khartoum on 11 December. In January Wingate's steamer, the *Abbas,* struck a rock in Sabaluka Gorge and collided with a wreck. Proceeding, he visited Geili to see the aged Zubayr Pasha before returning to Khartoum. On 3 February the duke of Brunswick arrived at the Palace for a fortnight, and on the seventh Grand Duke Boris. On the twenty-second Wingate went to Wad ban Naqa, returning to Khartoum on the twenty-fourth to more European tourists. He left for Cairo on 1 March and visited the Dongola Reach on his way back, arriving in Khartoum on 2 April. On the twenty-fourth he was off again to Cairo, and was present at the Opera House on 4 May for Cromer's farewell speech; on the sixth Cromer left for Europe,

---

[6] Ibid.

Wingate for the Sudan. He now went briefly to Erkowit in the Red
Sea Hills, which would become the Sudan Government's "hill station" and his warm-weather home. He went to Port Sudan and
Suakin on 14–16 May, then returned experimentally by automobile to
Erkowit for a few days. By the twenty-second he was in Khartoum, to
stay but two weeks before long leave. Between March 1906 and May
1907 Wingate thus went from Khartoum to Cairo—a five-day trip—
five times.[7]

This catalogue of arrivals and departures (which excludes day-
trips, sightseeing, and numerous overnight stays) leads to conclusions
about Wingate and the Sudan Government during a formative phase.
That he spent half or more of each year outside the Sudan indicates
the connection between Egypt and the Sudan and something of how
he viewed his duties. That even so much of his time in the Sudan was
spent away from Khartoum is remarkable. Inspection was valuable,
but repeated visits to towns accessible by steamer, often with a group
of European guests in tow, suggest personal rather than official
motives.[8] Provincial officials complained about the waste of time and
money. An officer's simple inspection of a White Nile district in 1901
cost £E750;[9] Wingate's tours were unavoidably more elaborate. A
mudir typically accompanied the governor-general in his province or
steamed ahead to greet him officially at each stop: two steamers were
therefore needed. Once, Wingate had to insist that the *mudir* of the
Upper Nile meet him as he steamed through: "inspection" having
been revealed as a facade for official tourism, the governor claimed
more important work to do; in the event he failed to appear, and had
to apologize.[10]

To what extent government business was hindered by Wingate's
traveling court is debatable. Certainly inconvenience was involved for
Khartoum officials. Whether at Gondokoro or Dunbar, El Obeid or
Marienbad, Wingate was in frequent—but not constant—telegraphic
touch with Khartoum and Cairo. In Cairo the Sudan Agency provided
a headquarters; in London an office performed similar functions when

---

[7] CB1; F.C.C. Balfour to his mother, 26 March and 17 April 1907, SAD 303/6.
[8] For favorable comments see, e.g., *The memoirs of Babikr Bedri*, 2, London 1980, 153.
[9] Fergusson to Wingate, 16 June 1902, SAD 272/4/2.
[10] Wingate to Matthews, 1 May 1904, SAD 275/4; Matthews to Wingate, 31 July 1904, SAD 275/5.

needed; at Dunbar officials came and went, staying at hotels and test-
ing the capacity of the local post office. Civilian and military secretaries
usually accompanied Wingate; on long trips a cipher clerk, Arabic secretary, Egyptian and British A.D.C.s, a military escort, and an array of
military and civilian servants went too, at great expense. High officials—one or another of the three secretaries, directors of departments
(lands, forests, game preservation, and so forth), Slatin Pasha—were
often brought along on provincial tours.[11] Their and Wingate's duties
in Khartoum fell to "acting" officials, who naturally dealt only with
routine matters; other questions pended or formed the substance of
dense telegraphic traffic. Complicated and generous leave arrangements left junior officers "acting" for even the highest officials. Once
Wingate was shocked to find that the legal secretary, a civilian, was pre-
sumed acting sirdar; at times it was difficult in retrospect to know who
had "acted" for whom—fortunately no crisis had demanded urgent
assertion of claims.

    At Khartoum itself Wingate's grand manner was evident from the
start, and soon became notorious. In 1901 Cromer got wind of his
wish for a "state coach"; it was "utterly unsuitable—indeed, ridicu-
lous—for the Sudan," he wrote, and the plan was apparently
dropped.[12] But Wingate went ahead with a "state barge," built locally;
this was a "yacht" (actually a steam launch) used mainly to ferry
Wingate and guests around the Three Towns.[13] He justified these
vehicles as needed if the khedive were to visit Khartoum, but as
Cromer pointed out, the khedive could ride,[14] and in any case the
British wished to prevent rather than dignify khedivial visits. In
Khartoum a large steamer was also kept for Wingate's use, and he
later added a converted tugboat (for Red Sea inspections and trips to
Egypt) to the gubernatorial fleet. Since all Wingate's travel in Egypt
and the Sudan was official, questions arose over expense, but not over
the necessity for the travel itself.

    More awkward were the affairs and expenses that even Wingate
termed "social." Until 1903 he kept a rented house in Cairo—
"Maison Rollo." He then hinted that, as sirdar, he needed a house

---

[11] See, e.g., "Diary of tour of inspection of White and Upper Nile stations, January
    9th to 27th. 1903," SAD 273/1.
[12] Cromer to Wingate, 20 June 1901, SAD 271/7.
[13] Watson to Wingate, 15 July 1901, SAD 271/7.
[14] Cromer to Wingate, 1 August 1901, SAD 271/8.

but could not afford the lease. Cromer dodged the hint: "Pray get rid of your Cairo house," he wrote. "I could never understand why you kept it up. You are not under the smallest obligation to entertain in Cairo and even in Khartoum."[15]

Indeed, much of Wingate's time in Khartoum was already occupied in what he called "social duties." In reminding him that he had no such duties Cromer missed—or perhaps evaded—the point. Partly through Wingate's and Slatin's efforts the Sudan was becoming a winter destination of European society. The "hospitality" Cromer disdained was for Wingate an end in itself. His frequent complaints about the necessity and expense of entertaining European royalty and others do not ring true. In 1905, after winning an additional £E500 per year entertainment allowance Wingate told Sir Vincent Corbett, then financial adviser to the Egyptian government: "These personal matters are always disagreeable and I have a special repugnance in coming *in forma pauperis* to you and Lord Cromer. . . . [But] the expenses of this appointment have grown with the growth of the place and it was as much as I could do to make both ends meet. . . . I know I am thought by some to be unecessarily [*sic*] lavish and even extravagant, but I must repudiate these charges. . . ."[16] Wingate argued that Khartoum's hotel was so poor that he had no choice but to entertain prominent visitors: "These Royalties are indeed cadgers," he told Cromer, "but what could one do?"[17] His wife echoed him: personal household expenses at the Palace were £9 per day in 1905, including the salaries of European cooks engaged solely in anticipation of important guests.[18]

Yet Wingate, aided by Slatin, continued to issue invitations and, when these were accepted, to provide hospitality at his own and the government's expense. Free transport, even private use of government steamers, was commonly granted. Justifications, when needed, were flimsy: politicians and high nobility would, it was hoped, sing the Sudan's praises in Europe and help the country economically. On several occasions there were medical emergencies: in March 1904 Wingate lent a steamer to take Prince Leopold to Cairo; he hoped Cromer would think him right to "say nothing of the cost of the trip,"

---

[15] Wingate to Cromer, 16 April 1903; Cromer to Wingate, 21 April 1903, SAD 273/4.
[16] 24 April 1905, SAD 276/4.
[17] 27 April 1905, SAD 276/4.
[18] Lady Wingate to Wingate, 27 April 1905, SAD 276/5.

which he proposed "to charge to the Sudan Government."[19] In 1905 Wingate invited the Prince of Wales; Cromer intervened, and no visit took place.[20] There was so much social activity that Slatin, whose frequent dinners at "Rowdy House" were reportedly the best in Khartoum, joked of a Sudan "season"; during the winter of 1908–09 Phipps, the civil secretary, himself entertained at dinners 170 people. More damaging than "cadgers" in Khartoum were their travels to the provinces, notably the Upper Nile, where they wasted officials' time, monopolized much-needed steamers and wood supplies, and were generally a nuisance.[21] Despite constant complaints by the governor, G. E. Matthews, Wingate allowed, indeed encouraged, tourists. "I fear I have been able to do little or nothing for all your various friends," an exasperated Matthews wrote in 1908, "about whom telegrams, letters, and notes of introduction have reached me." "Some unknown admirer of mine lurks at Khartoum who raises delusive hopes in many tourists' hearts."[22] Wingate ignored the sarcasm; one conciliatory reply reveals the extent to which his interest differed from his governor's:

> I am afraid that you have been rather inundated with tourists and others. I am always most reluctant to give them notes of introduction . . . , but you will see from the enclosed letter from M. Achille Fould (the French multi-millionaire) how very much he appreciated his reception at Renk. I am sure also that you will have found the Duke of Brunswick a very nice and agreeable fellow. . . . I much sympathise with you in the failure of the Shilluks to turn out when Winston Churchill passed through, but . . . they quite made up for their failure . . . by giving such an interesting show to the Duchess D'Aosta. . . . She will . . . be terribly distressed when she gets the news of the assassination of the King of Portugal and her nephew.[23]

A change in policy took place in 1905 after Cairo complained of an expensive visit by the duke and duchess of Connaught. Wingate acknowledged "a heavy drain on ones [*sic*] all too slender purse," but rather than "create a very disagreeable situation" he preferred "to fork out." (Cromer objected particularly to fireworks; Wingate

---

[19] Wingate to Cromer, 29 March 1904, SAD 275/3.

[20] Cromer to Wingate, 2 July 1905, SAD 234/4.

[21] See Daly, *Empire*, 99–104.

[22] Matthews to Wingate, 10 February 1908, SAD 282/2.

[23] Wingate to Matthews, 7 February 1908, SAD 282/2.

argued their value for government "prestige," but admitted the argument was not "very conclusive.")[24] It was agreed that thenceforth only official visits would be charged to the government: what Wingate called "ordinary royalties" would in future "pay for their tickets and food in the Sudan."[25] Costs of a trip by Prince Leopold, already under way, were split: the Sudan Government paid for his outward journey and Wingate himself for the prince's food on the return leg.[26]

Wingate's was a Sunday-morning conversion. In 1906 Cromer was "horrified to get a proposal from the Soudan Government that the relations of officers . . . who come out as tourists in the winter should be allowed to travel at 75 per cent. lower than the ordinary rates." The general financial situation was "extremely serious,"[27] yet Khartoum worried about tourist discounts! Wingate's true view of the "tourist problem" is evident in the fact that, following Cromer's retirement in 1907, travel to Khartoum only grew.

Wingate reveled in ceremony, as accessories to which European notables were invaluable. In 1898 the ruins of Gordon's palace had lain forlornly on the overgrown bank of the Blue Nile; by 1905 the society that revolved around Wingate's Palace astonished European visitors. After his first winter there, in 1900–01, Wingate had ordered emergency renovations to make it habitable; he had found a "palace" without lights or running water, and littered with the crated furniture he and others had sent from Cairo at Kitchener's command.[28] The Palace soon became, and remained until 1956, the focal point of the Anglo-Egyptian state.

The colonial Sudan's official ritual and social etiquette were largely creations of Wingate and his wife. While he presided over, indeed devised, state occasions, she established the domestic and social routine of a government house, and set the tone of expatriate society. A stickler for military detail and a student of precedence, Wingate arranged guards of honor, anthems, flags, "levees" and "durbars," inaugurals, and "illuminations"; his wife, a "great Victorian lady" (in her son's phrase), decided who should be received, where, and how, policed

---

[24] Wingate to Cecil, 6 January 1905, SAD 276/1.
[25] Wingate to Corbett, 27 May 1905, SAD 276/5.
[26] Wingate to Bernard, 4 May 1905, SAD 234/3.
[27] Cromer to Wingate, 16 April 1906, SAD 278/4.
[28] Maxwell to Wingate, 15 January 1900, SAD 270/1/1; Friend to Wingate, n.d. (August 1901), SAD 271/8.

church attendance, established dress codes, and, in an increasingly civilian government, imported or inspired those modifications of social
intercourse she deemed proper in the Sudan. The major's wife whose
"impertinent" Cairene servants had laughed at her in 1890[29] was by
1905 a formidable figure in her own right. With Society came its rules
and restraints: formal calls and the leaving of cards, dressing for dinner,
signing the Palace visitor's book and attending Sunday teas. In 1903 a
young official's wife described Lady Wingate as "very nice, kind, gra-
cious etc. but a very 'proper' person. High necked dresses must be
worn when dining at the Palace."[30] H. A. MacMichael, a newly-arrived
civilian official, recorded Wingate's return from leave in 1905: "[W]e
had to stand in rows outside the Palace and after coming over the river
. . . he had to salute, shake hands and grin familiarity at every single officer and official in turn—wretched man—as well as all the chief merchants, cadis, etc. . . ."[31] A few days later the king's birthday witnessed
a similar reception. Before the month was out, yet another "levee" was
held: "rather a boring affair," in MacMichael's words, it had "merely
consisted of walking past the Sirdar in rows and shaking hands. . . .
Every single official and officer in the place had to be there and also lots
of merchants and the sheikhs of various tribes. . . ."[32]

Similar ceremonies were held on public holidays, of which there
were many: British, Egyptian, Sudanese, Muslim, and Christian.
"Don't forget to have a good show on Coronation Day," Wingate
wrote his acting sirdar in June 1902: "Royal Standard to be hoisted,
parade of troops, Levee etc. and I think you might get . . . £50 from
Civil Funds for distribution amongst the poor."[33] (Wingate was in
London for the coronation, having asked, in a letter to the king's private secretary, for an invitation. The king's emergency appendectomy
forced postponement.)[34] When in 1903 the anniversary of Karari was
dropped as a "general holiday," a *mudir* remarked that there were
quite enough holidays without it.[35] In any case the famous statue of

[29] Kitty Wingate to Wingate, 11 March 1890, SAD 233/1.
[30] Grace Balfour to her mother-in-law, 1 February 1903, SAD 606/3.
[31] Letter home, 10 November 1905, SAD 578/4.
[32] Letter home, 1 December 1905, SAD 578/4.
[33] Wingate to Fergusson, 7 June 1902, SAD 272/4/1.
[34] Wingate to Bigge, 19 December 1901, SAD 271/2.
[35] Watson to Wingate, 1 September 1903, SAD 273/9.

General Gordon had been erected in front of the Palace that year, and would serve as a permanent focus of imperial religion.

Wingate built the first English church at Khartoum. Until it could be used, services—ending with "God Save the King"—were held in the Palace.[36] In 1903 Wingate appealed through the *Times* for funds to build a church, one "though simple, still not architecturally unworthy of the ground on which it will stand or the great historical associations which surround the capital of the Sudan."[37] A foundation stone was laid, with great fanfare, in February 1904, by Princess Henry of Battenberg. An official account gives details of the procession from the Palace, "escorted by the cavalry of the Governor General's Body Guard," and ends on a note consonant with Wingate's appeal: just as the stone slid into place "the setting sun . . . shot it's [*sic*] last and parting gleam through the grove of palm trees and past the bronze statue of General Gordon, lighting up the interior of the tent with it's [*sic*] rays."[38]

"Social duties," notwithstanding the expense borne by the Sudan Government (and thus the Sudanese and Egyptian taxpayer), cost Wingate a great deal of money. Even without a Cairo house his salary as sirdar and governor-general was insufficient for the role he had assumed. By 1907 this stood at £E4,584, a princely sum by his own previous standards. But Wingate was always a spender. He had bought land for a house at Dunbar, and begun construction. His sons Ronald and Malcolm were in school in England, and Victoria, born in 1899, soon would be. Nor were there ways to supplement his salary: experience, and his new dignity, had precluded acceptance of publishers' repeated offers of book contracts.[39] For years Wingate had worried that, because of the anomalies of his position, untimely death would leave his wife and children virtually penniless; in 1906 he even drafted a plea for his executors to make in that event.[40] A few days before Cromer finally retired from Egypt in 1907, Wingate, all the

---

[36] MacMichael to his father, 14 October 1905, SAD 578/4.

[37] Wingate to the Editor, the *Times*, 4 February 1903, SAD 273/2.

[38] "Ceremony of laying the Foundation Stone of All Saints Church in Khartoum," encl. in Owen to Charlton, 10 February 1904, SAD 275/2.

[39] See, e.g., Macmillan to Wingate, 3 January 1900; Arnold to Wingate, 25 January 1900, SAD 265/3; and Wingate to Churchill, 31 March 1899, SAD 269/3.

[40] Wingate to HBM's Agent and Consul General in Egypt (draft), 8 February 1906, SAD 234/5.

more concerned about the future, asked him directly for relief. At a difficult political juncture Cromer would not oblige, and Wingate settled for oral assurance of liberal treatment upon retirement, a promise that would haunt him years later. Indeed, Wingate recorded the conversation and sent copies to London, to be kept with his will.[41]

---

[41] "Maj. Gen. Sir F.R. Wingate . . . Pension and Gratuities," 21 July 1907; Wingate, "Note," 18 August 1907, SAD 234/5.

Chapter Eighteen
Weathering Storms,
1907–1911

⟶∞∞∞⟶

Lord Cromer had been so long in Egypt that departure in any circumstances would create uncertainty. He left in 1907 under a cloud of anti-British feeling after the Dinshawai incident, when villagers were tried and executed for an affray in which a British officer had died. Any successor was bound to chart a new course in Egypt, which in turn would mean changes in the Sudan. The years of Sir Eldon Gorst's consul-generalship were in fact the most vexed of Wingate's long tenure in Khartoum. His relations with Gorst were difficult personally, and involved disagreement over financial policy, security, the powers and authority of the governor-general, and indeed Egypt's role in the Sudan. For Wingate the strain of these disputes was worsened by illness and by rumors of impending dismissal.

By 1907 Gorst and Wingate already had a history of cool relations. As financial adviser to the Egyptian government (1898–1904) Gorst had been Cromer's understudy, with direct control of the Sudan budget. His remarkable autobiographical notes comment as early as 1900 on Wingate's "administrative incompetence," on his own hope of succeeding Cromer, and, in 1905, on Wingate's involvement in a "clique" to prevent that succession.[1] Aware of Gorst's uneasy relations with Cromer, Wingate had in fact made no secret of his own difficulties with the financial adviser; there was, indeed, a general anxiety in the Sudan Government at the prospect of Gorst.[2] This animus prejudiced Cairo-Khartoum relations, and gave to important political matters a personal aspect they should otherwise not have had.

It was this that lay behind rumors during Gorst's tenure that Wingate would resign or be dismissed. In 1908, after interference in Khartoum's handling of the Wad Habuba rising (see below), Sudan officials, including Slatin, threatened to resign, and there was pressure

---

[1] Gorst, Autobiography, Middle East Centre, Oxford.

[2] See, e.g., Cecil to Wingate, 7 August 1905, SAD 277/2.

171

on Wingate to follow suit. In 1909 the Egyptian press reported that Wingate had a ten-year contract: it was about to end and would not be renewed; Wingate put himself at the disposal of the co-domini, but Gorst expressed full confidence and did not hand up the letter.[3] Wingate fell ill in 1909 and in May 1910 had surgery in England; questions arose about his ability to continue. His promotion to lieutenant-general in 1909 incited further rumors.[4] On balance, however, it appears unlikely that Gorst seriously considered replacing Wingate, and there is no evidence at all that Wingate wished to resign.

Gorst's policy in Egypt, involving conciliation of the khedive and encouragement of representative institutions, had repercussions in the Sudan. Egyptians resented the annual subventions wrung from them for the Sudan; especially after failing to secure a British contribution, in the form of a loan, Gorst argued that these should be either eliminated or at least shown to benefit Egypt. Under Cromer, the Cairo connection had meant British control, not Egyptian interference; Wingate had taken steps to loosen ties with Egypt even as he expected an annual subvention. Now Gorst demanded the opposite: gradual elimination of the subsidy and strengthening of the ties.

While implications of this policy were evident in day-to-day financial disputes, one occasion especially illustrates the combined political and personal effects. For the opening in 1909 of Port Sudan, built at a cost to Egypt of almost £E1m, Wingate planned a largely Anglo-Sudanese ceremony. In rejecting this Gorst explained his wish "that the show should be made as Egyptian as possible"; he himself would not attend. The Sudan needed capital to progress: Britain would not provide it. The "only way" to persuade Egyptians that their money was well spent there was "to make them feel that the Soudan" was "part of Egypt." Wingate had to agree—no British battleship would anchor offshore, and the khedive, not a British royal, would preside—but it was a bitter pill.[5] Nor was it the last Wingate had to swallow, for by 1913 Gorst's course of treatment had eliminated the Egyptian civil subvention altogether. Wingate railed about consequences and criticized Gorst, openly to subordinates and more

[3] Wingate to Gorst, 26 January 1909, SAD 286/1; Gorst to Wingate, 31 January 1909, SAD 234/7.

[4] C.A. Willis to O, 22 April 1909, SAD 209/2.

[5] Gorst to Wingate, 18 February 1909; Wingate to Gorst, 28 [?] February 1909, SAD 286/2.

subtly to correspondents in England, but the Foreign Office supported Cairo. More significantly, the disappearing subvention had little discernible impact either on the Sudanese or on Wingate's own local policy.

That the Foreign Office placed Egyptian concerns over Khartoum's was borne out by the Wad Habuba crisis in 1908. Abd al-Qadir wad Habuba was a Mahdist veteran. After the battle of Omdurman he had returned to Katfia, near Kamlin on the Blue Nile, where resentment of the conqueror was heightened by the government's handling of land disputes in which he was involved. With others he killed a British deputy inspector in April 1908. A military force was dispatched, but in an ambush Abd al-Qadir's followers killed seventeen soldiers; several died later of their wounds. Public opinion was in no mood for a general rising, however, and Abd al-Qadir was handed over by villagers a few days later. On 17 May he was hanged. Local support for the rebel, and the army's heavy losses, make the incident stand out among many minor revolts of the Wingate years. While the crisis passed quickly, it caused another. Wingate's concern was twofold: rebels, especially with religious connections, must be treated harshly, to deter others; Egyptian officers wanted justice for dead comrades. Wad Habuba's confederates were tried, and twelve were sentenced to death. But Gorst consulted the Foreign Office, where, as in Egypt, the memory of Dinshawai was fresh. London ordered commutation. Wingate complied.[6] Subordinates were furious. Slatin resigned, claiming, in harsh language, that Wingate should have consulted his advisers before obeying the order; Wingate held that the result would have been the same, and Slatin withdrew the resignation. Others later claimed eagerness to resign if Wingate had given a lead.[7]

Wingate's private correspondence makes clear how differently he and his officials viewed the issue. To resign over such a matter was for Wingate inconceivable; his whole career shows how tenaciously he would cling to office. Nor, in any case, did the commutations raise a "constitutional" issue in the governor-general's relations with Cairo or London. Wingate viewed Slatin's reaction as typical of his emotional friend, and let it be known that others should not take

---

[6] The relevant correspondence is in FO 371/450–52.

[7] Slatin to Wingate, n.d., and Wingate to Slatin, 3 June 1908, SAD 451/124. See Daly, *Empire,* 125–27. Bonham Carter apparently also offered his resignation: Bonham Carter to Slatin, n.d., SAD 451/124.

such liberties.[8] Moreover Wingate knew (as subordinates could not) how much he relied on superiors' goodwill: a pension dependent on promises of "liberal treatment" rather than on contracted guarantees would be devalued by a political resignation. Instead of defying a direct order he therefore tried, in the months ahead, to turn it to his advantage, referring repeatedly to the fanaticism of the Sudanese to win British support for his policies. Improved conditions for Egyptian officers followed immediately; railway extension came later. When the duke of Connaught, as commander-in-chief of the British army, visited in February 1909, the "General Idea" of maneuvers was: "a state of insurrection. Khartoum, Khartoum North and Omdurman are isolated. The Railway is destroyed and the Garrisons are very short of provisions."[9]

The Wad Habuba controversy nonetheless weakened Wingate's position. That he took orders even in local political matters put a discount on his views; that he would obey orders rather than resign put a discount on his principles. The Foreign Office had preferred Gorst's advice to his own, while Cairo was left with an impression of overreaction, lack of control, and disarray in the ranks at Khartoum.[10] However it ends, a revolt rarely enhances the reputation of its target. It was in this context that new statutory limits to the governor-general's powers were born.

By temperament Wingate disliked sharing power. He would devolve authority—in a territory the size of the Sudan there was no choice—and gladly divided responsibility. But he resisted any limit to his ultimate exercise of power, whether by seeing off rivals or through bureaucratic rules. His Egyptian army career had by 1908 been so long—already twenty-five years— and his role in the Sudan so unprecedented, that he had developed a proprietary attitude. One aspect of this was paternalism; another was jealousy. Thus the boards and committees that proliferated within the Sudan Government had no share in the governor-general's executive authority: in some cases they were merely names given to irregular meetings of officials whose responsibilities overlapped. In 1908, amid the Wad Habuba controversy, Phipps, the civil secretary, told Wingate flatly that "these pre-

[8] Wingate to Stack, 4 June 1908, SAD 284/13; see also Stack to Wingate, 1 June 1908, SAD 234/6.
[9] SAD 286/2.
[10] Gorst, Autobiography.

sent arrangements cannot go on," that there must be "a sort of Governor General in Council arrangement" to meet regularly and consider all but routine business.[11] Such an "arrangement" would have insulated Wingate during the crisis. He heartily endorsed creation of a Central Government Board, which, however, had no power.[12]

Events in 1909, when Wingate was away from the Sudan even longer than usual, led to the board's early supersession. Gorst took a strong interest in this; Wingate's poor health (see below) argued for reform. In October Gorst recommended a council similar to that of the viceroy in India. An ordinance was enacted early in 1910. The Governor-General's Council, consisting of the three secretaries and other high officials, would vote on the annual budget and all legislation; the governor-general could still veto any decision. In practice, of course, vetoes were to be avoided, and indeed the council declined in importance throughout the remainder of Wingate's term, meeting infrequently. It proved useful in promoting his views in Cairo and London, and never threatened his exercise of power.[13]

That reform came from outside the Sudan, and that, once implemented, it had little real effect, indicates the degree of independence Wingate had under Gorst. As a bit of doggerel from early in Gorst's term had it:

> Bless Wingate, King, who no occasion loses
> Of doing here exactly what he chooses.
> Bless, bless King Gorst, and may he ne'er refuse
> To tell King Wingate what he's got to choose.[14]

When Cairo insisted, Khartoum must give way, but without external vigilance and local acquiescence Cairo's insistence rarely had practical effects. Wingate continued to hold power closely: in 1911, for example, he reprimanded the Permanent Selection Board for assuming "an opportunity of making a recommendation" for a vacancy—only he would decide what would be referred.[15]

---

[11] Phipps to Wingate, 7 June 1908, SAD 282/6.

[12] See Daly, *Empire*, 69.

[13] See Gorst to Grey, 14 November 1909, FO 371/664.

[14] Anon., "Eb-Ab-Win-Go. Rex Sudanorum," SAD 282/1.

[15] Wingate to Phipps, 16 April 1911, SAD 300/4/2.

The lack of flexibility Phipps had diagnosed in 1908 grew more serious thereafter. Wingate's insistence on using military personnel in administrative positions—the dual system epitomized in his own position—had only an appearance of efficiency. It caused constant difficulties: neglect of military matters, confusion about channels of communication, civilian disaffection over promotion.[16] During the Gorst years there was a constant undercurrent of civilian disaffection, and Wingate himself admitted that the quality of entrants to the civil service had consequently fallen off.[17] But he would not yield: "I see no particular reason for hurrying on this tendency towards separation," he wrote in 1911.[18] A related problem was his peripatetic life. As the government and its activities grew, absence of the governor-general—between Equatoria and Scotland—meant delay, inefficiency, and slackness. Even during his long stay (because of illness) in Cairo in 1910, Wingate deflected Gorst's suggestion of an acting sirdar and governor-general: everything would "go on just as usual" from Cairo.[19]

Both independence and difficulties grew too from Khartoum's secrecy and Cairo's waning interest in local issues. In a dozen ways Wingate acted quietly to reduce Cairo's influence, even as Gorst sought to emphasize Egypt's role in the Sudan. To circumvent Bernard, the financial secretary, Wingate would use the Sudan Agent in Cairo as a conduit to British authorities.[20] Intelligence officers were told to censor any of their own reports that might reach British authorities elsewhere: the intelligence department, Wingate wrote in 1908, was "not merely a news collection department but also . . . a political department."[21] "Patrols"—military expeditions in the unpacified South—went unreported: it "would be dangerous in the extreme" if word reached Westminster;[22] in one year there were six-

[16] See, e.g., Armbruster to Cromer, 24 September 1910, encl. in Wingate to Gorst, 28 September 1910, SAD 297/3.

[17] Wingate to Clayton, 2 September 1910, SAD 469/2/2. See also Bonham Carter to Wingate, 30 June 1910, SAD 469/2/1; Willis to O, 6 November 1910, SAD 209/2.

[18] Wingate to Phipps, 6 September 1911, SAD 301/3.

[19] Wingate to Gorst, 25 January 1910, SAD 290/1.

[20] Wingate to Stack, 3 April 1908, SAD 284/13.

[21] Wingate to Channer, 31 July 1908, SAD 283/7.

[22] Wingate to Asser, 27 October 1910, SAD 298/1.

teen such expeditions and Wingate was glad that almost nothing was known of this at home.[23] Big-game hunters Wingate wished to impress—Roosevelt, Prince Henri Liechtenstein—were allowed to shoot in reserves if they promised not to tell anyone;[24] in 1913 he chastised W. Steuart-Menzies, not for having shot three white rhinoceroses, but for disclosing the fact to others, who thereupon demanded "special permits" for themselves.[25] In 1911 Wingate decided that English, not Arabic, should be the official language in the multilingual South; this would be done "quietly and unostentatiously," lest word reach Egypt.[26] Unlike Cromer, Gorst really was interested only in the "big questions." While the Residency was preoccupied with Egyptian crises, the Sudan Government was left to create precedents.

London's ignorance and Cairo's unconcern left Wingate with only one other foreign troublemaker, the Church. But bishops and missionaries, anti-slavers or educationists were no match for him. He continued to limit proselytization to the south, and matched complaints about restrictions with reminders of missionaries' poor results. When a bishop argued that Sunday should be observed as a sabbath, Wingate agreed, then raised the practical point about two holidays and concluded frankly: "You must remember that the country is a Mohammedan country, and that we are governing it in the first instance in the interests of a Mohammedan population." Moreover "England" did "little for the Sudan"; if that changed, perhaps the policy could.[27] By the end of Gorst's tenure no such change had occurred, and Wingate's position was the same: he was, he told Llewellyn Gwynne, "the representative of the King and the Khedive, and . . . responsible for maintaining an even balance over all subjects in the Sudan, whether Christian or Moslem."[28] Cromer and Wingate had delayed creation of an Anglican bishopric in the Sudan; in 1911 when Gorst mused about joining the country ecclesiastically with Egypt, Wingate claimed that Khartoum could not be without its

---

[23] Wingate to General Dalton, 18 February 1911, SAD 300/1.

[24] Wingate to Butler, 19 August 1910, SAD 297/2.

[25] Wingate to Steuart-Menzies, 4 May 1913, SAD 186/2/2.

[26] Wingate to Feilden, 15 April 1911, SAD 300/4/2.

[27] Wingate to Bishop Taylor Smith, 25 March 1907, SAD 280/3.

[28] Wingate to Gwynne, 17 May 1911, SAD 300/5/1.

bishop half the year![29] So long as the missionaries, especially the Church Missionary Society, were unable to match admonitions with money and personnel, Wingate had no difficulty in controlling them.

There is no reason to conclude that Wingate, any more or less than other British governors of non-Christian populations, was cynical or irreligious. He was pragmatic, and had good reason for restricting missionary activity. His duties as a Christian were largely private. As a student of the Anglo-Egyptian scene has pointed out, Wingate was typical of his class of British officers, to whom the moral, ethical, and social values of Christianity took precedence over the narrowly spiritual.[30] Wingate was a regular church-goer, prayed daily in private, and kept a well-thumbed prayer-book. But he was not an agent of the Church, and when European or American missionaries attacked him he fell easily into the role of referee between two sides of fanatics, Christian and Muslim.

That Wingate had never willingly submitted to Cromer's views on "social duties" is borne out by his conduct during the Gorst years. The pattern of Wingate's life had by then been established: November through March he spent in the Sudan, at Khartoum or on tour; in the spring he went to Egypt, then to Europe and Britain on leave, to return to Egypt in October. There were variations on this theme: after construction of the government's modest "hill station" at Erkowit, Wingate went there with increasing frequency; flying visits to Egypt occurred as needed; trips to and from England altered in terms of route and sojourns; inspections in the Sudan always differed at least slightly, and depended too upon the press of business elsewhere.

Because of Cromer's retirement Wingate had taken leave in 1907 later than usual. He traveled in June via Vienna, where he dined with the emperor at Schönbrunn and was invested with the Grand Cross of the Order of Franz Josef. After the usual round of dinners in London (including one with the editor of the *Times* to meet Mark Twain) and a meeting of the Imperial Defence Committee, he went to Dunbar in early July. If their diaries are accurate, this was a quiet

[29] Blythe to Wingate, 28 January 1911; Wingate to Blyth, 14 February 1911, SAD 300/2; Wingate to Gorst, 29 December 1910, SAD 298/3.

[30] Richard Hill, "Government and Christian missions in the Anglo-Egyptian Sudan, 1899–1914," *Middle East Studies* 1, 2, 1965.

summer for the Wingates, and the first in which Knockenhair, the name they gave their new house at Dunbar, appears; their daughter would lay the foundation stone in November. They visited Balmoral in September, returning to Egypt via Vienna and Slatin in early October, and reached Khartoum on 5 November.[31]

A week later Wingate was off on his autumn tour, yet again up the scenic Blue Nile with his wife, to Kamlin, Wad Madani, Hilmi, Sinnar, Tisagi, Singa, Abu Naama, Rusayris, and Rufaa. By the time he returned to Khartoum the 1907–08 tourist season was under way. In December Wingate received the duchess d'Aosta, Winston Churchill, M. Fould, Garstin, and others; Gorst recorded a reception "with the customary Wingate pomp and circumstance."[32] Wingate then left on a tour remarkable even for him: al-Damir, Port Sudan, Sinkat, Suakin, Erkowit, Atbara, Abu Hamad, Karima, Marawi, Kurti, Gowari, al-Dabba, Old Dongola, Tangassi, and Gureid. He returned to Khartoum in time to welcome the duke of Brunswick at the end of January 1908. The duke of Connaught and others appeared in mid-February, and Wingate took them to the Red Sea Hills. He returned to Erkowit with his wife in early March—his third visit there in two months—and stayed a month. Unusually Wingate took a tour in mid-April, to the Upper Nile, and was at Tugr on the thirtieth when he got word of the Wad Habuba rising at Katfia. He nonetheless continued south, and returned to Khartoum only on 9 May. The ensuing controversy kept Wingate in Khartoum until mid-June, when he sailed from Port Sudan for the first time, and reached England on 25 June, the day before announcement of his promotion to lieut.-general. After visiting his sons at Winchester and attending official and social functions in London, he went to Dunbar on 11 July. Later that month Wingate attended a meeting of the Khartoum Church Fund (with Connaught in the chair), and had an audience with the king and an interview with the archbishop of Canterbury. In mid-September Slatin visited; they went together to Balmoral, where the other guests included Asquith and Grey, before Wingate departed for Egypt, via Vienna, on 29 September.[33]

---

[31] CB1.

[32] Gorst, Autobiography.

[33] CB1.

Wingate spent an unusually long time, a month, in Egypt before returning to Khartoum on 7 November 1908. His fear that the Wad Habuba rising might frighten off tourists[34] proved unfounded. On 20 November the royal procession began, in the familiar person of Leopold of Battenberg, this time with his brother. They stayed a month. The duke of Brunswick and the duke and duchess of Connaught and their entourage followed. A steamer was reserved to take the duchess up the White Nile, while the Upper Nile Province steamer would be held for the duke's "shooting party."[35] Lord Roberts and family were given a steamer, and railway passes, and stayed at the Palace; Wingate said that the "public and private expense" was justified because Roberts, "if favourably impressed," would "probably help . . . with the home authorities."[36] When Roberts's sailboat needed towing from Shellal to Wadi Halfa, Wingate billed the Sudan Government. In the convoluted style he often used when unconvinced he wrote: "[I]n view of the fact that Lord Roberts is such a distinguished soldier and one who has done so much for the Army and all connected with it, I feel this is a case in which I can well make this a charge against the Sudan Government . . . but . . . it is just as well that these little arrangements should be considered entirely private and should not get known. . . ."[37]

It was at this moment that the War Office gave Wingate a "Reward for Distinguished or Meritorious Service," with an annuity of £100 that could be waived if the honoree chose: Wingate took the cash.[38]

There was no January tour in 1909; Khartoum's calendar was too crowded. Wingate attended the consecration of the Coptic cathedral, and the foundation of the Catholic cathedral, both on 14 February. Sir William Mather—one of the few foreign visitors who was a certain benefactor of the Sudan—stayed at the Palace in mid-February. It was, as Wingate told Bigge, "a particularly heavy season," with an "exceptionally large number of distinguished visitors," including the duke and duchess of Schleswig-Holstein and "the Hohenlohes."[39]

[34] Wingate to Channer, 10 September 1908, SAD 283/9/3.

[35] Wingate to Maxwell, 27 December 1908, SAD 284/12/1.

[36] Wingate to Bernard, 28 July 1908, SAD 283/7/2.

[37] Wingate to Watson, 26 November 1908, SAD 284/11/1.

[38] War Office to Wingate, 10 December 1908; Wingate to War Office, 7 January 1909, SAD 115/10.

[39] Wingate to Bigge, 11 March 1909, SAD 285.

Expenses were heavy, but mainly for the Egyptian and Sudanese tax-payer. In January Wingate went so far as to authorize a special train to bring to Khartoum the gun and ammunition a duke had misplaced on tour; "I wish I could make him pay for" it, Wingate wrote.[40] Lord Winterton's steamer struck a rock; Wingate "bustled off the 'Elfin' in great haste."[41] (Later in the year, despite "reluctance to do anything which savours of personal advertisement," Wingate accepted Winterton's invitation for an extended illustrated article in the *World*'s "Celebrities at Home" feature.)[42] Great trouble and expense were incurred over ex-president Roosevelt: province officials acted as guides and beaters, steamers were placed at his disposal, the usual rail-way passes were provided, and he and his family were invited to stay at the Palace; "the only expenses . . . incurred by Mr. Roosevelt whilst in the Sudan will be those connected with his catering when he is not actually staying at the Palace," Wingate wrote. "I feel that it is only right that the Government should afford these facilities to so distin-guished a traveller."[43]

On 16 March the Wingates left for Erkowit. Lady Wingate left for England on the twenty-fourth, while he received the khedive for the official opening of Port Sudan on 1 April. A week later Wingate was ordered to Somaliland.[44]

By 1909 the protectorate of British Somaliland had become expen-sive detritus of the Scramble for Africa. Control was limited to the port of Berbera and its hinterland, to which, moreover, recalcitrant Somalis posed a constant threat. Their leader, Sayyid Muhammad Abdalla Hasan—dubbed "the Mad Mullah" by the British—denounced laxity among the Muslims and preached jihad against the Christians, European and Abyssinian alike. Successive campaigns against him

[40] Wingate to Kerr, 25 January 1909, SAD 286/1.

[41] Wingate to Stack, 18 February 1909, SAD 286/2.

[42] Wingate to Winterton, 19 September 1909. See also Winterton to Wingate, 17 September 1909; Robins (*The World*) to Clayton, 12 October 1909; SAD 234/7. The article appeared on 2 November 1909.

[43] Wingate to Leigh Hunt, 25 February 1909, SAD 286/2.

[44] CB1.

ended inconclusively. From 1904 Sayyid Muhammad was occupied in the south, but in August 1908 he again threatened the British protectorate. In London no policy recommended itself: another expedition would be expensive; abandonment of the interior would expose the coast to attack. Reconciliation with the Sayyid, or subsidizing him to ensure peace, would be difficult to defend in the light of the government's past pronouncements. By asking Wingate to inspect and report the Foreign Office bought time and, if he was not careful, a chance to shift the onus for eventual failure from Whitehall to Wingate.

Wingate, at Erkowit, quickly organized a mission. Accompanying him would be Slatin (whose "knowledge of dealing with such movements and . . . intimate acquaintance with the thoughts and ideas of native races would render him invaluable");[45] Gilbert Clayton, Wingate's private secretary; C. H. Armbruster, of the slavery-suppression department, who spoke Amharic and Italian; Dr. Atkey; and various secretaries, soldiers, and servants. The mission left Port Sudan aboard HMS *Hawke* on 18 April, and on the twentieth reached Aden, where London's formal instructions were awaited. They sailed again on the twenty-fifth aboard HMS *Philomel,* and reached Berbera the next morning. A letter, drafted by Slatin, was immediately dispatched to Sayyid Muhammad, inviting him to send envoys for discussions. After several days of interviewing officials and reading files, the mission moved to Shaykh, the main town between Berbera and Burao, arriving on 2 May. By then Wingate's relations with local British officials, who resented his presence, had deteriorated to noncooperation. The protectorate, he wrote privately, was in a "general muddle . . . whereby we have not only no real friends amongst the supposed Friendlies, but we have given the Mullah every opportunity of misjudging our real intentions." The whole Somali debacle was the fault of incompetent British officials and "the inaptitude of the Home Government to realize the situation."[46]

On 15 May the mission moved on to Burao, where another week of interviews and discussions took place, again informing the mission and irritating British officials, against whom scores of complaints were handed in to Slatin and Wingate. On the twenty-fourth the party went back to Shaykh, where they remained a month writing a long

---

[45] "Diary. Somaliland Mission—H.E. Lieutenant-General Sir Reginald Wingate," SAD 125/5.
[46] Ibid.

report and awaiting a reply from Sayyid Muhammad. On 16 June a temporizing letter finally arrived. The mission left Shaykh the next day, and sailed from Berbera on the twentieth. Wingate went directly to Egypt via Aden, arrived in Cairo on the twenty-fourth, and after a few days at Alexandria sailed from Port Said on the twenty-ninth.[47]

On 7 July Wingate met Sir Edward Grey and Lord Crewe in London to discuss his report and recommendations. These were framed as possible responses to the several courses open to Sayyid Muhammad. If the sayyid resumed hostilities, Wingate concluded that a military solution was likeliest to achieve success. But he avoided the trap of strongly advocating any policy. In the event, the stand-off continued: the British maintained a defensive posture on the coast, postponing until after the First World War the final, costly showdown with Sayyid Muhammad. Wingate's report, printed confidentially for circulation within the government, seems to have had no lasting influence.[48]

The next year was one of the most difficult of Wingate's life. He had been ill in Somaliland with "colic," and suffered gastro-intestinal upsets throughout the summer of 1909, most of which he spent at Dunbar in his new house, Knockenhair. The annual visit to Balmoral had to be canceled. Wingate nevertheless returned in October to Cairo, where he again fell ill on the twenty-ninth. On 3 November he entered the Victoria Nursing Home; he stayed for eighteen days, then spent a week at Mena recuperating. Gallstones were suspected, but after further consultations it was decided not to operate. Wingate returned to Khartoum in mid-December. On 2 February, in distress, he left for Cairo for further medical treatment. Thus Wingate was there on the twenty-first when Boutros Ghali, the prime minister, was assassinated, and with Lady Wingate he called at the hospital before Boutros died. As sirdar Wingate attended the funeral on the twenty-second. On the twenty-seventh his brother Frederick died unexpectedly in England. Wingate was able to entertain visitors during this extended stay in Cairo—Theodore Roosevelt and his family arrived from the Sudan in late March—but at the end of April his illness required him to go to England. An unsettling season in Egypt ended with the aged Zubayr Pasha, alarmed at rumors of an attempt on Wingate's life, at the docks to see him off.[49]

---

[47] Ibid.; CB1.

[48] *Lieutenant-General Sir R. Wingate's Special Mission to Somaliland*, SAD 125/7.

[49] CB1.

In London a decision was made for immediate surgery. Wingate entered the King Edward VII Hospital on 1 May and on the third underwent a successful operation for gallstones. There was a touching enquiry from the king on the fifth; Edward VII himself died the next day. Wingate's convalescence was lengthy. Pleurisy developed, and he remained hospitalized for a month; Roosevelt and Kitchener were among his visitors. On 2 June he was moved by ambulance to 19 Bryanston Square, the house of Dr. Acland, who had seen him through typhoid in 1883. There recovery was rapid, and marked by many visitors: the duke of Connaught, Prince George of Cumberland, Princess Henry, Prince Alexander, the bishop of London, Lord Grenfell, Cromer, Sir Edward Grey, Sir Evelyn Wood. On 18 June Wingate went with his wife and a nurse to Englemere near Ascot, to recuperate as Lord Roberts's guest. Slatin and Milo Talbot also came to stay. By the twenty-eighth he was well enough to travel to Dunbar.[50]

It was characteristic of Wingate that after this illness he remembered those who had helped him. As always, he dictated replies to hundreds of messages, and even second-hand wishes were acknowledged—"kind remembrance from me to Baron Fukushima and to Colonel Utsonomiya" was issued from Knockenhair.[51] But he sent letters of thanks also to station-masters for help with arrangements, and a testimonial to W. Zyczynski, who had shaved and barbered him for seven weeks. To Dr. and Mrs. Acland a silver tray was dispatched in September.[52]

Wingate stayed in Scotland until October. In early August Kitchener visited, and Slatin arrived on the thirty-first. He and Wingate went to Balmoral on 2 September, continuing with the new king a tradition of the old. He went with George V and Queen Mary to Mar Lodge on the fourth to see the Princess Royal, and on the seventh went with the queen on another outing. Wingate was at Dunbar on the eighth to welcome Milo Talbot and Sir William Mather. On

---

[50] Ibid. There is no better example of Wingate's record-keeping: his papers include complete day and night books for his hospitalization, test results, and receipts for all services. SAD 234/7.

[51] Wingate to Macdonald, 22 July 1910, SAD 291/3.

[52] Wingate to W. Zyczynski, 22 June 1910, SAD 291/2; to Dr. and Mrs. Acland, 11 September 1910, SAD 291/3. See also files of messages for recovery, SAD 234/8, 291/1.

the fourteenth he visited Asquith at Archerfield, and on the seventeenth went with his wife to Whittinghame as weekend guests of Arthur Balfour. They left Dunbar for Egypt on 5 October. There—after a summer in Scotland—Wingate played his first golf since the operation. He reached Khartoum, having crossed the new Blue Nile bridge for the first time, on 12 November.[53]

The 1910–11 season saw Wingate fully recovered. In mid-December he drove a ceremonial last rivet in the White Nile bridge at Kosti. He was there again two weeks later with Kitchener. On 16 January the Princess Royal and her husband, and Princesses Alexandra and Maud arrived. In early February the Wingates received Sir Ian Hamilton and the king of Saxony before setting out on a long tour to the Upper Nile. They called at al-Duaym, Renk, Kodok, Lul, Tawfiqiyya, Doleib Hill, Shambe, Bor, Mongalla, Gondokoro, and Rejaf, where Wingate gave a speech to assembled chiefs to mark formal acquisition of the Lado Enclave from Belgium. Wingate returned to Khartoum on 5 March. On the twentieth the king of the Belgians arrived; Wingate took him to Kosti to see the bridge. The Wingates then went to Erkowit. She sailed from Port Sudan, while he went on a tour of Red Sea towns: Trinkitat, al-Tab, Port Tawfiq, and Tokar—where three thousand camelmen paraded for him. Wingate returned to Khartoum for two weeks of business, then went back to Erkowit before going on long leave. The day of his arrival in London, 15 June, is marked in a diary with two brief notes: "Hear of Eldon Gorst's serious illness—no hope," and "Belsize Motor Landaulette (£450)."[54]

From Bryanston Square the Wingates attended the coronation of King George V at Westminster Abbey on 22 June 1911. They took their sons to the Naval Review at Gosport on the twenty-fourth, then left for Karlsbad, visiting Nijmegen, Cologne, Mainz, and Nuremberg en route.[55] Before returning to Britain in late July they lunched at Jagdhochloss Rehefeld, where the king of Saxony gave them some Meissen. They were in Dunbar again by 1 August; diaries record the arrival also of all three children, a rare gathering. On 1 September Wingate's sister Bessie died at Bedford. It was therefore in mourning that he went on the seventh with his wife and Kitchener to Balmoral, where Wingate won the king's agreement to visit the Sudan. Before

---

[53] CB1.

[54] Ibid.

[55] Ibid.

leaving for Egypt—in 1911 much earlier than usual—Wingate took his son Malcolm for a weekend visit to Sir Evelyn Wood. Wingate reached Egypt on 27 September, the same day Kitchener arrived to succeed Gorst.

The irony of the Gorst years, so far as the Sudan is concerned, is that others would reap credit for what he had so unpopularly sown. This was especially so in the economic sphere. Wingate and his officials never approved Gorst's policy of weaning the Sudan Government from Egyptian subventions, still less of his emphasizing Egypt's role in order to justify them. But neither had they offered any alternative. Egyptian dislike of lopsided condominium was real, not Gorst's invention. Annual negotiation of the Sudan budget had thus been increasingly unpleasant. Without some new source of revenue there would be little or no economic growth in the Sudan.

Gorst had therefore tried to win British financial help. After the Wad Habuba rising Wingate, in London, rested his argument on security.[56] It was an unstable basis: as often as London was reminded of Sudanese "fanaticism," so often did it note the Sudan Government's apparent ease in dealing with it. His pleas were rejected. Gorst's subsequent efforts to find revenue depended on his general policy of liberalization in Egypt; those efforts and that policy foundered with the assassination of Boutros Ghali in February 1910.

With Egyptian support declining, and British help denied, Wingate turned to private sources. The Sudan's potential had been extolled since (and even before) the conquest, but actual private investment had been slight. Ill-considered schemes to exploit non-existent mineral wealth had failed early. Experiments in agriculture had shown mixed results. Foreign speculators had given entrepreneurship a bad name, and the resulting climate of suspicion was inhospitable even for sensible schemes. Valuable private contributions, rather than investments—laboratories established at Khartoum by Sir Henry Wellcome, workshops funded by Sir William Mather, the Gordon Memorial College, and the many schools established by missionaries—would be important in training Sudanese, but not in supplying revenue. Tourism, export of animal products, the gum trade, and other traditional commerce could never provide the taxes needed even to replace diminishing Egyptian subventions. It was in this political and economic context that Wingate began to promote the idea of cotton-growing in the Gezira.

---

[56] Wingate to Herbert, 22 July 1908, SAD 283/7/1.

It had long been obvious that the rich grain-producing plain between the Blue and White Niles south of Khartoum—Gezira means "island"—had enormous cash-crop potential. Railway construction and the building of Port Sudan had in part been justified to bring the region closer to external markets. Research by Sir William Garstin and C. E. Dupuis between 1900 and 1903 made clear how suitable the Gezira was for irrigated agriculture: the natural slope of the land was good, and there were excellent sites for damming the Blue Nile. But Egypt had first claim to Nile water, a subject on which Wingate reflexively deferred to Cairo. Moreover the economic feasibility of an irrigation scheme with strict seasonal limits was uncertain; it was doubtful that the export market for cereal crops would justify the cost of infrastructure, while lengthy research would be needed before investment could be considered. Meanwhile the government encouraged experiments elsewhere in cotton-growing with basin irrigation. These, especially at Tukar and Zaydab, provided experience, not only agricultural but also in matters of land policy, taxation, labor, foreign concessionaires, and so forth. It was at this stage—not at the outset— that Wingate's contribution was made.[57]

Results of early tests coincided with reduction of the Egyptian subsidy and London's refusal to make up for it. "We shall be very soon at our beam ends," Wingate told Clayton in March 1910, and must therefore "do all we possibly can to induce British Capital . . . to have a vested interest in the country."[58] Wingate began quiet consultations with European businessmen and others with a view toward developing the Gezira, and called for a report on prospects to be prepared by officials in Khartoum. Meanwhile James Currie, director of education in the Sudan, contacted influential friends at home, including Lord Derby, president of the Cotton Growing Association.[59] Wingate himself, in conversation with Asquith and Lloyd George at Balmoral in September, found growing interest in the Sudan: "the wants of Manchester" was how he succinctly put it.[60]

---

[57] Arthur Gaitskell, *Gezira: a story of development in the Sudan*, London 1959, 34–53. Cf. Wingate, *Wingate of the Sudan*, 155.

[58] Wingate to Clayton, 6 March 1910, SAD 290/3/1.

[59] Wingate to Clayton, 13 March 1910, SAD 290/3/1; Clayton to Wingate, 20 March 1910, SAD 290/3/2; Gorst to Wingate, 19 April 1910, SAD 296/1/3; Wingate to Currie, 30 September 1910, SAD 297/3.

[60] Wingate to Kennedy, 20 September 1910, SAD 297/3.

Sir William Mather's address to the Cotton Growing Association at Manchester in October brought the Gezira to public notice, while behind the scenes Lord Milner apparently played a similarly important role. Sir Edward Grey himself took an interest, for domestic political reasons.[61] Half a century later a former manager of the Gezira Scheme would point out "how large a part the chance interests of individuals played in determining the final pattern of events."[62] The leading role remained to be filled, ironically by Gorst's successor and Wingate's old chief, Lord Kitchener.

---

[61] Wingate to Mather, 27 December 1910; and to Milner, 21 December 1910, SAD 298/3; for Grey's views see Grey to Gorst, 11 November 1910, Garstin to Gorst, 12 November 1910, and other papers in FO 141/578/540, an important source for the political history of the Gezira Scheme. See also Gaitskell, *Gezira*, 53–54.

[62] Gaitskell, *Gezira*, 54. For Wingate's initial view of Mather as someone to be mistrusted but "judiciously manipulated," see Wingate to Gorst, 21 February 1909, SAD 285.

Chapter Nineteen
"Quite Like the Good Old Times" (1911–1914)[1]

———◆◇◇◇◆———

It is safe to assume that Wingate had mixed feelings about Kitchener's appointment. During their previous association Wingate had damned him as "the quintessence of a coward," a "bounder," "utterly unscrupulous" and much else. Kitchener had gained intimate knowledge of the Egyptian army and the Sudan; he would never be cowed by claims of local expertise. Moreover, since 1899 he had achieved a degree of prestige and glamour almost unique in the empire. Kitchener had taken on Lord Curzon in India, and won; Wingate would not contest him. Now at last in Cromer's chair, and after the failed consulship of Gorst, Kitchener was in a powerful position. Wingate might well have dreaded his return.

Yet he did not. For the Gorst years had taught that the Sudan Government needed Cairo. Views shared by Lord Cromer had carried great weight in London; views forwarded by Gorst had carried less. Kitchener's powerful public and private support would be worth far more than Gorst's disinterested acquiescence; Kitchener's methods, however distasteful, were closer to the Anglo-Egyptian norm than Gorst's. Gorst had believed in measures; Kitchener believed in men. A reputation for toughness was a reason for his appointment in the wake of Gorst's liberal experiment. Kitchener, it was thought, would put the Egyptians in their place. This suited Wingate. If Kitchener were still impatient with administrative detail, and left the Sudan to his old understudy, good and useful relations would be possible. In the event, despite agreement on broad lines of policy, Kitchener's whims were as difficult to deal with as Gorst's reasoning.

While the foreign community and Anglo-Egyptian officials hoped for a return to Cromerian discipline, times had changed. Gorst's policy had not overthrown the old regime but had responded

---

[1] Kitchener to Wingate, 30 June 1910, SAD 234/8, on declining the offer of the Mediterranean command.

to its demise. Incipient Egyptian nationalism must be recognized and dealt with, not merely suppressed. The Dinshawai incident had epitomized a shift of the Egyptian masses, whose allegiance or support would in future have to be won rather than assumed. Kitchener's prestige should make the task easier, but only if his policies were palatable. Insofar as the Sudan was concerned, therefore, the premise of Gorst's regime would be upheld: Kitchener would not sacrifice the British interest in Egypt to please British officials in Khartoum; neither would he pander to Egyptian nationalists by encouraging their pretensions anywhere in the Nile Valley.

Two weeks after Wingate returned from leave in 1911 the change was exemplified by the greatest state occasion of his long governor-generalship. At Balmoral in September the king had accepted Wingate's invitation to visit the Sudan during his forthcoming trip to India. Much of Wingate's time for the next two months went into preparations. In mid-November he went to Egypt to meet the royal party on their way out; he attended a levee at Ras al-Tin palace in Alexandria on 18 November, and on the twentieth went with Kitchener to Port Said, where they dined with the king and queen aboard HMS *Medina* on the twenty-first and twenty-second. Wingate then sailed for Port Sudan, and returned to Khartoum on the twenty-seventh. After Christmas he paid a quick visit to El Obeid to mark the extension of the railway there. On 14 January he and his wife left for Port Sudan, meeting Kitchener, who had come up from Egypt, at Atbara. The king and queen dropped anchor at Port Sudan on 17 January.[2] Wingate had devised elaborate ceremonies and entertainments: Sudanese notables had been brought—without telling them why—from all over the country; Dinka dancers, Arab horsemen, Hadandua sword-dancers, and various military detachments performed. The day was declared a holiday in the Sudan, to be celebrated annually thereafter as King's Day. That Wingate used the visit to mark a new era is clear: with Kitchener's blessing the khedive was not invited, and Wingate made sure that Sudanese notables went away with medals, souvenirs, and impressions of Their Majesties' concern for the Sudan. The *African World* was paid for a commemorative issue, which was widely distributed.[3]

---

[2] CB1.

[3] Midwinter to Wingate, 1 May 1912, SAD 181/2/1.

In practical ways, however, Kitchener continued Gorst's policy in the Sudan. Egypt's annual subvention was not restored, indeed finally ended in 1913. Lobbying for British financial support, which Gorst had failed to win, went on relentlessly. Kitchener was a master at combining public and private, official and personal methods to get his way, and his support for British loans proved crucial. Nothing during his tenure better exemplifies the Sudan Government's need for a powerful advocate—and, therefore, Wingate's lack of influence in British political and social circles.

Even before taking up his post in Cairo, Kitchener began to lobby for a Sudan loan. In a memorandum of July 1911 he reviewed the Sudan Government's dependence on Egypt and the potential for trouble if foreign entrepreneurs took a strong position in the Sudan. He airily claimed that Gezira development would not only pay for itself but would also allow repayment of the debt to Egypt. The Foreign Office agreed. The solution would be a private loan guaranteed by the British government.[4] In June 1912 Kitchener submitted a sketch budget for a £3m loan, over half of it earmarked for railway construction, and it was with those terms that a bill was enacted by Parliament in 1913.[5]

Wingate's role in winning the guarantee was secondary; in arrangements for development of the Gezira he took a leading part. In 1910, after Gorst had failed to get British support, the Sudan Government had reached agreement with a private company, the Sudan Plantations Syndicate, to manage an experimental cotton farm at Tayiba. If it succeeded, the syndicate would be entitled to buy land in the eventual large-scale scheme. Gorst had approved this arrangement, which in 1913 Kitchener and his advisers strongly criticized, not least because it would alienate land. Wingate's defenders insisted, however, that "it was much better that the country should advance by means of private capital than that it should stand still."[6] Nonetheless, the impression was left that Wingate and his soldier-administrators had been tricked by sharp businessmen. When criticized he reminded Kitchener that he had "had to be prepared to

---

[4] Kitchener, Memorandum, n.d. (July 1911), FO 371/1114; Grey, minute, 14 May 1912, FO 371/1363.

[5] "Note respecting Soudan Loan," encl. in Kitchener to Grey, 16 June 1912, SAD 181/3; see also Kitchener to Cromer, 26 July 1912, FO 633/21/161.

[6] Currie to Director of Agriculture, 10 March 1913, FO 141/578/540.

dance on either leg."[7] "It would have been better," he admitted privately, "to have resorted to the help of a Company rather than not develop the Gezira at all, but in that case the Sudan would have eventually become something like Rhodesia is to-day," with a powerful chartered company to deal with.[8] The controversy reinforced Khartoum's distrust of foreign entrepreneurship, with far-reaching results; in 1914 Wingate would notice that "development" was "bringing to Khartoum a curious lot of the adventurer class, who will want somewhat careful watching."[9] Under his successors that distrust retarded development.[10]

In the event, Kitchener rescued Wingate from the Syndicate. Over objections by the British Cotton Growing Association he told the Sudan Government to assume management of the Tayiba scheme, putting the Syndicate on notice that it might be left out of the much more important Gezira Scheme. He then went further. After much discussion Kitchener proposed a partnership with the Syndicate, by which it would manage the Gezira scheme but not own the land or build the irrigation works; government, syndicate, and tenants would share the profits. Kitchener's command of the politicians, and British need for cotton, left little room for doubts about the financial viability of the scheme. By the end of 1913 estimates had already risen to the point where the non-Gezira purposes of the loan guarantee were to be postponed: a new Act was needed to allow this. And Kitchener answered queries with bluff assertions of the Sudan's ability, with the enormous revenue from a completed scheme, to finance any other projects wanted. That the size of the Gezira scheme itself had, in the planning stage, already been reduced by two-thirds, seems not to have worried anyone.[11] The war intervened, and when work was resumed soaring costs could be blamed on inflation.

Although cavalier with Gezira millions, Kitchener was as pennypinching in ordinary budget matters as he had been as sirdar.

---

[7] Wingate, 6 May 1913, cited in Gaitskell, *Gezira*, 65.

[8] Wingate to Stack, 10 April 1913, SAD 186/1.

[9] Wingate to Herbert, 29 January 1914, SAD 189/1.

[10] See, e.g., G.N. Sanderson, "The ghost of Adam Smith: ideology, bureaucracy, and the frustration of economic development in the Sudan, 1934–1940," in M.W. Daly, ed., *Modernization in the Sudan*, New York 1985, 101–20.

[11] Kitchener to Grey, 24 January 1914; Hamilton (Treasury) to Tyrrell, 9 March 1914; Kitchener to Foreign Office, 21 March 1914, FO 371/1965. See Gaitskell, *Gezira*, 65–73.

Financial disagreements marked his relations with Wingate. Although they both disliked Col. Bernard, and thus blamed much unpleasantness on him, the Sudan's weak finances multiplied difficulties. In confrontations Kitchener always won. The Egyptian subvention ended in 1913, and despite famine in the Sudan's northern provinces Kitchener was deaf to special pleas. (Even Wingate remarked that famine should lower labor costs at the Gezira works.) As with Cromer, Wingate had to acquiesce when his chief was adamant; and, like Cromer, Kitchener was frequently adamant.

As often as Wingate had cause to complain, however, he had reason to acknowledge Kitchener's support. In the Gezira negotiations this was crucial. In other ways too the contrast with Gorst was refreshing. In 1912 the Cairo newspaper *Wadi al-Nil* "made some bad remarks" about a patrol in the southern Sudan; Kitchener suppressed it.[12] Wingate complained about the Sudan's pared budget; Kitchener raised his salary by £500. Kitchener occasionally intervened in minor ways—demanding changes in the annual report of Gordon College, for instance[13]—but as often neglected matters Wingate put before him. A 1911 list of "Notes for [discussion with] Lord Kitchener" includes cotton-growing, punitive patrols, surveys, missionary and other religious matters, stores, customs, housing, special grants, overdrafts, British troops in Khartoum, press laws, Kitchener's statue, road building, cattle transport, medical matters, arrest of a German, "Princess Pless and Duchess of Westminster," rubber, telegraph conventions, dates of leave, and many other subjects.[14] It is unsurprising that by mid-1912 Wingate's liaison officers, especially Stack, the Sudan Agent in Cairo, complained that Kitchener did not find time to go into all the matters they wished to lay before him.[15] There was, in short, no system in Khartoum-Cairo relations at the highest level: Kitchener interfered at will, and in disputes prevailed; Wingate wanted support even in minor matters, but complained about interference. Wingate sometimes forgot,

[12] Kitchener to Wingate, 7 April 1912, SAD 181/1.
[13] Harvey to Bernard, 24 October 1911, SAD 235/3; Currie to Wingate, 19 November 1913; Wingate to Kitchener, 20 November 1913, SAD 188/2.
[14] Harvey to Bernard, 24 October 1911, SAD 235/3; Currie to Wingate, 19 November 1913; Wingate to Kitchener, 20 November 1913, SAD 188/2; N.d. (1911?), SAD 301/6.
[15] Wingate to Phipps, 29 April 1912, SAD 181/1.

but had to accept, that Kitchener, "no matter how sympathetic he may be to the Sudan," was "a good deal more sympathetic to Egypt."[16]

During his three-year consul-generalship Kitchener visited the Sudan four times. He was at Port Sudan for the visit of the king in January 1912. He returned in February to open the El Obeid railway. He visited in December 1912–January 1913, and in January 1914, when he went with Wingate to the Gezira works, then without him to El Obeid. (Wingate avoided return calls to the Residency in Cairo during Kitchener's tenure, resorting instead to "the Bungalow.")[17] About Kitchener's visit of February 1912 a British observer said a great deal about Wingate too, and about Cairo-Khartoum relations: "[T]o judge from the nervous way in which preparations are being made for his reception, one can feel that his eagle eye is feared as well as welcomed. Last year he came through here for a week as a 'tourist.' . . . He gave various suggestions, which were taken as orders, to the Sirdar and others; but as soon as he left for the North, people began to forget them, thinking it wd. be a long time before he was back again, if ever."[18]

An example of wishes becoming commands concerns the statue of Kitchener at Khartoum. During his private visit in 1911 Kitchener "suggested" a replica of a statue planned for the *maidan* at Calcutta. Wingate "readily acquiesced," and they selected a site. Kitchener would "arrange matters," but eventually Wingate got a bill for several thousand pounds. Kitchener told him to approach the likely casters in England and suggest that if they wanted the contract for Calcutta they should produce the replica free. Wingate did so and they agreed, provided he supply the brass.[19] In July 1914 Wingate was still corresponding with Kitchener on the type of pedestal he wanted;[20] war broke out a week later, and it fell to Wingate's successor to honor Kitchener posthumously.

The governor-general's relations with Cairo during Kitchener's term contrasted more starkly than ever with his status in the Sudan,

---

[16] Wingate to Palmer, 12 April 1912, SAD 181/1.

[17] Wingate to Stack, 24 April 1912, SAD 108/15.

[18] H.C. Bowman diary, 23 February 1912, MECOX.

[19] Wingate to Sandes, 10 February 1936, SAD 227/7. See also Wingate to Birdwood, 4 January 1911, SAD 300/1.

[20] Wingate to Kitchener, 25 July 1914, SAD 191/1.

where Wingate was by now a regal figure. His style and ritual were ever more elaborate and expensive. Events like the royal visit helped to create a Sudanese chapter of the imperial cult, in which the sirdar was both governor and high priest. His arrivals and departures became legendary. In November 1911, when Wingate returned from leave, in full dress uniform,

> the "higher officials" went to the Palace to greet him and Lady Wingate. We were there by 1/4 to 7: punctually at 7 they drove up in a double landau, with 4 ponies and postillions, and outriders, A.D.C.'s etc escorting them on horseback. . . . A guard of honour from the Yorkshire Regt. was drawn up facing the Palace: officers of the E.A. and the Yorks on the right, facing inwards, civilians and Sheikhs and ulemas [*sic*] on the left. . . . It was a pretty sight in the early morning sunshine, though rather theatrical; and I could not help being reminded of a Drury Lane melodrama. The Sirdar has got a wonderful "manner": he never forgets a face or a name, and has the royal faculty of saying the right thing to the right person. Here he is absolute ruler; he travels in kingly state, and is always accompanied by native orderlies and attendants as well as by his ADC's [*sic*] etc.[21]

Three reasons for such pomp in Sudanese circumstances are commonly offered. The first is that even a modest civil servant conforms with the routine in place. In this case, of course, Wingate created the routine. A second explanation is that a businesslike British soldier had to meet expectations of his "Oriental" subjects: rulers rule by inspiring awe. But Cromer and Kitchener (and Gordon) had largely done without it; tax rebates serve where regal ritual fails. Finally, Wingate himself argued that attempts to associate the British royal family with the Sudan were part of a policy to weaken the Egyptian connection and strengthen the British. This was true, but had nothing to do with Wingate's own style.

That style sometimes betrayed pettiness. In 1908 Wingate reminded officials that he should always be the last on and first off a steamer.[22] In 1912, a British visitor to Khartoum

---

[21] Bowman diary, 10 November 1911, MECOX.
[22] Clayton, "Steamers. Embarkations and Disembarkations," n.d. 1908, SAD 234/6.

met the Sirdar with his suite and escort . . . and as he passed, had raised his stick to his helmet in salutation. . . . He walked on, and was then surprised to hear an ADC galloping up to him, saluting, and saying gravely:—"I beg your pardon, Sir, but are you a stranger in Khartoum?" N. replied that he was a visitor, upon which the ADC said: "That was the Governor General you passed just now on the road. . . . It is customary for all civilians to take their hats off when the Gov. Gen. passes" said the ADC and rode off. . . . Would Lord Cromer ever have done such a thing? Or King Edward VII or King George?[23]

In 1913 Wingate, writing in the third person, asked permission to hang a banner with the royal arms over "the Governor-General's Chair" in the newly-consecrated Khartoum cathedral.[24] He commissioned a portrait of Gordon for the Palace (and showed embarrassment by writing that the Sudan Government had "voted" to pay for it), then commissioned one of himself.[25] For the coronations of both Edward VII and George V, Wingate wrote privately to have himself invited.

The consecration of Khartoum cathedral in 1912 was a notable event. Political arguments for a Sudanese bishopric had finally won the day. Wingate was active in raising money to complete a cathedral; his efforts were both world-wide and amateurish. In 1908 he had even written to J. P. Morgan, and when, in 1911, Morgan was to visit, Wingate asked an American journalist to intercede. (Kitchener urged directness: "Pierpont Morgan and a party . . . are going to Khartoum," he told Wingate: "Please see that he gives at least £1,000 to the college.")[26] An affected disdain for money, and reliance on middlemen, hampered this and other projects Wingate wished to support. When Lord Rosebery gave £100 for the cathedral, Wingate recruited others to ask for more.[27] When he heard that "Rockfeller [sic], or some other American millionaire" whose name he had not troubled to learn, had left millions for hookworm

---

[23] Bowman diary, 18 February 1912, MECOX.

[24] Wingate to Stamfordham, 30 August 1913, SAD 187/2.

[25] Wingate to Kitchener, 27 May 1911, SAD 300/5; Wingate to Ouless, 6 February 1912, SAD 180/2.

[26] Wingate to Bridgman, 24 November 1911, SAD 301/5; Kitchener to Wingate, 30 November 1913, SAD 188/2.

[27] Wingate to Stack, 18 March 1914, SAD 189/3.

research, he asked a prominent doctor to intervene,[28] with predictable results.

The consecration took place on 26 January 1912. The bishop of
London presided, and the Princess Royal was to be guest of honor.
In the event, she was detained in Egypt (where her husband died a
few days later). Again, H. C. Bowman was a witness:

> The ceremony was due to begin at 9.30, and by 9.15 we were all
> in our places, soldiers and govt. officials in white uniform, resi-
> dents of Khartoum . . . etc. and about 30 or 40 tourists. . . . Just
> before 9.30 we heard the National Anthem being played outside,
> and the Sirdar entered and walked up the central aisle to his spe-
> cial seat in the chancel, being preceded thither by the 2 church-
> wardens. . . . as judges they were wearing . . . kneebreeches, silk
> stockings, lace ruff and cut-away coat, with a legal gown over all.
> . . . The ceremony was impressive and went without a hitch, hav-
> ing been carefully rehearsed beforehand.[29]

These halcyon years before the First World War were probably
the happiest of Wingate's career. The world still saw the Sudan
Government against a backdrop of the Mahdiyya; defects, largely
unknown, would cause serious problems only after Wingate left. He
relied increasingly on officials, while assuming the style of a head of
state and immersing himself in social and private affairs. Indeed, like
Kitchener, he now addressed "big questions" such as Gezira development, but other matters only as they caught his fancy. At fifty he
had achieved a great deal; people and episodes of his early career—
Gordon, the Mahdi, the khalifa, Slatin's escape, Fashoda—had
already passed into semi-legend. Ironically the same status threatened
him, since under his rule the Sudan had attracted so little attention.
But he led a busy and varied life in his Blue Nile Palace, Red Sea hill-
station, and Scottish country house. He welcomed as guests the
nobility of Europe, some of whom—including, most gratifyingly,
members of the royal family—reciprocated. By 1913 he was a full
general and a G.C.V.O.; promotions and honors, British, Egyptian,
and European, came as a matter of course. His income was greater
than he would have dreamed possible a decade earlier. His eldest son,
with an Oxford degree, had won a place in the Indian civil service; his

---

[28] Wingate to Balfour, 20 August 1913, SAD 187/2.
[29] Diary, 1 February 1912, MECOX.

younger son had a promising career in the Royal Engineers. The Sudan, it seemed, was on the verge of important economic development which, with Port Sudan, the railways, and Khartoum itself, would comprise an impressive and lasting legacy. The last two years of peace thus appear in many ways, personal and public, as a culmination in Wingate's life.

They began ominously. On 23 February 1912, on his way to meet Kitchener at Khartoum station, Wingate was attacked by a madman. A blow to his left wrist was minor but caused occasional pain and debility for the rest of his life.[30] He was able to go with Kitchener to maneuvers at Karari the next day, and to El Obeid on the twenty-fifth to dedicate the new railway, an occasion marked by elaborate ceremonies, a levee, parade, and races. Kitchener returned to Egypt, while Wingate took an exhausting tour in the Nuba Mountains of southern Kordofan. After a fortnight in the *jabal*s he reached the Nile at Tonga, where his wife joined him, then returned by steamer to Khartoum. He spent seven of the next nine weeks at Erkowit, and went to Egypt at the end of May. A week later he was in Vienna, and on 12 June met his wife at Karlsbad, where they took a three-week "cure." On 5 July they attended a state ball in London and the baptism of Wingate's godson, Reginald Spencer Crawford. There followed a rare weekend with the whole family, at Digswell, after which Wingate went to Dunbar.[31]

As usual, Wingate's leave in 1912 was interrupted by several flying visits to London on business, but most of the summer was spent on golf, Sudan telegrams, and country-house visits in Scotland. It was apparently without irony that he told one correspondent he was too busy to "manage more than one round of golf a day."[32] Kitchener visited twice. Slatin came in September and went as usual with Wingate to Balmoral; Wingate asked permission to bring a Sudanese servant along. After another family weekend near London (and a visit to Farnborough in connection with Kitchener's statue), Wingate and his wife left for Cairo on 2 October and for the Sudan in mid-November.[33]

The winter of 1912–13 was unusual in that both the Wingates' sons, Ronald and Malcolm, paid long visits to the Sudan. They went

---

[30] CB1; *Wingate of the Sudan*, 164.

[31] CB1.

[32] Wingate to J. Kennedy, 14 August 1912, SAD 182/2.

[33] CB1; Wingate to Keppel, 6 August 1913, SAD 187/2.

with their parents and Lord Kitchener on a tour of Dongola after Christmas; Ronald then returned to England. At Khartoum, Malcolm learned that he had passed 10th out of Woolwich, following in his father's footsteps. The usual crowd of tourists demanded Wingate's attention too: Lord Desborough, the dowager duchess of Roxburghe, the Marchese Gentile-Farinola; Slatin was reportedly exhausted from nightly dinners, and the Palace was so crowded that Wingate wanted outside housing for his servants.[34] Malcolm and his mother left for Europe on 3 March, Wingate for a long tour of the eastern Sudan. He visited Tayiba, Wad Madani, Sharif Yakub, Fau, Rumayla, Gadaref, Tomat, Khashm al-Qirba, and Kassala, where he was received by Sayyid Ahmad al-Mirghani of the Khatmiyya sufis. The tour ended at Erkowit on 27 March, where Wingate remained for almost two months, interrupting his stay for a few days in Khartoum in mid-April before going on annual leave, via Khartoum, in mid-May. Traveling as usual via Trieste and Vienna, Wingate went to Karlsbad for a month's "cure" with his wife, who joined him from London. They celebrated their twenty-fifth wedding anniversary on 18 June. Wingate returned to London on 1 July, in time for the Egyptian army dinner that night. On the fourth he and his wife dined with the Princess Royal, on the fifth visited their daughter, Victoria, at her school, and on the sixth went to Dunbar. The summer was punctuated as usual by visits to London, where Wingate had a series of meetings on the Gezira scheme in mid-July; he was able to arrange a weekend at Digswell with Malcolm and Victoria too, and attended the inauguration of the Bath Chapel at Westminster Abbey on the twenty-second. After the state ball on the twenty-third, he and his wife returned to Dunbar. In mid-August they and their daughter visited the Princess Royal, who by now was a personal friend, at Mar Lodge for a few days. In September Kitchener came to Knockenhair, and Wingate went with Slatin for the annual visit to Balmoral. (The royal connection was now strengthened further when Wingate appointed as his A.D.C. the son of Lord Stamfordham, the king's private secretary.)[35] After a weekend with their sons in London, Wingate and his wife left England on 1 October for Egypt.

The last peacetime "season"—and thus the last of all—epitomized the good life Wingate had created for himself in the Sudan. He

---

[34] Wingate to Asser, 26 June 1912, SAD 181/3; to Acland, 21 January 1913; to Butler, 5 January 1913; and Phipps to Wingate, 24 March 1913, SAD 185/3.

[35] CB1; Wingate to Stamfordham, 16 October 1913, SAD 188/1.

and his wife returned to Khartoum in early November 1913, and presided over a calendar filled with official and private entertainment. There were garden parties for French and Austrian scientists, farewell dinners for retiring officials, balls for visiting notables. Kitchener visited in early January and went with Wingate to the dam site at Sinnar; he attended the annual accession parade and garden party, the Khartoum Horse Show, the final match of the Governor-General's Polo Cup, and the running of the Governor-General's Cup at the races. During Governor-General's Week—or "Joy Week"—the Khartoum Regatta took place, and the Wingates accepted anniversary gifts on King's Day at Gordon College; exhausted, Lady Wingate had to spend the next few days in bed.[36] In March Wingate rode the railway to El Obeid and back, in three days, then left immediately with his wife and Dr. and Mrs. Acland for Erkowit. After a two-week stay he saw them off at Port Sudan, then returned to Khartoum. He spent a fortnight in the capital, then went back to Erkowit for a month before going on leave.

Traveling as usual—but for the last time—via Trieste and Vienna, Wingate joined his wife at Karlsbad on 15 June. It was there that he got word of the king's Birthday Gazette, in which he was made a G.C.B. (and Kitchener received an earldom). And it was at Karlsbad that Wingate heard of the assassination at Sarajevo of the archduke of Austria. As the diplomats did their work Wingate and his wife, like the rest of Europe, went about their business. They returned to London on 6 July. Wingate attended a Gordon College board meeting and the Egyptian army dinner on the seventh. On the eighth the Sudan Plantations Syndicate met, and on the ninth the Wingates attended Lady Salisbury's ball. On 10 July they met for the first time Mary Vinogradoff, Ronald's fiancée, then dined and went to the theater (to see *An Ideal Husband*) with Malcolm and the Princess Royal. They went to Dunbar on the eleventh, a visit cut short by the European crisis.[37]

On 23 July, the day of the Austro-Hungarian ultimatum to Serbia, Wingate and his wife returned to London. On the twenty-fourth he met the prime minister. On the twenty-fifth and twenty-sixth the Wingates visited Malcolm at Chatham, and on the twenty-seventh Wingate saw Sir Evelyn Wood, his old patron, at Harlow. On

---

[36] Wingate to Penfield, 26 January 1914, SAD 189/1; CB1.

[37] CB1.

the twenty-eighth he had an interview with Sir Edward Grey about the looming crisis; later that day Austria-Hungary declared war on Serbia. Still life went on: on the twenty-ninth Wingate dined out and went to the theater with his wife, Malcolm, and Victoria, then took the night train to Dunbar. He had been there only a few hours when a state of war was declared in Germany. On 2 August, with war between Britain and Germany imminent, Wingate was ordered to return to Egypt immediately. He and his wife left Dunbar at 8:00 P.M. for London. He would not see Knockenhair again for six years.[38]

Like millions of others, Wingate now found his movements caught up in the crisis. On 3 August, Germany declared war on France. Passenger ships would not now sail without escorts: Wingate was at Victoria Station when an order came to postpone departure. Kitchener was already at Dover when a similar order reached him, and he returned to London, where he dined with Wingate. Malcolm Wingate arrived in London late that night, only to report for duty the next morning. On the fourth, Britain declared war on Germany. The next day Kitchener was appointed secretary of state for war. Wingate, trying to arrange passage to Egypt, lunched with Asquith; on the sixth he discussed problems with Kitchener and then with Winston Churchill at the Admiralty. Arrangements were made, and on the seventh Wingate embarked on the P&O liner *Mooltan* at Tilbury; some sixteen hundred officers and others (including sixteen generals and two Greek princes) were reportedly aboard. Wingate went ashore briefly at Gibraltar and again at Malta, where his brother-in-law, Leslie Rundle, was governor. The *Mooltan* reached Port Said on the morning of the eighteenth, and Wingate was in Cairo that afternoon. He remained there until 5 September when he set out for Khartoum.[39]

[38] Ibid.; CB2.
[39] CB1.

Chapter Twenty
A Forgotten War

The Great War reverberated even in the Sudan. Although European armies did not meet there, a campaign took place that determined the map of Africa. And although peripheral even to the "sideshow" of the Arab Revolt, the Sudan played an important and largely unknown role in that episode. In both respects Wingate's central part resulted from his own initiative. It is ironic that his wartime achievements were later ignored, while he won faint praise instead for keeping the Sudan's domestic peace as war swirled around it.

At the outbreak of war in Europe the Sudan's anomalous position gave cause for worry. The Condominium Agreement had established a government, but had not assigned sovereignty. In theory the co-domini shared power, but Egypt remained in international law a vassal-state of the Ottoman sultan. If the Ottoman Empire entered the war on Germany's side, to whom would Egyptians—and Sudanese—owe loyalty? If the sultan declared a *jihad* against Britain, would Muslims of the Nile Valley join him to oust their infidel overlords? In European warrooms these questions, when asked at all in the early days of the war, provoked speculation; in Egypt and the Sudan—and in India and other Muslim lands under European rule—they were more important. In the Sudan, where "fanaticism" had been touted as endemic, British officials viewed the possibility of Ottoman entry with great concern.

Upon returning to Khartoum on 9 September 1914, Wingate took steps to avert danger. Enemy nationals (including Charles Neufeld, the ex-Mahdist-prisoner who had long pestered him) were expelled or, in the case of some missionaries, sworn. (Slatin, in Austria, tried vainly and with Wingate's naive help to return; they exchanged letters despite their countries' war, and the friendship survived.)[1] Censorship was imposed; by the end of October fifty thousand letters had been opened. Propaganda poured out; Wingate reported "quietly engineering a species of Press campaign," both to

---

[1] See, e.g., Wingate to Slatin, 21 August 1914, SAD 191/2.

advertise Egyptian and Sudanese loyalty and "to tie up to some extent with the Government those who have made loyal speeches and addresses."[2] Wingate's long insistence on soldiers in civil posts now caused problems: those who were able rejoined their regiments, and Wingate had to ask London for a direct order to keep essential personnel. As the war went on it accomplished what Wingate had never allowed: demilitarization of the Sudan Government.

Wingate feared a local response to the sultan's call. This might take the form of a Sudanese tribal rising or a mutiny in the Egyptian army. In combating this the two-month gap between the outbreak of war and the entry of the Ottomans was well used. Wingate himself set out on a series of quick tours, addressing the Sudanese on the issues. On 17 September he gave his "war speech" at Omdurman, where he reported that the "excellent reception" was owed at least partly to the government's import and cheap distribution of Indian grain.[3] On 6 October he spoke at El Obeid, on 7 October at Wad Madani, on the twentieth at Port Sudan. "I am very particular," he told Clayton, "to avoid any reference to Turkey, but I unhesitatingly go for Germany and put all the blame on her. My idea would be that, if actual hostilities take place, we make every effort to show that Turkey's action is brought about by German machination and that, as such, it deserves no religious support. . . ."[4] Wingate therefore sought out and consulted religious leaders, both *ulama* and those *sufi shaykhs* who had cooperated with the regime. Although religiously-inspired unrest was no more common during the war than before it, Wingate blamed all such episodes on enemy propaganda,[5] and so redoubled efforts to conciliate religious shaykhs. Egyptian soldiers were given an option of non-combatant duty.

When the Ottomans went to war in November, Wingate had therefore done what he could to prepare the ground. A *Sudan Times* piece for 9 November depicted the kaiser gloating over corpses and writing a book "in blood on a parchment of human skulls" to compete with the Bible and Qur'an.[6] On the same day Wingate addressed

---

[2] Wingate to Clayton, 15 October 1914, SAD 192/1.

[3] Wingate to Clayton, 23 September 1914, SAD 191/3.

[4] Wingate to Clayton, 24 October 1914, SAD 157/10.

[5] See, e.g., Wingate to Clayton, 11 May 1915, SAD 195/4, wherein Wingate cites the "recrudescence of fikism" as evidence that "the poison is slowly working." There are many such examples.

[6] "Translation of an article that appeared in the 'Sudan Times' on the 9th November 1914," SAD 192/2.

the assembled *ulama* in apocalyptic terms, denouncing the Turkish government—not the sultan—as a "syndicate of Jews, financiers and low-born intriguers" who, "like broken gamblers" had "gone to war with the one Power who has ever been a true and sympathetic friend to the Moslems and to Islam." (This remark, in a speech drafted by Wingate's secretary, Stewart Symes, reflected a widely-held view of the Young Turk government, and caused trouble in Britain, where the editor of the *Jewish Chronicle* complained of the "monstrous insult." Wingate later explained lamely that no insult had been intended, and it was stricken from the record.)[7]

War with the Ottoman Turks had meanwhile forced the British to act in Egypt, for the Suez Canal was vital to the empire. Martial law was declared. The Legislative Assembly was prorogued in October. On 18 December Britain declared a protectorate over Egypt. The Khedive Abbas Hilmi was deposed; an uncle, Hussayn Kamil, was made sultan. In Kitchener's absence the new British representative in Egypt, Sir Henry McMahon, was styled high commissioner. Egyptians were told that Britain alone would sustain the effort of war, after which progress would be made toward self-government. In Khartoum Wingate read out the British proclamation of protectorate from the steps of the Palace on 20 December, and the next day held an accession parade for the Egyptian sultan.[8]

Absorbed in the task of defending Egypt and the Canal from Ottoman invasion, British officials in Cairo had little time for the Sudan. As on previous occasions, Wingate was both pleased and irked. He chose to see Egypt's new (and undefined) status as making the Sudan "more British than ever," and strove to take advantage of Cairo's preoccupation (and the new high commissioner's ignorance).[9] At the same time he complained of being uninformed and unconsulted, and detected a change in the Residency's attitude to him personally. This, he told Clayton, was "galling," but because of "very strong views on the absolute necessity of 'playing the game,'" he kept silent.[10] Even Clayton had to defend himself against Wingate's sensitivity to neglect. As usual in wartime, hierarchies of rank and senior-

---

[7] Daly, *Empire*, 486, n.56. See also Kedourie, *In the Anglo-Arab labyrinth*, 8–9.

[8] CB1.

[9] Wingate to Herbert, 23 December 1914, SAD 192/3.

[10] Wingate to Clayton, 19 November 1914, SAD 469/7.

ity were upset; Wingate saw erstwhile subordinates achieve power and prestige while he was forgotten. The great crisis of Wingate's career, in 1918–19, had political and personal roots in the events and emotions of 1914.

"When it is realised," Wingate wrote Clayton in November 1914, that "it might have been necessary to appeal for large British reinforcements in order to maintain our position in this country, . . . some acknowledgement should be forthcoming."[11] None was. In mid-1915 Wingate took personal responsibility for this success, telling Sir Ian Hamilton that "a man with less experience . . . would have probably felt it necessary to ask for thousands of British reinforcements."[12] But it is hardly surprising that Cairo, much less London, paid scant attention to the Sudan during the war. They saw the main task of the Sudan Government as ensuring domestic peace and supplying the war effort: failure in these respects might provoke censure, but success was not likely to attract much notice while millions fought in Europe. It is moreover difficult to credit war-time measures for the absence of a major revolt in the Sudan. An assumption that the peace was kept by censorship, propaganda, collaboration with Sudanese notables, and food distribution would unfairly indict a regime that had prided itself on good government. Wingate did not leave the Sudan, even to visit Egypt, until final departure in December 1916. He contended that his personal position was so important in maintaining order that even a few days' absence "would be the signal for a host of undesirable rumours."[13] Since no other political reason suggests itself, this contention cannot be dismissed. It is noteworthy, however, that Wingate spent long periods at Erkowit, and that, increasingly as the war went on, his time was occupied by matters unrelated to the Sudan's internal security. Whether there was also an element of self-exile, a reluctance on personal grounds to attend upon McMahon and his powerful advisers in Cairo, can only be surmised. Wingate's constant insistence, in correspondence, on his own importance leaves an impression of self-promotion or of sensitivity to remoteness from the war.[14] "They also

---

[11] Wingate to Clayton, 12 November 1914, SAD 192/2.

[12] Wingate to Hamilton, 11 August 1915, SAD 236/2.

[13] Wingate to Cromer, 31 March 1915, FO 633/24/67.

[14] See, in this regard, Wingate to Callwell, 1 September 1915, SAD 236/2, in which Wingate, in a "somewhat egotistical effusion," dismisses rumors that he wished to leave the Sudan for more active service.

serve" was hardly a motto for a sirdar; but calming the masses with singular prestige left an echo of Gordon.

Unlike that predecessor, Wingate had a family caught up in war. Unable to accompany her husband in August 1914, Lady Wingate had remained in Britain, dividing her time between Dunbar and various friends in and near London. Upon mobilization Malcolm Wingate had been appointed to the 26th field company, Royal Engineers; he left England for the front on 14 August 1914 and on the twenty-eighth spent his twenty-first birthday there. He took his first leave, in November, with his mother in London, after which she set out, via Paris and Marseilles, for Egypt. Lady Wingate reached Port Said on 19 December and was reunited with her husband at Khartoum on Christmas Eve. Malcolm meanwhile had seen action that led to a Military Cross in February 1915. His parents' commonplace books, which had often recorded their children's arrivals at school and departures from Knockenhair, would for the next three years note the many distinctions of Malcolm's active service.[15]

A personal disappointment with political ramifications was Wingate's inability to further the career of his elder son, Ronald. In February 1915 Ronald was appointed assistant to the commissioner at Lahore. He wished, however, after his marriage to transfer from the Indian civil service to the political service, which did not ordinarily admit married men. His father intervened with the viceroy, Lord Hardinge, and urged Ronald to write to him directly; although Hardinge was about to leave India, Wingate felt "sure" that his successor would "be kindly disposed to any request" he might make.[16] But Hardinge would not make an exception, and the new viceroy, Lord Chelmsford, declined Wingate's renewed request "in unequivocal terms." Wingate told Bonham Carter in London that his son had "been led to hope" (though not by whom); the result was disappointing and embarrassing to all concerned.[17]

The very quiescence of the Sudan during the first months of the war lends exaggerated importance to sundry reports and rumors of anti-British activity. Indeed an impression is left of Wingate's manipulating these in order to stress his government's achievements or even merely to keep its affairs from being forgotten in England. Within a few days Wingate might write that the Sudanese were both thor-

---

[15] CB1; CB2.

[16] Wingate to Ronald Wingate, 10 July 1915, SAD 236/2.

[17] Wingate to Bonham Carter, 10 August 1916, SAD 236/5.

oughly loyal and dangerously susceptible to Turco-German propaganda; that the army both knew where its interests lay and was riven with sedition. Bland reassurances were sometimes addressed to political and military superiors, while stark warnings went to the well-placed but indirectly concerned. As early danger from across the Red Sea ebbed, Wingate's attention turned increasingly to the west, to the lightly-administered tribes of Kordofan, and the sultanate of Darfur beyond.

Darfur was an unlikely ally of the kaiser. This remote territory had been annexed to Egypt only in 1874, and had been uneasily controlled from the Nile during the Mahdiyya. After the battle of Omdurman a prince of the old ruling house, Ali Dinar, had taken control. The Sudan Government was too weak, and Darfur too far away and unimportant, for the British to administer. They asserted formal claims for international recognition, but left Ali Dinar to govern; he sent an annual tribute to Khartoum, but otherwise ruled independently. His affairs came to Khartoum's notice in two main ways. Relations with the Baggara tribes, whose homelands straddled his borders with the Condominium, raised periodic questions of raiding and slaving, while the sultan's relations with the French in Wadai and the lands to the west added an international dimension that required Khartoum's attention. In negotiations France pressed the British to pacify the wild west by occupying the sphere they claimed; by 1914 diplomacy had achieved little but a British realization that such direct action could not be deferred forever.

The war in Europe both delayed and precipitated that action. Just as he moved gingerly to conciliate tribal and religious leaders, so Wingate tried to reassure Ali Dinar, lest the sultan answer an Ottoman call to jihad. Bizarre rumors from the far reaches of Kordofan fueled fears of tribal unrest, which in turn might indicate or provoke Ali Dinar's wrath. Wingate prompted religious notables in Khartoum to correspond with the sultan and urge loyalty. Yet relations deteriorated. As war-time alliances coalesced, a course seemed forced upon Ali Dinar: Britain was allied with France, his old enemy, and both opposed the Ottoman sultan, the premier Muslim ruler; in May 1915 Italy entered the war, driving another regional power, the Sanusi *tariqa* in Cyrenaica and the Fezzan, into the Ottoman embrace. Turkish agents were sent to enlist the support of Ali Dinar.

Wingate approached the problem methodically. There is no doubt he wished to regularize Darfur's position as a province of the Sudan, and that the war provided a pretext. But a campaign would be costly and dangerous: his forces, Muslims led by Christians, would have to cross waterless wastes inhabited by ill-assorted tribes to attack a Muslim ruler in his home territory. A reverse might spark tribal risings in Kordofan and require British reinforcements from Egypt or beyond, thus nullifying the Sudan Government's contribution to the war effort and humiliating Wingate and his officers. He—but not they—could recall the fate of Hicks's army at Shaykhan in 1883; as both civilian advisers and officers pressed him to move against Darfur,[18] Wingate therefore patiently prepared the ground. Propaganda was instigated, the Arab tribes of Kordofan were armed, agents were sent to stir up Ali Dinar's domestic opponents. Information was carefully selected for dispatch to Cairo and London—and notably, through private channels, to Kitchener—while a veil was drawn over military preparations. Tension increased, as Wingate made finely calibrated moves in the border region and Ali Dinar sent ever more insulting messages, duly forwarded by Wingate to superior authorities. The nuances of his thinking are evident in a secret letter to the governor of Kordofan in August 1915:

> until the military situation abroad is more favourable to us, in the eyes of the public . . . and until we can, if necessary, make good our declarations, we should be sparing of the latter. . . . We must be as vague as possible—and above all try to avoid giving the impression that we are greatly concerned or irritated at the Sultan's attitude, and to cultivate the idea that his present conduct is merely witness to sentiments which he has been known to bear secretly for years past. . . . That Government will tackle the situation one day . . . in her own way and in her own time should be the burden of our assurances to natives. . . . it is desirable to give the impression that Government, *as a logical outcome of the Sultan's attitude* will have to interfere in Darfur affairs before long rather than that Government *has decided to do so at the first favourable opportunity.*[19]

As confrontation loomed, Wingate stepped up the propaganda. Ali Dinar's renunciation of Anglo-Egyptian sovereignty seemed an insufficient reason for a campaign: Wingate began to include, in offi-

---

[18] See, e.g., Savile to Civil Secretary, 2 July 1915; Wingate to Savile, 1 August 1915, SAD 127/3, and Adjutant General to D.A.A.G., Erkowit, 26 June 1915, SAD 127/2.

[19] 19 August 1915, SAD 196/4.

cial and private correspondence, reports of the sultan's atrocities. One
story he circulated concerned Ali Dinar's having murdered a baby and
forced its mother to eat the remains. The tribes were said to be
"groaning" under his rule, which now increasingly was compared
with that of the Khalifa Abdallahi.[20]

On 26 February 1916 Wingate sanctioned an advance to two
Darfur border posts. He knew, and privately communicated the
knowledge to selected correspondents, that this ostensibly defensive
measure must lead to a showdown with Ali Dinar.[21] Wingate himself
went to Nahud, near the Darfur border—by train to El Obeid and
thence by camel or horse—to see off the invasion force, arriving there
on 8 March. (This was an extraordinary gesture—almost three weeks
of round-trip travel in order to have two days at Nahud.) By 10 April
the Darfur Field Force had taken Abiad, the main point between the
border and El Fasher, with only the slightest resistance. The road to
the Fur capital, where Ali Dinar was expected to make a stand, lay
open. A last-minute attempt to block it was now made in Cairo,
where political and financial objections arose, confirming Wingate's
reasons for having surrounded the campaign in secrecy. He now
therefore turned again privately to Kitchener, who had for months
been sent carefully-worded reports both directly and through his aide,
FitzGerald. Kitchener in turn cut through Cairo's objections, and an
advance to El Fasher was approved. The field force left Abiad on 15
May and defeated Ali Dinar's army before El Fasher on the twenty-
second. The sultan fled, and after months of fitful negotiation and
flight was ambushed and killed in November.[22]

Wingate's handling of the Darfur campaign allows insight into his
methods as soldier and administrator. Whether the campaign was necessary is debatable. An attack from Darfur would have provided a clear
justification against doubters in Cairo, but Wingate was right to consider the effects that perceived weakness might have had on the tribes
of Kordofan. The effects too of military success must be gauged: occupation of Darfur removed an irritant to Anglo-French relations in
Africa, and one moreover that Wingate had long suspected Cairo was
reluctant to deal with; would-be dissidents in the Sudan, tribal or reli-

---

[20] See Daly, *Empire*, 183.

[21] See, e.g., Wingate to Clayton, 21 February 1916, and to Kitchener, 22 February
1916, SAD 199/2.

[22] Daly, *Empire*, 181–82.

gious, were reminded of the government's power; the Egyptian army
was heaped with honors for its role in the campaign, and thus the less
likely to grumble; British officers, demoralized by news from Europe
and by their own inactivity, saw the campaign as a victory for Britain,
albeit on a distant front. Finally, while there is no question that
Wingate coveted a more direct role in the war than his position in the
Sudan provided, nor any question that he later exaggerated the Darfur
campaign's place in the history of the war,[23] there is yet no evidence of
mere self-advancement in his pressing forward when he did.

In planning and executing the conquest of Darfur, Wingate was
characteristically methodical. Typical of such campaigns, the military
results of success were dwarfed by the political effects of failure. This
in part accounts for the secrecy with which Wingate planned the
advance: it could be curtailed or canceled at virtually any moment
short of El Fasher; ultimate goals were neither communicated to the
outside world nor trumpeted in the Sudan. "In the event of a setback," he later told Phipps, "the less said the better."[24] And in another
private letter Wingate, giving credit to Kitchener, summed up the
larger reasons for secrecy that thirty years of Anglo-Egyptian experience had taught: "Had I not been able to privately apply for his powerful aid, politicians might have suddenly stopped our advance just as
it was about to mature. I purposely kept the movement very dark on
this account."[25] Indeed, during and after the campaign Wingate communicated directly with officers in the field, without reference even to
his own military intelligence. In June 1916 he told Lt. Col. P. V.
Kelly, commanding the field force, that

> In all these matters one's principal enemy is "routine". If the
> A.D.I. [assistant director of intelligence] gets these telegrams he at
> once repeats them to Cairo, Clayton takes them to the High
> Commissioner and probably to the French Minister, and before I
> know where I am I find my hands hopelessly tied by political inter-
> ference. I prefer in these cases, as in the case of the capture of El
> Fasher, to keep everything as much as possible in my own hands
> and only to declare publicly a "fait accompli".[26]

---

[23] See, e.g., Wingate to Grey, 8 June 1916, FO 800/48.
[24] 17 June 1916, SAD 200/5.
[25] Wingate to Garstin, 22 July 1916, SAD 201/3.
[26] Wingate to Kelly, 13 June 1916, SAD 200/6. See also Wingate to Clayton, 24
   March 1916, SAD 127/7.

Although he traveled to distant Nahud to see off the Darfur Field Force, Wingate had, since the beginning of the war, increasingly made his headquarters at Erkowit, the "hill station" near the Red Sea. This change of routine coincided with or caused others that give a different character to his final years as governor-general and sirdar. Beginning in April 1915 a London detective was assigned to him as a bodyguard; the Egyptian sultan had been shot at in Cairo earlier in the month. The war put an end to frivolous tourism; Wingate's commonplace book records no private visitors at all. After his round of flying visits to the provinces in the autumn of 1914, moreover, Wingate curtailed inspections. He visited the Gezira briefly in March 1915 to see the cotton crop, and again in October 1915, but otherwise his travels were limited to the Khartoum-Atbara-Port Sudan and Khartoum-Wadi Halfa axes. He spent almost the entire period between April and October 1915 at Erkowit, leaving only for brief visits to Khartoum, to Port Sudan, and to meet his wife at Wadi Halfa upon her return from England. As he told Clayton in April 1915, he would go to Khartoum occasionally "to see Heads of Departments and to show myself"; a special railway carriage was kept at "Summit," "ready to tack on to any train" if his presence in the capital was "urgently required."[27]

Two weeks after returning from Nahud in 1916, Wingate welcomed to the Sudan the Prince of Wales, who visited Port Sudan, Sinkat, Omdurman, and Khartoum, where pre-war ceremonial was revived for the occasion. (Whether Wingate's prohibition, from 1 June 1915, of alcohol at Palace dinners, a rule earlier adopted by George V, was relaxed for the prince is unknown.)[28] Wingate took advantage of the visit to distribute several hundred pounds to the urban poor, leaving the impression it came from the prince.[29] Wingate accompanied him also to Atbara and saw him off for Egypt while proceeding himself to Erkowit on 7 April. There Wingate received news of the fall of El Fasher and, on 5 June, of the death on the *Hampshire* of Lord Kitchener. Wingate visited Port Sudan for a day in late June, traveling to Khartoum only at the end of July, apparently—for there is an unexplained gap in his notebooks, perhaps the result of intense concentration on events in Arabia—only briefly for routine ceremo-

[27] Wingate to Clayton, 20 April 1915, SAD 195/1.
[28] CB1; CB2; Wingate to Drake, 29 May 1915, SAD 195/5.
[29] Wingate to Clayton, 9 April 1916, SAD 470/2.

nial duties. He left Erkowit for the last time on 4 October 1916; his appointment as high commissioner for Egypt was announced on 6 November.

By that time the war had taken a toll on Wingate personally. His cousins Alfred Wingate and Roger Wingate White were both killed at the front in May 1915. Another cousin, Benjamin Wingate Barrow, was taken prisoner after his ship hit a mine. His nephew, John Wingate Greany, was wounded at Gallipoli in August 1915 and killed in Mesopotamia in April 1916. Wingate's brother, Captain G. M. Wingate, died in England in April 1916. Malcolm Wingate's exploits at the front were a source of constant worry; his Military Cross in February 1915 was followed by a D.S.O. in March, which was awarded personally by the king in June. Lady Wingate was able to see her son for a few hours at Boulogne in July 1915 and in October when he had two weeks of sick leave, spent mainly at Knockenhair, owing to influenza. Wingate himself would never see Malcolm again. His other son, Ronald, whose marriage had been several times postponed during the war, married at Lahore on 11 November 1916 without any members of the family present.[30]

Wingate's long absences from Khartoum during the war caused difficulty for his staff and senior officials, and gave rise to unfavorable comment.[31] Events proved, however, that he was capable, through officials' exertions and constant telegraphy, of dealing from Erkowit with those matters that interested him. A greater problem for the Sudan Government was Wingate's very absorption in the war and concomitant neglect of other business. Regarding Darfur this amounted to detailed control, regarding Arabia almost obsessive preoccupation. For Wingate the real war was not on the western front, Darfur, but to the east, across the Red Sea, with the Arab Revolt and all that it implied for the Near East, the empire, and himself.

For questions remain about Wingate's ultimate ambitions during and after the war. While assuring private correspondents that he, and the Sudan, were best forgotten, Wingate constantly brought himself to attention. He had been mentioned in 1914 as a possible successor to Kitchener in Cairo; McMahon was soon by all accounts a failure there, and Wingate may well have seen himself as next in line. There

---

[30] CB1; CB2; Wingate to McKenzie, 1 July 1915, SAD 236/2. On his wedding Wingate gave Ronald £250 in war bonds and £100 in cash (Wingate to W.H. Bonham Carter, 10 August 1916, SAD 236/5).

[31] See, e.g., Willis to O, 27 July 1916, SAD 209/7.

seems, moreover, to have been in the back of his mind a far grander design to combine various territories, and great military and civilian posts, to create a British viceroyalty in the Near East. He had long held that both Aden and Somaliland should be "under the Sudan,"[32] and the war suggested vast new possibilities. With Egypt a protectorate, and the Sudan, as Wingate saw it, "more British than ever," the nucleus was there. Reverses in 1914–15 had led to discussion in military circles of the need for reorganization—what in 1916 Callwell at the War Office called a "British High Commissioner for the Middle East, co-ordinating Egypt, Arabia and Mesopotamia."[33] Who better than Wingate—already in nominal charge of the war effort in the Hijaz—to assume that role? That Wingate saw at least the possibility of grand reorganization, under himself, is proven by acts and statements after he became high commissioner in Egypt. That appointment allowed real scope for such designs, the seeds of which were planted in the irksome shadows of the Sudan.

[32] Wingate to Clayton, 13 April 1916, SAD 136/4.

[33] Callwell to Wingate, 7 August 1916, SAD 139/2; see also Clayton to Wingate, 9 October 1915, SAD 135/4.

Chapter Twenty-one
Arab Policy

In 1914 the tribes of Arabia were as disunited as ever. There, as else-where in their empire, the modernizing Turks had been strengthening control that had long been nearly nominal. This brought them into conflict with the Arabs of the Hijaz, where the sharifs of Mecca had enjoyed autonomy. The Arab Revolt, when it came, was not merely the local name for world war, but a local war of independence in which the world had interests.

Contacts between the British and the sharif's family began before the war. In February and April 1914, his son, Abdullah, had passed through Cairo and spoken with surprising candor to British officials. Behind the diplomatic correctness with which those officials discussed the affairs of a friendly power were hints of British sympathy for the Arabs. These were pursued when war broke out. As early as 6 September the Egyptian army intelligence department, true to form, produced a memorandum brimming with false information and Arabian possibilities. An order followed immediately from Kitchener, in London, to contact the sharif and ask his intentions. A messenger returned with the sharif's request for help against the Turks. This Kitchener quickly promised, raising as well the glittering prospect of an Arab caliphate.[1] Thus before the famous Husayn-McMahon cor-respondence, long before the Sykes-Picot agreement and Balfour dec-laration, and indeed even before a state of war between Britain and the Ottoman Empire, loose words and grand dreams were ensnaring the region.

Wingate's part in these opening gambits is unclear. If the intelli-gence department's "appreciation" of September 1914 was the work of Clayton, its director and Wingate's Agent, it would have reflected his wishes. In September 1914, however, Wingate was preparing the Sudanese for war with the Ottomans; when he looked over the Red Sea he saw enemy agents, not potential allies. But with Kitchener as

---

[1] Elie Kedourie, *In the Anglo-Arab labyrinth. The McMahon-Husayn correspondence and its interpretations 1914–1939*, Cambridge 1976, 4–18.

secretary of state for war, there was a vacuum at the Residency in Cairo. The acting agent, Sir Milne Cheetham, was unable to restrain powerful British officials; his successor (as high commissioner), Sir Henry McMahon, who arrived in January 1915, was an Indian civil servant intended to hold Kitchener's place. Conduct of affairs fell to Ronald Storrs, the oriental secretary; to Lord Edward Cecil, the financial adviser; and to various military commands. Wingate was not so much disregarded as forgotten. In pique he wrote to Clayton in January 1915: "I think it should be clear to anyone with a grain of sense that we in this country, with our long experience, have some knowledge of dealing with Arab tribes and Moslem Religious authorities, and if the British and Indian Governments think it undesirable to make any use of our experience, our geographical position, and our close connection with the other side of the Red Sea, that is their affair."[2]

Wingate was, in fact, by then already in contact with Arabia. He had for many years corresponded with one Abd al-Qadir al-Maccawi, a merchant of Aden who supplied him with intelligence. After the Ottomans entered the war, Wingate brought this to official attention and continued it, sending through Abd al-Qadir and others copies of British propaganda. At the end of 1914 the channel was disrupted at Aden, where a new British Resident intercepted Wingate's communications. Implicit in this action was the issue of control over Arabian policy, an interest of Egypt, the Sudan, Aden and, therefore, of the government of India. Wingate naturally held that Cairo should predominate, but McMahon's weakness and India's powerful insistence extended the debate.

A far more important correspondence ensued, with the sharif of Mecca himself. On 11 February 1915 Wingate told Clayton to ascertain whether the British government would approve his contacting the sharif and, if so, whether he or the Residency should draft a letter. Three months passed before London agreed. On 29 May Clayton wired Wingate the text of a message to be delivered verbally to the sharif. This asked only for a secure system for communicating on "important questions."[3] In July a message reached the Sudan from Abdallah, the sharif's son, asking if the British could supply

---

[2] Wingate to Clayton, 14 January 1914, SAD 469/8.
[3] Wingate to Clayton, 11 February 1915, SAD 134/2; Clayton to Wingate, 29 May 1915, SAD 134/6.

arms. This was completely overshadowed, however, by Abdallah's letter to Storrs, which reached Cairo on 18 August. In this, the first in what would be called the Husayn-McMahon correspondence, Abdallah, in Clayton's words, "opens his mouth pretty wide," demanding British recognition of Arab independence, an Arab caliphate, and an Anglo-Arab treaty of alliance.[4] The Residency was not cowed, but advised a temporizing reply urging the need to defeat the Turks before such matters were discussed. To this both the Foreign Office and India suggested qualifying amendments; Wingate urged action: "some more definite encouragement should be given" the sharif, he told Clayton,[5] and recommended "insertion of a pious aspiration on the subject of the Sherif's ideal of an Arab nation, in other words something might be added to ensure his remaining definitely on our side at any rate until our success in the Dardanelles enables us to give more authoritative expression to our views."[6] The object, he told Cromer, should be to keep the sharif "on the hook."[7]

Expediency thus lay at the heart of Wingate's own "Arab policy." When British officials in Cairo would snub representatives of embryonic Arab nationalism, Wingate urged conciliation. With the war going badly, he told Clayton, "we have need of all our Arab friends, and I think you would do well to give . . . at least the impression that you view" Arab Union "with some degree of sympathy."[8] In October he was more explicit. Britain, he told Clayton,

> should now unhesitatingly support the Sherif of Mecca. . . . We seem to be over-squeamish in not sympathising more readily with the aspirations of the Egyptian and Syrian Pan-Islamists. . . . The success of this policy requires the support of all parties. . . . The aspirations of the national idea . . . should be combined with those of the Arabic, Syrian[,] Egyptian pan Islamism . . . if the success of the movement is to be ensured.[9]

---

[4] Clayton to Wingate, 21 August 1915, SAD 135/2; Kedourie, *In the Anglo-Arab labyrinth*, 66–67.

[5] Wingate to Clayton, 27 August 1915, SAD 135/2.

[6] Wingate to Clayton, 30 August 1915, SAD 135/2.

[7] Wingate to Cromer, 18 September 1915, SAD 135/3.

[8] Wingate to Clayton, 1 September 1915, SAD 135/3.

[9] Wingate to Clayton, 18 October 1915, SAD 135/4.

In other words Britain should keep all strands of Arab sentiment "on the hook" until military developments made choices necessary or desirable.

The importance of Wingate's correspondence with the sharif is difficult to gauge. Its existence does not prove a decisive influence on the course of Anglo-Sharifian relations. The sharif's reply to Wingate's first message reached the Sudan only in mid-September 1915, the messenger having been greatly delayed at Jidda. He, however, had met the sharif at Ta'if in late August and arranged for regular and rapid communication with the Sudan. Upon receipt of this news Wingate urged dispatch of "a suitable message" and five thousand pounds.[10] He rightly wished to exploit an opening that, through the agency of Sayyid Ali al-Mirghani, would allow communication without the responsibility borne by official dispatches. As Wingate told Clayton on 1 November, after another letter from the sharif had reached Sayyid Ali:

> we can by this means give the Sherif some very useful advice without its actually coming from us. It is on these lines that I am getting Sayed Ali to reply and I have of course discussed with him the frontier questions and pointed out the necessity for reservations which we have made, in Syria, Palestine and Mesopotamia. . . . I think he [the sharif] is [a]cute enough to realize [sic] that through him [Sayyid Ali] he can fathom our ideas without having to apply directly to us for explanations.

Wingate was sure that his and Clayton's "combined work . . . in this Arab question" had "gone a long way to prepare the ground," and congratulated himself for having moved India in the direction of Anglo-Egyptian wishes.[11]

The delay that followed, and Wingate's reference to India, together hint at the complicated role he played in the diplomacy of the Arab Revolt. His call to exploit the new channel fell on deaf ears; a week after bringing it to Cairo's notice Wingate wrote to McMahon asking whether he had read his "various letters containing notes and memoranda on the Arab question, Khalifate, etc."[12] But the roots of

---

[10] Wingate to Clayton, 21 September 1915, SAD 135/3.

[11] Wingate to Clayton, 11 November 1915, SAD 135/5.

[12] Wingate to McMahon, 23 September 1915, SAD 135/3.

delay were in London, and entangled not only competing British views but also complex inter-allied interests.

From the outset Wingate had in fact undertaken to influence British policy in two ways: in supporting an Arab rising against the Turks and in securing Anglo-Egyptian (as against Anglo-Indian) interests. From the Sudan he pursued these aims through voluminous correspondence, in the same way he had tried to influence policy during earlier phases of his career. Frequent and detailed notes and memoranda on British policy in Arabia, on the future of the Arabs and of Islam, were dispatched to Britain, Egypt, and India. Wingate found it convenient at times to attribute his views to Stewart Symes, his private secretary and draftsman, but their origin is clear.[13]

The caliphate, leadership of the Muslim community, had been a mere shadow since extinction of the Abbasid dynasty in 1258. For political reasons the Ottomans had assumed the title, which was, however, largely unrecognized and even unknown in the wider Muslim world. Decline of the principal Muslim states and concomitant European encroachment in the eighteenth and nineteenth centuries had led, among other things, to Muslim interest in reviving the office. In 1914 both Muslims and Europeans thought that Arab resistance to the Turks might be incited by the prospect of such revival, and that candidates for the role would appear; indeed Khedive Abbas Hilmi had for years been said to covet it. When the Turks entered the war, they used the caliphate to summon all Muslims to jihad; the British looked for credible pretenders. Although Wingate touted the sharif of Mecca as most likely to succeed, he was privately casual about which potentate might someday fill the role. As late as September 1915 he told Wigram, the king's private secretary, that there would be "many more candidates when the critical moment comes—the Senussi, the Idrisi, Imam Yehia, Ibn Saud, Ibn Rashid, and a host of others"; the sharif had a strong claim, but was bound to need British help.[14]

Wingate's expressed views, characteristically embroidered, were as unrealistic as those of other British officials, or as cynical. An Arab caliphate with British sponsorship, an Arab (or "pan-Arab") state under British protection, was the stuff of dreams when war in Europe ground to stalemate. Storrs in Cairo "evoked the splendid vision of a

[13] See, e.g., Symes's Notes of 11 and 15 February 1915, SAD 134/2.
[14] Wingate to Wigram, 6 September 1915, SAD 236/2.

North African or Near Eastern vice-royalty . . . from Aden to Alexandretta."[15] Clayton, the chief conduit between Wingate and the Residency, was himself a strong advocate of the sharif as caliph, and gave prominence to Wingate's arguments. When the (Egyptian) grand qadi of the Sudan, Shaykh Mustafa al-Maraghi, wrote in support of the sharif, his views were widely circulated; when Sayyid Ali al-Mirghani, the Sudanese religious notable, wrote similarly, he was touted as a figure of global significance. It is likely that Wingate induced both expressions, and certain that had they not buttressed his own they would have been suppressed. In this intramural war, officials in distant centers of British power supported their own cases with wild predictions and loose promises. As usual Wingate worked indirectly, his views reaching the king through Wigram, Kitchener through FitzGerald, Curzon through Cromer,[16] Storrs and McMahon through Clayton, the sharif through Sayyid Ali, the War Office through military intelligence, and various others through Symes.

Opposition at home to the use of British troops in remote theaters was always strong, and was cited repeatedly to support the government of India's political objections. Wingate therefore sent intelligence "appreciations" on Arabia not only to the Foreign Office and War Office, but also to the viceroy in private correspondence. Just as Wingate feared Sudanese reaction to war with the Ottomans, so Lord Hardinge in Calcutta had millions of Indian Muslims to account for. Then too old issues arose of where India's western interests should give way to the Foreign Office's responsibilities; when Kitchener had written in 1914 of an Arab caliphate, had he considered the ties that would bind Indian Muslims to it? Or India's interests in the Persian Gulf and Mesopotamia? What of Aden? India balked at the prospect of a large Arab state on its borders, and of a caliphal potentate with claims upon Indian Muslims. Why upset the East when the war would be won or lost on the Western Front?

Thus in March 1915 Hardinge told Wingate that Symes's memorandum on the future of Arabia was all very well, but that the "wisest course" was "to let the Arabs in Arabia work out their own salvation," so long as other European powers were excluded.[17] In

---

[15] Kedourie, *In the Anglo-Arab labyrinth*, 33.

[16] As late as June 1915 Curzon wrote Cromer: "We ought to know more about this Sharif of Mecca. His family and position are impeccable. But what of the man?" (Curzon to Cromer, 9 June 1915, SAD 134/7).

[17] Hardinge to Wingate, 18 March 1915, SAD 134/4.

May, enclosing notes by the grand qadi and Sayyid Ali al-Mirghani, Wingate claimed that, having discussed Hardinge's concern about British control of Mesopotamia, "Muslim leaders here" (the Sudan) "now realise the necessity for this and would make no further opposition."[18] What Hardinge thought of Sudanese notables' deliberating over his policy is unknown; he replied merely that it was still "too soon to make any move" in Arabia; the British "must wait till Constantinople has fallen" before prompting the sharif "to declare himself."[19] In August Wingate wrote again on British war aims and ways in which these might be compatible with Arab and Muslim aspirations. "I am increasingly drawn," he said, "to an attempted solution on Pan-Arabian lines." But an Arab union needed a religious basis for cohesion, while an Arab caliphate, "buried away in the sands of the Arabian Peninsula," would have no appeal. What he foresaw he expressed with typical circumlocution: "a federation of semi-independent Arab States . . . under European guidance and supervision, linked together by racial and linguistic bonds, owing spiritual allegiance to a single Arab Primate, and looking to Great Britain as its Patron and Protector."[20]

It was in Cairo, not Calcutta, that Wingate's influence was most easily brought to bear. The prestige of long service ensured that his views were heard and prompted others to make use of them. Clayton, still Sudan Agent, was in constant touch, and oversaw political and military intelligence in Egypt. Open disagreement between the two was rare; Wingate's doubts about Clayton were born of misunderstanding created by long absence from Egypt. Wingate relied on correspondence and intermediaries, refused frequent requests to come to Egypt himself for consultation, and even balked when officials would come to him; in late 1915 he excused Mark Sykes on the grounds that Sykes's time was too valuable to be spent on the long journey to Khartoum: through Clayton and correspondence Sykes would be fully informed of his views. Wingate even declined to meet McMahon at Wadi Halfa. It is doubtful that Cairo and London took his reason—the Sudanese upheaval his absence might cause—at face value. He may have calculated that the benefits of a brief visit or two could not justify the taint of involvement in Cairo's confusion: pitching and snip-

[18] Wingate to Hardinge, 14 May 1915, SAD 134/6.
[19] Hardinge to Wingate, 10 June 1915, SAD 134/7.
[20] Wingate to Hardinge, 26 August 1915, SAD 139/6.

ing from afar carried fewer risks while affording ample opportunity to influence a debate that, in the end, would be settled in London.

In forming the Arab policy that finally emerged in late 1915 and early 1916, Wingate thus played an indirect but important role. His method had been perfected over thirty years: he provided political intelligence to support a particular policy. As he had during the 1890s, and indeed as he continued to do in 1915–16 regarding Darfur, Wingate drew from a mass of obfuscating detail clear indicators of the direction he wished to pursue. Subordinates, notably Clayton and Symes, followed in his footsteps. Both had served as his private secretary. In October 1915 Clayton, in a long letter criticizing British policy in the Near East, told Wingate: "The whole situation in this part of the world should be dealt with . . . by one head and everything should conform to one definite line of policy. I am horribly afraid that they will make a muddle of it and the issues involved are such that failure will mean shaking our Empire to its very base."

He went on:

> I have had some extremely interesting discussions with an Arab officer who deserted to us at the Dardenelles. . . . the G.O.C. has told me to prepare a note for him on the officer's views. . . . I shall take the opportunity of rubbing in the fact that if we definitely refuse to consider the aspirations of the Arabs we are running a grave risk of throwing them into the arms of our enemies which would mean that the Jehad, which so far has been a failure, would probably become a reality.[21]

Analysis of this episode[22] shows that Clayton did what he said he would, and that Wingate, McMahon, and British officers in Egypt used the resulting "intelligence" to urge the necessity of immediate action in Arabia. The Foreign Office was led to understand that that alone would prevent the Arabs from rising in support of the Turks. On 20 October, therefore, Grey told McMahon to "give assurances that will prevent Arabs from being alienated"; since this was "urgent," details were left to the high commissioner. McMahon was told also to keep Wingate informed.[23]

---

[21] Clayton to Wingate, 9 October 1915, SAD 135/4. The officer was Muhammad Sharif al-Faruqi. See Kedourie, *In the Anglo-Arab labyrinth*, 73–76.

[22] Kedourie, *In the Anglo-Arab labyrinth*, 73–83.

[23] Ibid., 92–94.

At this crucial juncture Wingate was indeed kept informed, but his advice went unheeded. On 23 October he cabled Clayton a "formula" which, with "necessary verbal explanations" by a messenger, he thought would satisfy the sharif:

> His Majesty's Government will recognise and support, and further will exercise Her good offices with Her Allies to this end, the principle of Arabian independence within the boundaries defined, on behalf of the Arab people, by the Sherif of Mecca; without prejudice to the claims by Great Britain and Her Allies to exercise such local measures of protection and control over certain districts as may be necessary to secure these territories from foreign aggression, to promote the welfare of the local populations, and to safeguard their economic interests.[24]

Instead of this general "formula," McMahon sent the sharif a poorly-worded and badly-translated letter distended with cagey circumlocution. This centerpiece of the "Husayn-McMahon correspondence" would have dire results after the war. Cairo had been caught up in the sense of urgency created by its own intelligence reports. The outcome was a series of concessions to the sharif, correspondence with whom was now referred to as "policy."

But the sharif was in no hurry to rise. Despite the deadline for British acceptance of his terms, he was naturally swayed more by military and political reality than by British promises. Constantinople did not fall. The Gallipoli campaign dragged on to costly failure at the end of 1915. In that context McMahon's letters seemed desperate, and so may have forestalled rather than incited the sharif. In any case, the correspondence continued, both through Cairo and the Sudan. The Anglo-Egyptian leadership's object remained the entry of the Arabs, and any other potential enemies of Turkey, into the war. Intramural arguments over the wording of correspondence involved practical issues of how best to bring that about, not whether words would be honored after the war. As Wingate told Clayton in November: "After all what harm can our acceptance of his [the sharif's] proposals do? If the embryonic Arab State comes to nothing, all our promises vanish and we are absolved from them—if the Arab State becomes a reality, we have quite sufficient safeguards to

---

[24] Wingate to Clayton, 23 October 1915, SAD 135/4. The version quoted in Kedourie, *In the Anglo-Arab labyrinth,* differs slightly.

control it. . . . In other words the cards seem to be in our hands and we have only to play them carefully. . . ." The important thing, he argued, was not to force the sharif's hand: like other neutrals he awaited proof of which way the war would go; once the British showed success, in Mesopotamia, for example, the time would be right.[25]

On 26 November 1915 Clayton told Wingate (in a "very private" letter marked with the Masonic star they used for "eyes-only" correspondence) that a new Near Eastern intelligence office would be established in Cairo. This—the Arab Bureau—Clayton had been asked to head while keeping all his other roles.[26] Such concentration of intelligence under one official was sensible, or would have been if intelligence had been separated from policy-making. But by 1916 Clayton was already a formidable advocate. The Arab Bureau, which he described as "independent" and meant to "furnish information of all kinds, rather than express views,"[27] became coordinator of Arab policy. Clayton, now director of military intelligence for the Egyptian army, Sudan Agent and assistant director of the Sudan Government's intelligence department, and intelligence officer for the G.O.C. Egypt, would be, in the words of T. E. Lawrence, who later joined the bureau, "like water, or permeating oil, creeping silently and insistently through everything."[28] Relations with Wingate deteriorated. As early as January 1916 Wingate told E. S. Herbert that Clayton had become a "judicious Staff Officer," who kept him in the dark. By September Clayton was refuting charges that he had "not put forward" Wingate's views and had neglected his duties as Sudan Agent.[29] Although close correspondence continued, Wingate increasingly relied on Herbert for "the real jam of Cairo news."[30] But the volume of Clayton's manuscript correspondence with Wingate absolves him of the charge of neglect which, even had it been true, might with understanding have been forgiven of one so fully engaged in the war

---

[25] Wingate to Clayton, 15 November 1915, SAD 135/5.

[26] Clayton to Wingate, 26 November 1915, SAD 135/6.

[27] Clayton to Wingate, 11 February 1916, SAD 136/2.

[28] *Seven pillars of wisdom*, Garden City, N.Y. 1936, 57.

[29] Wingate to Herbert, 20 January 1916, SAD 136/1; Clayton to Wingate, 24 September 1916, SAD 140/6.

[30] Wingate to Herbert, 22 October 1916, SAD 141/4.

effort. It rather appears that Wingate, as he had and would in the cases of other successful subordinates, saw in Clayton's independence an inevitable disloyalty, as if allegiance depended on subordination.

Just as it seems to have struck Wingate again that the war had passed him by, the sharif of Mecca finally raised his revolt.

Chapter Twenty-two
The Arab Revolt

◄─────∞◊∞────►

That Wingate's conquest of Darfur has found no prominence in military history is unsurprising. But neglect of his role in the Arab Revolt calls into question the way in which historical consensus is reached about persons and events. It is ironic that Wingate, who did as much as anyone to burnish the aura of General Gordon, would be overshadowed completely by another legendary figure, T. E. Lawrence. The two misfits yoke his long career, which extended from Mahdism to nationalism, the one he fought to destroy and the other that was used to destroy him. Wingate's role in the Arab Revolt was central and creative, yet even after the war he was forbidden to acknowledge that he had once been in command. Immured at Erkowit, far from scribes and cameras, Wingate fought by telegram.

During 1916, his last year in the Sudan, Wingate was preoccupied with war. In February–March a lull in Arabian affairs allowed him to go to Nahud to see off the Darfur expedition; otherwise he divided his time between Khartoum and Erkowit, where he was able not only to maintain easy communication with Egypt but also conveniently to oversee operations in the Hijaz. From Erkowit, early in 1916, Wingate continued his campaign to incite the sharif of Mecca and to win over British waverers. Chief among these remained the viceroy of India and his advisers, who saw any allied effort against the Ottomans as misguided: even successful campaigns in the east, they argued, would delay victory in the west and make more acute those political questions—the future status of the Ottoman lands—that so concerned them. Wingate's patient efforts failed to convince, but were not entirely wasted.

Those efforts, extending over two years and involving constant commentary on the war and inter-allied diplomacy, were occasionally misinterpreted and are still easy to belittle. They had, however, a consistent end: destruction of the Ottoman Empire, and British control of its post-war affairs. In supporting the sharif, Arab nationalists, and others, Wingate nursed no notion of Islamic renaissance

or Arab empire; if such prospects incited revolt against the
Ottomans, he promoted them. In April 1916 he wrote with irrita-
tion to Clayton:

> I am afraid both the High Commissioner and Lord Hardinge are
> under the impression that I am a believer in the creation of a con-
> solidated Arabian Kingdom under the Sharif—Of course any such
> notion is altogether remote from my real views, but it has suited
> me, as I believe it has suited all of us, to give the leaders of the Arab
> movement this impression and we are quite sufficiently covered by
> the correspondence which has taken place to show that we are act-
> ing in good faith with the Arabs as far as we have gone—It may be
> very difficult to make either the Foreign Office or the Indian
> Government appreciate the somewhat subtle distinction, but I
> think we ought to be given the credit of a certain amount of ordi-
> nary common sense and prescience. . . . [1]

Wingate thus "advocated" what he deemed unlikely—creation of a
large and stable Arab state—not romantically in spite of the unlikeli-
hood but optimistically because of it.

Ignorance, poor Intelligence, equivocation, wishful thinking,
misunderstanding, miscalculation, bloated circumlocution and bad
translation, secrets and partial revelations were by the end of 1915 the
coin of allied-Arab relations in any case. The sharif's decision, in
December, finally to rise in revolt was relayed to the British in mid-
February 1916, and taken up triumphally by Anglo-Egyptian officials.
Ironically by the time the sharif acted, in June 1916, the Sykes-Picot
agreement had been reached (though not revealed to him), and his
was the position of beleaguered client rather than eager ally; hoped-
for revolt in Syria had not occurred, and Ottoman reinforcements had
been sent to the Hijaz. When, therefore, the British finally began to
send material support, prospects for significant success against the
Turks had already dimmed.[2]

Wingate was exasperated with this turn of events, and with intramural British disagreements that continued even after the sharif had
revolted. The desperate need for coordination of British political
activity in the Middle East had finally led to the establishment in

---

[1] Wingate to Clayton, 24 April 1916, SAD 136/5.
[2] For the Sykes-Picot agreement see Elie Kedourie, *England and the Middle East.
The destruction of the Ottoman Empire 1914–1921,* London 1956.

January 1916 of the Arab Bureau in Cairo.[3] But it was slow in getting started and in any case—notwithstanding the formidable mythology that has grown up around it since—never fully superseded the various other centers of British military and administrative authority. In mid-June 1916 Wingate told Clayton he was "bombarded with telegrams from all parts, none of which quite tally with each other"; there was "a general air of confusion and uncertainty." Instead of definite action in Arabia, the British had "made about twenty bites out of the cherry," the result, he wrote, of "pusillanimity," "personal motives," and "indecision and uncertainty."[4] From Erkowit Wingate nevertheless took up the arming of the Arabs. He had for months urged dispatch of arms, ammunition, and money; now he sent Egyptian army artillery and mooted dispatch of Egyptian troops. The relief of action was tempered by continuing ineptness in the chain of command: he learned, for example, from Cairo only by letter rather than wire, that complete batteries were needed in the Hijaz, thus wasting a week and much effort of overworked staff. "Want of a directing hand" was his sustained diagnosis; the Arab Bureau had not, indeed could not have, provided it. Only "the mercy of Providence and the success of the Darfur operations" had allowed him to meet dilatory demands from his own meager stores.[5]

Wingate nonetheless took personal satisfaction in the start of the Arab Revolt. His still-copious personal and semi-official correspondence from mid-1916 brims with reminders of early and consistent advocacy of the policy so lately adopted. He had, he told the Chief of the Imperial General Staff in London, "been doing all I could ever since the war began to help to bring about what has now occurred in Arabia, realizing [*sic*], as I did, the immense effect that a successful movement of this sort would have throughout the whole Islamic world and how seriously it would upset the nefarious and lying propaganda of our Turco-German enemies. . . ."[6]

Such flourishes indicate the elevation of Wingate's mood after long months of finger-tapping. Whether momentous or not, events in the Hijaz would at least open a new front, and would permit some

---

[3] For a history see Bruce Westrate, *The Arab Bureau*, University Park, Pennsylvania 1992.

[4] Wingate to Clayton, 15 June 1916, SAD 137/4.

[5] Wingate to Clayton, 19 June 1916, SAD 137/3.

[6] Wingate to Robertson, 22 June 1916, SAD 137/5.

outlet for a general's energies. Wingate's correspondence now became enormous: by mid-July he was filling one or two files a day.[7] Erkowit became the nexus for the revolt, and Wingate the coordinator of its political and military intelligence, supply, and strategic planning. On 24 June he sent Col. C. E. Wilson, governor of the Sudan's Red Sea Province, to Jidda as his representative. Chain of command—from Wingate as sirdar through Wilson and officers of the Egyptian army—was clear, but above Wingate it was not, for there had not yet been an appointment to overall command of Hijaz operations. The situation fully justified Wingate's pressure now for a decision in this respect. As late as the end of June the War Office in London, citing multiple interests, British and foreign, in the Arab movement, refused to sanction a unified British command. Wingate argued indirectly for his own appointment to such a post; McMahon held that military and political direction should remain in Egypt.[8] Between 26 and 28 June, however, he abruptly changed his mind, and asked Wingate to assume "direction of military matters connected with our assistance to the Sharif." He, McMahon, would "retain direction of political dealings."[9] The apparent off-handedness of this sudden change warned Wingate to demur. The web of Anglo-Egyptian intrigue stood out clearly against the sunny sky of Erkowit. McMahon's shaky authority was almost spent; to fall in eagerly with his plans might mean going down with him. Wingate temporized, and posed a series of questions to the high commissioner. Had the Foreign and War offices been consulted? Would London meet the Arabs' need for guns, ammunition, airplanes, food, and money? Would the sharif's demand be met for a diversion against the Turks on the Mediterranean coast? Was London willing to send an expeditionary force? What "promises, verbal or other," had been given the sharif? Finally Wingate asked: "[W]hat are the respective functions of the High Commissioner, the Commander-in-Chief in Egypt, the Arab Bureau. . . . unless I am given full discretionary powers and am assured that my recommendations will meet with immediate consideration, little benefit and possibly more confusion than exists at present, will result from the proposed change."[10]

----

[7] See, e.g., SAD 138/3, 138/5–6.

[8] Chief Egypforce to Sirdar, 25 June 1916; Sirdar to Chief Egypforce, 26 June 1916, SAD 137/5.

[9] High Commissioner to Sirdar, 28 June 1916, SAD 137/5.

[10] Sirdar to High Commissioner, 30 June 1916, SAD 137/5.

Wingate was playing for time. Some of his points McMahon answered directly, some he could not. On the one that concerned Wingate most, authority, McMahon merely repeated that political control would remain with the high commissioner. Wingate complained that his responsibility would therefore be merely "nominal," and his "utility and capacity to assist would be almost nullified"; he should not have to act as a post office between Cairo and the sharif, but should have "full discretionary powers" in matters where policy had been already settled.[11] McMahon's delay in responding further forced Wingate to postpone urgent decisions himself, and indeed seemed to agitate him unduly. Had he gone too far in his demands? On 8 July he told Parker at the Arab Bureau that although he would be glad to continue in an "advisory" role, he would in that case *assume no responsibility whatever*"; indeed, he admitted none for anything that had happened so far. "Had Lord Kitchener or Lord Cromer been in the chair," he continued, "they would have long ago handed the whole affair, stock, lock and barrel, over to the Governor General of the Sudan."[12]

McMahon's delay was one more example of British dithering, the result of which, Wingate continued to argue, might be the collapse of the sharif's movement.[13] On 9 July 1916 he wrote "privately" to General Robertson, Chief of the Imperial General Staff, enclosing copies of the relevant telegrams, and ominously absolving himself of responsibility.[14] The issue was ostensibly resolved when McMahon told Wingate on the tenth that operations beyond the Hijaz were now contemplated, and that therefore military and political control would remain in Cairo after all.[15] Wingate's "directing hand" (as Hogarth at the Arab Bureau had called it, with relief and enthusiasm), was now removed before it could be formally applied.[16]

Nor did the matter rest. Indeed, in the confusion that characterized British conduct of the war in the Near East the question of com-

---

[11] High Commissioner to Sirdar, 3 July 1916; Sirdar to High Commissioner, 3 July 1916, SAD 138/2.

[12] Wingate to Parker, 8 July 1916, SAD 138/4.

[13] Wingate to Parker, 8 July 1916, SAD 138/4.

[14] Wingate to Robertson, 9 July 1916, SAD 138/5.

[15] High Commissioner to Sirdar, 10 July 1916; Sirdar to High Commissioner, 11 July 1916, Wingate, SAD 138/7; Wingate to Robertson, 12 July 1916, SAD 138/9.

[16] Hogarth to Wingate, 29 June 1916, SAD 137/6.

mand continued to arise. Wingate's part in resurrecting it was characteristic too: while protesting his single interest in the war, he yet acted to promote himself. After McMahon resumed control in July, Wingate expressed relief, while nonetheless continuing to press for a unified command in the Hijaz and to cultivate the idea that he was in the best position to occupy it. After he and General Murray, the G.O.C. Egypt, exchanged plaintive letters about the unworkability of divided responsibility and the hope that one or the other would have combined control,[17] Wingate on 31 August 1916 wrote twice to Robertson in London. One letter gave a brief history of the Arab Bureau—"I venture to think," he wrote, "that the Arab Bureau owes its inception to my efforts"; claimed credit for Clayton's work by praising him as a mere liaison officer; and protested uninterest in a unified Hijaz command and his wish that Lord Grey be informed of that uninterest![18] Wingate's second letter to Robertson had a similarly unsubtle sub-text. Modestly allowing that on strategic questions he was "out of [his] depth," Wingate yet went on to survey difficulties in the Hijaz, recommend a landing on the "Northern Arabian coast," and refer in passing to the Dardanelles, India, Afghanistan, Persia, Egypt, Darfur, the Turkish garrisons in Arabia, German designs on the Holy Places of Islam, and General Murray's willingness but inability to "cope" with the present situation in Egypt.[19] On 2 September Wingate followed up with a long letter to his old colleague General Callwell, praising him and the prime minister, commenting on strategy in the Balkans, detailing the help he had given the sharif, and mentioning Murray's inability to send further help.[20] After learning that the sharif's forces had taken Taif, Wingate wrote even to Cromer, Grenfell, and others claiming credit which, although they must not acknowledge it publicly, he had no objection to their making known "privately."[21]

While Wingate's private campaign continued, so did the Arab Revolt; intriguing correspondence was no substitute for progress on the ground. Wingate's ambition may have hampered the Anglo-

---

[17] Murray to Wingate, 16 August 1916, SAD 139/4; Wingate to Murray, 23 August 1916, SAD 139/5.

[18] Wingate to Robertson, 31 August 1916, SAD 139/7.

[19] Wingate to Robertson, 31 August 1916, SAD 139/7. The typed text has the word "co-operate" lined out, and "cope" inserted in Wingate's hand.

[20] Wingate to Callwell, 2 September 1916, SAD 140/1.

[21] Wingate to Cromer, Wingate to Grenfell, 25 September 1916, SAD 140/7.

Egyptian war effort. Despite the confusion that multiple commands and conflicting British and allied interests had created there, Wingate still refused to visit Cairo, even briefly. His stated reasons were always the same: pressure of work and the risk to security in the Sudan if his steadying hand were removed. The former point contradicted the fact that much of his work involved correspondence with Cairo necessitated by his refusal to go there. The latter point, valid in 1914, may have been still in late 1916. But Wingate could easily have traveled secretly, or met relevant officials at Aswan or even Wadi Halfa; when he was appointed high commissioner in November, security risks were cited only to justify designation of a successor at Khartoum as "acting"—Wingate left the Sudan and never returned. At the end of August 1916 Clayton had begged him to attend a conference in Cairo, convened to settle just such long-standing questions as Hijaz command. "I do know how distasteful it would be to you personally," Clayton wrote revealingly, "but you could do such an immense amount of good here."[22] To depict Wingate sulking in his tent may seem inaptly to exaggerate one of several motives (and indeed his own importance), but the confusion that hampered the British war effort benefited Wingate personally. An important reason for his appointment as high commissioner was to put an end to that confusion.

The Cairo conference involved Murray, McMahon, Clayton, Storrs, Admiral Wemyss, Col. Wilson, and representatives of British G.H.Q. Egypt and the Arab Bureau. Private accounts reveal the personal differences that characterized British affairs in Cairo; these were now rehearsed rather than settled. Indeed, if avoiding this quagmire was Wingate's reason for staying away, his absence was more justifiable than military circumstances alone would allow. Murray's caution, to the point of inactivity, was more fully exposed (and soon more widely broadcast to London), but otherwise the conference settled little.[23] The continuing disagreements of the men on the spot only emphasized the need for the British government to act.

Decisions were now finally made. After insistent refusal to give much assistance to the sharif, the British government at last decided fully to support his revolt. On 4 October 1916 Wingate was again appointed to command the Hijaz operations. McMahon strenuously

----

[22] Clayton to Wingate, 24 August 1916, SAD 139/6. See also Clayton to Wingate, 31 August 1916, SAD 139/7.

[23] Wilson to Wingate, 20–25 September 1916, SAD 140/5.

objected to the Foreign Office that divided political and military control had already been tried, and had failed. Asked for his views,
Wingate could only disagree: he had never fully accepted military
responsibility precisely because McMahon had insisted on retaining
political control. Now Wingate went further, deploying strong arguments that he himself should hold dual command and requesting that
relevant papers on the vexed subject be supplied the War Council in
London.[24] In complying, McMahon told the Foreign Office:

> I used the term "full trial" from my point of view and I think with
> justification in that I gave the arrangement a trial sufficiently full to
> prove that it was unworkable. . . . The whole of the correspon-
> dence follows by post. It will show that so far from shirking any
> responsibility the Sirdar shows a generous disposition to assume
> both political and military responsibilities which in my opinion his
> geographical position and the dearth of military resources ren-
> dered him and still render him incapable of discharging. . . . [25]

Both men knew that the Hijaz operations were but one example
of the larger issue of divided control, resolution of which would soon
result in Wingate's replacement of McMahon in Cairo.[26] On 10
October the Foreign Office told McMahon that the decision stood,
and, for good measure, that London had accepted Murray's advice
over his own; McMahon was to give Wingate "whatever authority" he
needed.[27] To Murray, Wingate wrote with the same small-mindedness
with which he had (privately) taxed his correspondent for so long: it
was "rather late in the day to make the change," he said, and if he
failed in the Hijaz, this could not be "fairly laid to my charge"; as
usual when writing in this vein, Wingate added that he "deprecate[d]
in the strongest possible terms the introduction of the personal element into such considerations."[28]

[24] McMahon to Sirdar, 4 October 1916, SAD 142/11; Sirdar to High
Commissioner, 3 October 1916, SAD 142/11.

[25] McMahon to Sirdar (quoting his telegram to the Foreign Office), 6 October
1916, SAD 142/11.

[26] On the continuing confusion in Egypt see Clayton to Wingate, 28 September
1916, SAD 140/8.

[27] McMahon to Sirdar, 10 October 1916, quoting Foreign Office telegram 812,
SAD 142/11.

[28] Wingate to Murray, 12 October 1916, SAD 141/3.

Having at last a definite task, and the authority to carry it out, Wingate acted with characteristic energy. In reply to McMahon's wire of the tenth, Wingate told him, without apology, that he planned an immediate trip outside the Sudan—to the Hijaz—to discuss "the military and political situation" with British officials and representatives of the sharif. (To avoid speculation he would "give out locally" that he would be inspecting Port Sudan.)[29] The views so freely given for two years had, after all, carried no responsibility for consequences their adoption might have; now at last in authority, Wingate evidently saw a need to separate the chaff of his own and others' propaganda from the grain of military facts.[30] Asked by McMahon to come to Egypt instead to confer, Wingate emphatically refused, on the novel grounds that a visit must entail an audience with Sultan Hussayn; he would, however, postpone the Hijaz trip if necessary. But with studied casualness he let McMahon know which way the wind was blowing: regarding political authority over Hijaz affairs, Wingate wrote, "My own view is that it would be simpler if you gave me *carte blanche*."[31]

Wingate was soon reminded that formal designation of command meant little in the Anglo-Egyptian labyrinth. As early as 14 October 1916 McMahon, expressing diffidence because of the new regime, yet told the Foreign Office he opposed strong action to help the sharif; the British could "await developments before taking further action."[32] Two days later he intervened again: when Wingate suggested greater discretionary powers for the Arab Bureau, to streamline conduct of Hijaz affairs, McMahon demurred, suggesting instead that Clayton (who was still answerable in one of his capacities to McMahon) take on that role.[33] These matters were not trivial. London now decided to send no British troops to the Hijaz, nor to back up Wingate in the Sudan, whence Egyptians might have been sent for the same purpose. Wingate canceled his proposed visit to Rabegh, instead concentrating efforts anew on providing the disconcerted Sharifians with material

---

[29] Wingate to McMahon, 10 October 1916, SAD 142/11. The words quoted have been underlined, with the heavy pencil Wingate used, in his copy of the wire.

[30] See, e.g., Wingate to Wilson, 12 October 1916, SAD 141/3.

[31] Sirdar to McMahon, 13 October 1916, SAD 142/11.

[32] McMahon to Sirdar, 14 October 1916, repeated to Foreign Office, SAD 142/11. Wingate's marginal comment: "Wait and see!"

[33] McMahon to Sirdar, 16 October 1916, SAD 141/1.

and money. Having at last won overall command, Wingate was thus left with little military activity to oversee. The danger of an Arabian collapse, always possible, seemed greater than it had in the spring, when the dual control had first been seriously mooted. As difficult as relations between Murray and McMahon had been, they still agreed on the secondary importance of the Hijaz, and in this they were still widely supported in London. Indeed, the War Office seemed to hold that the appointment of Wingate was an end in itself: British policy, Robertson told him in late October, should be to "avoid any military commitments" and to confine assistance to supplying the sharif. "If we develop our resources to the full," he concluded pointedly, "reduce our commitments in secondary theatres to a minimum and devote our energies whole-heartedly to fighting Germans, we shall win through."[34]

The same sense of change without difference, of substituting personnel for policy, was about to result in Wingate's appointment to Cairo. In the few weeks remaining to him in the Sudan, however, his Hijazi efforts continued. On 6 November Admiral Wemyss and Lawrence arrived in Khartoum to discuss the revolt. Lawrence's account of the meeting is perfunctory, and indeed took as much notice of his surroundings during the train journey to Khartoum as it did of his encounter with Wingate.[35]

While Wingate conferred with Wemyss and Lawrence in Khartoum, his appointment to Cairo was being settled. Upon arrival there Wemyss found, as he reported to Wingate, that McMahon had been sent a "'Decypher yourself' telegram, and had the mortification of himself slowly and laboriously word by word spelling out" his own dismissal.[36] It might be said that this established a precedent in the Foreign Office's relations with its representative in Cairo: McMahon was the first to be so treated; now, and at last, it was Wingate's turn.

[34] Robertson to Wingate, 27 October 1916, SAD 141/4.
[35] *Seven pillars*, 109–11.
[36] Wemyss to Wingate, 19 November 1916, SAD 143/5.

PART THREE: EGYPT AND BEYOND

Chapter Twenty-three
The Legacy of Cromer

⤜∞⤛

By the time Wingate took up his appointment at the end of December 1916, Egypt had had enough of war. Events that would lead to his departure in 1919 flowed directly from wartime policies and problems that had created that disaffection. Incompatible imperial interests, failure at the front, disarray in the bureaucracies of multiple commands, rising discontent among the Egyptian masses, and bitter personal rivalries among British officials resulted from years of pent-up frustration and mismanagement. Few British observers were naive enough to blame Sir Henry McMahon alone for these problems, nor could anyone realistically expect Wingate to solve them. The war and its conduct in Egypt had made the glittering vice-regency of Cromer a bureaucratic nightmare, a proconsular graveyard that would claim not only McMahon and Wingate but also most of their successors.

We have seen that in 1914 the British took steps, even before the Ottoman Empire entered the war, to secure their anomalous position in Egypt. These were designed to regularize Britain's legal position, strengthen its administrative control, and placate Egyptians loyal to the Ottoman sultan, their sovereign. Martial law was declared. When Turkey entered the war in November further steps were taken. In December a protectorate was proclaimed, supposedly weakening (yet still not legally severing) the tie between Egypt and the Ottomans.[1] Khedive Abbas Hilmi was deposed and replaced by an uncle, Hussayn Kamil, whom the British raised to the dignity of sultan. Further to ease Egyptian fears the British declared that they, not Egypt, would bear the full weight of the war effort, and that the protectorate would, at war's end, "accelerate progress towards self-government." In

---

[1] Egyptian politicians' claims, published years later and repeated in secondary accounts, that Wingate advised acceptance of British terms, cannot be true. Wingate left Cairo for the Sudan on 5 September 1914; conversations about a protectorate could not have taken place. Cf. Janice Terry, *The Wafd 1919–1952*, London 1982, 11–12.

assessing the wisdom of these steps the threat not only of the
Ottoman sultan's call to jihad but also of Ottoman armies on the borders of Egypt must be borne in mind.

Whether or not the British promise to bear the burden of war
was realistic was less important than the extent to which Egyptians
were forced to take part. For the first year of the war they were largely
left alone. The growing importance of Egypt as a British base—home
by the end of 1915 to three general headquarters and thirteen divisions—inevitably brought demands upon Egypt. By all accounts
these were harshly enforced. The enormous engineering works connected first with Egypt's defense and then especially with plans to
invade Ottoman Palestine required large numbers of laborers. These
were at first obtained through recruitment of volunteers. When this
method proved inadequate, a form of conscription was devised, and
hundreds of thousands entered into forced labor, causing deep
resentment in a people who remembered the corvée; corruption
crept in, terms of employment were changed arbitrarily, and civilian
workers became casualties of a war that held little interest to
Egyptians. Similar methods were used to requisition draft animals,
further alienating the Egyptian peasantry. Feeding large armies
inflated prices, while British attempts to control these involved reduction in the acreage under cotton, for which there was booming foreign demand. Ham-fisted fund-raising campaigns for the Red Cross
caused offense, bearing witness to the myopia of British officials who
so frittered away their credit with the Egyptians. With the results of
these abuses, and indeed with their continuation, Wingate would
have to deal.

Other administrative and personal problems connected with the
war made his task more difficult. Even in the days of Gorst (to say
nothing of Cromer and Kitchener), the authority of the British agent
in Cairo was undisputed by other British officials, civilian or military.
McMahon's weakness and the appearance on the scene of powerful
soldiers blurred the distinctions between civil and military administration and confused chains of command. We have seen, for instance,
how Gilbert Clayton occupied several offices at the same time, not
merely nominally but indeed often with little or no executive assistance; his occasional difficulties with Wingate indicate not only competition for his time but also the divided loyalties involved in simul-
taneous service to three governments and two armies. Furthermore
McMahon, and after him Wingate, would have thankless responsibility for civilian administration when that was judged by London

mainly in terms of its contribution to the war effort. Maintenance of domestic peace was a minimal requirement, not an extraordinary achievement. In this respect Wingate's role was little different in Egypt from the one he occupied in the Sudan. But in the remote Sudan he could remove himself from attention simply by choice; in Egypt he would occupy the eye of a storm.

That position differed further from Khartoum and Erkowit because of the extraordinary supporting cast that awaited him in Cairo. The protectorate had not changed the form of Egypt's government, and just as the sultan did not rule, so his ministers did not govern, without British advice and consent. Sultan Hussayn Kamil proved the dignified figurehead the British had hoped for. The Legislative Assembly had been prorogued in October 1914. The prime minister throughout the war, Hussayn Pasha Rushdi, was a moderate politician of the old school who worked faithfully with the British in difficult circumstances. Indeed, during the first two years of the war and protectorate, Britain enjoyed widespread if not enthusiastic cooperation from Egyptian political notables; their patience had worn thin by the time Wingate arrived. And by then too Wingate had to face entrenched and disaffected British officials far more dangerous to him personally than Egyptian nationalists.

Britain's decision in 1882 not to annex Egypt had created as many administrative difficulties as it had solved diplomatic ones. In theory the khedive had remained an absolute ruler, subject only to the Ottoman sultan. He legislated, appointed and dismissed ministers, was commander in chief and court of final appeal. With British occupation the exercise of those powers was made subject to British approval, but they were not revoked. In theory the khedive and his ministers merely consulted the British agent and a few advisers before acting. During Cromer's long tenure, however, procedures were established by which the approval of the relevant adviser and the agent himself was needed before a minister could act. The advisers—to the Ministries of Finance, Justice, Interior, Education, and Public Works—thus became powerful figures in their own right. Cromer's immense personal prestige ensured his own ultimate control.

Changes that began during Cromer's last years in Egypt accelerated under Sir Eldon Gorst, his successor. Gorst had himself served as financial adviser, a position second only to the consul-generalship in importance. He had long nursed ambitions to succeed Cromer, and by doing so established the precedent that Egyptian experience was a requirement for the post. (McMahon's appointment in 1914 would be the exception to prove the rule.) On the constitutional level Gorst soon faced the dilemma of all enlightened despots: how to liberalize a regime without surrendering control. His untimely death foreshortened an experiment that found few defenders among the British. During that brief tenure, however, the principles of trusteeship (if not the word) first informed British policy, and these would prove impossible later to deny.

It was "Kitchener's luck" to succeed Gorst. To many his appointment heralded a turning back of the clock, but his resemblance to Cromer was largely superficial, a similarity of manner rather than of method. Indeed, a civilian agent would likely have found greater difficulty than the conquering hero did in pursuing liberalizing policies in Egypt. The Legislative Assembly established in 1913 seemed an earnest of British intentions. More ominous was reversal of Gorst's policy of increasing Egyptian participation in the higher ranks of the administration: the tendency of Cromer's last years, of growing dependence on British personnel, was thus resumed, and would continue with important consequences during and after the war. Nonetheless Kitchener's masterful personality was an effective instrument of policy. Seeming to disdain approval, he more easily inspired fear; whereas a civilian might curse a Cairo newspaper, Kitchener closed it down. With British officials he avoided battles as carefully as he had with Sudanese amirs: he secured his line of retreat with powerful political support at home, and for all his bravado he attacked only when the balance of force was overwhelmingly in his favor.

If, then, even in peacetime Sir Henry McMahon would have faced a formidable task in Cairo, the war complicated it to the point of impossibility. His personal quirks and professional defects have been so exaggerated as to explain the multiple failures of British wartime administration in Egypt. But even a dilatory chief had a right to subordinates' loyalty; an inexperienced one must have expected officials' sympathetic cooperation, not back-biting contempt. Part of Kitchener's legacy was, as usual, the anger and frustration of disaffected officials. These McMahon was left to face alone, unarmed with the personal weapons Kitchener had always been able to deploy.

None of this is the fruit of hindsight. When Wingate was offered Cairo in October 1916 he knew the personal risk he would assume along with one of the most important positions in the empire. To that point his career had, at its most crucial turns, always depended at least in part upon an interplay of politics and personality. That he, tireless servant of the empire, should have been so dependent was no doubt galling, but it is no defense of Wingate that he played the game less well than others. In the Sudan for long years he had grown more knowledgeable but less adept, perhaps reasoning that the solid achievements of his long career would, at last, allow him to act the way Cromer and Kitchener had. But whereas the promotion from Khartoum to Cairo may have seemed to release him at last from petty politics, may have convinced him that now he would be above all that, in fact only the stakes had changed.

Chapter Twenty-four
High Commissioner

On 11 October 1916 Sir Edward Grey cabled Wingate to offer him the high commissionership of Egypt: "In my opinion there is no one so well fitted as yourself, by your special knowledge, experience and personal qualities, to fill the post, and I should like to submit your name for the appointment. Before doing so, however, I should like you to consider who would replace you in the Sudan and whether you can leave the country at the present time."[1]

The succession had been under review at least since June, when Kitchener, who had been expected to return at war's end, was killed in the North Sea. McMahon's administration had been judged a failure; there was no question of confirming him in the position. That London took so long to act must indicate, however, that the Foreign Office retained some confidence in him: to no current business, civilian or military, was his personal attention so crucial as to postpone a change. In July Lord Hardinge, now permanent under-secretary of state at the Foreign Office, had told Ronald Graham, adviser to the Egyptian ministry of the interior, that both he and Wingate were under consideration. In the end Wingate was preferred, and Graham was brought back to the Foreign Office.

Wingate seemed a sensible choice. In terms of experience he stood alone. At a time of stress in Egypt he might be expected, by British and Egyptians alike, to reassure, to stabilize, and to end the disarray of recent years. Wingate took only a few hours to consider Grey's offer. There had been rumors about a change in Egypt, and he had long been mentioned as an eventual successor; an appointment considered "obvious" to so many could not have come as a "complete surprise" to him.[2] The appointment was announced on 6 November, as was that of Lee Stack, civil secretary in the Sudan Government, to

---

[1] Grey to Wingate, 11 October 1916, SAD 160/4.

[2] Cf. Wingate, *Wingate of the Sudan,* 201–02. See Stack to Wingate, 24 August 1916, SAD 130/2.

succeed him as acting sirdar and acting governor-general of the Sudan. Wingate's motives for recommending "acting" status are unclear; several suggest themselves: to justify departure after years of claiming that the Sudan could not risk his absence; to ensure continued control of Sudan affairs; to allow return to Khartoum in the event of failure in Egypt; even to continue a process of consolidation that his own joint appointments suggested. In any case Stack's "acting" status continued until after the war, hampering his own effectiveness and adding nothing to Wingate's panoply: as high commissioner he did not still style himself sirdar and governor-general, and within weeks of arrival in Egypt he was so occupied with its affairs that Stack was left with as free a hand in the Sudan as Wingate himself had had.[3]

If Wingate now foresaw a vice-royalty of the Near East, London took no steps to realize it. Stack's "acting" status meant little to the Foreign Office, where peace and quiet remained the only object in the Sudan. Wingate's more important suggestion, that he be made commander-in-chief of British forces in Egypt as well as high commissioner, was rejected, with important results. Throughout the war the division of military and civilian responsibility in Egypt had caused problems, as had the further division of military authority among several commands. Personal rivalries and bureaucratic confusion had beset military administration. General Archibald Murray had survived these as commander of the Egyptian Expeditionary Force. His relations with Wingate during the early stages of the Hijaz revolt had been mixed, the result at least in part of the very division of authority Wingate would now personify. Succession to McMahon meant succession to a system in which the high commissioner lacked full control of British activities in Egypt.

Other evidence of change since Cromer came in the manner of the succession. A "decypher yourself" telegram was rare bureaucratic torture indeed, even for so hapless a figure as McMahon.[4] His expressed doubts about Wingate's suitability to succeed might be dismissed as pique, but for the fact that Wingate would indeed soon be stuck in the quagmire of Anglo-Egyptian politics. The otherwise "real universal approval" that his appointment elicited,[5] in Egypt and

---

[3] See M.W. Daly, *British administration and the Northern Sudan, 1917–1914*, Leiden 1980, 5–18.

[4] Wemyss to Wingate, 19 November 1916, SAD 143/5.

[5] Grenfell to Wingate, 9 November 1916, SAD 236/5.

Britain, was born of war-time frustration and desire for a fresh start. The frustration continued, and grew worse, because Egypt's problems, and British problems in Egypt, were not soluble by a mere change at the top.

Wingate spent his last weeks in the Sudan fully occupied in Hijaz affairs, in preparations for departure, and in dealing with his now massive personal correspondence. The affairs of the Sudan itself, or at any rate those unconnected with the war, had been largely delegated since early 1915.[6] Wingate and his wife had left Erkowit for the last time on 4 October for Khartoum, and remained there until 18 December when, with much fanfare, they entrained for Egypt. On the nineteenth they boarded the Sudan Government steamer *Ibis* at Wadi Halfa, and on the twentieth landed at Shellal. Wingate, whose career had for three decades revolved around the Sudan and who for sixteen years had lived there as its ruler, had left for the last time. At Aswan on 21 December, Sultan Hussayn received Wingate on his yacht off Elephantine Island. The *Ibis* proceeded to Luxor on the twenty-second, Assiut on the twenty-third, and Bani Suef on Christmas Day. On 27 December the Wingates were officially received in Cairo.[7] Debate over implications of Wingate's clothes—military or civilian—for the occasion had been settled by London: Wingate arrived in uniform.[8]

In personal terms Wingate's appointment to Cairo was as much vindication as promotion. Years of disagreeable toil under difficult masters, of useful and important administration in the Sudan, and, lately, of waiting in the wings, had finally culminated in his occupying what was generally agreed to be the second post in the empire. Moreover, as energetically as Wingate would pursue his new duties, there was at this pinnacle a sense of ending, as though the Residency were more of a reward than an opportunity. Whether this impression is owed to Wingate's undoubted exhaustion in early 1917 or to some deeper cause is unknown. It had been suggested that Wingate take leave before assuming his duties in Cairo; he declined. Later in 1917, however, his health deteriorated and he offered to resign. After the Foreign Office consulted his doctors, that offer was refused, and although Wingate still took no leave until 1919 his health improved. Relevant correspondence is so delicate as to leave unclear the nature

---

[6] Daly, *British administration*, 9–11.

[7] CB1; CB2; Cf. Wingate, *Wingate of the Sudan*, 204.

[8] Terry, *The Wafd*, 18.

of the illness, but Wingate referred to recurring effects of his 1898 attack of typhoid.[9]

Other private concerns weighed on Wingate in his hour of triumph. Finances were a constant worry. In the Sudan he had made viceregal pomp a pillar of the regime, and had grown accustomed to viewing personal matters as government service. In Cairo, even in wartime, he would continue to maintain an elaborate household. But the line there between private and public obligations was more distinct than in Khartoum. During his first six months in Cairo, Wingate claimed that expenses exceeded income by £1,200. His salary as high commissioner stood at £6,460 (£4,698 after income tax), and a "special allowance" brought disposable income to £6,698. That allowance was inadequate for the purpose intended: servants' wages, upkeep of stables and automobiles, and other expenses that, Wingate pointed out, were not elsewhere met from the salary or emoluments of the British representative. Even the "outfit allowance" for readying the Residency had been insufficient: the Wingates had overspent it by some £373, even though they had brought their own furniture, china, and other household goods from Khartoum.[10] Nor was allowance made for expenses incurred while traveling in Egypt,[11] a disagreeable departure from Sudan practice. Wingate's ability to meet these expenses stemmed from a gratuity he received upon relinquishing his appointments as sirdar and governor-general of the Sudan. This—in lieu of pension—amounted to £E15,507 (or £18,000),[12] a considerable sum but one that would not long support Wingate's style, nor compensate during his long retirement for the lack of an annuity.

In August 1917 Wingate took the opportunity presented by ill health and discussions of his salary to recommend changes in the high commissionership. The protectorate had inaugurated a new era; this should be reflected in more than a changed title for Britain's representative. The post "should be held by someone highly placed in the social world—e.g. a member of the Royal Family or a wealthy Peer," assisted by an expert deputy high commissioner. In that way the work of government would go on, while British prestige would be upheld

---

[9] See "Appendix 'E'. Health Question," SAD 236/7.

[10] "Appendix 'D,'" SAD 236/7.

[11] Wingate, draft note, n.d. (1917), SAD 236/7.

[12] Alexander to Garsia, 25 April 1917, SAD 164/4.

by a Resident "of such social standing as to impress on the Native and Foreign elements—from the Sultan downwards—a sense of his personal distinction and eminence."[13] Wingate may have felt that the time had come for his ennoblement; if so, the Foreign Office ignored the hint. Nor would the division of functions he recommended ever take place. The one result of these wartime musings came in December, when London raised Wingate's "total emoluments" (before tax) to £10,000,[14] a figure Wingate continued to describe as inadequate, and which was apparently intended to last only until the war ended.[15]

Wingate's financial problems were never solved. During the summer the Egyptian court usually moved to Alexandria, so Wingate needed a house there. In the past, the Residency's Secret Service Fund had apparently been misused to pay for the British representative's quarters, a practice Wingate now both deprecated and revealed to the Foreign Office.[16] In his case an agreement was reached with the Zervudachi family to rent their villa, at terms suspiciously favorable to the government. Wingate complained that this created a personal obligation; at the end of the war "the whole question of an Alexandria Residency" would have to be taken up.[17] Knockenhair too had to be maintained during the war. Worst of all, when the offer of the high commissionership had been made, Wingate had not asked about pension terms. Such enquiries need not have raised eyebrows at the Foreign Office, but would have been both ordinary and sensible. Wingate would have long and bitter years in which to regret this omission.

In wartime the high commissioner's social functions were not so much reduced as altered. The large number of British officers in Egypt meant that dinners and luncheons largely replaced banquets and balls. Cairo was more than ever at the nexus of the British Empire, and official travelers naturally stopped there; the prominent among them had to be shown hospitality. Within a few days in early 1918, the Wingates were hosts to the duke of Connaught, General

[13] "Extracts from a private letter from General Sir Reginald Wingate to the Lord Hardinge of Penhurst dated 4 Aug. '17," SAD 236/7.
[14] F.O. to Wingate, 14 December 1917, SAD 236/7.
[15] Balfour to Wingate (personal), 5 December 1917, SAD 236/7.
[16] Hardinge to Wingate, April 1917, SAD 145/5.
[17] Wingate to Despina Zervudachi, 25 March 1917, SAD 145/3; Wingate to Graham, 9 June 1918, SAD 169/1.

Smuts and his staff, Sir Percy Cox, General Stewart from Aden, and the sultan of Lahaj.[18] Egyptian notables and members of the large foreign communities in Egypt had to be entertained at garden parties and receptions. On 24 May 1917—Empire Day—the Wingates had a thousand convalescent soldiers to tea in the Residency garden.[19] Wingate's personal correspondence, his principal recreation, lapsed. In a letter to his son Ronald, in March 1917, Wingate noted that he "had to see hundreds of people," and "numbers of deputations"; only his "absolute rule of getting out on most afternoons for a couple of hours and playing nine or eleven holes of golf" had allowed him to "survive the ordeal."[20] Wingate's own official visits were usually war-related. He toured convalescent camps and hospitals, and attended Red Cross events and charity affairs as well as making the usual visits to government agencies, schools, and foreign clubs.[21]

The war took its toll on the Wingates personally. On the Western Front their son Malcolm had continued to serve with distinction. In May 1917 he was again mentioned in dispatches, and in November was promoted captain. Father and son were so busy that contact waned: in March 1917 Wingate told Dr. Acland, in London, that it had been a year since he and his wife had heard from Malcolm; in May he thanked Acland for acting "in loco parentis" to both Malcolm and his sister, Victoria.[22] Late in 1917 Malcolm and his parents had a long-distance argument about his wish to leave the tedious regimental staff work in which he was immured and return to the front. But as Wingate told Lord Stamfordham, Malcolm had had "the first year of it [the front] continuously and as far as parents' feelings are concerned, this would seem to have been enough."[23] Wingate had already used personal influence to have his other son, Ronald, appointed to the new Mesopotamian administration; he now tried discreetly to arrange Malcolm's appointment to the General Staff. Malcolm learned of this and in embarrassment returned to the front.[24] On 21

---

[18] Wingate to Wood, 25 March 1918, SAD 148/7.

[19] CB1.

[20] 25 March 1917, SAD 145/3.

[21] CB1.

[22] [Wingate to Acland], 25 March 1917, SAD 145/3; 19 May 1917, SAD 145/7.

[23] 21 October 1917, SAD 146/7.

[24] Private information; CB1. For Ronald's appointment see "private and personal" postscript to Wingate to Hardinge, 2 April 1917, SAD 145/4.

March 1918 he was killed in action. In one of many letters his father wrote about his death, Wingate stated:

> He was killed instantaneously by [a] shell splinter . . . as he and his Field Company (the 459th) were moving up from billets to battle position, and was buried where he fell. . . . He could have had no suffering and was saved all the anguish of having to retreat. We know that in his short and strenuous career, he gallantly did his duty and his leaving his Staff billet at G.H.Q. was, I know, a matter of conscience—he wrote me very fully about it, but the upshot of it all was that he thought a less able-bodied man could do his staff work and that he ought to return to the fighting line. When I knew and understood how much he was worrying, I did my best to help him, though we all realized [sic] what it might mean—but neither his mother nor I—nor he—would have wished it otherwise. . . . And he has left behind him a fine example of a good British officer—*sans peur et sans reproche.* God rest his soul.[25]

The ways in which Wingate and his wife dealt with this blow are instructive of their characters. Lady Wingate never recovered. Malcolm had been her favorite; his memory upset relations with her grandchildren thirty years after his death, and in the matter of his insistent return to the front she would always blame herself. After the war she and her husband made annual visits to his graveside at Lagnicourt. Her own ashes are buried there.[26]

In grief as ever Wingate himself was active. News of his son's death reached him only on 1 April.[27] On the sixth he produced a flurry of letters. One went to Winchester, offering up to £300 for a memorial to the fallen Wykhamist. Another he wrote to Dunbar about a memorial service scheduled for the tenth, with instructions about disbursement of £50 to charities and about a memorial tablet in the local church. To Chatham, Wingate wrote too about a tablet for the garrison church and for advice about other suitable memorials.[28] He had already begun to consider tablets for churches in Cairo and Khartoum, and changes to his own will. A detailed correspon-

---

[25] Wingate to Carey, 6 April 1918, SAD 168/2.

[26] Private information.

[27] CB2. Cf. Wingate, *Wingate of the Sudan,* 226.

[28] Wingate to M.J. Rendall, Headmaster of Winchester College; to Carey, Dunbar; to Capper, Chatham, 6 April 1918, SAD 168/2.

dence began about Malcolm's personal effects, about the condition of his grave, and, as soon as the war ended, plans for a stone there.[29] Hundreds of messages of condolence poured in; typically, Wingate appears to have answered them all, often at length. The king wrote on the day he heard the news; Theodore Roosevelt sent a long and intimate letter in July. Sir Evelyn Wood told Wingate there is no death: "what seems so is transition."[30]

Other transitions marked Wingate's Cairo years. On 30 January 1917 Lord Cromer died in London; Wingate had continued to correspond with his former chief, but even in retirement Cromer had never been more to Wingate than that, either personally or politically. On 16 June Wingate's old friend Abd al-Qadir al-Maccawi died at Aden. On 9 October 1917 the Egyptian sultan died after a long illness; immediate political consequences notwithstanding, Wingate remembered Hussayn Kamil as a friend.

The grim toll of life and war, and the intense pressure of the Cairo years, were not without an echo of personal satisfaction. In May 1917 Wingate was appointed colonel commandant of the Royal Regiment of Artillery. In December he learned that he (and the viceroy of India) would receive the GBE, a distinction which, he minuted, was not a "war honour" but was given in recognition of his services in Egypt and was "something that had to be done."[31] When in July 1917 Wingate saw his first battle tanks, he recorded in his diary that two of them involved in the capture of Gaza had been named *Sir Reginald* and *Lady Wingate*.[32]

That Wingate saw his namesake during an official inspection hints at the awkwardness of his role as high commissioner: a general in a civilian administrative position near the front. Between his arrival in Cairo in December 1916 and his recall to London in February

---

[29] See Wingate to Goldney, 16 October; to Bonham Carter, 23 October; and to the Graves Registration Department, 23 October 1918, SAD 170/2. See also Wingate to Bonham Carter, 6 April 1918, SAD 168/2. Wingate later learned that no body had been found beneath the original marker. Exhumations were made, but Malcolm Wingate's remains were apparently never positively identified (CB1).

[30] King George V to Wingate, 1 April 1918; Roosevelt to Wingate, 28 July 1918; Wood to Wingate, 3 April 1918, SAD 236/8.

[31] F.O. to Wingate, 20 December 1917, SAD 164/4; minute, n.d.

[32] CB1.

1919, Wingate left Egypt only to visit the front in Palestine. In correspondence about his appointment the possibility had been raised of his visiting England before taking up his new duties; he had not had home leave since 1914 and needed rest. It later became clear that a visit in late 1916 would also have given him a useful opportunity to consult leading members of the government at a time of important ministerial changes; Asquith resigned on 7 December and Lloyd George became prime minister.[33] But at the time this did not appear to signal important changes in policy toward Egypt or in attitudes toward Wingate. Grey at the Foreign Office gave way to Arthur Balfour, a cousin of Lord Edward Cecil, the financial adviser in Egypt, and of Lord Robert Cecil, who now became parliamentary under-secretary at the Foreign Office. The potential difficulties for Wingate represented in this change at the top seemed mitigated by the appointment of Lord Hardinge, the former viceroy, as permanent under-secretary, and of Sir Ronald Graham, the former adviser to the Egyptian Interior Ministry, as assistant under-secretary. Wingate already knew Balfour slightly, and it is unlikely that a few official meetings on general policy would have neutralized the effect of any personal bias. It was Wingate's misfortune to have been appointed by a waning government, and therefore when crisis came to be all the more expendable for that reason. In any case, Wingate had deflected Grey's suggestion of a visit home with his own of a tour of the Red Sea, combining a restful change of scene with official inspection. The trip was planned and re-planned several times, but never took place.[34]

Wingate visited British forces in Palestine thrice as high commissioner. In September 1917 he spent three days at Allenby's headquarters near Khan Yunis. Attended only by Symes, his private secretary, and Captain Ulick Alexander, Wingate went by special train to Kantara on 2–3 September, crossed the canal, then continued on the new military railway to Kalab, whence brief side-trips were arranged. Allenby's expressed hope that "the holiday" had done him good was apparently not facetious: an anonymous report on the visit speaks of it as a diversion from the cares of office, and it was evidently timed to coincide with the Foreign Office's consideration of Wingate's

---

[33] See, e.g., Wingate, *Wingate,* 202–04; Terry, *The Wafd,* 20.
[34] See Wingate to Hardinge, 17 September 1916, SAD 123/11; Hardinge to Wingate, 11 October 1917; Wingate to Hardinge, 21 October 1917, SAD 166/1; Wingate to Hardinge, 29 November 1917, SAD 146/10.

health.[35] In mid-November he paid another, six-day visit. With
Allenby and Clayton he inspected a number of Jewish colonies; from
the hills above Ascalon he glimpsed Jerusalem. Wingate's enthusiasm
near the front and away from the Residency is evident in letters to his
wife: "We have actually been to Jaffa!" was how he commenced one
of them.[36] But the possibility of his entering Jerusalem in December
with Allenby's victorious forces was vetoed by the Foreign Office so
as not to offend the French.[37] In late February 1918 Wingate took a
few days at Luxor to recover from influenza, and in late spring he
spent five days at Sollum, "a refresher—though it was not much
rest."[38] In early September 1918 he was able finally to visit
Jerusalem.[39] Wingate's visits to the front were somewhat awkward.
His status as British high commissioner in Egypt might unnecessarily
signal or pointlessly imply troublesome post-war intentions. Of more
immediate concern was his own continuing military role and the ways
in which this related to that of the British commander-in-chief of the
Egyptian Expeditionary Force. The appointment in June 1917 of
Allenby to succeed General Murray had at least removed an irritating
personal element from those relations. But the problem was systemic,
and resulted from the division of command that placed one general
(Wingate) in command of the war in the Hijaz, and another in charge
in the north.

So long as British efforts to achieve a breakthrough in Palestine
were thwarted, this division, while difficult, was manageable. Indeed,
in January 1917 Murray told Wingate curtly that the War Office's
decision to allow Wingate a brigade of British troops for service in the
Hijaz would "seriously hamper" his own operations, "if not entirely
bring them to a standstill":[40] blame, as well as responsibility, could be
divided. The sharif's long reluctance to use non-Muslim troops now

---

[35] Allenby to Wingate, 7 September 1917, SAD 146/4; "(X) Notes on a visit to
the Palestine Front," 2–6 September 1917, n.d., SAD 236/7.

[36] 20 November 1917, SAD 236/7; see letter of 18 November in the same file. A
detailed itinerary is "Palestine 1917," n.d., SAD 146/10.

[37] Wingate to FO, 21 November 1917; Prodrome (Cairo) to Alexander (GHQ, for
Wingate), 22 November 1917, SAD 146/10.

[38] Wingate to Hardinge, 7 March 1918, SAD 148/6; Wingate to Graham, 9 June
1918, SAD 168/1.

[39] Wingate to Allenby, 18 August 1918, SAD 149/5.

[40] Murray to Wingate, 5 January 1917, SAD 145/1.

reasserted itself, and, to Wingate's and his lieutenants' great dismay, the force's departure was canceled. In February the respective spheres of operation between Wingate's and Murray's commands were defined by a line from Aqaba to Maan, but even then it was recognized that important political questions could not be so divided. Thus a political officer assigned then to Murray was to report on Hijaz affairs to Wingate.[41]

In fact, Sharif Hussayn's refusal of British troops continued to limit Wingate's role. The failure of the sharif's forces to take Medina, and the continuing threat to his position at Mecca that resulted partly from that failure, made it essential to prevent reinforcement of Turkish positions by disrupting communications. The sharif's forces thus concentrated their attention on the Hijaz railway. In this effort the British helped mainly with supplies, money, and training in demolition and other tactics, and Wingate's efforts were concentrated on the often difficult task of securing these from the Egyptian Expeditionary Force, the Egyptian army, the Sudan Government, and the War Office.[42] In this essential effort, involving as it did massive correspondence and constant arm-twisting, he was notably successful. But Wingate knew better than most that in wartime the active soldier, not the successful bureaucrat, reaps credit for success. In this case the office-bound commander in Cairo competed with Lawrence of Arabia.

The very success of the Arab Revolt in the Hijaz combined with the limitation of Wingate's authority to render his command increasingly insignificant after July 1917. The fall of Aqaba then led to attachment of the main Sharifian force, under the Amir Faysal, to Allenby's Egyptian Expeditionary Force in the north. For the remainder of the war the Hijaz was truly a backwater, where useful efforts continued against the Turks in Medina and the railway, but where ultimate success would have little impact on the British campaign against the Ottomans to the north, in Palestine, and in Syria. The functions of the Hedjaz Mission and the political activities of the Arab Bureau relating to the Hijaz were both absorbed in November 1917 by a Hedjaz Operations Staff in Cairo, which continued to report to both Wingate and Allenby on affairs in their respective spheres.[43]

---

[41] Robertson to General Officer Commanding-in-Chief, British Force in Egypt, 21 February 1917, SAD 145/2.

[42] See Wingate to Secretary of State for War, 25 June 1917, SAD 145/8.

[43] Wingate to War Office, 14 March 1918, SAD 148/6.

It was this division of authority, albeit over increasingly lopsided areas of operations, that carried potential for conflict, as the whole history of the war effort in Egypt had shown. That Wingate praised Allenby unstintingly even in private correspondence speaks well of his willingness to accept diminished status, and perhaps more clearly attests to Allenby's generous treatment of the man he would soon succeed. But the fact remains that Wingate's role in the Arab Revolt has never been properly appreciated. Its beginnings and indeed most of its activities were necessarily secret. His successes have largely been credited, especially in popular history, to other, more colorful figures. Official recognition, which should normally have come to Wingate at the end of the war, was meanly withheld by a small-minded government in the wake of the Egyptian revolution. Even Wingate's Hijaz dispatches went unpublished until late 1919, by which time public interest in the subject had dimmed.

Chapter Twenty-five
Administration and Intrigue

━━━◆∞◆━━━

The seeds of Wingate's downfall in Egypt were planted before he became high commissioner. Although his dismissal in 1919 came in the wake of political crisis, old personal animosities unrelated to the issues of the day are what brought him down. In hoping that he could master Anglo-Egyptian intrigue he discounted new combinations ambition would create, and fatally misjudged the tenor of politics in Britain. Wingate had long experience of the right and weak losing to the strong and wrong, and when in 1917–18 he purported to disdain the personal in politics he was not naive but disingenuous. His failure in Egypt was therefore itself personal, not political.

That as high commissioner Wingate would not revive the glory days of Cromer was clear in many ways. Division of British authority between his office and the military was not only inefficient but also encouraged rivalry and intrigue. It meant that in his civilian capacity Wingate had to enforce the military's unpopular wartime requirements of the Egyptians, and to accept the blame. Since 1914 he had signaled awareness of intramural British conflicts by staying away from Egypt altogether. As high commissioner he tried first to avoid rather than settle those differences, then to remove rather than conciliate the trouble-makers. From Khartoum he brought with him senior officials including Stewart Symes, his private secretary, and Alexander Keown-Boyd, his assistant private secretary; his intention to bypass channels within the British establishment was clear. At the time of his appointment that hierarchy had already been in flux; within weeks of his arrival it was in ferment.

The chief British officials in Egypt were the advisers to the ministries of Justice, Finance, and the Interior, the oriental secretary, and the head of the Chancery. During McMahon's absences and after his dismissal the acting high commissioner had been Sir Milne Cheetham, head of the Chancery. The powerful financial adviser was Lord Edward Cecil, whose acquaintance with Wingate dated to the Nile campaigns. Son of the third marquess of Salisbury and brother of Lord Robert Cecil (parliamentary under-secretary at the Foreign Office), and cousin of A. J. Balfour, now foreign secretary, Lord Edward had long since fallen out with Wingate. Sir Ronald Graham, adviser to the Interior Ministry, having been passed over in the succession to McMahon, became instead assistant under-secretary at the Foreign Office, and left Egypt three months before Wingate arrived. His post in turn was contested, and went in the end to James Haines, supported by McMahon and Cecil and opposed by Graham. The adviser to the Ministry of Justice, William Brunyate, was an old hand who, however, had alienated British and Egyptians alike with a brusque and sarcastic manner. The oriental secretary was Sir Ronald Storrs. All of these figures had personal and political supporters and official and private contacts with Egyptians, with the foreign communities in Egypt, and in Britain; had definite views on the policies that had been and should be pursued during the war; and nourished incompatible ambitions. Even before Wingate arrived in Cairo the sultan himself had referred privately to Cecil's clique as a *camorra*.[1]

The relief with which tired bureaucrats greet a change at the top is often matched by worry. That McMahon had failed was taken for granted; debate about the failure's causes went on, too easily focusing on his own weakness. His faults had been others' opportunity. British officials had increased their authority at the expense of the high commissioner and the Egyptian government. Cecil especially had concentrated power in his own office, since Cromer the most important in the Anglo-Egyptian regime. The war had contributed by deflecting attention from the nuances of a system wherein advisers, however powerful, were still nominally servants, not masters, of the Egyptian government. McMahon had been glad to share the burden of Egypt's domestic affairs, of which on arrival he had been entirely ignorant. The result was greater independence for advisers and their officials. These had positions to protect when Wingate arrived in the unlikely role of new broom. Even before he reached Cairo the resignations began, not only of personal enemies and failed office-seekers. These continued thereafter, giving rise to unfavorable comment among even loyal supporters. In February 1917 Stack wrote privately to Clayton: "It looks as if, like [in] the Sudan,

---

[1] Sultan Hussayn to Wingate, 23 November 1916, SAD 153/7. Wingate interpreted the remark to mean "camera" (Wingate to his wife, 10 October 1919, SAD 238/1).

the elimination of the outstanding personalities around him was beginning."[2]

Shuffling of the bureaucratic deck was complicated by a bitter struggle between Wingate and Cecil. In surviving it Wingate was severely weakened. At issue, ostensibly, was the role of the financial adviser; in fact the personal element is so obvious as to obscure the political. Wingate knew that in Cecil he had a powerful rival; Cecil had nursed his own ambition to succeed McMahon, and despised Wingate.[3] As governor-general of the Sudan, Wingate had been disagreeably reminded that his former assistant was, as financial adviser in Cairo, supervisor of his official and indeed private finances; it was Cecil with whom he had to correspond about salary and allowances. With another shift in their respective positions it remained to be seen whether Wingate would follow the example of Cromer or of McMahon—whether he would try to rule or merely preside. In any case there was bound to be trouble. Within weeks of Wingate's taking office he urged approval of Lord Edward's standing request for secondment for military service. Even the correspondence over this matter should have alerted Wingate to the dangers he courted. Lord Hardinge, who had passed through Cairo in April 1916 on his way home from India and had freely commented upon the undue influence Cecil wielded, now told Wingate that "the Cecil interest [in the Foreign Office] fully grasped the meaning of Edward Cecil going away for five months." Yet Hardinge gave the correspondence to Balfour, Cecil's cousin, "purely in the interests of the Public Service and of your own [Wingate's] position."[4] Wingate won this first skirmish—Cecil took leave—but could scarcely afford another such victory.

Indeed, by arranging Cecil's leave Wingate transferred his archenemy from Cairo, where at least he could be watched, to London, where the Cecil "comorra" flourished. As early as 21 February Ronald Graham cabled Wingate: "Bob Cecil has put forward a proposal that Egypt should now be handed over to the Colonial Office!"[5] Quite apart from its impertinence during the war this plan was, in Graham's phrase, "mainly personal."[6] In July Balfour decided

[2] Stack to Clayton, 22 February 1917, SAD 470/6.
[3] Edward Cecil to Salisbury, 28 July 1917, quoted in Kenneth Rose, *The later Cecils,* New York 1975, 225. For Cecil's dislike of Wingate see 224–26.
[4] Hardinge to Wingate, 14 February 1917, SAD 163/2.
[5] Graham to Wingate, 21 February (1917), SAD 236/6.
[6] Graham to Wingate, 4 October 1917, SAD 166/1.

that his cousin should return to Egypt. In notifying Wingate the foreign secretary referred openly to "difficulties" Cecil had had with him, and expressed confidence that personal differences would not stand in the way of working together; any "real divergence in official matters" should be referred to the Foreign Office.[7] Cecil's return, Balfour's role as referee, and, in September, the formation of a cabinet committee in London to discuss reorganization of Egyptian affairs, were ominous.

During Cecil's leave R. L. Lindsay, under-secretary in the Egyptian finance ministry, had served as acting financial adviser, and fallen out with Wingate as surely as Cecil had. In July he quietly asked for permission to revert to the diplomatic service and leave Egypt. As he later told Wingate:

> My action was simply a resignation, but put in the form least likely to arouse comment. . . . And this resignation was due purely to the fact that in the course of the last six months I have become convinced that your views and mine on the principles of finance and on the manner of carrying them out are entirely irreconcilable. I am therefore unwilling to remain a day longer than absolutely necessary in a position of responsibility where I have to do things which I cannot regard as justifiable.

Wingate demanded an official explanation, and, while awaiting a reply, privately insisted that political disagreements between them had involved, on his part, no personal bias.[8] After a meeting, Lindsay gave in writing his reasons for resigning.

Coming from a high official—albeit Edward Cecil's deputy—Lindsay's criticisms (and Wingate's marginal notes on them) give evidence of Wingate's personal rule in the Sudan, and of his incompatibility with a bureaucratic regime in Cairo. Wingate, Lindsay wrote, had encouraged Egyptian complaints about the Finance Ministry, and by other actions shown loss of confidence in the ministry and himself, leaving him no alternative but to resign. (Wingate minuted: "I should not have spoken so bluntly perhaps—especially as L. was only in an acting position, and it is on that account that I have can-

---

[7] Balfour to Wingate, 18 July 1917, SAD 165/1.

[8] Lindsay to Wingate, 26 August 1917; Wingate to Lindsay, 27 August 1917, SAD 165/2; Wingate to Lindsay, 1 September 1917, SAD 165/3.

celled my acceptance of his resignation.") Where Lindsay had urged parsimony, Wingate had intervened to spend, arguing, in Lindsay's words, that "it was important to reduce the Reserve Fund quickly because if at the end of the war Egypt was found with a large sum in reserve, His Majesty's Government would undoubtedly take it"! Wingate's minute to this charge is revealing: "Clearly a mutual misunderstanding of my remarks on reduction of RF. [These] were made in an entirely confidential manner. I had no idea L. had taken them as he has until I received this letter." (Lindsay claimed that Wingate had expressed the view twice, on separate occasions.) Finally Lindsay complained about Wingate's interference in pension matters: "You have informed me," he wrote, "that Pension questions are an administrative and not a financial matter," and should be submitted to a "special Board." But Wingate had repeatedly overruled the Finance Ministry—and without reference to a board. To this Wingate minuted: "Look up the past!" and "This may be so but political considerations must come in now—as they have done in innumerable cases in the past."[9]

Even if Lindsay's charges were baseless—the matter of rumormongering would have been unprovable even at the time—they show Wingate in an unflattering light. Imputation of intrigue, of inviting criticism of political enemies, is not inconsistent with Wingate's methods. His wish to spend more than advisers thought prudent was characteristic; it would have required discipline to resist that temptation as high commissioner. Circumventing regulations in pension matters was nothing new, and Wingate's minutes make no apologies for it. Lindsay's reference to the reserve fund elicited two responses typical of Wingate: first that he had been misunderstood; second that he had spoken "confidentially," and, as he argued, thus irrelevantly. Finally, Wingate's refusal of Lindsay's resignation was a sign of weakness, not generosity, at a time when his high commissionership seemed in danger of unraveling and he had (for health reasons) made his own offer to resign.[10]

Indeed, in canceling acceptance of Lindsay's resignation Wingate signaled his own defeat. The system, not Lindsay, was responsible for

---

[9] Lindsay to Wingate, 2 September 1917, SAD 165/3.

[10] For continuing difficulty caused by Wingate's distinctions between "private" and "official," "confidential" and "official" communications, see Graham to Wingate, 10 August 1917, and Wingate to Graham, 26 August 1917, SAD 165/2.

the problem, he said; an innocent man should not be made to suffer. But in conveying this message to the Foreign Office, Wingate went on:

> I am quite prepared that he should continue to act as Under Secretary for Finance on CECIL's return and that the existing system should go on until the war is over. However much I may differ with that system, I feel that any drastic changes are not at present feasible and we are all too immersed in war work to give up the time and thought which these impirtant [*sic*] changes will require.

"The whole question of the govt of this country," he concluded, would "have to be taken up . . . as soon as matters become normal," probably by a royal commission.[11]

Wingate's about-turn anticipated deliberations of the Egyptian Administration Committee created in the Foreign Office at Robert Cecil's request. By expressing willingness to postpone changes in Egypt, Wingate in fact defended his own position against changes the Cecils wanted. Lindsay's criticisms showed how easily the high commissioner could manipulate the present system; Wingate prudently retreated in the hope that his ability to do so would not be curtailed. The committee—Balfour, Curzon, and Milner—sat in late September 1917 and heard Edward Cecil, Cheetham, and Sir Henry McMahon. "It will be impossible in the future always to obtain men of the qualities and experience of Lord Cromer and Lord Kitchener to fill the position of High Commissioner," Lord Edward wrote in his memorandum for the committee; "an effective and adequate system of control . . . should be instituted and the necessary machinery set up." He called for a new department, temporarily under the Foreign Office but detachable after the war: "The Dept. must be capable of advising the Sec. of State on all matters connected with Egypt, and must act as the channel between him and the Egyptian Govt., but it will in no sense form a portion of the regular Foreign Office. It is even advisable to keep the the [*sic*] offices of the two bodies entirely separate." Cecil went on to suggest qualifications of the official to head the new department, notably that he not be drawn from the Foreign Office.[12]

---

[11] Wingate to Hardinge, 4 September 1917, SAD 165/3.

[12] "Memorandum by Lord Edward Cecil respecting the future government of Egypt," n.d., SAD 165/3.

Cecil's arguments, poorly conceived, badly expressed, and weakened by personal animus, were thoroughly demolished in memoranda by Graham and Hardinge.[13] He had ineptly put them in the enviable position of refuting him by defending their superiors.

The immediate results of the Egyptian Administration Committee were meager. Members of the War Cabinet were too busy to deliberate. A draft report, prepared by Storrs, the committee's secretary, called for a new Egyptian department within the Foreign Office, as the nucleus of a possible Near Eastern department later, and for rotation of officials between Cairo and the Foreign Office to add to the expertise available in London. Milner, who corresponded privately with Edward Cecil on the matter, dissented from this summary. Egypt's political and constitutional affairs would soon loom larger, he argued, and the Foreign Office was not equipped to deal with the questions that would result.[14] With this Edward Cecil, indeed Wingate and others, agreed, but the weakness of Cecil's presentation allowed a legitimate question to be shelved for the duration of the war. Wingate's victory was again costly. Rumors of Wingate's financial ineptness had spread in London,[15] and his methods in general been brought to official attention; any new troubles would add to a record of controversy.

Cecil returned to Egypt in early October 1917. In mid-November he was diagnosed with tuberculosis, and went on leave again.[16] He did not resign, nor did Wingate feel able under the circumstances to ask this. New controversy arose over who should act in his place. Lindsay, having withdrawn his resignation, should normally have assumed the role, but Wingate insisted he take leave, and that the judicial adviser, Brunyate, act for Cecil.[17] This was approved, and Brunyate was appointed. There the matter stood until Cecil, dying, finally resigned.

Questions of political significance were obscured by the animosity between Wingate and the Cecils. As the war wore on, Egyptian

---

[13] Graham, "Future administration of Egypt," 2 September 1917, encl. in Graham to Hardinge, 2 September 1917; Hardinge, minute, 6 September 1917, SAD 165/3.

[14] Memorandum, 31 October 1917, SAD 165/3. See also Milner to E. Cecil, 31 December 1917, quoted in Rose, *The later Cecils,* 226.

[15] Wingate to Hardinge, 20 October 1917, SAD 166/1.

[16] Wingate to Robert Cecil (draft), 15 November 1917, SAD 166/2.

[17] Wingate to Foreign Office, 20 November 1917, SAD 166/2.

discontent increased and found expression in the stirrings of nationalism. These in turn were inseparable from the question of Egypt's
future status and administration. It was natural that the harried war
cabinet in London gave more prominence to channels of imperial
communication than to currents in Egyptian politics. It was just as
natural that thoughtful Egyptians queried the future of their country
rather than the details of British rule. Wingate had to concern himself
with both. In 1917 a political crisis in Egypt made ominously clear
the connection between Egypt's domestic politics and international
status. While Wingate's handling of the immediate problem was deft,
proposals for the longer term were unconsonant with changes in
Egypt's political mood.

A pillar of the protectorate since its inception had been the sultan, Hussayn Kamil. It was not only fortunate for the British but
also determinant of their plans, that that prince had been available
to succeed Abbas Hilmi in 1914.[18] He had openly supported the
British war effort in the face of bitter denunciation, not least from
within his own family. By the time of Wingate's arrival in Egypt in
December 1916 the sultan had been in failing health for some time.
This raised concerns about the succession and reopened the question of Egypt's status; absence of a suitable heir rendered the protectorate debatable, with annexation the logical alternative. In April
1917 the sultan himself raised the issue with Wingate, and they
returned to it in June, by which time the Foreign Office had asked
for an official appreciation. Wingate consulted Cheetham and
Brunyate, both of whom, on balance, continued to favor protectorate; Graham at the Foreign Office pointed out that annexation
would be a breach of faith: promises had been made in 1914 to win
Egyptian support in the war.[19]

Wingate, by his own admission, had always been an "annexationist"; everything in his Sudan experience showed the disadvantages
of Egypt's complex administration.[20] In May 1917 he expressed
doubt that "any member of the Mohammed Ali family [was] in any
way fitted for" succession; if the sultan died, the opportunity arose of

---

[18] W.E. Brunyate, "Future political status of Egypt," 13 July 1917, SAD 237/10.

[19] Brunyate, "Future political status of Egypt"; Wingate to Hardinge, 17 June
1917, SAD 164/8; "Extract from a private letter from Sir Ronald Graham to
General Sir Reginald Wingate . . . ," 25 June 1917, SAD 164/8.

[20] Wingate to Hardinge, 17 June 1917, SAD 164/8.

"settling with the family once and for all" and annexing Egypt.[21] The Foreign Office understandably wished to postpone consideration of such drastic action until after the war. While Wingate had to accept this, he continued to argue that in the event of the sultan's sudden death, annexation would be the safest policy. What, he asked, would Britain do with a "Turcophile" sultan and an "Anglophobe" Egyptian ruling class after the war?[22] "The local difficulties in the way of annexation," he told Balfour, "need not be over-estimated nor regarded as in any way insuperable."[23]

On 9 October 1917 Sultan Hussayn died at Abdin Palace. His brother, Ahmad Fu'ad, was chosen over a son, Kamal al-Din, to succeed him. Wingate had at various times expressed a preference for each and worry about both. Only a month earlier he had told London that "the bulk of the better class Egyptians" shared the view of Sirri Pasha that Ahmad Fu'ad was "practically unknown in Egypt, could not even speak the language, was notorious for the company he kept amongst Jews and other dagoes," knew little about the country, and had "unsound judgment and autocratic methods."[24] But Graham at the Foreign Office expressed what was evidently the more important concern that while Prince Kamal al-Din "might have proved useful but was more likely to prove dangerous," Ahmad Fu'ad was "unlikely to prove either the one or the other."[25] Even during the brief time remaining to Wingate in Egypt this view was proven wrong; over the long term King Fuad, as he was styled after 1922, would be a constant irritant to the British.

The accession of Ahmad Fu'ad led to a political crisis that both foreshadowed and fueled the explosion of a year later. The new sultan lost no time in champing at the British bit, while Wingate and his advisers were naturally sensitive to any tug on the reins. Ahmad Fu'ad sneered at British reminders of his relative autonomy; he early promised to become the center of anti-British agitation. This impelled his ministers, and none more than the prime minister, Hussayn Rushdi Pasha, to bid against him for public support. Rushdi had already petitioned Wingate in May 1917—as indeed Sultan Hussayn

---

[21] Wingate to Hardinge, 6 May 1917, SAD 145/6.

[22] Wingate to Hardinge, 17 June 1917, SAD 164/8.

[23] Wingate to Balfour, 23 July 1917, SAD 165/1.

[24] Wingate to Graham, 12 September 1917, SAD 165/3.

[25] Graham to Wingate, 12 October 1917, SAD 166/1.

had asked the Foreign Office in April—about the appointment of
more Egyptians to important posts, with no result. By late 1917
Rushdi was so fully identified with the protectorate that only visible
and important British concessions could safeguard his own position.
In mid-December the sultan forced two members of the council of
ministers to resign, and, advised by Rushdi, proposed to appoint in
their places "a couple of Ministers who," in Graham's words, "had
distinguished themselves by their violent attacks on Lord Kitchener
and his policy":[26] Sa'd Zaghlul Pasha and Abd al-Aziz Fahmi Bey.
Wingate argued, though not strongly, that Zaghlul's membership of
the cabinet would at this point be less dangerous than his exclusion,
but London overruled him.[27] Wingate thereupon had to remind both
Ahmad Fu'ad and Rushdi that ministers could be replaced only upon
British advice. It would appear that this insistence upon past procedure, as much as dislike of the nationalist nominees, was behind
London's instruction that Wingate not give way. In the end a compromise was reached, by which one of the ministers was replaced; the
other remained, and neither Zaghlul nor Abd al-Aziz was brought
into the government.

Wingate's annexationism was consistent with a strategic and personal vision he had nourished for years, which now seemed closer
than ever to fruition. Wingate was an archimperialist. Acquisition and
administration of territories and peoples are the context of his career.
Whether in planning and executing the Nile campaigns, securing the
southern Sudan against France and Belgium, conquering Darfur,
directing the Arab Revolt, or musing frequently about reorganizing
East African and Asian dependencies, Wingate's unshakable principle
was the superiority of British rule. Where it could be imposed, it
should be. His experience in the Sudan was celebrated by others as
proof of the contention. Even so he had chafed there under a condominium implying less than total British rule, and tried to diminish or
preclude Egyptian influence. During the war his views on territorial
questions were invariable: British wishes were preeminent; others'
"pretensions" should be resisted. That he favored annexation of
Egypt in 1917 is thus unsurprising, however unrealistic the view
would appear even a year later.

---

[26] Graham to Wingate, 20 December 1917, SAD 166/3. Regarding Sultan
   Hussayn's request see Hardinge to Wingate, 19 April 1917, SAD 145/5.
[27] Wingate to Hardinge, 29 November 1917, SAD 146/10.

More intriguing are Wingate's views on the future political organization of the Near East. He was not only annexationist but also amal-
gamator. Again, his early career holds clues: in the 1890s Wingate had
seen in the Egyptian army's intelligence department the possible
nucleus of a vast northeast African organization. Soon after the Anglo-
Egyptian conquest of 1898 he had advocated "Aden and Somaliland
coming under" the Sudan.[28] In 1915–16 Wingate's memoranda on the
future of the Arabs, an Arab or "pan-Arab" state, and the caliphate, all
foresaw British patronage if not formal rule. The long debate with the
government of India over the Arab Revolt was widely if tacitly seen as
territorial—in the sense of involving distribution and rule of Ottoman
lands after the war—rather than strategic. By 1916 the possibility of a
"British High Commissioner for the Middle East, co-ordinating Egypt,
Arabia and Mesopotamia"[29] was openly mooted at the War Office, as it
had been in Wingate's Anglo-Egyptian circle. At that point Wingate
was already sirdar of the Egyptian army, governor-general of the Sudan,
and commander-in-chief of the Hijaz operations; his Agent in Cairo,
Clayton, directed the Arab Bureau, and had already suggested Wingate
as the best candidate for the coordinating role they held necessary.

Wingate's promotion to Cairo made it likelier that grand musings
might be realized. He may have had this in mind when arranging
Stack's appointment as acting sirdar and acting governor-general of
the Sudan, and when he tried but failed to have himself appointed
commander-in-chief of British forces in Egypt as well as high commissioner. In any case he continued to extend his nominal authority and
to argue for greater amalgamation. He retained command over Hijaz
operations, to which was added in 1917 political authority over Aden.
In the spring of that year he corresponded with Hardinge about the
possibility of an exchange of territory that would leave Eritrea in
British hands and France out of Djibouti, "thus securing . . . the Red
Sea as an All-British lake" and improving the chances for a favorable
arrangement with Abyssinia over Lake Tana, the source of the Blue
Nile. At the same time discussions began about amalgamating the
Sudan civil service with a nascent Mesopotamian service; Wingate
rashly offered essential senior officials, including Clayton and E. E.
Bonham Carter, the Sudan Government's legal secretary.[30] Foreign

---

[28] Wingate to Clayton, 13 April 1916, SAD 136/4.
[29] Callwell to Wingate, 7 August 1916, SAD 139/2.
[30] Wingate to Hardinge, 2 April 1917, SAD 145/4.

Office discussions during the summer of 1917, and the documents prepared for the Egyptian Administration Committee that met in September, shared recognition of the need, after the war if not immediately, for some overarching Near Eastern organization; largely to forestall the Cecils, Hardinge began to set up in the Foreign Office an "Egyptian and Mesopotamian Department."[31]

Even as the Cecils' Egyptian Administration Committee was about to meet at the Foreign Office to clip his wings, Wingate's horizons had been expanding. In mid-September 1917 he proposed a tour:

> I should start off with a small staff . . . [he told Lord Hardinge] to visit in the first instance Aden. . . . I feel that I ought to see the Resident and local people now that the political work passes through my hands. . . . I should [then] arrange with Admiral Gaunt to take me in one of his cruisers up the Persian Gulf and to fix up a meeting with Sir Percy Cox somewhere in Mesopotamia. I should hope also to see some of the principal Arab Chiefs in that neighbourhood, especially Ibn Saoud. It seems to me that with the eventual consolidation of our administration in Mesopotamia, some system of combination and co-ordination with the Aden Protectorate, Yemen, the Hedjaz and the Sudan will be very necessary. . . . On the way back I might perhaps look in at Jeddah . . . to discuss Arabian policy with the Sherif. . . .[32]

Events in Egypt forced Wingate to cancel the trip, but its intention seems clear. As he told Hardinge in January 1918, "As Delhi is very certainly the centre of our Eastern Moslem world, so Cairo will inevitably become the Western centre."[33] Who would be viceroy?

It has been argued that Arabophilia—"whether sentimental or utilitarian"—lay behind Wingate's opposition to the Sykes-Picot agreement in particular, and in general to plans to divide the Arab lands of the Ottoman Empire between or among the victors in the war.[34] But a conviction that British rule was better than French need not be ascribed to love of Arabs. Allied diplomacy with the Arabs was complicated mainly by the number of voices that conducted it, not by

---

[31] Hardinge to Wingate, 9 November 1917, SAD 166/2.

[32] Wingate to Hardinge, 17 September 1917, SAD 123/11.

[33] Wingate to Hardinge, 25 January 1918, SAD 148/3.

[34] Elie Kedourie, "Cairo and Khartoum on the Arab Question," in *The Chatham House version and other Middle-Eastern Studies,* 2nd ed. New York 1984, 32.

the double-dealing that subsequent events have implied. As we have seen, Wingate himself saw advocacy of the Arab cause—or of Arab causes, or of pan-Arabism, or pan-Islamism—largely as a tactic by which to win support for the war effort against the Turks. That he viewed the Sykes-Picot agreement in the same way, as a temporizing, wartime concoction necessary for good inter-allied relations but changeable or disposable later, is not surprising. Thus in 1916 he had worried that even rumors of the agreement might deflect the sharif of Mecca from the course of revolt, might even, as Clayton claimed to fear, drive him and others into the arms of the Turks. When that danger had passed it was perfectly consistent for Wingate and others in Anglo-Egyptian circles to argue against the agreement itself; the sharif had been made promises, and these must be kept. But the promises that Wingate had thought mere wartime expediency acquired their solemn character only as the French replaced the Turks as Britain's Near East rival.

As high commissioner Wingate's ability to be heard on such large political questions was much greater than it had been in the Sudan. In February 1917, a few weeks after his arrival in Cairo, Wingate wrote Balfour about their "Allies' activities in the Hedjaz." The French, he claimed, were willing to "sacrifice the success of the Hedjaz revolt . . . in the belief that this success . . . might militate against the full realization [*sic*] of their territorial aims in Syria."[35] For this and other reasons he pressed for "amendment" of the Sykes-Picot agreement, first to secure Britain's advantage in Arabia, then to alter arrangements for Palestine, and finally, by advocating a "facade" of Arab rule in Mesopotamia, to modify even the nature of future French control in Syria, since by Anglo-French agreement the degree of European control was to be similar in both territories. It is likely that Wingate's expressions were concerted with those of the Arab Bureau; there was no disagreement in Anglo-Egyptian circles about the desirability of limiting French influence in the region. By mid-1918 Cairo called for open renunciation of the Sykes-Picot agreement. Although this never came, by the end of the war the Foreign Office too saw the agreement as having outlived its usefulness. The "solemn" character of British commitments to the sharif of Mecca was then valuable toward that end. In 1918–19 as in 1915–16 Wingate's and others' advocacy of Arab causes was pursued in a search for local collaborators against successive rivals,

---

[35] Wingate to Balfour, 11 February 1917, SAD 145/2.

the Turks, then the French.[36] Sentimental attachment to the Arabs, that is to the Arabs of the desert, there may well have been—Wingate and chief lieutenants had long and formative experience with them—but the simpler explanation may here as usual be the better. That Wingate supported the "Arab cause" against the Turks, against the French, and against the Italians and other would-be interlopers, but not against the British, would seem to prove the point.

The central importance of Wingate in the planning and execution of the Arab Revolt lends further irony to the vitality with which the legend of Lawrence impinges upon scholarly discussion of Britain's war aims in the Middle East. This is not to say that Lawrence's role has been exaggerated, although it has, and at the expense more of colleagues in the Arab Bureau, notably Clayton, than of Wingate. Rather the myth survives that romantic idealism was a motive of those who opposed the inter-allied agreements that would divide the Arab lands among the European powers. Of Wingate, at any rate, if not of all his famous lieutenants, it has to be said that "the Arab cause" was a weapon against the Turks and those who threatened British inheritance of the Turkish domains. Wingate's numerous memoranda and enormous correspondence yield little in the way of enthusiasm for the Arabs except as fifth columnists against their Turkish masters. (Lawrence, he said in November 1916, was "a visionary," whose "amateur soldiering" had "evidently given him an exaggerated idea of the soundness of his views on purely military matters.")[37] Wingate was above all practical, a believer in and long-time practitioner of the arts of propaganda, not a partisan of national revolution. "Purely military matters" concerned him most; the war really did "come first." In December 1918 Wingate told Hardinge:

> I admit to having been sufficiently opportunist to take the fullest advantage of the situation to treat the Sherif's revolt rather as a really useful war measure than as a means to an end for the renaissance of a great united Arab Empire. . . . There are others who may still retain such beliefs and hopes and I admire their enthusiasm, but, personally . . . as long as the movement served its purpose in knocking out one or two of the stones of the arch of the Central Powers, I am satisfied that its object (as far as my intervention is concerned) has been achieved.[38]

---

[36] See Kedourie, "Cairo and Khartoum on the Arab Question," 27–30.
[37] Wingate to Clayton, 23 November 1916, SAD 143/6.
[38] Wingate to Hardinge, 28 December 1918, SAD 171/6.

After his dismissal in 1919, Wingate continued to argue for a Near Eastern viceroyalty in all but name. By then his arguments were tainted by his advocacy, and events had unfolded in ways that rendered his schemes reactionary. But a note he wrote in July 1919, while still nominally high commissioner, and sent to various ministers, politicians, and the king, usefully summarizes views that seemed tailored to his personal circumstances. After complaining bitterly about his treatment Wingate wrote:

> Some form of administration must be organised before long for the Near East. Mesopotamia, Palestine and Arabia must necessarily come under a more or less unified form of administration. The head waters of the Euphrates and Tigris come from among Kurds and Armenians. Persia needs reconstruction so as to become a good neighbour. The new communications with Egypt will bring that country and the Sudan into the ancient close connection with the eastward lands. . . . While there may be governors of Provinces, Government will stand in need of some high official with vision and an all-embracing purpose—someone in close touch with a Near Eastern Department or Ministry in London, but who for some part of each year would be moving through and inspecting the localities for which such an administration will be responsible. Associated with him, a strong staff would be necessary.[39]

What Wingate proposed now was an echo of the old duke of Connaught, "inspecting" warm places in winters. But by 1919 a scheme that would in any case have seemed self-serving now appeared derisorily so, a discredited official's plea for employment.

---

[39] "R.W.'s note of 21 July (1919) re Refusal of S.S. and Organization [*sic*] of N. and M. East," SAD 237/7.

Chapter Twenty-six
Prelude to Revolution

Wingate's preoccupation with the war did not limit his activities to foreign affairs. Britain's main concern in the Near East had been the defense of Egypt against Ottoman invasion, not its use as a base from which to attack. Egypt was involved in the war from the start, and the military, political, and diplomatic activities of the whole Anglo-Egyptian regime, whether in the eastern Mediterranean, Arabia, Mesopotamia, or North Africa, were conceived of in an Egyptian context. In turn, Britain's ability to prosecute the war from Egypt depended on Egypt's ability to supply men, animals, food, and other goods. The domestic policy adopted and pursued under McMahon and Wingate was therefore directly connected to the war effort, and Egyptian opposition to the one was inseparable from the other. When, at the end of the war, that developed from elite politics to mass nationalism, British officials who confronted it, including Wingate, were taken by surprise.

When Wingate became high commissioner at the end of 1916 a war regime had been in place for two years. Institutions of the protectorate were entrenched. Policies had been devised to tap Egypt's reserves of human and animal labor, its crops, and its surplus wealth. British fears of Egyptian loyalty to the Ottoman sultan as caliph had given way to the stereotype of the docile fallahin. Maxwell's promise that Britain, not Egypt, would bear the burden of the war had given way to apologies for Egypt's involvement, then to indignation at hints of Egyptian "disloyalty." Hundreds of thousands of Egyptian men were drafted as laborers, millions of farm animals were requisitioned, crops (and their prices) were determined by British needs rather than by the market, contributions to war charities became taxes in all but name, and provincial administration became expedient and corrupt. Just as the war justified lip-service to Arab nationalism, an Arab caliphate, a Zionist homeland, and other schemes, so it was used to excuse recklessness in the administration of Egypt. And just as Wingate wearily reassured doubters that international contradictions could be made right by a victorious Britain, so in Egypt

Maxwell had promised self-government in Egypt after the war. The legacy in the Near East of the allies' wartime diplomacy is well known; in Egypt the bill for promises unfulfilled was submitted the day the war ended.

While the protectorate implied closer British control of Egypt, the war in fact brought a rapid decline in the quality of administration. This was evident especially in policies toward labor and agriculture. In these areas Wingate mainly continued and elaborated on policies already adopted before his arrival; his freedom of action was limited. On the other hand he was no McMahon, ignorant of Egyptian economic conditions and political realities. As sirdar he had long been concerned with Egyptian labor questions and indeed with military recruitment; in 1915 he had concurred in a plan to conscript twenty-five thousand men into the Egyptian army to work on fortifications along the Suez Canal.[1] As governor-general of the Sudan during the first two years of the war, he had been closely involved in supplying British forces in Egypt, and indeed had ample experience with the bureaucratic improvisations the war occasioned everywhere. British demands for Egyptian laborers had at first been indirect and limited to volunteers. When, early in 1916, British forces prepared to go on the offensive in Sinai, however, the need for labor increased. Military works, including roads, railways, and fortifications were labor-intensive. To meet the needs of the military a Labour Corps was established. This at first recruited Egyptian volunteers by contract. As the campaign progressed, however, demand increased but recruitment fell; casualties had been incurred, and terms of employment, which now involved service far from home, were less attractive— thousands of workers were in fact sent abroad, to Mesopotamia, Greece, and even France. New methods of recruitment were debated. In 1917 Wingate approved a scheme by which Egyptian provincial officials would supply recruits, who were conscripts in all but name. In 1918 even the fiction of volunteerism was dropped, as Wingate endorsed "a sort of corvee system"[2] and Egyptian authorities were told to carry it out. Thus was revived one of the most feared and hated practices of the old regime, abolition of which had been cited to justify British occupation.

---

[1] Maxwell to Wingate, 26 November 1915 and Wingate to Maxwell, 26 November 1915, SAD 135/6.

[2] Terry, *The Wafd*, 26; see also Marlowe, *Anglo-Egyptian relations*, 221–23.

Feeding the allied armies in Egypt was another burden on the local economy. Early in the war the British had acted to limit the acreage planted in cotton, lest a world boom in fiber markets cause a decline in Egyptian cereal production. This restriction was later strengthened. While Lancashire complained of the high price of cotton,[3] the brunt of this policy was borne by Egyptian farmers and consumers. A Cotton Seed Control Board organized the marketing of Egyptian cotton in England and helped to enforce crop restrictions, in effect insulating the British forces from the world market price of grain and protecting British manufacturers from the world market price of cotton. In 1918 the Cotton Control Commission was established to buy up and sell the Egyptian cotton crop at prices it set itself, thus monopolizing the market. Confiscation of farm animals caused hardship, inefficiency, and bad feelings. By 1918 Egypt was unable to meet the demand for food of both the home market and British forces; grain was requisitioned for the army at fixed prices, while in the towns the price skyrocketed because of shortage. Prices of essential commodities doubled during the war. By 1918 British officials warned of the danger of food riots in the towns.[4]

To these major causes of Egyptian discontent were added miscellaneous grievances that together brought Egypt to the brink of revolt even as Britain approached victory in the war. British war charities took on the character of taxes, as local officials wrung "contributions" from unwilling fallahin. Burdensome wartime regulations interposed a new layer of increasingly corrupt bureaucracy. Price controls led to black marketeering. Conscription of peasants disrupted not only their own lives but those of their families and communities. Inflation alienated urban workers, whose wages failed to match rising prices of essentials. Thus an identity of interest was forged between the rural masses, who for a generation had enjoyed security under British rule, and the towns, where opposition to occupation had been strong from the start. What was required to unite these previously disparate elements was leadership.

There was no shortage of candidates for the role. We have seen that the new sultan, Ahmad Fu'ad, had from his accession in October 1917 looked for ways to improve his position relative to the British and his own ministers. In the "cabinet crisis" of 1917 he had been

---

[3] Graham to Wingate, 4 October 1917, SAD 166/1.
[4] Terry, *The Wafd*, 27–30.

stymied by Wingate's and the Foreign Office's insistence that he accept British advice on appointments to the cabinet. As Wingate pointed out then and later, however, Ahmad Fu'ad's very weakness encouraged him in disagreement with the British, if only to establish a reputation among his own people. He therefore appears to have maintained close, though necessarily quiet, relations with notables opposed to the protectorate. Several times in 1917–18 he gave proof of dislike for the current regime. In a much-cited interview in 1917 with Edwin Montagu, the visiting secretary of state for India, the new sultan sneered at the "autonomy" of his current status, and expressed hope for improvement.[5] He deliberately embarrassed the prime minister, Rushdi Pasha, publicly criticized ministers, insulted foreign dignitaries, and in other ways made clear his impatience with limits on his authority. In August 1918 Wingate told the Foreign Office that when the war ended, Ahmad Fu'ad "might be tempted to encourage the opposition of a more or less Nationalist character"; his personal weakness might lead him to "take a line which would bring him popularity and the position which he lacks."[6] Indeed only the extent, not the fact, of Ahmad Fu'ad's contacts with the nascent nationalist opposition are in doubt.

The leading figure in that opposition, and the man who came to symbolize and embody it, was Sa'd Zaghlul Pasha. Revered in Egypt as the father of independence, he was reviled by British contemporaries as a demagogue. His background gave little hint of demonism. Born in the late 1850s to a prosperous Delta farming family, he had studied at al-Azhar and been made an editor of the *Egyptian Gazette* under Muhammad Abduh. He became a lawyer, then a civil judge, gaining a reputation for honesty and moderation. In 1906 Cromer made him minister of education. In that post, true to the spirit of Muhammad Abduh, Zaghlul clashed with Khedive Abbas Hilmi over educational reform. He was later minister of justice, and a founding member of the Umma party, which called for constitutional limits on the monarchy. Having left the cabinet after a confrontation with the khedive in 1912, he was elected in 1913 to the new Legislative Assembly, and was its vice-president when that body was prorogued at the outbreak of war. He had been involved in the cabinet crisis of late 1917, as one the new sultan wished but failed to appoint to the

---

[5] Wingate to Graham, 3 November 1917, SAD 236/7.

[6] Wingate to F.O., 31 August 1918, See also Kedourie, *The Chatham House version,* 88–89.

cabinet. Wingate had advised London then that while Zaghlul's appointment would have given the new ministry "a somewhat stronger Nationalistic tendency," he was "not altogether averse to this": it might be better to "secure his support on the side of the government rather than have him in opposition."[7] Instead, Wingate later said, Zaghlul remained a member of the sultan's *"officine nocturne."* [8]

Wingate's confrontation with the sultan in 1917 was only one straw in the rising wind of Egyptian political discontent. With the sultan and his associates coalescing into a focus of opposition to the British, the prime minister, Hussayn Rushdi, and his principal ministers feared their own isolation. They had cooperated with the British as the weight of the war effort had grown ever heavier, and could not afford to be seen as stooges. They had, moreover, notwithstanding their cooperation, seen their own positions diminish as the British, for reasons of wartime expediency, had usurped their functions. In late 1917 Rushdi himself began to call for revision of the protectorate regime, and while his ideas remained inchoate, this was ominous. Wingate took that opportunity again to warn London of the nationalist pressure that would be brought to bear after the war.[9]

As the war neared its end that pressure grew. In January 1918 President Wilson's Fourteen Points gave heart to nationalists and ammunition to politicians. During the summer the sultan continued to voice dissatisfaction with the protectorate. In October he told Wingate that Egypt should have Home Rule. On 5 November Wingate received Zaghlul, who asked that the Legislative Assembly be reconvened. In reply Wingate cited the Qur'an: God is with the patient, if they are patient. "I cannot say that this entirely satisfied him," he added, but he had nothing else to tell him. On the sixth the sultan, of all people, spoke expansively of constitutional monarchy and a new parliament. On the seventh the Anglo-French declaration about the future status of the Arabs showered sparks on the Egyptian tinder. Wingate told Graham at the Foreign Office: "[W]e must expect a repercussion of this statement in Native circles here who will argue that as self-government is to be allowed to all territories liberated during the war, why should the same principle not be followed as regards Egypt, which was also liberated but placed under British

---

[7] Wingate to Hardinge, 29 November 1917, SAD 146/10.

[8] Wingate to Graham, 9 June 1918, quoted in Kedourie, *The Chatham House version*, 88.

[9] Kedourie, *The Chatham House version*, 93.

protection *after* the war began?" With the tone he had used in Sudan days when he felt left out of higher councils he added: "I have no doubt that H.M.G. has a ready answer for all such criticisms, but it would help me greatly to know, as soon as possible, the line I should adopt when they come, as they undoubtedly will."[10]

In fact the Foreign Office had no "ready answer." The war had made evident even to ardent Liberals that Egypt was the lynchpin of the British Empire. Autonomy, semi-independence, and other contrivances were one thing when applied to the wastes of Arabia, quite another in Egypt. Moreover Wingate's arguments in 1917 for annexation had failed not only to carry London but also to inaugurate serious debate about a post-war policy. Even Edward Cecil's and his allies' self-interested attempt to embarrass Wingate and wrest Egypt from Foreign Office oversight might have led indirectly to such a debate, but did not. In dissenting from Graham's report of the Egyptian Administration Committee, Lord Milner had warned that steps must be taken to prepare for post-war constitutional and administrative problems in Egypt.[11] Nothing was done. To preserve his own position against the attack of the Cecils, Wingate had adopted the line that all effort should be focused on winning the war and that changes should be delayed. Although since then he had repeatedly warned that nationalist sentiment was increasing, and had (as in 1917 when he suggested Zaghlul's inclusion in the cabinet) advised temporizing measures, he had offered no fundamental proposals to stem it. He had, however, continued to ask London for direction. On 19 October 1918 he told Hardinge privately that "by adopting an opportunist method of keeping the peace" they might "stave off a crisis" until after the war: he hoped Hardinge would give him some "sort of indication of 'how the cat is going to jump.'"[12] Thus when, a week before the armistice, Wingate referred to the Foreign Office's "ready answer" to the nationalists, he asked for something he knew did not exist.

In confronting Egyptian nationalism Wingate was no neophyte. During his years as sirdar and governor-general Wingate had formed definite views. In 1900 he had defused the Egyptian army mutiny at Omdurman by judicious compromise. In 1908 after the Wad Habuba

---

[10] Wingate to Graham, 6 November 1918, SAD 170/3.

[11] War Cabinet. Egyptian Administration Committee. Memorandum by Lord Milner, n.d., SAD 165/3.

[12] Wingate to Hardinge, 19 October 1918, SAD 150/3.

rising he had placated Egyptian officers when Sudanese death-sentences were commuted. When the First World War had broken out he had assigned conscience-stricken officers to non-combatant duty, and conciliated the Sudanese through deft measures. In directing the Arab Revolt he had shown concern for Muslim feelings. Two common themes emerge. First, to Wingate, religion, not secular nationalism, was the most potent danger. Second, in political crises sensitivity to others' dignity was essential in avoiding confrontation. This in turn could be misinterpreted as—or made by enemies to seem—a sign of weakness; in 1900 where Kitchener might have shot mutineers and precipitated a general rising, Wingate compromised and prevented bloodshed. In November 1918 he told Graham of "growing unrest on the part of the British Officials" in Egypt, who criticized him "for encouraging Native Nationalistic aspirations." As an example Wingate cited his recent insistence, after intimations that it would please the sultan, that Cheetham, rather than a lower-ranking official, represent him on official occasions. Cheetham "took very strong objection," an attitude Wingate knew was shared: "I run the risk," he told Graham, "of making a cleavage between them and the High Commissioner." But it was British policy to prop up the sultan, and it was common sense to defer in insubstantial ways.[13]

It was against that background of British grumbling, and with the same practical attitude, that Wingate received at the Residency, on 13 November, two days after the armistice in France, Zaghlul Pasha and two associates, Abd al-Aziz Fahmi and Ali Sharawi. Abd al-Aziz Bey had, with Zaghlul, been nominated by the sultan for the cabinet in 1917; Ali Sharawi was a prominent landowner and member of the old Legislative Assembly. In what Wingate described as an hour's "somewhat stormy, but entirely friendly, discussion," they put the case for Egyptian independence. Wingate's summary of this controversial meeting is worth quoting at length.

> They do not deny the great benefits conferred on Egypt by the British occupation and administration, but they claim that the well-educated and intelligent section have not had sufficient scope hitherto; they consider themselves far more capable of conducting a well-ordered government than the Arabs, Syrians and Mesopotamians to whom the Anglo-French Governments [*sic*] have granted self-determination as expressed in the recently pub-

---

[13] Wingate to Graham, 6 November 1918, SAD 170/3.

lished official statement. (You will remember that . . . I pointed out that this statement would almost certainly lead to the raising of questions in regard to the future government of Egypt.)

He continued:

> They further argued that Egypt had shown a spirit of great loyalty during the War; that they had helped forward its prosecution by men and money, and that now all danger from Turkish aggression was over, they expected their reward, viz: —independence. When I pressed them to explain exactly what they meant by this and in what respect they regarded the future connection of England with their country, they said "We look on England as our closest friend and ally by whose strong right arm we have been set free; we shall ever be loyal and faithful to her and we should make an alliance with her of perpetual peace and friendship; we should be prepared to sacrifice our men and money should she require them in future wars, and we should range ourselves with her, by treaty, in such a manner as to place our mutual relations on an entirely different footing to that of any other nation. In return for this we should expect to be given complete autonomy, though we should probably accept a measure of financial supervision on the part of His Majesty's Government, such as existed . . . prior to 1882. We should also guarantee special facilities for British ships traversing the Suez Canal."

Wingate told Hardinge at the Foreign Office that he had offered "frank criticism," and had counseled patience while the affairs of the world were in turmoil. In parting, the Egyptians disclosed their intention to go to London to put their case; Wingate replied that "with liberty-loving people like the British—no serious opposition was likely to be raised and in any case they were free agents."[14] Thus was born the Egyptian *wafd* (delegation), the nucleus of the party that would dominate Egyptian politics for the next thirty years. And thus began the end of Wingate's career.

Three hours after the delegation departed, Wingate received the prime minister, Rushdi, who said that Zaghlul and his associates had seen him immediately after leaving the Residency. He proposed that he and another minister, Adli Pasha, go immediately to London themselves, not instead of but as well as the *wafd:* if the latter were

---

[14] Wingate to Hardinge, 14 November 1918, ts copy, SAD 237/10.

denied, he and his ministers would appear creatures of the British. "He urged," Wingate told Hardinge, "that there could not be a more favourable time than the present to settle once and for all the future of Egypt—and I think he is right." Wingate went on: "If these burning questions are not settled now, we are likely to have considerable difficulty in the future. The general spirit of self-determination to which the war has given birth, has taken a firm hold in Egypt and I think it is only just that the Sultan, his Ministers and the Egyptians generally should be told how they stand. . . ."[15] Wingate made clear in this early letter his suspicion that the ministers, the *wafd,* and indeed the sultan had concerted an approach; this was later confirmed.[16] His ignorance of this in advance was later taken in London as evidence of failure at the Residency.

On 17 November Wingate told the Foreign Office by telegram of these interviews and warned that "the new movement" would probably "soon take a more pronounced form"; prominent Egyptians were planning to hold meetings. He asked for instructions.[17] On the twentieth he wrote a long letter to the Foreign Office on the state of Egyptian public opinion. He reported "strange stories" of impending British evacuation, the return of the ex-khedive, even the end of the war on terms favorable to Turkey. It was said that the Legislative Assembly would be soon recalled, that the Americans, French, and others supported Egyptian aspirations; President Wilson, especially, was invoked. More seriously, political meetings were being held, petitions drawn up. Yet Wingate reported that there had been "no apparent disposition to engage in secret agitation or revolutionary propaganda," no "signs whatever of a militant spirit nor of attempts to excite religious fanaticism or anti-European feeling." Wingate advised that at this stage most educated Egyptians looked for "a change of form rather than of system," concessions that would "flatter their national and religious sentiment by giving Egyptians the appearance of increased political responsibility."[18]

On 24 November Wingate wrote again at length to Hardinge on the unfolding political situation. He had learned that petitions were circulating in the provinces, and propaganda in the schools; Rushdi

---

[15] Wingate to Hardinge, 14 November 1918, ts copy, SAD 237/10.

[16] See Kedourie, *The Chatham House version,* 95.

[17] Wingate to F.O., 17 November 1918, ts copy, SAD 237/10.

[18] Wingate to Hardinge, 20 November 1918, ts copy, SAD 237/10.

was warned, and Wingate took steps to put a stop to this. Zaghlul and thirteen associates had asked officially for permission under martial law to go to London. Wingate presented various options regarding a possible Egyptian delegation, and repeated his own

> conviction that the present appears to me a favourable time to grasp the nettle. . . . Meanwhile the absence of any reply from the Foreign Office to our telegrams is somewhat disquieting. . . . Pending some such expression of views, I am not replying to the application of the Extremists to go, and have also told Ruchdi [*sic*], that the question . . . is still under consideration.[19]

The next day he cabled more forcefully. There were "indications of a campaign directed against the Protectorate." He had ordered a ban on public meetings and demonstrations. He still urged that "a hearing should be given in London to any Egyptian politicians who wish[ed] to address themselves directly to the Foreign Office." Zaghlul, he said, had been "taking advantage of the fact that they were received at the Residency to represent their movement as a lawful one . . . while simultaneously appeal[ing] to extreme Nationalist sentiment."[20]

In understanding the nature of the crisis that was to engulf Wingate these many and direct expressions of his views are essential. It was only on 27 November that the Foreign Office finally cabled some indication of its own. This was uncompromising. "As you are well aware," Wingate was told in a message signed by Balfour, Egypt was unready for self-government; Britain had no intention of abandoning her responsibility for the good government of the country and the welfare of her people and foreign interests. The message concluded:

> No useful purpose would be served by allowing Nationalist leaders to come to London and advance immoderate demands which can be entertained [*sic*]. H.M.G. would always be ready to listen (?with) [*sic*] sympathy to any reasonable proposals on the part of other Egyptians and would welcome a visit from Rushdi Pasha and Adly Pasha to express their views. . . . But proposed visit of two Ministers would not be opportune at present moment.

The Foreign Office would be fully occupied with the peace negotiations; in Egypt it was important to move ahead with new legal

---

[19] Wingate to Hardinge, 24 November 1918, SAD 170/3.
[20] Wingate to Foreign Office, 25 November 1918, ts copy, SAD 237/10.

codes and the work of the Capitulations Commission.[21] There was no indication in this curt message that the seriousness of the situation was understood.

There had been other hints of the Foreign Office's dissatisfaction with Wingate's handling of the affair. As early as 14 November, in reply to a cable a week earlier that warned of Egyptian repercussions from the Anglo-French declaration, the Foreign Office had blithely wired: "We have had up to now no indication of such Native aspirations"; Wingate was told to keep London "*fully* informed,"[22] thus implying that he had not done so. He had, and continued to do so. But on 2 December Balfour wired:

> I note extremist leaders are exploiting fact of your having received them at Residency which was unfortunate. You will of course make it perfectly clear that you view this agitation and all those who participate in it with extreme disfavour. . . . I understand leaders of movement do not carry much weight but it might easily become mischievous and even seditious . . . if left unchecked. You will no doubt adopt all . . . measures to prevent any such developments.[23]

Ensuing controversy over the phrase "which was unfortunate" has obscured the carefully-worded evasions of this telegram, which implied that Wingate had not until then been doing what he was now instructed to do. The documentary evidence is clear that he had not only taken the required steps but had also kept the Foreign Office fully informed of them.

Wingate might well have suspected that the hints expressed to him of Foreign Office dissatisfaction were only echoes of louder, private expressions. As early as 25 November Graham had in a minute purported to see in recent events evidence of the Residency's failure to maintain close relations with the Palace, and also criticized Wingate's weakness in the interview with Zaghlul. Graham repeated and expanded upon those views in the following weeks,[24] but not to Wingate, with whom he continued in private as well as official corre-

---

[21] F.O. to Wingate, 27 November 1918, SAD 237/10.

[22] Wingate to F.O., 8 November 1918; F.O. to Wingate, 14 November 1918, SAD 237/10.

[23] F.O. to Wingate, 2 December 1918, SAD 237/10.

[24] Kedourie, *The Chatham House version*, 108–09.

spondence. The common theme was of Wingate's weakness: he had
failed to call to order an ambitious young sultan, and entertained
obnoxious views of extremist politicians. As the Foreign Office's
expert on Egypt, Graham necessarily carried weight, more especially
at a time when official attention was distracted by events elsewhere.

On 4 December, having been told by Wingate of London's position on his proposed visit, Rushdi submitted his resignation as prime
minister. In interviews with him and the sultan, Wingate argued at great
length for him to stay, but had nothing to offer. Wingate may have been
surprised at this outcome,[25] in which case he miscalculated Rushdi's own
freedom of action in the light of the sultan's and Zaghlul's maneuvers.
Had the Foreign Office but set a date for a ministerial visit, a basis for
negotiation in Cairo would have been laid. But Wingate found it impossible to refute the view, in the sultan's words, that Britain would welcome an Egyptian delegation on "the Greek kalends," that is never.[26]

On 7 December Wingate wrote to Hardinge to offer his own resignation. In an eloquent defense of his methods he wrote:

> If it is really the view of H.M.G. that I should not see representa-
> tives of all shades of opinion at the Residency, I feel that I ought
> not to be here, for my conception of how best to serve my
> Country in my present position, is to act as I have done hitherto.
> . . . the High Commissioner here must have the complete support
> of the British Government, the British officials and the [British]
> Community. . . . [27]

Graham later told Wingate that the phrase "which was unfortunate"
in Balfour's message of 2 December had been added to his
(Graham's) draft "by the higher authorities," an exculpation unlikely
to ease Wingate's mind. Graham said that the real cause for concern
was not that Wingate had met certain Egyptians, but that he had had
no previous intimation of the objects of the *wafd*'s visit or of the
apparent alliance of the sultan with the politicians.[28] Having made his

---

[25] See Wingate to Hardinge, 1 December 1918, SAD 170/3.

[26] Wingate to Balfour, 5 December 1918, ts copy, SAD 171/2; see also Wingate to
Rushdi, 1 December 1918, SAD 237/10.

[27] Wingate to Hardinge, 7 December 1918, SAD 237/10.

[28] Graham to Wingate, January 1919, SAD 171/2. The "higher authority" was Sir
Eyre Crowe, who had earlier minuted: "Sir R. Wingate seems deplorably weak."
(Kedourie, *The Chatham House version*, 109.)

name as an intelligence officer in Egypt, and after some thirty-five years of Egyptian experience, Wingate was now criticized for ignorance and neglect.

Awaiting a vote of confidence from London, Wingate continued to cajole Rushdi to withdraw his resignation, which the sultan had not formally accepted. The Foreign Office purported to expect Wingate to bring pressure on the sultan to coax Rushdi, but the sultan continued to play a double game. In the end London authorized acceptance of Rushdi's resignation and the search for a successor.[29] None could readily be found. The impasse, Wingate still believed, could be most easily broken by some symbolic concession to the late ministers. In a private letter characteristic not only of Wingate's views but also of his methods, he told Hardinge on 28 December that Rushdi and Adli could be invited to London not to discuss "internal reforms in Egypt" but "larger questions which had arisen owing to the defeat of Turkey"—in other words matters that would be considered at the peace conference. "This would be a sop to their vanity and enable them to save their faces, without bringing against H.M.G. the charge of having given way to Nationalist pressure." Moreover Wingate repeated that "more good than harm" would still result from allowing the "Extremists" to travel to London for a "straight talk." Interestingly, these views were expressed in a private letter that would take a week or more to reach London. Indeed, Wingate wrote therein that he "would make no further reference to the contents of this letter in a public despatch—nor will it be recorded in this office['s] files. I feel that these ideas may not perhaps be palatable to H.M.G. and in that case they can be treated as if they had not been written."[30] This ambivalence—urgent advice diffidently offered in a private letter—cannot have helped Wingate's falling star at the Foreign Office. The fall was accelerated when, on the thirtieth, Wingate told the sultan that there was still a possibility that London would reverse itself over the visit of an Egyptian delegation and the ministerial resignations.[31]

London did. On 1 January Balfour wired Wingate that if the "mere presence" of Egyptian ministers in London "would have a

---

[29] F.O. to Wingate, 24 December 1918, ts copy, SAD 237/10.

[30] Wingate to Hardinge, 28 December 1918, ts copy, SAD 171/6.

[31] Wingate, "Notes of a conversation with H.H. the sultan on 30th December . . . ," 31 December 1918, ts copy, SAD 171/6.

pacifying effect in Egypt" and not appear to constitute British concession to pressure, they could come in February.[32] By now, however,
Rushdi and Adli were adamant that their visiting London without
members of the *wafd* would brand them indelibly as creatures of the
British. Negotiations ensued, therefore, about the composition of an
Egyptian delegation and an agenda for its conversations in London.
Various possibilities arose, were discussed, and were superseded: Adli
might be made prime minister and travel to London in that capacity;
an Egyptian minister might travel immediately to London as a "technical adviser"; the Egyptians wished guarantees that no vital Egyptian
interest would be discussed at the Peace Conference. In the midst of
these discussions, involving the sultan, ex-ministers, and others,
Wingate himself received a summons to London, ostensibly to consult the government in advance of the Egyptians' arrival. Graham had
first suggested in mid-December that he should come when the ministers did.[33] There is ample evidence that by early January, if not
before, plans were mooted that he should not return. Wingate's
papers give no indication that he suspected the personal disaster that
would now befall him. He made secret preparations to leave Egypt on
21 January, meanwhile continuing his negotiations. On the fifteenth
he reached a tentative agreement with Rushdi and Adli. Immediately
upon his arrival in London he would put the case for allowing members of the *wafd* to travel too, and they would then proceed on or
about 10 February; if London refused to remove the "veto" over the
nationalists' travel, the ex-ministers would also decline to come.
Meanwhile their resignations, still not officially accepted, would
stand.[34] Wingate now advised the Foreign Office to accept this solution, but added that no decision was necessary before his own arrival
in London.[35]

   While Wingate strove to resolve a situation which, at the time of
his departure, was still a "cabinet crisis," the Foreign Office played for
time. There is no doubt that officials there were preoccupied with the

---

[32] Balfour to Wingate, 1 January 1919, ts copy, SAD 237/10.

[33] Graham to Wingate, 13 December 1918, SAD 171/3. Hardinge implied in his
   aptly-titled memoirs that Wingate went to England for his health: *Old diplomacy,*
   London 1947, 233.

[34] Wingate, "Notes on conversations on 14th and 15th January 1919," 15 January
   1919, ts copy, SAD 237/10.

[35] Wingate to F.O., 16 January 1919, SAD 132/1.

impending negotiations in Paris, nor that they had, without exception, failed to grasp the seriousness of the situation in Egypt. That failure itself may have been either a cause or an effect of the personal animosities that now asserted themselves. As early as 3 January Lord Robert Cecil, whose interventions in Egyptian affairs we have already noted, told his cousin, Balfour, the foreign secretary: "I spoke to the P.M. and suggested that if Wingate was recalled home Allenby would be a suitable successor. This he warmly approved . . . [.] But the P.M. wanted nothing done which would preclude Wingate's return to Egypt if that were decided on . . . [.] But I ought to add that everyone to whom I have spoken about W. is confident that he is not up to the job."[36]

Such opposition Wingate might have expected. But within the Foreign Office itself Graham and even Hardinge were withdrawing support. On 19 January Graham told Wingate that the government "continue[d] to have every confidence" in his "skill and judgment."[37] Yet three days later, in a letter to Hardinge, Graham criticized Wingate's methods and rejected his policy. Hardinge passed these criticisms to Balfour, and told Graham that he (Hardinge) agreed with them.[38] Thus the main point Wingate was to raise in London had been rejected before he left Cairo, and for reasons that inextricably linked the political and the personal.

---

[36] Cited in Terry, *The Wafd*, 93.

[37] "Extract from a private letter from Sir Ronald Graham to General Sir Reginald Wingate . . . 19 January 1919," SAD 237/10.

[38] Terry, *The Wafd*, 95.

Chapter Twenty-seven
Services Hardly Required

>——≪◯◯◯◇—

Wingate and his wife sailed from Port Said on 21 January aboard HMS *Juno*. After a night as guests of Lord Methuen at Malta they landed at Marseilles on the twenty-eighth, and on the twenty-ninth reached Paris. Wingate went directly to Lord Hardinge, who, with other senior officials, was there for the peace negotiations. On the thirtieth Wingate lunched with Balfour, and "gathered . . . [he] was generally in agreement" with his policy. But Balfour told him to go into details in London with Lord Curzon who, in Balfour's absence, was in charge at the Foreign Office. Before leaving Paris, Wingate met also Lord Robert Cecil, Sir Eyre Crowe, and other officials, and had a lunch meeting with the prime minister, Lloyd George. There was time too for private meetings. Victoria Wingate was working as an archivist for the British delegation to the peace conference. And on 2 February, before they left for London, Wingate and his wife and daughter, in a borrowed car, went to Lagnicourt to see the spot where Malcolm had fallen in battle.[1]

On 3 February Wingate reached England. There was little time to celebrate a return after four and a half years of wartime absence. On the fourth he called at the Foreign Office. Pleading pressing business, Curzon would not see him. During the next two weeks Wingate saw Graham and other officials frequently and was shown the correspondence with Cairo. This indicated a worsening situation. As Wingate's arrival in London had been expected to lead quickly to resolution of the impasse over the ministers' and nationalists' visit, so London's silence deepened the crisis. Finally on 17 February, two weeks after he had arrived in London, Wingate was received by Curzon. At that unpleasant interview it was clear, Wingate wrote

---

[1] Wingate, "Note on the departure from Egypt and arrival in Paris and London of Sir R. Wingate," 31 August 1919, SAD 237/10; Wingate to Cheetham, 1 February 1919, SAD 237/2; Wingate to Andrew Balfour, 7 February 1919, SAD 172/4.

later, "from the outset that I had failed to carry conviction." Having
expected this, Wingate handed Curzon a draft telegram to Cheetham,
which would invite the Egyptian ministers to London and place no
barrier in the way of the nationalists' traveling as "private individuals."
Wingate argued that this telegram would immediately relieve the tension by allowing Rushdi and Adli to resume office, pacifying some of
the nationalists, and pleasing the sultan. According to Wingate,
Curzon replied that the government could not let the nationalists
"hold a pistol to our head"; Curzon would send Wingate's draft to
Balfour in Paris, but would argue against it.[2] His view, clearly shared
by Graham, was that the nationalists had no right to make demands,
the Egyptian ministers had no right to dictate the terms of their own
reception in London, and that acceptance of Wingate's advice would
be seen in Egypt as a sign of weakness. The ministers should be
invited, the nationalists barred.[3]

For another ten days the situation was allowed to deteriorate.
Wingate, who with his wife was staying in a borrowed house in Great
Cumberland Place, "called daily at the Foreign Office to ascertain if a
reply had been received from Paris." On 24 February Cheetham wired
from Cairo that "a change in atmosphere" had "lately become increasingly obvious." Rushdi and Adli had lost the "popularity acquired by
their resignations"; having "to wait so long for a decision from
London . . . [had] made their position an undignified one and . . .
[had] considerably diminished" their prestige.[4] When a reply finally
came from Balfour it rejected Wingate's draft and accepted the
Foreign Office's alternative. A telegram was duly sent to Cheetham on
26 February, inviting the ministers but refusing to receive the nationalists. Wingate, having seen the telegram and warned of its consequences, was left to consider his own position.[5] Repeatedly his advice
on a major issue had been rejected, most recently at the highest level
and after personal consultation. Although he recorded no official hint
that resignation would be accepted, Wingate later wrote that he had
considered but rejected that course. His grounds are unpersuasive:

---

[2] "Note on the departure from Egypt."

[3] Kedourie, *The Chatham House version,* 99. Cf. ibid., 100: Kedourie states incorrectly that the Foreign Office version "refused permission to any Egyptian to leave
Egypt for any reason whatever."

[4] Cheetham to Curzon, 24 February 1919, ts copy, SAD 237/10.

[5] "Note on the departure from Egypt."

having regard to the fact that the War was not definitely over, that I was still holding the post of General Officer Commanding the Hedjaz Operations and that the preoccupations of His Majesty's Government in Paris were of paramount importance, the most patriotic course I could adopt was to continue to place my knowledge and experience of affairs in the Near and Middle East at the disposal of my country.[6]

On 1 March in Cairo, Cheetham met Rushdi and delivered the British government's long-awaited decision. Rushdi thereupon saw the sultan, who immediately accepted his long-pending resignation. In attempting to organize a new government Cheetham was predictably hampered by the efforts of Zaghlul and his associates, who publicly warned the sultan of the dangers of a new ministry's accepting British terms.[7] Cheetham therefore recommended deportation of Zaghlul, who had "long ceased to listen to reason"; indeed, Cheetham wired, in a possible reference to Wingate, "moderate and more sensible Egyptians" wondered why the British had let Zaghlul "go so long unchecked."[8] For once the Foreign Office wasted no time in replying; Cheetham had correctly read the prevailing mood there, if not in Egypt. On the seventh, without consulting Wingate, the Foreign Office authorized Cheetham to arrange with the military authorities the arrest and deportation to Malta of Zaghlul and his associates.[9] On the ninth Zaghlul and three others were banished.

His advice rejected, his presence in London virtually ignored at the Foreign Office, Wingate awaited developments and saw to his private affairs. Petitioners took advantage of this rare opportunity to apply for employment in Egypt and the Sudan for themselves or relatives; Wingate obliged in at least two cases: a royal friend and one of his own in-laws. He did his somber duty with lawyers and military officials to settle his dead son's affairs, collect his belongings, and search for missing letters. He found time to help his old friend Slatin Pasha: before leaving Cairo he had arranged for a monthly sum to be forwarded; now he intervened with Stack in Khartoum, and others, to have money placed in a special bank account in London, and

---

[6] "Note on the departure from Egypt."

[7] Cheetham to F.O., 5 March 1919, ts copy, SAD 237/10.

[8] Cheetham to F.O., 6 March 1919, ts copy, SAD 237/10.

[9] F.O. to Cheetham, 7 March 1919, ts copy, SAD 237/10.

arranged with the crown princess of Sweden for the money to be passed to Slatin. The London social life Wingate had enjoyed so much he was now free to resume. On 16 February he lunched at Clarence House; on the twenty-fifth went to a party at St. James's Palace; and on the twenty-seventh attended a royal wedding.[10] When his benefactors at Great Cumberland Place needed the house, Wingate decided to go to Dunbar. Indicative of either his usual attention to detail or his usual shortage of funds, Wingate asked a well-connected friend for free railway passes: he had written himself and been refused, and now argued that his "relations with the Egyptian State Railways as High Commissioner" were "similar to those of Chairmen of Railway Companies in England, who would undoubtedly possess a free pass over all systems."[11] From Knockenhair, where the Wingates arrived on 13 March, he wired his A.D.C. to send money: there was only £30 in the bank at Dunbar, which would "not last long."[12]

Wingate's departure for Scotland on 10 March, the day after Zaghlul was deported, indicates either that what followed in Egypt surprised him as much as it did other British authorities, or that he presciently expected his own urgent recall. In any event, in Egypt a firestorm of protest erupted. In Cairo, Alexandria, and provincial centers in the Delta demonstrations and riots broke out. These soon spread to the towns of Upper Egypt. Europeans, including British soldiers and civilians, were killed by mobs, Egyptian demonstrators were killed by troops, and great destruction of property took place. On 19 March Wingate was called urgently to London.

Now, on 20 March, he was immediately received by Lord Curzon. Wingate argued that he should return at once to Egypt, but Curzon claimed that developments more than ever required his presence in London for advice. The situation in Egypt clearly called for drastic action, and the tenor of urgent wires from Cairo made it increasingly clear that Cheetham lacked the personal resources

---

[10] Wingate to Marsh, 24 February 1919, SAD 151/2. Wingate to Watson, 17 February 1919, SAD 172/4; Wingate to Slatin, 28 February 1919; Wingate to Stack, 18 February 1919, SAD 172/4. Wingate to Stack, 7 March 1919; Wingate to W.H. Bonham Carter, 10 March 1919, SAD 172/5.

[11] Wingate to F.S. Jackson, M.P., 2 March 1919, SAD 172/5. Wingate got free passes for most of the journey, having "only to travel as an ordinary soldier passenger between London and Doncaster" (Wingate to Jackson, 14 March 1919, SAD 172/6).

[12] Wingate to Alexander, 14 March 1919, SAD 172/6.

needed to prevail. Even while Wingate was at Dunbar, Curzon had reminded Balfour of General Allenby's imminent arrival in Paris. The hint was taken, and on 20 March, as Wingate put his own case to Curzon, Balfour announced Allenby's immediate return to Egypt as Special High Commissioner with supreme civil and military control. In informing Wingate Balfour wired: "This makes no technical change in your position," and promised details later. To Curzon, however, Balfour admitted that it was "probable" Wingate would never return, but that there was no need for an immediate decision.[13] Indeed, Balfour's explanation, in a letter to Wingate a week later, was merely temporizing. Allenby's appointment, he wrote, did not "require much more to be said about it"; while Allenby dealt with the present crisis, Wingate's "services will hardly be required. How long this exceptional period will continue" no one could say.[14]

Indeed, what followed in the treatment of Wingate was exceptional by any standard. The Foreign Office's attitude toward him, especially since his return from Egypt, should have engendered the deepest suspicions. At the end of March publication of Wingate's glowing Hijaz dispatches was postponed, at the Foreign Office's request, for what the War Office called "political reasons."[15] Yet the fact that his resignation had not been requested gave hope that his position was retrievable. Friends reminded him that the government was, after all, sorely in need of Egyptian expertise. Publicly he gave no sign that he had been superseded. He wrote thoughtfully to Cairo, placing his personal property (and his son Ronald, who was due to arrive there) at the Allenbys' disposal. Rather than retire to Dunbar, he and his wife took a flat at Queen Anne's Mansions,[16] and on 6 April he told Grenfell that he was "very much occupied with Egyptian affairs and . . . constantly in consultation with the Foreign Office."[17]

---

[13] Balfour to Wingate, 20 March 1919, SAD 237/10; Kedourie, *The Chatham House version*, 111. See also "Rough notes by Sir R. Wingate on the situation in Egypt," 21 March 1919, ts copy, SAD 162/1, and Wingate to Balfour, 29 March 1919, ts copy, SAD 237/10.

[14] Balfour to Wingate, 26 March 1919, ts copy, SAD 172/5.

[15] W.O. to Wingate, 29 March 1919, SAD 151/3.

[16] Wingate to Cheetham, 22 March 1919, SAD 172/7; Wingate to Balfour, 31 March 1919, SAD 237/10; J. St. Loe Strachey to Wingate, 1 April 1919, Wingate to Grenfell, 3 April 1919, SAD 151/4.

[17] Wingate to Grenfell, 6 April 1919, SAD 151/4.

But it was with clerks, not Curzon, that he consulted. Although he was shown the Egyptian cables, his letters to Curzon as early as mid-April carry the stamp of a petitioner begging recognition.[18]

Meanwhile events in Egypt developed quickly. Order had largely been restored before Allenby arrived in Cairo on 25 March. He reached hasty conclusions. Having discussed the situation with Cheetham, Clayton, and others, he proposed on the thirty-first releasing Zaghlul and his colleagues and allowing "any respectable Egyptians" wishing to travel to Europe to do so. This, he confidently expected, would allow a new Egyptian ministry to be formed, end the immediate political crisis, and lay a basis for fruitful negotiation. In other words Allenby advocated the policy that had branded Cheetham with "weakness," and would grant to the nationalists the demand they had been refused before the disturbances. This might well be seen as vindicating Wingate, whose own "weakness" in suggesting permission for the nationalists to travel had at least been exhibited *before* Zaghlul's deportation and the consequent explosion. Ironically, politics and personality combined in support of a weak policy demanded by a military strongman, as they had in opposition to the firmer policy of the seasoned administrator.

Allenby's advice, Wingate later wrote, caused "some consternation" at the Foreign Office. Curzon, having shunned him, now called him to his house for urgent consultation. "It would be a very grave mistake," Wingate said, "to give in to the Extremists *after* they had been guilty of the grossest acts of lawlessness and bloodshed," advice he had tendered in vain as early as 20 March. Now at last Wingate had said what Curzon wished to hear: Curzon cabled Balfour in Paris that Wingate supported him in opposing Allenby's proposal.[19] On 3 April Curzon and Wingate visited Bonar Law, who in Lloyd George's absence was acting prime minister, to argue against Allenby's policy. Details of that interview are few, but years later Wingate claimed that Curzon had threatened to resign if his (and thus Wingate's) advice was rejected, that Bonar Law had upbraided Curzon for dealing with "Cabinet matters" in Wingate's presence, and that it was then left to Wingate himself to make the

---

[18] See, e.g., Wingate to Curzon, draft, 11 April 1919, SAD 237/6.

[19] "Note on the departure from Egypt"; "Rough notes by Sir R. Wingate on the situation in Egypt," 21 March 1919, ts copy, SAD 162/1; Kedourie, *The Chatham House version*, 112–25.

case against Allenby's advice.[20] Bonar Law thereupon told Lloyd George that he had formed a "poor impression" of Wingate: "I would have no faith whatever in his judgment. On the face of it I should be inclined to agree with Allenby."[21] Curzon nonetheless asked Wingate for a memorandum of his views. This was sent to Paris on the third. "To give way *immediately*, as is now suggested, would be fraught with the gravest dangers," Wingate wrote. "Our real power and authority will have practically gone, and we shall be at the mercy of agitators any time they care to repeat the methods by which they will say they have obtained their ends in the present crisis." But having made the extraordinary appointment of Allenby only a fortnight ago, Balfour argued that he and Lloyd George could hardly reject his advice. In cabling him their "fullest support," Lloyd George left the final decision to Allenby, suggesting as an alternative the dispatch of a special mission, under Milner, to investigate and report on the future of the protectorate.[22]

This proved to be Wingate's last active intervention in the affairs of Egypt. The Foreign Office's attention, when fixed on Egypt at all, now necessarily focused on Allenby's policy and its disastrous consequences. As Allenby had predicted, a new Egyptian ministry was soon formed, but it lasted less than two weeks amid strikes, demonstrations, and new outrages. Zaghlul and his associates, once released, had gone to Paris, where they tried unsuccessfully to influence the peace conference. In Egypt, however, Zaghlul's influence grew rapidly. As Wingate had foreseen, the British concession was widely interpreted as a victory for Zaghlul and violence. The new ministry, its successors, and indeed "moderate" politicians generally, whom Allenby had expected to cooperate, now increasingly took their lead from Zaghlul and dared not oppose him without further concessions from the British. Thus the process had begun, of successive rounds of crisis and negotiation, that would lead to Britain's unilateral declaration of Egyptian independence in 1922. As the failure of Allenby's policy became clear, Wingate's very presence in Britain became embarrassing. Disdained when he had been called weak, Wingate would be insufferable when he was proved right.

---

[20] Wingate, "Note of a conversation . . . between Lord Stonehaven and Sir Reginald Wingate," 14 December 1939, SAD 176/7.

[21] Quoted in Kedourie, *The Chatham House version*, 115.

[22] "Note on the departure from Egypt." See also Hardinge, *Old diplomacy*, 233–34.

Amid continuing crisis in Egypt, plans went ahead for Milner's mission. Its formation was announced publicly by Curzon on 15 May. Debates in both houses of parliament that day included no statement of the government's support of Wingate or endorsement of his long-rejected advice. Wingate took this opportunity to write to Curzon to ask when he would be returning to Egypt. When "anything definite" had been decided, Graham replied, he would be informed.[23] After months of pretense the Foreign Office finally hinted that Wingate should resign. On 2 June he met Graham and "gathered" that there had been "certain criticisms" of his "conduct of affairs in Egypt." Wingate refused to go without a fight. On the third he wrote to Curzon, demanding a full explanation of such criticism, the names of those who had voiced it, and an opportunity to refute it. He threatened to call for a "full and complete judicial enquiry" if "any reflection" were cast on his "personal character or official reputation," and asserted "no intention whatever of resigning . . . without such judicial enquiry."[24]

In thus challenging the government, Wingate gambled that its difficulties in Egypt would salvage his own career. The last thing the Foreign Office wished was public scrutiny of its conduct during the Egyptian crisis. On the other hand it was clear that Wingate could never return to Egypt as high commissioner. The Foreign Office's solution was to damn Wingate with faint praise, and to put him in the position of rejecting honorable treatment. On 14 July Curzon called him to the Foreign Office, assured him of the government's "entire approbation" of his conduct in office, but told him that Allenby would "remain in charge in Egypt, in view of the impending despatch" of Milner's mission. Curzon then offered Wingate the governorship of the Straits Settlements, an offer he repeated in writing a few days later.[25]

Wingate now gambled again. On 23 July he wrote to Curzon to decline the Straits governorship, explaining that his "transfer in such circumstances . . . must inevitably tend to confirm the impression in the public mind" that his conduct in Egypt had been disapproved. But he did not resign. Rather, he asked for leave of absence until the

---

[23] Wingate to Curzon, 19 May 1919, SAD 237/10; "Note on the departure from Egypt."

[24] Wingate to Curzon, 3 June 1919, ts copy, SAD 237/7.

[25] "Note on the departure from Egypt."

end of the year, "by which time the report of the Special Mission should be available": it would "then be possible for His Majesty's Government to appreciate the causes of the present situation in Egypt."[26] Curzon's strategy had been clever. So long as the government did not publicly criticize Wingate, he had no grounds for demanding exoneration; meanwhile his supersession by Allenby spoke for itself. Similarly, while Wingate was clearly justified in seeing the Straits governorship as a demotion, it was an important post he could not disparage publicly. Wingate might have been wise to use the offer as a bargaining point in winning further concessions from the government. By refusing it outright and not resigning he tried instead to buy time, and thus misjudged the importance attached by the public and the parliamentary opposition to the Egyptian question and to himself. In this misjudgment Wingate was evidently supported by the tenor of private comment.[27]

Indeed, Wingate appears unrealistically to have expected to win his battle with the Foreign Office. In draft notes dated 15 July 1919 he set terms for his own return to Egypt: "Increased powers and prestige. Higher salary—or more things paid by Govt. e.g. mil. escort, carriages and horses, motor cars etc. Staff increased and specially selected. . . . Steamer on Nile—and launch. More travelling in Provinces—E. Govt. to take a share in the higher expenditure. . . . Improvement of Residency by Office of Works." In the event he did not return to Egypt, Wingate's notes go on: "If N. and M.E. Ministry formed—necessity for Inspector General with considerable prestige and well-paid—good staff. . . . To travel six months in year (winter) and have other six months at home office in London."[28]

A week later, in a letter to Lloyd George, Balfour, Curzon, Milner, Winston Churchill, and Lord Stamfordham, the king's private secretary, Wingate argued his case for Near Eastern reorganization and his own place in it. His reputation had suffered unfairly; he had had to defend himself to the government rather than be defended by it. It was therefore up to the government to rescue his reputation "by some signal mark of His Majesty's approval." The proposed inspec-

---

[26] Wingate to Curzon, 23 July 1919, SAD 237/10.

[27] See, e.g., Symes to Wingate, 31 July [1919], SAD 237/7; Stamfordham to Wingate, 7 August 1919, and Wood to Wingate, 19 August 1919, SAD 237/8; and Alexander to Wingate, SAD 237 passim.

[28] Wingate, MS notes, 15 July 1919, SAD 237/7.

tor-generalship would serve this purpose during "the ripening years" of his life.[29] Explicitly tying his own fate to policy recommendations ensured that they would be given short shrift.

At Dunbar, Wingate busied himself with extraordinarily long and detailed memoranda on the Egyptian crisis and its aftermath. Rough notes for a memorandum covering a "dossier" he submitted for the Milner Mission clearly indicate how inseparable, in his mind, the Egyptian crisis and his own future had become. These notes refer to the "intrigues" of the Egyptian sultan, the Residency, the Foreign Office, army headquarters in Cairo, Lawrence, Robert Cecil, Graham, Brunyate, and others.[30] In preparing this dossier, which consisted largely of correspondence between himself and the Foreign Office, he further alienated the very officials whose favor he demanded. Hardinge and Graham both objected to his inclusion of their private correspondence. Again, however, Wingate, badly advised by Alexander, his aide de camp in London, misjudged the importance that would be attached to such correspondence, even if it were published. At this early stage in a long and unedifying controversy the Foreign Office had not yet discovered how to buy Wingate's silence.[31]

That stage was soon reached. Wingate's request for a leave of absence had been granted from 1 September until the end of 1919. Beyond that nothing had been settled. Departure for Egypt of the Milner Mission was repeatedly postponed; it would not begin its work until December. In mid-September, his dossier for the mission having elicited no official comment from the Foreign Office, Wingate wrote to Balfour, who had just returned from Paris, and asked him to read it. "I am at a loss," he wrote, "to understand the reason of my treatment." Balfour replied that since the beginning of 1919 he himself had "had nothing to do with the administration of the Foreign Office, as distinct from the work of the Peace Conference": he had therefore forwarded Wingate's letter to Curzon. This reply evidently infuriated Wingate, who rightly disputed Balfour's claim to detachment and again called attention to his personal predicament. "I am

---

[29] "R.W.'s note of 21 July re Refusal of S.S. and Organization [*sic*] of N. and M. East," SAD 237/7.

[30] Wingate, "Notes (Rough) for Covering Memo," 2 August 1919, SAD 237/8.

[31] Hardinge to Wingate, 30 August 1919; Graham to Wingate, 30 August 1919, SAD 237/8. See Alexander to Wingate, 2, 7, 10 August 1919, SAD 237/8, and 5 September 1919, SAD 237/9.

virtually made a scapegoat," he wrote on 30 September, and again threatened to demand a public enquiry if he were dismissed.[32]

On 2 October Curzon finally wrote to Wingate officially of Allenby's confirmation as high commissioner in Egypt, effective the fifteenth. After rehearsing the reasons for Allenby's initial assignment, Curzon merely stated that they remained valid, and thus justified Allenby's permanent appointment. His succession involved "no reflection whatever" on Wingate, whose services had been "of no common order": especially in the Sudan had he performed with distinction—his "services" in Egypt went unmentioned.[33]

---

[32] Wingate to Balfour, 18 September 1919; Balfour to Wingate, 22 September 1919; Wingate to Balfour, 30 September 1919, SAD 237/9.

[33] Curzon to Wingate, 2 October 1919, ts copy, SAD 238/1.

Chapter Twenty-eight
Patience Denied

———◆◇◇◇◆———

Wingate's supersession as high commissioner, even though impending for months, was a blow from which he never fully recovered. With previous setbacks or disappointments in a long career he had dealt by submerging himself in work and awaiting the next opportunity. Now, however, aged fifty-eight, with no work to do, he faced permanent retirement from government service. The injustice of his position infuriated him, and vindication obsessed him. Ironically, however, his very doggedness may have ensured his failure. Without private means, Wingate needed employment; vain, he craved titles and honors: his enemies knew this, and in the end were able to avoid his public criticism by privately dangling before him the prospect of redress.

During the summer of 1919, most of which he spent at Dunbar, Wingate had already begun to produce extraordinarily long memoranda, indeed "dossiers," defending his conduct of Egyptian affairs. One such dossier he submitted (in triplicate) to the Foreign Office for the Milner Mission. Other notes and memoranda written for his own use make plain his view that he was the victim of a conspiracy of personal enemies.[1] Since this was all but impossible to prove, Wingate evidently thought it necessary to make his position unassailable on any but personal grounds.[2] Thus to ordinary longwindedness was added a lawyerly concern to dredge up every document, every cable and private letter, to support his case. In the months ahead, bundles of papers, with covering memoranda and dozens of appendices, would be dispatched to government ministers and others to support his demands.

On 2 October Curzon told Wingate by letter of his permanent replacement by Allenby, effective the fifteenth. Wingate went immediately to London. He wrote formally to Curzon to protest, and to

---

[1] See, e.g., "Notes (rough) for covering memo," 2 August 1919, SAD 237/8.
[2] See Wingate to Milner, 29 August 1919, SAD 237/8.

Lloyd George[3] who, however, simply referred him to the Foreign Office. At the same time Wingate wrote to Curzon privately, again threatening to press for a public enquiry into the events leading up to his dismissal. On 10 October he had a long interview with Milner—who had tried to avoid seeing him[4]—and rehearsed developments since he had left Khartoum at the end of 1916. Milner tried to calm him: "You can probably inflict some harm on the Govt. but they can harm you far more—they will stick at nothing in attacking you and they must eventually down you—and when they do you will be down and out and would never have a chance of re-employment. You are far too young to give up work. Be patient and this temporary eclipse may soon pass." "He implored me again and again," Wingate wrote his wife, "as an old friend not to put myself in the wrong by an open public attack—I said it was cruel to be placed in such a position," but Milner "harped on the fact that . . . by keeping silent, I was sure to get re-employment at some later date." Wingate noted that Milner had discussed the situation that morning with Curzon, who was certain to succeed Balfour at the Foreign Office in the imminent re-shuffle. Wingate told his wife that "the Govt. are thoroughly frightened—my letters have had a startling effect and I am sure M[ilner] has been put on to stop me." After leaving Milner Wingate discussed the matter with Alexander, his A.D.C., who agreed that his "*private* attack" had done "much good," and that it was "better to give up the *public* attack—at any rate for the present till we see how the cat is going to jump."[5]

Wingate's interview with Milner at this critical moment foreshadows his failure in the months ahead. Wingate was not persuaded by the appeal of an "old friend": he remained convinced of Milner's "close Cecil connection." What seems to have induced him to follow Milner's advice was the suggestion that the government would reward him if he did. At this early stage he could not expect a definite offer, but the belief that his threats had had "a bombshell effect"[6] led him to conclude that in giving general assurance of future consideration

[3] Wingate to Curzon, 19 October 1919, ts copy; Wingate to Lloyd George, 9 October 1919, SAD 238/1.

[4] H.C. Thornton, Colonial Office, to E.M.B. Ingram, 9 October 1919, SAD 238/1.

[5] Wingate to his wife, 10 October 1919, SAD 238/1.

[6] Ibid.

Milner represented the government. Wingate now wrote official vale-
dictions to Hardinge, Balfour, and Allenby—to whom he added congratulations "on the splendid welcome" he had recently received in
England—with copies to Milner. To be sure the point was made he
told Milner on 19 October: "These will show you the attitude I propose to adopt, viz. 'conditional silence provided outside pressure is not
too strong.'"[7] By revealing that it was not vindication he wanted so
much as re-employment, Wingate gave an advantage to his enemies.

Not for the first time, Wingate's finances influenced his decisions.
Nor was this aspect of his predicament unknown at the Foreign
Office, even as his threats were under consideration there. As early as
mid-summer Wingate had expressed concern about financial implications of his recall: continuing expenses in Egypt, arrears of reim-
bursements, tax matters, pension questions. Correspondence began
between the Foreign Office and the Treasury.[8] On 17 September
Wingate wrote to Curzon that the government owed him almost
£3,000, and that his bank account was "considerably overdrawn." It
was not until mid-October (that is, after notice of his supersession)
that he was told his salary and official allowance would be paid to the
end of August, less taxes and other charges, and that from that date
the allowance would cease until his leave of absence expired at the end
of the year.[9]

Wingate's circumstances did not allow him to separate his personal finances from the political issue of dismissal. On 31 October he
told Hardinge that the £1,200 deficit he had incurred during his first
year in Egypt had not been diminished since. "I have always gone on
the principle," he averred, "that it is a duty to spend the official salary
in the proper maintenance of one's position, and consequently,
throughout my career, I have been unable to increase my private
resources from my official pay and emoluments." To this remarkable
statement Wingate added that he would soon have only a general's
half-pay to live on, and that he was now forced to sell his car and otherwise "economise rigidly in all directions." Lest there be doubt

---

[7] Wingate to Allenby, 16 October 1919, Wingate to Milner, 19 October 1919,
SAD 238/1. See also Wingate to Balfour, 19 October 1919, SAD 238/2.

[8] Spicer, F.O., to Wingate, 14 August 1919; Graham to Wingate, 2 September
1919; Wingate to Curzon, 9 September 1919, SAD 237/9.

[9] Wingate to Curzon, 17 September 1919; Wellesley, F.O., to Wingate, 23
September and 20 October 1919, SAD 237/9.

about his reasons for raising these points Wingate went on: "You have advised silence, but pressure from outside to make me speak is strong." Hardinge replied on 19 November that he would make the case to the Treasury for reimbursement of Wingate's 1917 deficit.[10] Even though the difference between the amount demanded by Wingate and that suggested by Hardinge was only £45, Wingate now took legal advice in London on the matter. Finally, in January 1920, he appears to have settled for £1,393.[11]

Wingate was perhaps surprised at how little "outside pressure"— by which he meant press criticism of his Egyptian policy—arose. This was partly attributable to the drawn-out method of his supersession. Friends fell into two groups: those who railed against his "abominable" treatment, and those who advised patience until the offer of another post; all properly congratulated him, upon his official retirement, for distinguished service.[12] "The manner of my severance from Egypt," he told one of them, had shown him that he had "a greater circle of true friends" than he had suspected.[13]

One who now came to the fore was Henry Craik, M.P.,[14] who exerted great effort on Wingate's behalf. "The refusal of [the governorship of] the Straits," he pointed out to Wingate in mid-November 1919, "was an obstacle," but he was optimistic. Above all, he counseled, Wingate should concentrate on the practical problem of getting another post,[15] not on "fixing the blame" for the "wrong committed."[16] But Wingate pressed for more. On 18 November he wrote to Milner, rehearsed his mistreatment, again coupling this with his views on "Middle and Near East organization [sic]," and reminded Milner that "Lord Cromer was given a grant of £50,000 on leaving Egypt";

---

[10] Wingate to Hardinge, 31 October 1919; Hardinge to Wingate, 19 November 1919, SAD 237/9.

[11] Wingate to Bonham Carter, 20 November 1919, SAD 237/9; Bonham Carter to Wingate, 28 January 1920, SAD 238/7.

[12] See, e.g., Wood to Wingate, 30 October 1919; Stamfordham to Wingate, 16 October 1919; Edward Arnold to Wingate, 23 October 1919, SAD 238/2; Sidney Low to Wingate, 3 November 1919, SAD 238/3.

[13] Wingate to Dr. Robertson, 2 November 1919, SAD 238/3.

[14] Sir Henry Craik (1846–1927), M.P. for Glasgow and Aberdeen universities, 1906–27, created baronet 1926.

[15] Craik to Wingate, 13 November 1919, SAD 238/3.

[16] Craik to Wingate, 20 November 1919, SAD 238/3.

his own service in the Sudan and during the war deserved "public recognition," a "monetary grant," and "re-employment."[17] There was understandable confusion within the government as to what Wingate really required: Bonar Law thought "recognition" was all he wanted.[18] Indeed, Wingate was not sure himself: in the months ahead he would variously suggest positions, titles, grants, promotion to field marshal, and apologies in parliament, all the while forfeiting time, the one advantage he had. Throughout the winter of 1919–20 it seemed Wingate might be offered another post. In early December Lloyd George, Bonar Law, Balfour, and Milner discussed the matter, without conclusions. Craik continued to act behind the scenes. He reported that Balfour was a stumbling-block, then Milner, then that royal intervention might help. Others took up the case: the bishop of St. Asaph promised to intervene with the prime minister, and Lord Stamfordham with Curzon; Grenfell spoke on his behalf. All expressed hope, counseled patience, warned against the dangers and, as time passed, against the futility of a public campaign.[19]

A notion arising from time to time was that Wingate should return to the Sudan. In reply to one such suggestion, by Grenfell (to whom he had written bitterly about the government's failure to confer honors on him), Wingate wrote in January 1920: "I am mainly responsible for the success of the Arab Revolt. . . . Allenby was guided by me in the whole of his Palestine and Syria policy. . . . [H]e saw the chance . . . of stepping into my shoes and then ruthlessly kicked [me] down the ladder by which he had climbed to eminence. . . . [A]s things have turned out, he gets everything. I lose my appointment and my reputation. . . ." Quoting his own report to the Milner Mission, Wingate went on to consider his return to the Sudan, a prospect "in many respects attractive . . . but under present conditions quite impossible":

> Allenby is "High Commissioner for Egypt *and* the Sudan", and
> Stack . . . has been definitely appointed, on my recommendation,

---

[17] Wingate to Milner, 18 November 1919, SAD 238/3.

[18] Craik to Wingate, 13 November 1919, SAD 238/3.

[19] Craik to Wingate, 7 December 1919, SAD 238/4; 28 December 1919, SAD 238/5; 21 January 1920, and 31 January 1919, SAD 238/7; and 13 February 1920, SAD 238/8; Grenfell to Wingate, 27 December 1919, SAD 238/5 and 15 January 1920, SAD 238/6; Stamfordham to Wingate, 4 February 1920, SAD 238/8. See also Balfour to Craik, 13 January 1920, SAD 238/7.

to be Sirdar and governor-general. . . . [But] if, as I have strongly
recommended, the Sudan could be separated from Egypt . . . and
if Uganda and East Africa and the greater part of Arabia were combined into one general oversight, then I think that some such
proposition would be both feasible and practicable and I should
not be afraid of trying my hand at running it. . . . Allenby could
retain the oversight of Egypt and Palestine, and India could watch
over Mesopotamia.[20]

Apart from further evidence of Wingate's expedient views on the
Arab Revolt and his fitful musings on imperial reorganization, this
and similar missives betray an unrealistic assessment of his own importance. Perhaps such flights of fancy allowed escape from the injustice
and many small indignities of his present position; faced with fights
over pension rights and railway passes, Wingate dreamt of his place in
a grand imperial triumvirate.

Meanwhile his financial prospects worsened. At the end of 1919
Wingate's salary as high commissioner ceased, and he was left with a
general's half-pay, in his case less than £800 a year, and income from
investments, most of which was taken up by life-insurance premiums.
At the end of November a war gratuity of £666 was paid him.[21]
Immediately after his supersession in October he had sent his A.D.C.,
Alexander, to Egypt to wind up the Wingates' personal affairs. By
early January some forty-two crates had been shipped; much of their
furniture at the Residency was sold to Allenby for about £1,900.[22]
Alexander sold Wingate's Sozaire Benwich car for more than £1,000,
and another car, a piano, wine, and other goods for another £1,450.
But upon arrival in Cairo, Alexander had discovered that Wingate's
private bank account was overdrawn by almost £600, and that there
were outstanding bills amounting to another £500. Thus the liquida-

---

[20] Grenfell to Wingate, 27 December 1919, SAD 238/5; Wingate to Grenfell, 2
January 1920, SAD 238/6. See also Wingate to Grenfell, 16 December 1919,
SAD 238/5.

[21] Wingate to Hardinge, 31 October 1919, SAD 237/9; War Office to Wingate,
28 November 1919, SAD 238/3; Wingate to Crawley, 2 January 1920, SAD
238/6. See also Chetwode, War Office, to Wingate, 18 December 1919, SAD
238/5.

[22] Wingate to Allenby, 16 October 1919, SAD 238/2; Alexander to Wingate, 16
November 1919, SAD 238/3; 14 February 1920, SAD 238/8; Wingate to
Earle, 4 January 1920, SAD 238/6.

tion produced about £3,250.[23] This, with proceeds from other sales already mentioned, the Foreign Office reimbursement and war gratuity, meant that Wingate had at least several thousand pounds available at the beginning of his retirement. But his style of life, and a threat that arose in 1920 even to his pension, made the future insecure. Attempts by Grenfell, Craik, Stamfordham, and others to arrange a special grant came to nothing.[24]

As early as January 1920 Wingate therefore began to consider company directorships, but quietly lest he seem to withdraw from the pursuit of office. On a manuscript "List of companies in which I may become interested"[25] are the names of well-connected acquaintances—notably few after such a long time in high office and a further hint of the personal isolation that lay at the heart of Wingate's treatment by the government. He asked Sir John Cargill for membership of the board of Burmah Oil, and was politely turned down.[26] Cautioned by his lawyer, he himself felt bound to refuse several offers.[27] Yet he was not above writing personally to the general managers of British railways asking for renewal of free passes.[28]

In Honours announced on 6 July 1920 Wingate was awarded a baronetcy. The circumstances of the award, and his acceptance, were part of his continuing struggle with the government. For years Wingate had hinted at a peerage. His services merited one; in an era of inflated honors he had a right to expect it. But a peerage might be seen as vindication, when the government preferred to see him blamed, and would moreover have given Wingate a platform in the House of Lords from which to trumpet complaints about government policy in Egypt. A baronetcy, on the other hand, if accepted,

[23] Alexander to Wingate, 5 April 1920, SAD 251/5.
[24] See Grenfell to Wingate, 15 January 1920, SAD 238/6; Stamfordham to Wingate, 20 January 1920, SAD 238/7 and 4 February 1920, SAD 238/8.
[25] Wingate to Chetwode, 11 January 1920, SAD 238/5; "List . . . ," n.d. (1920), SAD 238/6.
[26] Cargill to Wingate, 6 January 1920, SAD 238/6. See also Wingate to Balfour of Burleigh, 2 February 1920, SAD 238/8.
[27] See Wingate to Midleton, 2 February 1920, SAD 238/8; Bonham Carter to Wingate, 9 March 1920 and Wingate to James Little, 10 March 1920, SAD 238/9.
[28] Wingate to Kaye Butterworth, 1 January 1920; Wingate to General Manager, Glasgow and South-Western Railway, 2 January 1920; Wingate to General Manager, Great Central Railway, 2 January 1920, SAD 238/6.

would vindicate the government, while leaving the impression that
Wingate's services had been in some way flawed. In 1927 he told a
relative that he had been "recommended for a Peerage," but that
Curzon had "with his own hand crossed out Peerage and substituted
a Baronetcy," a version of events later repeated by his son.[29] It seems
more likely that the baronetcy, like the Straits governorship, had been
carefully tendered as bait which, whether accepted or rejected,
absolved the Foreign Office and tainted Wingate.[30] Some confidants
advised rejection but, ostensibly in the interest of his son, Wingate
accepted.[31] He took the title Baronet of Dunbar and Port Sudan.

There the government must have expected relations with
Wingate to end. That they continued reveals not so much persever-
ance on Wingate's part as naivete, and the small-mindedness of officials who made him fight for a pension. That the battle would continue was signaled immediately: in a private letter to Wingate on the
day the baronetcy was announced Curzon noted that he was trying to
settle the "question of your pension . . . in a manner consonant with
the dignity conferred upon you." And in reply Wingate pointedly
expressed a hope that his services would be re-employed.[32] But acceptance of the baronetcy left Wingate nothing to bargain with, except a
claim to sympathy and the threat of nuisance.

Between mid-1920 and the end of 1921 it seemed on several
occasions that those last arrows might hit the mark. In July 1920
Wingate corresponded with Milner about a highly remunerative seat
on the board of the Suez Canal Company, but this was in the gift of
the prime minister and Wingate was eventually passed over in favor of
Lloyd George's secretary, J. T. Davies.[33] In October Wingate wrote to
Crowe at the Foreign Office asking to be considered for an ambas-
sadorship to Constantinople: "Apart from my contact with Near and

[29] Wingate to Dan Wingate, 21 November 1927, SAD 115/13; author's interview
with Sir Ronald Wingate, 24 April 1975.

[30] See Wingate, "Note of a conversation . . . between Lord Stonehaven and Sir
Reginald Wingate," 14 December 1939, SAD 176/7, in which Bonar Law is
blamed for the refusal to grant a peerage.

[31] Wingate to F. Milner, draft, 9 January 1925, SAD 241/5. See F. Milner to
Wingate, 8 January 1915, SAD 241/5.

[32] Curzon to Wingate, 5 June 1920; Wingate to Curzon, 17 June 1920, SAD
251/5.

[33] See correspondence with Milner, Craik, Balfour, Vansittart, and Cromer, SAD
239/4, 240/8–10, 251/6–7.

Middle Eastern problems," he wrote, "I passed for Interpreter in Turkish many years ago."[34] In ceaseless letters he mentioned Indian governorships—"I began my military career in Bombay," he told Milner, "and passed the H.S. in Hindustani"[35]—military missions, boards of directors. In mid-1921 Wingate approached Winston Churchill, then colonial secretary, about the governorship of Gibraltar, which would not fall vacant for a year or more; Churchill offered no hope.[36]

Those who would help him began now to counsel acceptance of defeat and concentration on practical matters; some who could help began to disappear from the scene. Principal among these was Milner, who in February 1921 had resigned as colonial secretary. If his object, since the crisis of 1919, had been to keep Wingate quiet, he had succeeded. By urging patience, holding out a prospect of re-employment, arguing against publicity, and seeming to take Wingate's part, Milner had kept the government informed and protected himself. In 1917 he had supported Edward and Robert Cecil over Egyptian administration; in 1919 he had supported Curzon and Balfour in rejecting Wingate's advice. If Wingate had subsequently criticized the government publicly, Milner would have attracted a share of blame, so in advising Wingate he had had his own interests as well as the government's to consider. After his mission returned from Egypt in March 1920 Milner had embarked on a round of negotiations with the Egyptian nationalists and others that paved the way for the early demise of the protectorate, thus reversing the policy he had supported. Having concluded those negotiations during the autumn of 1920, Milner finally issued the report of his mission. This endorsed the rightness of Wingate's advice about the Egyptian ministers in 1919, but held that Wingate "would have done well . . . to urge his views with even greater insistency."[37] Thus when in July 1921, after resigning from the government he advised Wingate to consider company work, since "as now seems to be the case, the Govt. have noth-

---

[34] Wingate to Crowe, 2 October 1920, ts copy, SAD 251/7.

[35] Wingate to Milner, 6 October 1920, SAD 251/7. See also Wingate to Cromer, 1 September 1921, SAD 239/3.

[36] Wingate to Churchill, 30 July 1921, SAD 239/2. Craik to Wingate, 2 August 1921; Churchill to Wingate, 22 August 1921; and Smith-Dorrien to Wingate, 8 September 1921, SAD 239/3.

[37] Report of the special mission. . . .

ing to offer you," Wingate justifiably taxed him with having given false hopes.[38] What Wingate had called Milner's "close Cecil connection" took a final turn when, in February 1921, Milner married the widow of Lord Edward Cecil.[39]

The Report of the Special Mission to Egypt indeed provided Wingate's last opportunity to make a public case. He did not take it. The report was circulated privately for several months before publication. Wingate saw a draft in March 1921, and immediately wrote to Curzon to protest its wording in regard to himself. Curzon's reply, four months later, gave no satisfaction.[40] Wingate later learned that the mild criticism of him in the report had been inserted at the suggestion of Milner himself, in order to give the government "some excuse for their action."[41] He deliberated anew the possibility of a public campaign for exoneration: Craik told him that there were, in fact, a number of M.P.s "fully prepared to fight" on Wingate's behalf.[42] But in the wake of the Milner report, as before, Wingate's waning hopes of re-employment and continuing difficulties over pension stood in the way. As Craik himself had told him in July 1921, Wingate gave "too much effort to trying to get the past cleared up, instead of *looking ahead*."[43]

In his financial affairs Wingate had always looked ahead with hope rather than caution. In forty years as a soldier and administrator he had saved little. His salary as high commissioner for Egypt ceased on 31 December 1919. Small legacies that had come to him and his wife over the years, and the gratuity of some £18,000 he received in 1917 upon retirement from the Egyptian army, were supplemented in 1919–20 by liquidation of his property in Egypt. But Wingate had always lived beyond his means, and although the total value of his investments by 1920 is unknown, the income produced from these

---

[38] Milner to Wingate, 21 July 1921; Wingate to Milner, 22 July 1921, SAD 239/2.

[39] See Craik to Wingate, 11 July 1921, SAD 239/2; Alexander to Wingate, 22 December 1921, SAD 239/6. Eight months after Milner married Violet Cecil, she, presumably with his agreement, published Lord Edward's *The leisure of an Egyptian official*, adding nothing to his record as an administrator. See Rose, *The later Cecils*, 218.

[40] Curzon to Wingate, 4 July 1921, ts copy, SAD 239/1.

[41] Wingate to Frederick Milner, 14 May 1922, SAD 240/5.

[42] Craik to Wingate, 22 February 1922, SAD 240/2.

[43] Craik to Wingate, 14 July 1921, SAD 239/2.

was, he said, barely sufficient to pay life insurance premiums. If he were not quickly to use up his capital he was faced with the prospect of living on army half-pay of £800 a year, and if he found no further government employment even that would last only until 1923, for under War Office regulations he must retire after three years of unemployment. Worse still, after further controversy the War Office ruled in 1921 that Wingate's years as high commissioner did not constitute military employment, and he was therefore forced to accept retirement from the army at the end of January 1922.[44] Wingate tried to take advantage of this further setback by putting his case for promotion to field marshal, the rank attained by all his predecessors as sirdar of the Egyptian army.[45] This too was denied him.

It was therefore for financial reasons as much as for vindication that Wingate continued to press for a special grant. Legal grounds for his claim were weak; verbal assurances from Lord Cromer dating to 1907 carried little weight with Lord Curzon in 1922.[46] Wingate argued that by taking up the high commissionership he had—owing to the Foreign Office's dismissal of him and the War Office's rulings—forfeited the pay and pension benefits of six and a half years of active military duty.[47] Yet the Foreign Office not only rejected the idea of a special grant, but also left Wingate to plead with the War Office for his pension. There an exhaustive review of the various terms and regulations under which Wingate had served since 1883 concluded that the latest at which his services in the British army could be counted toward a pension was 1903. Any claim for service beyond then should be made of the Egyptian government. Although Wingate had, in fact, privately investigated that possibility, political complications obviously obtruded. The War Office conceded, however, that Wingate's case was "so exceptional" as to deserve "special consideration."[48] That was given only after further extended argument, intercession by concerned

[44] War Office to Wingate, 3 December 1921, SAD 239/5. See also Wingate to Secretary, War Office, 4 December 1921, SAD 239/5.

[45] Wingate to Wilson, W.O., 30 November 1921, SAD 239/4; Wingate to Curzon, 6 December 1921, SAD 239/5.

[46] D.G. Osborne, F.O., to Wingate, 2 February 1922, ts copy, SAD 240/2.

[47] Wingate to Curzon, 8 February 1922, SAD 240/2.

[48] C. Harris, "Note on Sir R. Wingate's Retired Pay," ts copy, 21 February 1922, encl. in Harris, War Office, to Wingate, 21 February 1922, ts copy, SAD 240/2. See also Alexander to Wingate, 16 October 1920, SAD 251/7.

friends, and more inter-departmental wrangling.[49] In June 1922 the Army Council, having considered Wingate's "very eminent services," agreed to Curzon's suggestion of a pension equivalent to that of a "Minister in the Diplomatic Service retiring from a first class Mission," or £1,300.[50] Wingate was later told that opposition to his improved pension had been "'civilian' not 'military.'"[51]

While this humiliation proceeded, Wingate was forced to look to his immediate circumstances. In the spring of 1921 he and his wife decided to give up their London flat, and would have sold the furniture but for a depressed market. The embarrassing quest for railway passes having failed, he now routinely traveled third-class.[52] Adding to his woes, Knockenhair was "looted" by burglars in May, and the happy prospect of his daughter's marriage was clouded by the fact that she and her intended would be "so badly off."[53] Despite his anger at Milner's suggestion, in July, that he "contemplate City work," Wingate now therefore had little choice. A final attempt at interesting the government in employing him in some Eastern capacity failed during the summer; Wingate even visited Balfour at Whittingehame in October to plead his case.[54]

Although he nursed his grievances for the rest of his life, it seems that during the autumn of 1922 Wingate finally began to accept his fate. A manuscript note dated 11 September 1922 reads: "This dossier contains correspondence . . . relating to the Egyptian Crisis and my treatment by HM's Govt. . . . [I]n case of my death, there is much in it that could be published—should my family consider it desirable to have the facts made known publicly. . . . "[55]

---

[49] See Wingate to Wigram, 15 January 1922; Alexander to Wingate, 21 February 1922, SAD 240/1. Alexander to Wingate, 7 and 13 April 1922, SAD 240/4.

[50] H.J. Creedy, W.O., to Wingate, 21 June 1922, SAD 240/6. Wingate continued to argue for £1,400: see Bonham Carter to War Office, 28 September 1922, and Creedy, W.O., to Bonham Carter, 18 October 1922, SAD 240/10.

[51] Moyne to Wingate, 10 August 1923, SAD 241/2.

[52] Alexander to Wingate, 19 May and 23 June 1921, SAD 239/1; and 20 December 1921, SAD 239/6.

[53] Regarding the burglary: Alexander to Wingate, 19 May 1921, SAD 239/1; the marriage: Alexander to Wingate, 21 February 1922, SAD 240/2.

[54] See Churchill to Wingate, 11 September 1921, and Alexander to Wingate, 16 September 1921, SAD 239/3. Wingate to Balfour, 17 October 1921; Alice Balfour to Wingate, 18 October 1921; Wingate to Balfour, 22 October 1921, SAD 239/4.

[55] Wingate, note, 11 September 1922, SAD 240/9.

Chapter Twenty-nine
The Business of Living

⊰◌◌◌⊱

Once he accepted that the government would do nothing for him, Wingate was able to look ahead at the possibilities open to him. In the event, the killing frost of 1919–21 gave way to a long and active Indian summer. For twenty years Wingate immersed himself in business, family, society, and travel in Britain and abroad. By successive governments he was treated correctly but rarely consulted—and on Sudanese, not Egyptian, affairs. He routinely devoted hours a day to private correspondence. He and his wife lived simply but well, dividing their time between London and Dunbar, with a foreign holiday almost every year. It was a pleasant, busy, and comfortable life, the sort to which Wingate had perhaps looked forward, lacking only the official honors to which he had always aspired.

In 1924–25 friends made a final attempt to win a peerage for Wingate. The Sennar Dam on the Blue Nile was to be inaugurated in January 1926, realizing the dream of Wingate and others to irrigate the Gezira plain south of Khartoum. Sir Frederick Milner used the occasion to argue that Wingate should be honored for his Sudanese work alone, regardless of past controversies over Egypt. Lord Stamfordham secured the interest of the king, and Milner and Wingate drafted an appeal, over Milner's name, to Austen Chamberlain, then foreign secretary. This lauded Wingate's achievement in the Sudan; Egypt was mentioned only to point out "one of the greatest sacrifices man ever made": Wingate's leaving Khartoum to take up the high commissionership.[1] But Chamberlain followed the Foreign Office line: a baronetcy had been conferred; if the prime minister wished to recommend a peerage, he would offer no objection. After this rebuff, and recognizing that another drawn-out campaign would end in failure, Wingate asked Milner to desist.[2] Citing pressing

---

[1] F. Milner to Chamberlain, draft, 16 December 1925, SAD 241/5; see Wingate to Milner 17 December 1925, SAD 241/5.

[2] Chamberlain to Milner, 2 February 1926; Milner to Wingate, 17 March 1926, SAD 241/6.

business but in fact to avoid embarrassment, Wingate declined an
official invitation to attend the opening of the Sennar Dam.[3]

Meanwhile Wingate had joined the boards of several companies
with African interests. These included the Rhodesia-Katanga
Junction Railway and Mineral Co., which first approached him in
November 1922; the African Railways Finance Co.; the British (Non-
Ferrous) Mining Corp. and the Allihies Copper Mines, Ltd.; and,
most importantly, as chairman, the companies of the Tanganyika
Concessions. This was a working chairmanship, the gift of Robert
Williams, the engineer and entrepreneur, and involved regular business in the City and frequent trips to Brussels for board meetings of
the Union Minière du Haut Katanga. Membership of the board of
the Benguela Railway Co. involved annual trips to Lisbon. Travel
farther afield on business Wingate avoided: in 1929 he declined a trip
to Angola for the opening of the Benguela Railway.[4] On several trips
to Brussels, Lady Wingate went too, and they visited Malcolm's grave
at Lagnicourt, when possible on the anniversary of his death.[5] More
usually they stopped there on the way to or from a springtime "cure"
at Karlsbad or another spa.[6]

Until September 1940 the Wingates' London home was the
small flat at Queen Anne's Mansions that they had tried to sell in
1921. As Wingate's business activities increased he spent as much as
nine months a year there, and holidays at Dunbar were often interrupted by brief visits to London. He and his wife resumed the social
life he reveled in. There were frequent occasions to which he added
interest and prestige: lunches for Near Eastern dignitaries, dinners for
visiting royalty. The Wingates liked the theater and exhibits, and went
often to large formal dinners. They spent an occasional weekend in

---

[3] Archer to Wingate, 13 October 1925; Wingate to Archer, 19 October 1925,
SAD 241/5. See Milner to Wingate, 16 November 1925, SAD 241/5.

[4] Secretary, Rhodesia-Katanga Junction Railway and Mineral Co. to Wingate, 17
November 1922, SAD 241/4; see Report of the Board, 23 July 1924, SAD
241/4; Wingate to W.G. Hollyhoke, 29 April 1926, SAD 241/6; Wingate to
Anderson, 5 February 1934, SAD 242/8; Wingate to Slatin, 1 January 1929,
SAD 223/14; Minutes of Board Meeting of the British (Non-Ferrous) Mining
Corp., Ltd., held on 19 March 1929, SAD 242/2; Wingate, *Wingate of the
Sudan*, 254.

[5] See, e.g., Wingate to Slatin, 6 May 1931, SAD 223/16; Wingate to Asser, 16
March 1933, SAD 242/7.

[6] Wingate to Slatin, 6 April 1927, SAD 223/12.

the country with friends from Sudan days; Christmas was often celebrated at the country house of Milo Talbot. Wingate's correspondence from the late 1920s and early 1930s is crowded with parties,
dinners, receptions, board meetings, comings and goings: the tone is
that of Khartoum before the First World War:

> I have had a bad cold [he told Slatin in March 1930], but only
> stayed two days in bed and now I am up and off to the office and
> then to a big Luncheon party given by the Portuguese
> Ambassador. . . . I think I got cold by getting very hot at the
> Persian Minister's New Year's Day and then going to see another
> invalid—The Princess Royal who has been in bed . . . for five or
> six weeks. . . . I am off to Brussels on Sunday for a Meeting and
> hope to be back again a few days later.[7]

In London Wingate maintained unofficial connections with the
Sudan. In 1919 he was interpreter and guide for a Sudanese delega-
tion congratulating the king on victory in the war. Unless abroad
Wingate never missed the annual Egyptian Army and (after 1925)
Sudan Defence Force Dinner; with the deaths of Grenfell, Wood, and
Stack, he was for almost the last thirty years of his life the only sur-
viving sirdar.[8] In 1929 he presided at the inauguration of the Sudan
Club Dinner Club, which thereafter he attended regularly; in 1930 it
met on his sixty-ninth birthday.[9] He chaired the governing body of
Gordon Memorial College in Khartoum from 1917 to 1933; then, it
was belatedly discovered that the trust's by-laws specified the incum-
bent governor-general as president, and Wingate resigned in pique.
In 1926 he was awarded the Gold Medal of the African Society.[10] At
Queen Anne's Mansions he and his wife often entertained to tea
active or retired officers and officials, both British and Sudanese.

Although Wingate found time for the Sudan, and for charitable
and honorary work connected with the army, he dissociated himself
from Egyptian affairs. In 1930 he was "otherwise engaged" when

---

[7] Wingate to Slatin, 28 March 1930, SAD 223/15.

[8] See Clayton to Wingate, 29 March 1926, SAD 124/14.

[9] Wingate to Slatin, 7 May 1929, SAD 223/14; 9 July 1930, SAD 223/15.

[10] For the Gordon College incident see minutes of a meeting of the Trustees and
Executive Committee, 21 September 1933, SAD 572/5. For details of the
medal see Martin to Wingate, 15 June 1926, SAD 241/6 and other papers in
the same file.

invited to meet an Egyptian delegation and an Arab delegation from
Palestine. And in 1936, when the Foreign Office asked him to
accompany Egyptian representatives to the funeral of King George
V—a request his old A.D.C., Alexander, called "gross impertinence"—he excused himself;[11] he, his wife, and daughter attended by
invitation of the War Office.[12] He was honorary colonel of several battalions, including one of the Manchester regiment, which had been
at Khartoum in 1914; this was a duty he took seriously: he made regular inspections, and represented the battalion at wreath-layings and
other ceremonial occasions.[13] Wingate was also vice-president of the
Officers' Housing Association in London, a member of the committee of the Empire Day Movement, and an officer of the Royal
National Lifeboat Institution.[14]

Memories of the Sudan were enlivened by renewed contact with
Slatin Pasha. Immediately after the war, while Wingate was still high
commissioner for Egypt, this was delicate. Rumors had circulated that
Slatin's wartime activities in his native Austria had not been entirely
humanitarian. Refusing to believe these, Wingate had corresponded
with him during the war and helped to settle his affairs.[15] When in May
1919 the Foreign Office asked him about Slatin's "attitude towards
England," Wingate sprang to his friend's defense. But in September,
when Slatin wished to visit London and Wingate asked for official
guidance, the Foreign Office advised doing "nothing to facilitate" a
visit. Pointedly addressing him—bereft now of his British decorations—as "Mr. Slatin," the Foreign Office barred him.[16] After further
consideration Slatin was admitted in January 1920. During a two-

---

[11] On the 1930 Egyptian delegation: Wingate to Slatin, 15 April 1930, SAD
223/15. On the Arab delegation: Wingate to Slatin, 28 March 1930, SAD
223/15. On the 1936 delegation: Wingate, draft note, 25 January 1936;
Alexander to Wingate, 27 January 1936, SAD 243/2.

[12] Wingate to Creedy, W.O., 29 January 1936, SAD 243/2.

[13] Wingate to Slatin, 3 December 1930, SAD 223/15; Wingate to Spencer, 11
November 1933, SAD 242/7; Wingate, *Wingate of the Sudan*, 255.

[14] Wingate to Huddleston, 24 March 1928, SAD 242/1; Wingate to Slatin, 18
June 1931, SAD 223/16; Wingate, *Wingate of the Sudan*, 255; Wingate to
Maffey, 9 February 1927, SAD 241/7.

[15] For Slatin's war service see Brook-Shepherd, *Between two flags*, 251–71, 275–93.

[16] Loyd, F.O., to Wingate, 16 May 1919; Wingate to Loyd, 18 May 1919; Slatin
to Wingate, 16 September 1919, SAD 223/6; Hardinge to Wingate, 20
September 1919; Slatin to Wingate (quoting F.O. note), 5 October 1919, SAD
223/6. See also Brook-Shepherd, *Between two flags*, 294–301.

month visit he rehabilitated himself socially, a process hastened by Wingate's loyal friendship. For allies in the ensuing battle to resume his British decorations, however, Slatin had to turn elsewhere, and Wingate's help in arranging naturalization as a British subject was likewise inadequate.[17]

During the inter-war years Wingate's long association with the royal family continued, and grew more intimate. He and his wife not only attended occasional state functions but also were guests at royal lunch and dinner parties. Lady Wingate especially was close to the Princess Royal, duchess of Fife, who had visited the Sudan. During the 1920s they exchanged frequent visits at Knockenhair and Mar Lodge. For nearly ten years, until the Princess Royal's death in January 1931, Wingate served as trustee of the Fife estates, time-consuming work that involved "many snags and curious family considerations."[18] In connection with the Union Minière Wingate renewed acquaintance with the king of the Belgians, whom he had also entertained in Khartoum.[19]

Both Wingate and his wife enjoyed good health well into old age. In January 1928 both had influenza and bronchitis; they recuperated with a trip to Madeira, where, however, in a "distinctly inferior" hotel, they "both promptly got ill with Madeira sickness."[20] A year later Lady Wingate's illness recurred, and day and night nurses had to be employed. In December 1932 both had "gastric 'flu."[21] In 1933 Wingate began wearing eyeglasses for golf, and in 1935 he needed false teeth.[22] Wingate's stature (about 5'6") emphasized lifelong overweight, which he controlled through exercise, not diet. He indulged a love of cigars until late in life, at dinner preferred whisky to wine,[23] and apparently suffered no lasting effects from the abdominal surgery of 1910.

---

[17] See Brook-Shepherd, *Between two flags*, 305–23.

[18] Wingate to Hohler, 21 January 1931, SAD 242/4. See also Wingate to "Jack," 28 July 1932, SAD 242/6.

[19] See, e.g., Wingate to Slatin, 6 May 1931, SAD 223/16.

[20] Wingate to F. Milner, 15 March 1928, SAD 242/1. See also Wingate to Rodd, 14 January 1928, SAD 242/1.

[21] Wingate to Slatin, 20 February 1929, SAD 223/14; Wingate to Brittain, 22 December 1932, SAD 242/6.

[22] Wingate to Cowan, 11 November 1933, SAD 242/7; Wingate to Alexander, 6 December 1935, SAD 243/1.

[23] Interview with Mrs. Guy Street, 15 July 1991.

Life in Britain provided fewer opportunities for Wingate to see his children than he had had while posted abroad. When Ronald arrived from India in October 1930 his parents had not seen him for six years. In March 1922 in London Victoria Wingate had married Captain Henry Dane, son of Sir Louis Dane, a retired Indian official; they had then left for India, where the Wingate's first grandchild, Josephine, was born at Poona in January 1923. Two grandsons followed: Paul, born at Rugby in 1924, and Martin, born in Malaya in 1936.[24] While her husband served in the Indian army and, after 1930, when he took up business in Malaya, Victoria was in England on leave only every two or three years. Her children were put in school there, however, and saw their grandparents more frequently.[25]

As a company director Wingate was personally insulated from the worst effects of the Depression. Directors' fees were reduced, and Wingate tried to curtail company expenses by missing some board meetings. "*Ma fish felus*" ("There is no money"). "I am at my wits' end to know how to carry on," he wrote to Slatin in 1931, exaggerating for the sake of his poorer friend.[26] The Wingates still had their "cure" at Karlsbad in 1932 (although they traveled second class), and when the fields between Knockenhair and the sea were developed into golf links in 1933, Wingate invested in the scheme.[27] Indeed, financial problems were, as usual, the result of Wingate's determination to maintain a certain standard of living.

Although until the Second World War, Wingate spent more time in London than at Dunbar, Knockenhair remained his true home. Lady Wingate spent the summer there, and Wingate himself, once annual general meetings were over, usually had from late July until late October with her. The flat in Queen Anne's Mansions was small—bedroom, sitting-room, bathroom, and no kitchen: meals were taken in a private restaurant[28]—so it was only at Knockenhair that they could have house-parties, and overnight visits of their son and daughter, grandchildren, and other relatives; the Rundles were

---

[24] CB1.

[25] Wingate to Slatin, 6 May 1931, SAD 223/16; CB1.

[26] Wingate to Slatin, 25 June 1931; Wingate to Slatin, 8 December 1931, SAD 223/16.

[27] Wingate to Acland, 27 June 1932, SAD 223/17; Wingate to Goodland, 23 January 1934, SAD 242/8.

[28] Wingate to Slatin, 10 May 1932, SAD 223/17; interview with Mrs. Guy Street, 15 July 1991.

regular visitors for long stays. Wingate's collection of Sudanese, mainly Mahdist, memorabilia was displayed there, and his archives were spread around the house. There was a staff of five or six, including a secretary-stenographer. At Knockenhair Wingate indulged a life-long passion for golf, and, with his wife and guests, became a regular bridge-player. There were long and bountiful afternoon teas, and occasionally in the evenings films from Sudan days, showing, among other things, Wingate riding through the streets and tossing coins to crowds.[29]

Even at Knockenhair informality, absent elsewhere from the Wingates' lives, was limited. After leading society for many years in Khartoum and Cairo it was difficult for Wingate, and much more so for his wife, to relax Victorian standards. In the Sudan, Lady Wingate had been famous for rigid propriety; in old age she remained "extremely sensitive" behind a "severe front." She never recovered from Malcolm's death in 1918; a corner of the drawing room at Knockenhair was reserved as a "shrine," his name was never mentioned, and a grandson who resembled him suffered for it. Mornings began with prayers in the dining room, which family, guests, and servants were expected to attend.[30] Wingate shared with Edward VII and George V a concern with medals and uniforms, forms of address, and points of etiquette. Even during international crises he noticed an Order listed incorrectly in the Court Circular, or engaged in correspondence over a minor medal. In old age he remained unerringly fastidious, taking "immense care" of his clothes: he wore spats over highly-polished shoes,[31] and was, he thought, one of the last men in London to wear a top hat to Sunday services. "I rather like the old ideas," he told Slatin in 1932; "all this slackness in dress is to my mind a mistake."[32] From Khartoum he had sent to Paris for hair oils and moustache wax, and to London for monocle glasses; in retirement at Knockenhair he had a manicurist call regularly from Dunbar—decades later he was remembered for his "beautiful hands"—and he always smelled of lavender. He shaved himself with seven cut-throat razors, numbered for each day of the week.[33]

---

[29] Interview with Mrs. Guy Street, 15 July 1991; J. Street to the author, 11 April 1991.
[30] Interview with Mrs. Guy Street, 15 July 1991.
[31] Ibid.
[32] Wingate to Slatin, 13 May 1932, SAD 223/17.
[33] Interview with Mrs. Guy Street, 15 July 1991.

In a letter to Slatin in July 1931 describing a garden party at Buckingham Palace, Wingate remarked that "so many old friends have gone west that there is occasionally an element of sadness" in such occasions.[34] In September 1930 Wingate's "dear old friend" General Mahon had died,[35] and in 1931 the Princess Royal, Sir Frederick Milner, and Dr. Acland, Wingate's friend for half a century, followed. On 4 October 1932 Slatin Pasha died in Vienna. In November 1934 Lady Wingate's brother, General Rundle, died in London. Sir Henry Wellcome, another old friend from Sudan days, died in July 1936, and in February 1937 Wingate's last surviving aunt, "Minipin," to whom he had grown close, died in London.

On 18 June 1938 the Wingates celebrated their fiftieth wedding anniversary. The day began with morning service at St. Mary Abbott's in Kensington, where, in Wingate's words, they "thanked God together for 50 very happy years of married life." At Queen Anne's Mansions they received a deputation from Wingate's regiment; after speeches a silver dish was presented. Telegrams, including one from the king and queen, and letters poured in.[36] In the evening the Sudan Government held a golden wedding reception at the Royal Empire Society, attended by more than two hundred "old officials, officers and old friends of Egypt and the Sudan."[37] The next day Victoria brought Josephine and Paul to lunch, and there was a family gathering at which Sir Louis Dane, Victoria's father-in-law, proposed the toast.[38]

This was the last great occasion before the Second World War. As early as September 1938 the manager of Queen Anne's Mansions gave air-raid instructions, and Wingate offered Knockenhair Hill to the army as a look-out.[39] But the old soldier did not relish the prospect of war. Wingate opposed intervention to save Czechoslovakia, and was unstinting in praise of Chamberlain and Mussolini after the Munich crisis.[40] When war broke out in September 1939, however, Wingate, aged sev-

---

[34] Wingate to Slatin, 25 July 1931, SAD 223/16.

[35] CB1.

[36] Ibid.

[37] Wingate to Armbruster, 25 June 1938, SAD 243/4.

[38] CB1.

[39] Manager, Queen Anne's Mansions, to Wingate, 19 September 1938; Wingate to Colonel Becket, 27 September 1938, SAD 243/4.

[40] Wingate to ?, 22 March 1938; Wingate to Armbruster, 20 October 1938, SAD 243/4.

enty-nine, answered the call, and increased the scope of his inspections as honorary colonel of several battalions; in October he went to the War Office and argued in vain for free railway passes for honorary colonels.[41] During the first months of war Wingate was based at Dunbar, whence he conducted inspections and took the salute after Sunday church services, and where Lady Wingate hosted local ladies' knitting-parties for the troops.[42] Wingate occasionally sent unsolicited advice to government ministers about the war in the Near East, once even suggesting that Ronald might be of use there as "the son of Wingate Pasha."[43]

The Wingates were in London on 13 September 1940 when Queen Anne's Mansions was wrecked in a German air raid. They had taken shelter and were playing bezique when a bomb struck the building. Though shaken, they were uninjured and were led with other residents through "a heavy bombardment" to a shelter under Westminster Central Hall.[44] The next day they moved to the Goring Hotel in Ebury Street, Belgravia, where they remained, despite bombing in that vicinity too, for almost a year. After some months at Froyle Place, near Alton, where the widow of Wingate's old friend, Milo Talbot, lived, they returned to the Goring. Meanwhile Victoria, who had fled Ipoh in Malaya and been evacuated with two of her children from Singapore two months before it fell, had arrived in Britain in March 1942.[45] In March 1944 Wingate, aged eighty-two, was hospitalized with a serious illness, apparently of the prostate; surgery was required, and his son later reported that only penicillin saved him.[46] Recovery was slow, and doctors advised retirement from business. Early in 1945 Wingate therefore resigned his board memberships, and with his wife "settle[d] down again—permanently—in Dunbar."[47]

---

[41] Wingate, note to his wife, 23 October 1939, SAD 243/5.

[42] Wingate to F. Balfour, 2 January 1940, SAD 243/6; see also Wingate to "Peterborough" (*Daily Telegraph*), 24 January 1941, SAD 243/7.

[43] Wingate to Lloyd, 6 August 1940, SAD 243/6.

[44] Wingate, "Our experiences at Queen Anne's Mansions S.W.1 on the night of Friday, 13th September 1940," n.d., SAD 115/13.

[45] Wingate to Leslie, 16 April 1941; Alexander to Wingate, 18 April 1941, SAD 243/7. Wingate to Cromer, 10 April 1942, SAD 243/8.

[46] Interview with Mrs. Guy Street, 15 July 1991; Wingate to Elizabeth Alexander, 11 June 1945, SAD 243/11. Cf. Wingate, *Wingate of the Sudan*, 257.

[47] Wingate to Elizabeth Alexander, 11 June 1945, SAD 243/11. See also Wingate to Jamieson, 12 October 1944, SAD 243/10, and Staff, Princes House, to Wingate, 29 March 1945, SAD 243/11.

On 10 June 1946 Lady Wingate died at Knockenhair in her eighty-eighth year. She had suffered from circulatory problems for some time,[48] and a nurse was in residence at the end. A family friend brought a letter Lady Wingate had written in 1937, expressing her wish to be cremated and that her ashes be buried at the memorial to Malcolm at Lagnicourt. The funeral was held in the dining room at Knockenhair on the thirteenth, and cremation followed in Edinburgh. Poignant diary entries record the rites, and Wingate's grief after almost sixty years of marriage.[49]

The death of his wife briefly revived Wingate's oft-deferred memoirs, which she had pressed him to write. The project had a long history. As governor-general of the Sudan and high commissioner in Egypt, Wingate had declined all invitations to write another book.[50] Within days of his supersession in 1919, however, Edward Arnold had tactlessly asked him to "write the book we have so often talked of on the transformation of the Soudan since Slatin's day."[51] Wingate declined. A few days later Percy Martin asked if Wingate would write a memoir, and reminded him that they had once discussed Martin's writing a biography; Seeley, Service expressed interest in an autobiography.[52] Wingate was uninterested. In June 1920 Gleichen asked him to write a few pages for a volume on Egypt and the Sudan in Hodder and Stoughton's "Nations of Today" series; Wingate felt "too keenly the treatment . . . meted out" to him, he told his old colleague, "to write dispassionately on the subject."[53] In 1922 Wingate's literary agent, A. P. Watt, offered an advance of £750 for a volume of "reminiscences"; Wingate declined.[54] In 1923 the *Encyclopaedia Britannica* asked Wingate to write an entry on Egypt for the new edition; he consulted the Foreign Office, but Curzon held that one "so prominently connected" with the subject "in an official capacity" could not "fairly or properly" write about it, so

---

[48] Wingate to Keppel, 24 August 1939, SAD 243/5.

[49] CB1.

[50] See, e.g., Arnold to Wingate, 18 February 1898, SAD 227/1.

[51] Arnold to Wingate, 23 October 1919, SAD 238/2.

[52] Martin to Wingate, 13 November 1919; Seeley, Service to Wingate, 16 February 1920, SAD 227/2.

[53] Gleichen to Wingate, 24 June 1920; Wingate to Gleichen, 26 June 1920, SAD 251/5.

[54] Watt to Wingate, 10 January 1922, SAD 225/1.

Wingate declined.[55] At the height of the Anglo-Egyptian crisis in 1924 he declined Williams and Norgate's invitation to write a short book on the Sudan, and in 1925 when Arnold wrote yet again, and the *Britannica* asked for a "short political history of the Sudan" for its supplements, he refused them both.[56]

Yet Wingate remained keenly interested in his place in history. In the 1920s he had begun to accept small writing assignments connected with the Sudan. He wrote a foreword for Percy Martin's *The Sudan in evolution* (1921), an introduction to H. C. Jackson's *Osman Digna* (1926), and a preface and introduction for C. H. Stigand's *Equatoria: the Lado Enclave* (1923). In 1930 he wrote a long foreword for *The story of Fergie Bey*, a book about Captain V. H. Ferguson, who had been killed on duty in the southern Sudan. In 1932 he supplied a foreword for *The people of the book*, a collection of stories by A. J. Pott, who had served with him in the Sudan campaigns.[57] He wrote brief memoirs of Col. H. D. Pearson (1923), Milo Talbot (1931), and Wellcome (1936), and helped E. W. Sandes with *The Royal Engineers in Egypt and the Sudan*, published in 1937. For that book he wrote a foreword, commented on drafts, and met Sandes to discuss details; his letters refer repeatedly to secrets that he could not commit to writing and that must never be published.[58]

In 1939 Wingate finally submitted to Edward Arnold's entreaties and signed a contract for his memoirs. He intended to collaborate with his son,[59] but the war immediately intruded. Wingate's interest was briefly rekindled by publication in 1943 of Wavell's *Allenby in Egypt*, which he found unfairly critical of himself.[60] But his illness and Ronald's absence allowed little progress. Indeed from Knockenhair in July 1945 he told his son that he was "as fully occupied as ever," and

[55] Wingate to Foreign Office, 1 August 1923; S. Gaselee, F.O., to Wingate, 15 August 1923; Wingate to Britannica, 17 August 1923, SAD 241/2.

[56] Williams and Norgate to Wingate, 25 November 1924, SAD 227/3; Arnold to Wingate, 9 October 1925; Bryant to Wingate, 23 September 1925; Wingate to Bryant, draft, 29 September 1925, SAD 225/5.

[57] Wingate to Slatin, 23 September 1930, SAD 223/15; and 23 March 1932, SAD 223/17.

[58] See correspondence in SAD 227/7.

[59] Wingate to Armbruster, 9 August 1939, SAD 243/5.

[60] Wingate to Ronald Wingate, 21 January 1944, SAD 243/10. See also Selby to Wingate, 12 January 1944, SAD 243/10.

"as unprepared as ever" to write a book.[61] Having discussed it with H. C. Jackson, a retired Sudan official and prolific writer, Wingate therefore suggested a collaboration. Admitting he was "weak on" the Sudan, Ronald agreed.[62] Violet Dinsmore was hired in 1946 as writer or editor. In a procedure reminiscent of Wingate's books on the Mahdiyya all three—she, Jackson, and Ronald—apparently wrote drafts of his "memoirs" for Wingate to correct.[63] By late 1946 Jackson and Ronald had despaired of this method,[64] and the project was shelved again. When Edward Arnold, most patient of publishers, enquired in 1951 they were told that Wingate was simply too old to complete the book.[65]

After the death of his wife Wingate's declining health gradually restricted his activities. In October 1947 he made his last trip abroad, to visit Ronald in Brussels. During a winter with Victoria at Eden Bridge, Kent, he missed his independence; visits to her and other relatives continued, but he never again took up residence with any. Knockenhair was too big and expensive (and cold in the winter), so Wingate lived in hotels, accompanied by Nurse Hutton, to whom he had grown close during his wife's last illness. He settled finally at the Bellevue Hotel in Dunbar,[66] where he spent the last few years of his life as an invalid. Attended by Nurse Hutton, he continued to receive visitors and to correspond; as late as 1950 he was officially consulted on a point in Anglo-Egyptian relations.[67]

Francis Reginald Wingate died at Dunbar on 29 January 1953, aged ninety-one. Preliminary plans for a full military funeral had been

---

[61] Wingate to Ronald Wingate, 24 July 1945, SAD 243/1.

[62] Wingate to Ronald Wingate, draft, 24 July 1945; Ronald Wingate to Wingate, 1 August 1945, SAD 243/11.

[63] See correspondence and drafts in SAD 457 and 467/1. See also historical notes prepared by H.C. Jackson for Ronald Wingate, SAD 245/7. "One gets no help from the old man," Ronald told Jackson on 30 September 1946 (SAD 467/1).

[64] Ronald Wingate to Jackson, 30 September 1946, SAD 467/1; Jackson to Ronald Wingate, 4 March 1947, SAD 219/7.

[65] Watt to Ronald Wingate, 2 January 1951, SAD 219/7. What Ronald Wingate's *Wingate of the Sudan,* published in 1955, owed to Jackson is unclear, but he is unmentioned in it, and felt badly treated over the memoirs. See Jackson to Ronald Wingate, 18 May 1955, SAD 457.

[66] SAD 244/2; Interview with Mrs. Guy Street, 15 July 1991.

[67] Alexander to Wingate, 6 February 1950, SAD 244/2.

drawn up the previous August.[68] At the ceremony in St. Anne's Church, eulogies stressed the names attached to his baronetcy, Dunbar and Port Sudan, and recalled especially his work in the Sudan; even now Wingate was praised for having "continued the great work . . . which Kitchener had begun." The pipes and drums of the Argyll and Sutherland Highlanders led the procession to the cemetery, through streets shown in contemporary photographs to have been almost empty.[69] He, and his achievements long ago, had by then been mostly forgotten. But having been witness to, and actor in, so much history, Wingate had never given up hope that history would render a verdict, and that he would someday be vindicated.

---

[68] HQ, Royal Army, Scottish Command, "Funeral of General Sir F. Reginald Wingate, Bt.," August 1952, SAD G//s 583.

[69] Unidentified local newspaper, n.d., SAD 764/9; Cf. Wingate, *Wingate of the Sudan*, 258.

Bibliography

I. Archival Sources

A. Sudan Archive, Durham

This study is based mainly on the papers of F. R. Wingate, deposited in the Sudan Archive of the University of Durham Library. A revised, comprehensive guide to the Wingate Papers has been published. They include not only private papers but much official correspondence and Wingate's copies of government documents. In the Notes I have referred to the Wingate Papers and other papers at Durham thus: SAD [box number]/[file number]/[folio number (rarely)].

B. Public Record Office, London

1. FO 78: Turkey, including Egypt, 1895–1905.
2. FO 141: Egypt, consular correspondence, 1896–1922.
3. FO 371: Egypt, political, 1906–1922.
4. FO 403: Confidential prints, north–east Africa and the Sudan, to 1904.
5. FO 407: Confidential prints, Egypt and the Sudan.
6. FO 633: Cromer papers.
7. FO 800: Miscellaneous papers.
8. WO 32: Papers on the Omdurman mutiny.
9. WO 106: Papers on the defence of Egypt.

C. National Records Office, Khartoum

1. CAIRINT: Papers on intelligence and administration.
2. REPORTS: Unpublished official reports.

D. Middle East Centre, St. Antony's College, Oxford

1. H. C. Bowman papers.
2. Cheetham papers.
3. Gorst papers.
4. Letters of F. R. Wingate to H. A. MacMichael.

E. Rhodes House Library, Oxford

1. Talbot papers.

F. Hatfield House

1. Papers of the third Marquess of Salisbury.

G. Other Privately Held Papers

1. Bible and commonplace books of F. R . Wingate and Catherine Wingate, in the possession of the author.

II. Published Primary Sources

A. Egypt

1. Intelligence Reports
    a. Frontier Series, 1–285, August 1885–February 1892.
    b. Suakin Series, 1–127, April 1886–February 1892.
    c. *Intelligence Report, Egypt:* 1–59, April 1892–May 1898.
    d. *Sudan Intelligence Report:* 60, 25 May–31 December 1898.

B. Great Britain

1. War office
    a. *General military report on the Egyptian Sudan,* 1891, 1892.
2. Foreign Office
    a. *General report on the Egyptian Sudan, March 1895.*
    b. *Report of the Special Mission to Egypt,* 1921.
    c. *Reports by His Majesty's agent and consul-general on the finances, administration, and conditions of Egypt and the Soudan, 1899–1919.*

C. Memoirs

Bedri, Babikr, *The memoirs of Babikr Bedri,* vol. 1, London 1969; vol. 2, London 1980.

Bennett, E. N., *The downfall of the dervishes,* London 1899.

Burleigh, Bennet, *Khartoum campaign 1898, or the re-conquest of the Soudan,* London 3rd ed., 1899.

Gordon, C. G., *The journals of Major-Gen. C. G. Gordon , C.B., at Khartoum*, London 1885.

Hardinge of Penhurst, Lord, *Old Diplomacy*, London 1947.

Letters of Queen Victoria, The, third series, London 1932.

Neufeld, Charles, *A prisoner of the Khaleefa*, London, 3rd ed., 1899.

Rodd, James Rennell, *Social and diplomatic memories* (second series) *1894–1901. Egypt and Abyssinia*, London 1923.

Slatin, Rudolf C., *Fire and sword in the Sudan*, London 1896.

Steevens, G. W., *With Kitchener to Khartum*, London 1898.

Storrs, Ronald, *Orientations*, London 1937.

Symes, Stewart, *Tour of duty*, London 1946.

Winterton, Earl, *Orders of the day*, London 1953.

Wood, Evelyn, *Winnowed memories*, London 1918.

III. Secondary works

Alford, Henry S. L. and Sword, W. Dennistoun, *The Egyptian Soudan. Its loss and recovery*, London 1898.

Arthur, George, *Life of Lord Kitchener*, London 1920.

Bates, Darrell, *The Fashoda incident of 1898*, Oxford 1984.

Brook-Shepherd, Gordon, *Between two flags. The life of Baron Sir Rudolf von Slatin Pasha*, London 1972.

Churchill, Winston, *The river war*, London 1899.

Cromer, Earl of, *Modern Egypt*, London 1908.

Daly, M. W., *British administration and the Northern Sudan*, Leiden 1980.

———, "The Egyptian Army mutiny at Omdurman, January–February 1900," *Bulletin of the British Society for Middle Eastern Studies* 8, 1, 1981, 3–12.

———, *Empire on the Nile. The Anglo-Egyptian condominium in the Sudan, 1898–1934*, Cambridge 1986.

Darwin, John, *Britain, Egypt and the Middle East. Imperial policy in the aftermath of war 1918–1922*, New York 1981.

Doolittle, Duncan H., *A soldier's hero. General Sir Archibald Hunter*, Narragansett, Rhode Island 1991.

Fergusson, V. H., *The story of Fergie Bey (Awaraquay). Told by himself and some of his friends*, London 1930.

Gaitskell, Arthur, *Gezira: a story of development in the Sudan*, London 1959.

Hallam, W.K.R., *The life and times of Rabih Fadl Allah*, Ilfracombe, Devon 1977.

Hill, Richard, *Egypt in the Sudan 1820–1881*, London 1959.

———, "Government and Christian missions in the Anglo-Egyptian Sudan, 1899–1914," *Middle East Studies* 1, 2, 1965.

———, *Slatin Pasha*, London 1965.

Holt, P. M., *Egypt and the fertile crescent 1516–1922*, London 1966.

———, *The Mahdist state in the Sudan*, Oxford, 2nd ed., 1970.

———, "The source-materials of the Sudanese Mahdia," *St. Antony's Papers, Number 4: Middle Eastern Affairs, Number 1*, London 1958, 107–18.

Jackson, H. C., *Behind the modern Sudan*, London 1955.

———, *Pastor on the Nile*, London 1960.

———, *Sudan days and ways*, London 1954.

Johnson, Douglas H., "The death of Gordon: a Victorian myth," *Journal of imperial and commonwealth history* X, 3, May 1992, 285–310.

Kedourie, Elie, *The Chatham House version and other Middle-Eastern studies*, London 1984.

———, *England and the Middle East. The destruction of the Ottoman Empire, 1914–1921*, London 1956.

———, *In the Anglo-Arab labyrinth. The McMahon-Husayn correspondence and its interpretations 1914–1939*, Cambridge 1976.

Keown-Boyd, Henry, *A good dusting. The Sudan campaigns 1883–1899*, London 1986.

Lawrence, T. E., *Seven pillars of wisdom*, Garden City, N.J., 1936.

Magnus, Philip, *Kitchener. Portrait of an imperialist*, New York, 2nd ed.,1968.

Marlowe, John, *Anglo-Egyptian relations 1800–1953*, London 1954.

———, *Cromer in Egypt*, London 1970.

Milner, Alfred, *England in Egypt*, London 1892.

Perkins, Kenneth, *Port Sudan. The evolution of a colonial city*, Boulder, Colorado, 1993.

Rose, Kenneth, *The later Cecils*, New York 1975.

Sanderson, G. N., "Contributions from African sources to the history of European competition in the Upper Valley of the Nile," *Journal of African History* III, 1, 1962, 69–90.

———, *England, Europe and the Upper Nile 1882–1899*, Edinburgh 1965.

———, "The foreign policy of the Negus Menelik, 1896–1898," *Journal of African History* V, 1, 1964, 87–97.

———, "The ghost of Adam Smith: ideology, bureaucracy, and the frustration of economic development in the Sudan, 1934–1940," in M. W. Daly, ed., *Modernization in the Sudan*, New York 1985, 101–20.

Sandes, E.W.C., *The Royal Engineers in Egypt and the Sudan*, Chatham 1937.

Shoucair, Naum, *Ta'rikh al-Sudan al-qadim wa-l-hadith wa-jughrafiyatuh*, Cairo, n.d.

Terry, Janice, *The Wafd 1919–1952*, London 1982.

Theobald, A. B., *Ali Dinar. Last sultan of Darfur 1898–1916*, London, 1965.

Warburg, Gabriel, *The Sudan under Wingate. Administration in the Anglo-Egyptian Sudan 1899–1916*, London 1971.

Wavell, Viscount, *Allenby in Egypt*, London 1943.

Westrate, Bruce, *The Arab Bureau. British policy in the Middle East 1916–1920*, University Park, Pennsylvania 1992.

Wilson, Jeremy, *Lawrence*, London 1989.

Wingate, F. R., *Mahdiism and the Egyptian Sudan*, London 1891, 2nd ed. 1968.

———, *Ten years' captivity in the Mahdi's camp 1882–1892*, London 1892.

Wingate, Ronald, *Wingate of the Sudan*, London 1955.

Ziegler, Philip, *Omdurman*, London 1973.

Zulfo, Ismat Hasan, *Karari, The Sudanese account of the battle of Omdurman*, London 1980.

Index

267, 268, 270, 278, 280–2,
284, 285, 287, 289, 298,
303, 304
Harper's Magazine, 44
Henry of Battenberg,
Princess, 158, 159. 168,
184
Herbert, E.S., 224
Hicks, William, 18, 21–2
Hijaz, 215, 227, 232, 233,
234, 235, 236, 254, 255,
256
Hohenlohes, 180
Holled-Smith, Charles, 40
Holt, P.M., 42n
Hunter, Archibald, 62–3, 90,
101, 118, 119, 132
Hussayn, Sharif (of Mecca),
215, 216–7, 218, 223–4,
225, 227, 228, 230, 231,
254–5, 269
Hussayn Kamil, 205, 235,
239, 241, 247, 252, 258,
264, 265, 270
Hussayn Rushdi, 241, 265–6,
276, 277, 280–2, 284, 285,
286, 290, 291
Hutton, Nurse, 324

Iqayqa, 106
Isma'il Pasha, 13, 14–15, 20
Italy, Italians, 61, 65, 67, 81,
84, 91, 92
Itang, 160

Jackson. H.C., 323, 324
Jackson, H.W., 64, 141,
142–3 147
Jerusalem, 254
Jewish Chronicle, 205

Jidda, 218, 230
Joachim, Miss, 72

Kamal al-Din, Prince, 265
Kamlin, 159, 179
Kannur, 103
Karai, 106
Karima, 161, 179
Karlsbad, 185, 198, 199, 200,
314, 318
Karma, 86
Kassala, 61, 65, 67. 82, 158,
160, 199
Kawa, 133, 161
Kelly, P.V., 211
Keown-Boyd, Alexander, 257
Khartoum, 20, 23–4, 25,
107, 121–2, 131, 140, 152,
158, 159, 160, 161, 162,
163–4, 166, 180–1, 190,
194, 198, 205, 212, 251
Khashm al-Qirba, 199
Khatmiyya tariqa, 154, 199
Kimberley, Lord, 75n, 76, 81
Kitchener, Herbert, 15, 44,
49–50, 52, 54, 55, 56,
57–9, 64–5, 66, 67, 74. 76,
76n, 78, 82, 84–8, 89, 94,
96, 97, 98, 99–100, 101,
102–4, 106, 107–8,
109–16, 117–9, 120, 142,
146, 150, 158, 184, 185,
200, 325
As governor-general of the
Sudan, 121–2, 123, 124,
125–6, 127, 131–2,
134–5, 137, 138, 142,
143–4, 145, 166
As agent and consul-general in Egypt, 186,